LANCHESTER LIBRARY

3 8001 00636 9247

D0588826

Lanchester Library

WITHDRAWN

Coventry University Library

# Politics

## *Made Simple*

The Made Simple series
has been created
especially for self-education
but can equally well
be used as
an aid to group study.
However complex the subject,
the reader is taken
step by step,
clearly and methodically,
through the course. Each volume
has been prepared by experts,
taking account of
modern educational requirements,
to ensure the most
effective way of
acquiring knowledge.

# In the same series

Accounting
Advertising
Auditing
Biology
Book-keeping
British Constitution
Business Calculations
Business and Enterprise Studies
Business Law
Calculus
Chemistry
Child Development
Commerce
Computer Electronics
Computer Programming
Computer Typing
Cost and Management Accounting
Economic and Social Geography
Economics
Education
Electricity
Electronics
Elements of Banking
English
Financial Management
First Aid
French
German
Graphic Communication

Italian
Latin
Law
Management
Marketing
Mathematics
Modern European History
Modern World History
MSX
Music
Office Practice
Personnel Management
Philosophy
Photography
Physical Geography
Physics
Politics
Psychiatry
Psychology
Russian
Salesmanship
Secretarial Practice
Social Services
Sociology
Spanish
Statistics
Teeline Shorthand
Typing

# Politics

## *Made Simple*

J. R. Thackrah, BA, PG Cert. Ed., MA

MADE SIMPLE
**BOOKS**

Made Simple Books
An imprint of Heinemann Professional Publishing Ltd
Halley Court, Jordan Hill, Oxford OX2 8EJ

OXFORD   LONDON   MELBOURNE   AUCKLAND   SINGAPORE
IBADAN   NAIROBI   GABORONE   KINGSTON

First published 1987
Reprinted 1989
Reprinted 1990

© J. R. Thackrah 1987

This book is sold subject to the
condition that it shall not, by
way of trade or otherwise, be lent,
re-sold, hired out or otherwise
circulated without the publisher's
prior consent in any form of binding
or cover other than that in which it is
published and without a similar condition
including this condition being imposed
on the subsequent purchaser.

**British Library Cataloguing in Publication Data**
Thackrah, J. R.
  Politics Made Simple. – (Made simple books)
  1. Political science
  I. Title   II. Series
  320        JA66
ISBN 0 434 98514 7

Printed in England by Clays Ltd, St Ives plc

# Contents

# Preface

This book is about the historical ideas, modern political ideas and assumptions, political activities, and international issues which encompass the overall study of politics, a subject which affects the lives of every person, country and international organization.

It is hoped that readers will be both specialist and non-specialist alike – either studying for an examination or just requiring an overall grasp of politics for general interest. For academic purposes it covers the syllabuses of school examining bodies as well as degree courses at university level.

I am particularly grateful to Mr Robert Postema, who prior to leaving Heinemann, gave me invaluable advice and encouragement; Mr Douglas Fox, the Publishing Director of Made Simple Books, and my Editor, Anne Martin. A sincere debt of gratitude must go to my parents for their help with checking, typing and proof reading.

*J. R. Thackrah*
April 1987

# Part 1  Historical Ideas

# 1
# What is politics?

## Politics

The term **politics** is derived from the Greek *polis* meaning city state or simply state. As an activity, politics is the process in a social system by which the goals of that system are selected and ordered in terms of priority of the allocation of available resources. It involves cooperation and the resolution of conflict by means of the exercise of political authority and coercion. Politics involves the activities of groups of various kinds, including groups of a specifically political type, such as political parties. Politics is concerned with the 'public' goals of the society. The study of politics attempts to describe, classify, analyse and explain political activity and the values which are implemented by political decisions. This study is also sometimes termed government, but this is normally the title of a more restricted field of study, namely the politics of formal institutions at the level of the state.

A study of politics can be undertaken with the aim of an understanding of the interrelationships between government and the political system on the one hand and the individual citizen and general public on the other; or, in constitutional terms, the aim can be to attain an acquaintance with the institutions and procedures of central and local government, including the legal system. Through politics one can understand the place of the individual in society and study the character of the society (industrial, economic, social and cultural) and the fundamentals of a democratic society. There has to be a ready and unashamed recognition that politics is about conflict as well as consensus. The more detailed a person's knowledge of political activity, the less one is at the mercy of plausible but mistaken alternatives, or false and irrelevant ideas. The more readily a person understands mankind's own political tradition, the more readily its whole resources are available, the less likely a person will be to embrace illusions which wait for the ignorant and the unwary, for example, the illusion that in politics a person can get on without a tradition of behaviour. In politics, the world is the best of all possible worlds and everything in it is a necessary evil.

Politics makes call upon knowledge. Political activity is impossible without a certain kind of knowledge and a certain sort of education. Connections between commitment, bias and doctrination on the one hand, and between neutrality and objectivity on the other hand are close and concepts tend to overlap. Politics has a strong element of controversy and can be divisive, splitting families, fellowships and friendships. Government is associated with three primary concepts: force, authority and order. Human identity is seen in terms of four primary concepts: rights, individuality, freedom and welfare.

**Political education** has to provide a basic vocabulary. Respect for truth and reasoning is invaluable and this respect can be achieved by studying a broad range of political concepts. Politics must be more than institutional analysis and must be built upon a conceptual framework. Ideas are a logical starting point but are powerless without an administrative network to bring them realization. At international level one has international institutions and at a national level federal and unitary systems of government. Another concept involves a look at the rise of the leader and his or her social origins and the process of his or her rise to power plus an understanding of the activity of the leader in power. The role of the individual as another concept is important. The individual's value depends on the degree of participation allowed for in the political system. Overlapping the concept of leader is one of conflict – causes of which can be ideological, social, economic and political. If violent, conflict can take the form of civil war, revolution, *coup d'etat*, rebellion or demonstration. Internationally there is the ideological dimension plus the naked struggle for power.

A lay view of politics rests on three assumptions. First, there is the **perception** of what is done to us by government and external forces, that is force, authority and order. Second, there are the perceptions of our human identity, i.e. what we think we are, what is done to us and what should not be done to us. These concern rights, individuality, freedom and welfare. Last there are perceptions of different kinds of relationships, between 'them' and 'us' or between 'order' and 'individuality' or government and the governed, i.e. concern with justice, representation and influence.

If every country has the government it deserves, each society develops the forms of political education it wants. The student of both politics and history cannot but be saddened by the tremendous amount of human energy and the colossal quantities of the earth's resources which have been dissipated in attempts to resolve political conflicts throughout human history. If man is a rational creature his best hope for more enlightened approaches to political affairs would seem to be education. Without leadership, people are unlikely to have settled conditions for their mutual welfare and protection. Leaders enjoy power but need the goodwill of the people to continue in office. The more a government tries to do the more agents and support it needs.

Politics comes into all aspects of global society in the world. **Political behaviour** as an area of study within political science is concerned with those aspects of human behaviour that take place within political contexts i.e. within a state or other political community, for political purposes or with political motivation. Its focus is the individual person – as voter, leader, revolutionary, party member, opinion leader – rather than the group or the political system, but it necessarily takes account of the influences of the group on the individual's behaviour, the constraints of the system on the individual's opportunities for action, and the effects of the political culture on his or her attitudes and political habits. The major areas of interest for political scientists who have undertaken the study of political behaviour have been the psychological and social influences on behaviour, e.g. political socialization, the political ideologies, attitudes and opinions of individuals and their manifestations; the relationship between individuals as political actors and the groups to which they belong, political activity such as voting and other forms of political participation, leadership, decision making, political violence, etc.; the methods of political communication used by individuals, and the relationship between individual behaviour and the political system and its environment.

Behaviour is related to communication, the process whereby components of a political system, such as groups, institutions or individual political actors, transmit and receive information relevant to the functioning of the system. The information can be of any type, e.g. statistics, intelligence reports, statements of opinion, and decisions. Behaviour can be closely related to the anthropological background of the group and the ways in which political functions are carried out in various ethnic communities. Such functions are performed by various structures in most if not all ethnic groups, though formal political structures may be absent. **Political anthropology** studies the effects of cultural tradition, the interaction of a society with its physical environment, the effects of social and technological change, and similar factors on the ways in which political structures arise and change and functions are performed. Behaviour and communication are vital aspects of **political culture**, which is the set of orientations concerning the political process, such as ideologies, attitudes and beliefs and their expression, as they are related to members of a political system and set in the context of norms of that system. The form of political culture in any society is a product of the historical experiences that have affected the political system and the results of the political socialization processes experienced by members of the political system. Thus it is possible to study the interrelationships between ideological and attitudinal values concerning politics and the rules and procedures of the political system; orientations towards political leadership and the political process itself; the focus of political identity of individuals and groups. A political culture will generally contain identifiable subcultures based on religion, regional differences, ethnic groups, social status, etc. These subcultures will consist of political attitudes and values distinct from those of the general political culture with respect to particular political institutions and processes. Should these subcultures become dominant, the political integration of the community may be threatened, e.g. the nationalist subculture in Northern Ireland, the French subculture in Quebec and the Greek and Turkish subcultures in Cyprus.

Culture can be strong where political development is new. The study of political development focuses on the effects of rapid social and economic change on the political arrangements of society and the role that is played by political institutions and forces in affecting the course of developmental change. Such study is associated with newly independent states. The study of development change can include the effects of economic and social change on the institutions of government and on the methods and levels of political participation; the roles of elites and styles of leadership in developing nations; the search for equality in social and political relationships; the influence of the military; the relationship between ideology and development especially concerning nationalism, communism and democracy; political communication and the mass media; political socialization and the role of education as a developmental force; the integration of minorities, and the role of the bureaucracy. Several trends are associated with the processes of political development, such as the increased complexity and specialization of political roles and institutions, the enlargement of an educated political elite, the increased politicization of the population and the emergence of national rather than parochial political issues.

In all developing as well as developed countries the political process must be interrelated with the economic policy; and there has to be a linkage between political and economic factors in public policy and related matters. All societies have political elites, that is social groups, consisting of a small minority of the total population of a community, which exercise a predominant influence on political outcomes by virtue of their occupancy of important political offices. They are also members of influential social classes or castes, have common educational background and are members of social or economic elite groups.

Within any political community some cohesion is necessary, and political integration is the state of cohesion existing in a political community as demonstrated by a high degree of mutual political interaction among the members of that community based on consent rather than coercion. The degree of integration of a community is related to several factors, including the dominance of a political culture of the community or system over the subcultures within it. The degree also depends on the efficacy of political institutions and processes of the community in meeting expectations, and the ease and frequency of political communication among members of the community. Malintegration occurs when the range of shared political values is diminished, coercion becomes necessary to obtain compliance with the law, and demands are made by sections of the community for secession. Stresses which lead to a weakening of political integration must be reduced by appropriate responses from the political authorities, otherwise the system will tend to divide or will collapse entirely. Such stresses may result from societal change, extreme threat, failure to remove sources of cleavage, inability to satisfy the demands of members of some salient subculture, and economic deprivation.

The study of stress within political integration is closely related to the study of **political psychology**. This is a branch of political science that focuses on the psychological foundations of human behaviour in its political aspects and manifestations. It is based on the premise that since political actions are ultimately the actions of individuals, the explanation of those actions must include psychological factors. Political actions are concerned with the preferences that individuals have concerning goals and values, and methods of attaining them, and their choice of persons to represent or lead them. Political psychology assumes that such actions are directly related to the attitudes that individuals possess regarding these matters, and that such attitudes are, in part, determined by more fundamental ideological beliefs and personality styles. Thus the interests of political psychologists include the relationships between personality factors and political behaviour, the classification and scaling of political attitudes; the processes of political learning and political socialization, the psychological bases of leadership styles, and the agglomeration or association of political attitudes.

The study of the moral and metaphysical aspects of politics is grounded almost invariably in a familiarity with the history of political thought. **Political philosophy** employs the methods of philosophy and history to deal with questions of, *inter alia*, the nature of the state and of political life, the philosophic aspects of the study of politics, the grounds of political obligation, the moral qualities of different forms of government, and the relationship between morality and political policy.

The term **political theory** is usually applied to those areas of the study of politics otherwise termed political philosophy and empirical political analysis. Political philosophy is concerned with the study of the normative and ethical aspects of political problems, the philosophic aspects of the processes by which political data or phenomena are studied, and the historical and contemporary study of political thought. Empirical political analysis involves the attempt to construct empirically based theories about political systems, political processes and political behaviour. Such theories are built up by the means of description of political phenomena, their classification, hypothesis-testing, and the establishment of laws about political behaviour, and they are justified by reference to observable experience and objective data, rather than appeals to divine or other abstract sources.

In close alliance with political theory, **political thought** is often taken as an equivalent term to political philosophy though in fact it omits the study of philosophic problems in its concentration on thinkers and the ideas, or to political theory, though it has little interest in the development of empirical or analytical theories. Thus political thought is usually approached in one of two ways: either as the study of important thinkers, e.g. Aristotle, Hobbes, Rousseau, Marx; or as the study of the development of important concepts, e.g. natural law, democracy, nationalism, socialism, sovereignty. Political theory is closely linked with **political history** which is the study of past political systems, events, processes, institutions, actors and behaviour, that is, of the chronological dimension of political science itself. Such study includes the establishment of facts from the evidence provided by historical records and the estimation of the causes of events through the explanation of relationships between political actors, institutions and processes. Such explanation may of necessity draw on facts regarding the effects of the environment – physical and social – on the political system. Political history has traditionally been studied in parallel with **political geography**. This aspect of geography is the study of the relationship between political areas, principally states, and their physical environment. It is based on the fact that the major political units of the world – empires, states, provinces, townships, colonies – are territorial areas and are influenced by geographic factors.

Within any political history one can find a **system**. This is a set of structures, processes and institutions which interact with each other and, across the boundaries of the system, with the environment to allocate values authoritatively for a society, or to attain the goals of society and generally to perform those functions which may be defined as political. It is a subsystem of the wider societal system such as a state, the international system, a political party, a trade union, or a tribe. It is usually regarded as an open system, involved in exchanges with its environment and an adaptive system capable of adaptation to changing circumstances, regulation of its own components, response to stress and, through feedback mechanisms, able to adjust its outputs to input conditions.

The study of political thought and theory has helped people to become politically socialized. **Political socialization** is the process whereby, on the one hand, an individual acquires attitudes and orientations towards political phenomena, and, on the other hand, society transmits political norms and beliefs from one generation to the next. These two aspects may be in contradiction where an individual has apparently acquired deviant attitudes and orientations. The socialization process tends to be gradual and to extend from early childhood into adulthood. It appears that basic political attitudes are acquired first: loyalty toward the society or race, nation state, etc., recognition of authority and predisposition towards its exercise; then come more specific attitudes such as broad identification with a political party; then attitudes that may be as specific as a stance on some particular policy or programme. While this process normally occurs in sequence through the life of an individual, major societal changes or his entry into a new society (for example, through emigration) may involve a new socialization process at a relatively late age.

Political socialization can occur through direct or indirect processes. Among these are: personal political experiences, imitation and political education. Agencies of political socialization include the family, peer groups, educational institutions and large groups, both political, such as political parties, and non-political, such as churches. The attitudes and values of these various agencies change in content and direction over time and may well be dissimilar relative to each other. Thus an individual may experience problems of reconciling the socialization processes to which he or she is submitted, for example rural inhabitants of modernizing societies on taking up residence in a city, and immigrants from a traditional culture on moving into an industrialized society.

Political socialization is often confused with **political sociology**. Political scientists see political sociology as the study of the effects of the social environment on the political subsystem, while sociologists are more inclined to describe it in terms of the interrelationships of political and social institutions. Political sociology is that branch of sociology which is concerned with the social causes and consequences of given power distributions within or between societies, and with the social and political conflicts that lead to changes in the allocation of power. Studies that fall within this definition include those that concentrate on political consensus and cleavage and their social causes, the relations between social structure and political power, the analysis of elites, the social bases of political groups such as parties and pressure groups, the relationship between social and political change, the social bases of political ideologies and the influences of social institutions on political behaviour, such as political socialization and political participation.

The political scientists' interest would focus on the social causes of political ideology differences, the effects of social change on political institutions and policies, the social bases of voting behaviour and party membership, problems of political culture, political integration and social causes of political stress, such as revolutions, civil war, military interventions in politics. Political scientists can also be concerned with politicization which is the process of drawing into political activity, if only temporarily, groups or individuals previously uninterested in politics. In other contexts it can refer to the process of making an issue a matter for political determination, rather than for example social or economic determination. An issue or question can be depoliticized when it no longer is regarded as a matter for political debate and decision, for example religion in many Western countries today.

The broad study of politics can be defined within the term political science. The term '**political science**' can be used to distinguish the study of political institutions and processes from the study of political ideas. In its use as the title of a discipline, 'political science' refers to the imprecisely defined body of knowledge involving the study of political ideas, institutions, processes and events mainly concerned with the government of states. Such governments have the power to use political resources, which are those values possessed by political actors which are capable of being used or exchanged in order to produce desired political outcomes.

The very nature of the word science also implies that 'analysis' is involved in politics. **Political analysis** can be seen as the intellectual process of defining, classifying and explaining political phenomena and political problems. To undertake these tasks, it makes use of the range of concepts, methods, approaches, models and theories, available at the time. It is a major dimension of political science, alongside political history, political description and political philosophy. Sub-areas of political analysis can be identified both in terms of subject, e.g. policy analysis, electoral analysis, systems analysis; and in terms of the stage or method of analysis, e.g. methodology, taxonomy, theory construction, comparative analysis and mathematical analysis.

What has been emphasized in this introductory chapter is that politics is both an activity and a study of that activity. As an **activity**, politics is the process in a social system by which the goals of that system are selected, ordered in terms of priority both temporally and concerning resource allocation, and implemented. It thus involves both cooperation and the resolution of conflict, by means of the exercise of political authority and, if necessary, coercion. Politics usually involves the activities of groups of various kinds, including sometimes groups of a specifically political type, such as political parties. It is distinguished from other social processes by its concern with the public goals of the society. The study of politics attempts to describe, classify, analyse and explain political activity and the values which are implemented by political decisions. The essence of politics is the examination of the various conflicting interests and views among human beings. This issue was examined by the Greeks with the creation of the city states such as at Athens, Troy and Sparta.

## Questions

1  Why do people study politics?
2  Compare and contrast the lay and specialist views of politics.
3  Why is behaviour an important facet in political analysis?
4  Examine why the political process must be interrelated with economic policy.
5  Give reasons why every society needs a political culture.
6  'Political theory is the basis of politics.' Do you agree?
7  What are the pros and cons of political socialization?
8  Is excessive political activity dangerous?

## Further reading

Bullock, A. and Stallybrass, O. (eds), *Fontana Dictionary of Modern Thought*, Fontana, London, 1982.
Bullock, A. and Woodings, R. B. (eds), *The Fontana Biographical Companion to Modern Thought*, Fontana, London, 1983.
Deutsch, K. W., *Politics and Government, How People Decide their Fate*, Houghton Mifflin & Co., Boston, 1980.
Dworkin, R., *Taking Rights Seriously*, Harvard University Press, Harvard, 1978.
Elliott, F., *A Dictionary of Politics*, Penguin, London, 1965.
Field, G. C., *Political Theory*, University Publishers, London, 1965.
Flew, A., *Dictionary of Philosophy*, Pan-MacMillan, London, 1979.
Goodwin, B., *Using Political Ideas*, John Wiley & Sons, London, 1983.
Lacqueur, W. (ed.), *A Dictionary of Politics*, Pan, London, 1973.
Laski, H. J., *An Introduction to Politics*, George Allen & Unwin, London, 1960.
Laver, M., *Invitation to Politics*, Martin Robertson, Oxford, 1983.
Leeds, C. A., *Political Studies* (3rd edn), Macdonald & Evans, Plymouth, 1982.
Leftwich, A. (ed.), *What is Politics? The Activity and its Study*, Basil Blackwell, Oxford, 1984.
Ponton, G. and Gill, P., *Introduction to Politics*, Basil Blackwell, Oxford, 1984.
Popkin, R. H. and Stroll, A., *Philosophy Made Simple* (2nd edn), Heinemann, London, 1986.
Redhead, B., *Political Thought from Plato to NATO*, Ariel Books, London, 1984.
Renwick, A. and Swinburn, I., *Basic Political Concepts*, Hutchinson, London, 1983.
Robertson, D., *Dictionary of Modern Politics*, Europa, London, 1985.
Robins, L. (ed.), *Introducing Political Science: Themes and Concepts in Studying Politics*, Longman, London, 1985.
Rodee, C. C., Christol, C. Q., Anderson, T. J. and Greene, T. H., *Introduction to Political Science*, McGraw Hill & Co., New York, 1983.
Runes, D. D., *Dictionary of Philosophy*, Philosophical Library, New York, 1942.

Safire, W., *Safire's Political Dictionary*, Ballantine Books, New York, 1978.

Scruton, R., *A Dictionary of Political Thought*, Pan, London, 1942.

Wiener, P. P., *Dictionary of the History of Ideas: Studies of Selected Pivotal Ideas* (4 vols), Charles Scribner's Sons, New York, 1973.

Wintle, J. (ed.), *Dictionary of Modern Culture*, Ark Paperbacks, London, 1981.

# 2
# Origins of political thought

## City state

Western political thought began with the study of the Greek **city state**, or
**polis**, i.e. a system of independent jurisdiction over a city. Jurisdiction is
the sphere of authority exercised by a state. Hence in international law it
has been applied to the right of a sovereign state to determine rights and
duties of persons by legislation and to enforce those rights and duties. The
idea of jurisdiction forms an essential part of the notion of a state as
embodied in a territory.

To the Greeks, political organization appeared most efficient, elaborate
and perfect; different not only quantitatively but qualitatively from all
other types of organized social life. Thus when Aristotle says at the beginning of his *Politics*, that the *polis* or political association is 'the most
sovereign and inclusive association' he adds that it is not size nor numbers
alone that distinguish political power from all other powers that men exercise over men, but a peculiar quality which that power possesses, a particular aim which it pursues; the attainment of justice, that is of a system
of relations between men ensuring certain standards and determined by
law. The idea of the state is inspired by awareness that, among all human
associations there is one that stands out for combining, however differently
in proportions, might, power and authority; might, in order to be able to
defend itself from outside dangers and to impose upon its members, if
necessary, conformity by force; power, in so far as that force is exercised in
the name of and in accordance with certain rules; authority, in as much as
that power should be considered legitimate and entail an obligation on
those who are called to obey its commands.

To the Greeks, the advantages to be obtained by means of the state were
of supreme importance and such as fully justify its power. Greek political
experience was summed up in the *polis*; a small territorial unit leading a
precarious existence among a number of rival cities and increasingly threatened by the appearance of a new and larger type of state. Yet in the Greek
view of life, this small and exclusive concern was the very embodiment of
perfection. Although Aristotle was euphoric about the *polis*, pessimistic
views about politics were certainly not lacking among Greek writers. The
importance of force was not overlooked. Might indeed seems at times to
be conceived as equivalent to right, especially in international relations.
Thus doubt could arise about the origin of political power, however great

the benefits which the existence of the state entailed. How could this existence be explained? Was it grounded on reason or force, on nature or convention? The question which the Sophists (professional philosophers) asked
simply could not be raised so long as the state was conceived (as it was by
Plato and Aristotle) as the necessary complement of man. As the bearer of
the highest values, the state stood in no need of any further legitimation.

The Greek city state was so different from the political communities in
which modern men live, that the Greek philosophers were thinking of
political practices far different from any that have prevailed commonly in
the modern world, and the whole climate of opinion varied.

As compared with modern states, the ancient city state was exceedingly
small both in area and in population. The population was divided into
three main classes that were politically and legally distinct. At the bottom
of the social scale were the slaves, for slavery was a universal institution in
the ancient world – for example, of all the inhabitants of Athens perhaps
one-third were slaves. The second main group was resident foreigners or
*metics*. Although in a commercial city like Athens the number of such
persons might be large, the *metic*, like the slave, had no part in the political
life of the city, although he was a freeman and his exclusion implied no
social discrimination against him. Finally, there was the body of citizens
entitled to take part in its political life. This was a privilege attained by
birth, for a Greek remained a citizen of the city to which his parents
belonged. What **citizenship** entitled a man to was membership; that is,
some minimum share of political activity or participation in public business. Aristotle considered that eligibility to jury duty was the best criterion
of citizenship. The modern notion of a citizen as a man to whom certain
rights are legally guaranteed would have been better understood by the
Roman than by the Greek, for the Latin term *ius* does partly imply the
possession of private right. The Greek thought of his citizenship not as a
possession but as something shared. This fact had a profound influence
upon Greek political philosophy. It meant that the problem as they conceived it was not to gain a man his rights, but to ensure him the place to
which he was entitled.

Athens became the best known type of the **democratic constitution**. The
whole body of male citizens formed the Assembly, which met ten times a
year. Political means had been designed to make the magistrates and
officials responsible to the citizen body and answerable to its control. The
device by which this was effected was a species of representation. What it
aimed at was the selection of a body sufficiently large to form a sort of
cross-section or sample of the whole body of citizens, which was permitted
in a given case or for a short term to act in the name of the people. The
terms were short and the magistracies were held as a rule not by individuals
but by boards of ten, one chosen from each of the tribes into which citizens
were divided. For purposes of local government, the Athenians were
divided into about a hundred *demes*, or as they might be called, wards or
parishes or townships. The *demes*' most important function was the pre-
sentation of candidates to fill the various bodies by which the central
government was carried on. The system was a combination of election and
lot. The *demes* elected candidates in proportion to their size and the actual
holders of office were chosen by lot from the panel thus formed by election.

Outside this scheme of choice by lot were ten generals chosen by direct election and, moreover, eligible to repeated re-elections. Not only were they military officers, but they exercised great influence over the decisions of the Council and the Assembly at home. The office was not really a military post but in certain cases a political office of the highest importance.

The really essential governing bodies at Athens were the **Council of Five Hundred**, which formed a key to popular control of government; and the courts with their large popularly chosen juries. Some sort of Council was a characteristic part of all forms of the Greek city state but in the aristocratic states, as at Sparta, the Council was a senate composed of elders chosen for life and without responsibility to the Assembly. The Council of the Areopagus was the remnant of an aristocratic senate which had been shorn of its powers by the rising democracy. In substance the Council of Five Hundred was an executive and steering committee for the Assembly.

The actual work of government was really centred in this committee. But 500 was still far too large for the transaction of business and it was reduced to a working size by the favourite device of rotation in office. The great powers of the Council, however, were always dependent upon the goodwill of the Assembly. The Assembly passed judgement upon matters which the Council presented to it, enacting, amending or rejecting them, as it saw fit. It was through the courts that popular control both of magistrates and of the law itself was fulfilled. This control was secured in three ways. First there was the power of examination before a candidate could take office. Second an official could be made subject at the conclusion of his term of office to a review of all the acts performed by him, and this review also took place before a court. Finally there was a special auditing of accounts and a review of the handling of public money for every magistrate at the end of his term.

The popularly chosen Council and its responsibility to the Assembly and the independent popularly chosen juries, were the characteristic institutions of Athenian democracy. The meaning democracy had for thoughtful Athenians, is epitomized in the famous Funeral Oration attributed to Pericles, who was the leader of the democracy, and represented as having been delivered in honour of soldiers who had fallen in the first year of the great war with Sparta. Until the time of Thucydides, there had never before been such a passage of incomparable brilliance in historical literature, also his commentary on the Oration. The statement emphasized a political ideal. The main purpose of Pericles's speech was evidently to awaken in his hearers' minds the consciousness of the city itself as their supremely valuable possession and as the highest interest to which they could devote themselves. In the Athenian conception annunciated by Pericles, the city was a community in which its members were to live a harmonious common life, in which as many citizens as possible were to be permitted to take an active part with no discrimination because of rank or wealth, and in which the capacities of its individual members found a natural and spontaneous and happy outlet.

On the wider issue of achieving a harmonious common life it must be admitted that the city state was only a qualified success. The very intimacy and pervasiveness of its life which was responsible for much of the moral greatness of the ideal led to defects which were the reverse of its virtues. In general, city states were likely to be prey to bitter factional quarrels and party rivalries. It is because the ideal of harmony was only partly realized that it forms so persistently a part of Greek political thought. Loyalty tended constantly to be paid to a particular form of government or to a party rather than to the city, and this too easily opened the way to sheer political egotism which was not even loyal to a party.

Nevertheless within the circle set by the conception of civil harmony and a life in common the Athenian ideal found a place for two fundamental political values: freedom and respect for law. The Athenian did not imagine himself to be wholly unrestrained but he drew the sharpest distinction between the restraint which is merely subjection to another man's arbitrary will and that which recognizes in the law a rule which has a right to be respected and hence is in this sense self-imposed.

The Athenian ideal might be summed up as the conception of free citizenship in a free state. The processes of government are the processes of impartial law which is binding because it is right. The citizen's freedom is his freedom to understand, to discuss, and to contribute, not according to his rank or his wealth but according to his innate capacity and his merit. In a life such as this, the supreme value for the individual lies just in his ability and his freedom to contribute significantly to fill a place however humble in the common enterprise of civic life.

Turning from the Greeks to the Romans, one finds the restricted vision of the city state gradually broadening out into that of a **universal empire**. There is a new and quite different emphasis on law as the constituent element of the state. One sees the state itself is no longer a bearer of ultimate values. It is rather nothing but a means for obtaining certain ends. Cicero's treatment of the problem in his *De re publica* is particularly significant in this respect. The accent is here shifted from the goal to the structure of the state; it is a partnership in law and not common interest alone that makes a people into a state. There exists in any political community a supreme power from which law emanates. In turn this 'positive' law which expresses the supreme values of justice, and does not vary from city to city, but remains eternal and unchangeable, valid for all nations and for all times.

The idea of law was thus definitely inserted in the idea of the state. Roman lawyers of the imperial age developed further the legal theory of the state by singling out, among innumerable rules that determine human conduct, those particular rules which define the use and the distribution of power in the community. They gave these rules a name, public law. These rules expressed in their view the very essence of the state. Yet on the other hand, these lawyers bear witness to the radical change that had occurred in the general view of life and of the role which political institutions play in it. The contrast between nature and convention has now become the basic assumption of political theory. And the state, like law itself and all other institutions that contradict or limit the 'natural' equality and liberty of men, had to be justified either by examining its origin or by making it an instrument for the attainment of particular values. Both philosophy and religion were at hand to provide the necessary ingredients as proved by the Stoics.

## Stoicism

This philosophical school was founded about 300 BC at Athens by Zeno. **Stoics** believed that God (identified with reason) was the basis of the universe, that human souls were sparks of the divine fire and that the wise man lived 'in harmony with nature'. Knowledge of virtue was all-important. Stoicism was subsequently modified to stress the primacy of active virtue and duty. Epictetus taught that all men were brothers. Stoicism appealed strongly to many prominent Romans including Marcus Brutus and Marcus Aurelius and its doctrines influenced many later thinkers. Under the Stoic influence political thought became less legalistic and cosmopolitan, especially the postulation of a natural law by the Stoics, which was popularized by such major thinkers as Cicero. It was Christianity in large measure which gave the Stoic and Roman idea of cosmopolitanism much more real expression. Indeed Christianity, Stoicism, Buddhism, and other religions and philosophies have always taught that morality is not a matter of frontiers, but that in some sense benevolence and other duties are owed equally to all human beings just because they are human. Stoicism is thus one of the great moral systems that have most influenced human conduct.

Two important principles of Stoicism have influenced later political theory: namely the doctrine that all men are equal, one of the roots of anarchist thinking, and the belief in a universal law of nature. It was considered that all people have been endowed with sufficient reasoning faculties to understand the basic principles of justice, which transcend any human laws. Stoicism was antithetical to the concept of feudal government.

## Feudal government

**Feudal government** flourished during the age of feudalism – the type of land tenure, characteristic of medieval Europe, in which property was held by a vassal of a lord in return for military service and a pledge of homage. Feudalism originated with the collapse of public order in Western Europe during the eighth and ninth centuries. Both kings and great lords distributed life grants of lands and offices in return for promises of loyalty and service. This practice developed into the grant of hereditary fiefs or fees (Latin word: *feoda*, from which the word feudalism is derived) in return for military service. The resulting fragmentation of authority was reflected in the rapid growth of feudal armies often engaged in private wars, the development of the castle as an administrative and military centre, and the growth of private justice administered by local lords rather than central authority. From the twelfth century, these implications of feudal tenure were challenged by the growing power of Western rulers, especially in England, where it was abolished in 1661. Their governments increasingly depended on a royal bureaucracy and an army of mercenaries rather than the feudal bands. The growth of towns, outside the feudal framework, also contributed to the decline of feudalism.

In the Marxist view within the scheme of class struggle between economic groups, feudalism led to mercantilism and finally to capitalism. An important influence on a political system is the degree of 'modernity' of a state. It has been suggested that the British and Japanese systems show a blend of tradition and modernity. Rapid industrialization and democratic institutions were superimposed on predemocratic or feudal societies and elements of tradition such as 'deference' remained. Deference is anathema to any Marxist. That a bourgeois revolution is necessary to overthrow feudalism, and a socialist revolution to overturn capitalism, are fundamental tenets of Marx's philosophy of the dialectical progression of the historical process. It would be scarcely possible to reject this idea and remain a Marxist. Mao Ze Dong (Tse Tung) in China just kept within the rules by propounding his theory of the new democratic revolution in which both processes occur simultaneously, bourgeoisie, proletariat and peasantry joining forces to overthrow the hated *ancien regime*.

Medieval Europe was based on the power and influence of the Holy Roman Empire and the reality of feudalism – that hierarchical form of society and state whose connecting links stretched from king to peasant. Feudal society was based on a complex of rights and duties in which no man had absolute authority. The king was merely *primus inter pares* and had responsibilities to his nobles as well as rights over them. If the king broke the contract of customary right and duties he could be forcibly reminded that there were bounds to his power. Magna Carta was just such a reminder. The first third of the Charter defined the feudal rights to which the king was entitled. It was the law which was supreme. This was the tradition of the legal structure of the state revived – a tradition which had to a certain extent been obscured by the Christian emphasis on the religious purpose of the state. In many cases liberty had been acquired by the abolition of institutions restraining personal freedom, such as laws against religions, remnants of feudal obligations, etc. With the exceptions, however, of the social concept of feudalism and the cynical ideas of the Renaissance, the whole Western tradition of political theory was essentially Christian in its preconceptions and language. Nationalism and the formation of nation states depended upon the development of popular sovereignty, to such an extent that in Western Europe, and subsequently in other parts of the world, they emerged in opposition to the existing political arrangements of empires or feudal societies as aspects of a broad democratic movement.

Feudal government was matched by production for use rather than exchange and by the absence of wage labour or freedom of movement. A challenge was posed to the benefits which feudal government gave to mankind's creativity by the onset of the Renaissance.

## Questions

### City state

1  Account for the importance of the city state to the ancient Greeks.
2  Compare and contrast the city state with the modern state.
3  Describe the actual work of government in the city state.

4    'Pericles's oration is important'. Why?
5    Assess the differences between the Roman perceptions of a city state and those of the Greeks.

## Stoicism

1    What was the appeal of Stoicism?

## Feudal government
1    Analyse the strengths and weaknesses of feudal government.

## Further reading

Crick, B., *Political Theory and Practice*, Penguin, London, 1971.
Dunning, W. A., *A History of Political Theories: Luther to Montesquieu*, Macmillan, London, 1957.
Jones, W. T., *Masters of Political Thought*, Vol. II, Machiavelli to Bentham, Harrap, London, 1963.
Locke, J., *Social Contract essays by Locke, Hume & Rousseau*, Oxford University Press, 1971.
Sabine, G. H. and Thorson, T. L., *A History of Political Theory*, Holt-Saunders, New York, 1973.
Strauss, L., *The Political Philosophy of Hobbes*, University of Chicago Press, Chicago, 1973.

# 3
# Renaissance

## Renaissance: the idea

Today the word **Renaissance** (rebirth) is generally applied to a series of cultural changes which began in Italy in the fourteenth century and spread to the rest of Europe in the late fifteenth century, colouring and perhaps conditioning many fundamental assumptions about art, scholarship and morality until at least the eighteenth century. The word is also applied to the period when these innovations occurred and assumed a dominant position. Classical elements were prominent in speculation, artistic literature and the fine arts of Europe between the fall of Rome and the fourteenth century; and it is also true that in the twelfth and thirteenth centuries the works of Aristotle had come to play a dominant role in the study and teaching of logic, metaphysics and theology. But, until the end of the fifteenth century, Greek and Roman influences were at least in theory subordinated to the requirements of clerical education. Florence to many people is considered the home of the Renaissance, yet none of the Renaissance ideals could have been implemented without the active support of the leading oligarchs of the city, hardheaded businessmen intent on prosecuting their own interests and the welfare of the city whose affairs they managed. Following the lead of Florence and Tuscany one after another, the courts of Italy accepted the new learning and literature, the new paintings and architecture, and the new moral values which they exemplified. In the early sixteenth century Rome was the greatest centre of scholarship and artistic patronage and Venice had begun to understand the message. By this time trans-Alpine Europe was beginning to be interested. The basis was Latin; the aim was the perfection of what we would nowadays call 'communication'. Cicero filled the educational role which had been occupied in the schools of the Middle Ages by Aristotle. The slow and subtle adaptation of Renaissance techniques and attitudes in France and Germany, in England and Spain, produced endless variations of the basic theme; as indeed had the earlier reception in the various Italian centres. But the assumption that all culture depended on a mastery of Latin (for scholars Greek was added) and a thorough knowledge of the main classical writers was pervasive and was to colour European society for centuries to come. A gentleman was by definition well educated in the 'humanities'. The humanities were grammar, rhetoric, history, poetry and moral philosophy studied in Latin and to a lesser extent Greek. The aim was an illuminated and public-spirited elite. Clearly the non-Italian peoples of Europe identified themselves less passionately with classical Rome than the Italians had done. Indeed the Germans, the French and the rest looked back to an antiquity in which their ancestors had been subjugated by the legions. Nothing is more remarkable therefore than the rapid and irrevocable penetration of Italian ideas and practices among the 'barbarians'.

Obviously the tensions were produced in the Middle Ages by an official condemnation of the world so that natural beauty of artistic achievement became an end in itself, wealth and education became more than mere embellishments or social display. The contrast between how men actually lived and how they ought to have lived was not confined to Italy. This fact explains the movement of Florentine discoveries from Tuscany to Italy and from Italy to Europe. Italy solved the moral problems of the continent.

The most significant single treatment of the Renaissance was provided by the Swiss theologian, Jacob Burckhardt, in 1860. He fairly and firmly asserted four propositions: there was indeed a Renaissance, a definable and important moment in the spiritual and material evolution of Western humankind; this moment was sharply opposed to the Middle Ages; the Renaissance inaugurated the modern world; and it was a product initially of the Italian people.

Post-Burckhardt Renaissance argument centred around the emergence of other Renaissances besides that which started in Italy in the Trecento; and the problem of the Renaissance as a radical transformation of society in all its aspects. While the rival Renaissances have been forgotten now, this cannot be said for the question of the Renaissance as a fundamental reorientation of the human predicament. If it was significant (so runs the argument) then it must have been significant in the fields of politics, of science, of religion, as well as in those of literature, morality and the arts. Yet in these spheres the innovations of the Italians, even as developed at large through Europe, had little direct influence. The devices of governments were perhaps enriched a little by the humanities but they were hardly transformed. Man, however, helped in the development of the Renaissance idea.

## Dignity of man

**The dignity of man** attained its greatest prominence and was given its characteristic meaning in the Italian Renaissance. As an idea it is usually ill defined and tends to express a complex of notions, classical and Christian, which writers of the period desired to assert. Certain elements in the history and culture of the Renaissance favoured its development into a definitive literary and philosophical genre. One element was the humanist movement which, in its commitment to a revival of classical motifs in literature and classical attitudes in history and moral philosophy, was eager to demonstrate its equally strong conviction that antique rhetoric poetry, history and philosophy were not in conflict with Christianity but could actually strengthen religion. Second, the very notion of dignity involved the question of relative status as its medieval comparison of man and angel had shown. Last, in the eyes of many people there was an inherent tension between the increasing secularism manifested in the expanding economic, political and social activities of late medieval Europe and those elements of medieval Christianity which stressed asceticism, withdrawal, contemplation, poverty, humility, the anguish, misery and worthlessness of *homo viator*, earthly man. There was no such tension between these new manifestations of the historical dynamism of human energy and the equally Christian vision of the dignity and excellence of man. This theme must be considered as a deeply formative pattern of Renaissance thought and expression through its capacity to offer a resolution of this tension.

Later humanist and Platonic discussions of the dignity of man were extensive and elaborate, involving complex theological and philosophical concepts. Through all their variations, however, the two basic arguments presented by Francisco Petrarch, the fourteenth century Italian poet and scholar, with rhetorical succinctness remained fundamental. Theologically and philosophically, man's dignity derived from the character and purpose of his creation and the resulting position and role this gave man in the universe, from the freedom and the capacity to ascend toward the divine conditions inherent in the image of God in which he was created and restored to man in the Incarnation. Historically and existentially, man's dignity derived from his individual and collective actions and creations in this world from which came his earthly fame and greatness, tokens of the individual's contributions to the high cultures and civilizations which mankind invented and constructed.

It was the revival of Platonism (the philosophical theory that the meanings of general words are real existing abstract entities (forms) and describe particular objects, etc., by virtue of some relationship of these to the form) in the late fourteenth century in Florence under the guidance of Marsilio Ficino which gave new life to the dignity of man. He stressed the role of reason in man as a free faculty, plus man's natural appetite for immortality and deification. These themes, the dignity of man in his pursuit of deification and the universality of all human traditions in this pursuit, were central to the development of Renaissance culture.

The idea of the dignity of man did not cease to find exponents among both philosophers and writers in the sixteenth and seventeenth centuries. More important changes however in relation to the dignity of man were to be the impact of the Protestant Reformation and Catholic Reformation on the one hand and of the emergence of a new science on the other. These sixteenth century developments were drastically to alter the conception of man and his place in the universe and consequently the entire conception of the dignity of man, though the Renaissance concept of man itself had important implications for both these developments.

## Renaissance humanism

This is the name for an intellectual movement that developed in Italy from the mid-fourteenth to the end of the fifteenth centuries and which had as its aim a new evaluation of man, of his place in nature and in history, and of the disciplines which concern him. A characteristic feature of the movement was that it originated and was carried on not by professional philosophers but by men of letters, historians, moralists, statesmen in dispute with the philosophers of the time, to whom they opposed the golden wisdom of the philosophers and writers of the classical period. The debate between humanists and scholastics appeared as a debate between two cultures – between a culture of a scientific tendency and one of rhetorical or literary tendency.

**Humanism** did constitute a force of radical innovation and it alone laid the foundations of what today we call the modern world. The humanists did not accept classical antiquity in the form which it had assumed during the preceding centuries. Primarily, they wished to discover its authenticity and its original sources, both in their true perspective. The humanists were aware that they were living in a world which was rapidly changing and in which the medieval structures (the Empire, the Church, feudalism) had lost their validity. The Italian republics and signorial states were headed by the new bourgeois class which, moreover, was beginning to acquire political importance in the great monarchies of France, England and Spain. It was the era in which trade, voyages, and exchanges of all sorts came to the forefront.

Italian Renaissance humanism was an attempt to regain possession of the authentic legacy of the classical world and hence of the techniques suitable to discovering this legacy. It was an effort to rescue human knowledge from the authority which still oppressed it and to vindicate its freedom. It was ultimately the first attempt to construct a body of knowledge which met the demands of man's daily life, private and public, and therefore could serve as an effective instrument for his plans in the future. Historiography was just one aspect of this knowledge.

## Renaissance historiography

History is a mirror by means of which the present peers into the past in order to see itself as it would wish to be seen by the future. The Renaissance deprecated the Middle Ages in order to assert its own identity. The Renaissance rewrote history; and ultimately it was a revolutionary force which succeeded in destroying a static hierarchical and reactionary mode of thought and behaviour and replaced it with one which broke open the way to the comparatively unhindered exercise of individual virtue in private and public life alike. There was the freedom, if not always the possibility of the person to move in many directions, economic, social, political, emotional, intellectual and moral. Methodological assumptions arose about the course of history – the idea of progress, the theory of perfectibility, the climate theory, the cyclical theory of history, the doctrine of uniformitarianism and the idea of decline.

Although the last three are in ideological opposition to the first three, all are fundamental to our understanding of the ways in which the Renaissance thought. The idea of progress is of most consequence, for it is involved in the rise of the idea of science which marks out the modern world from the preceding eras. The concept of modernity, of the modern world emerging in the Renaissance and continuing as a unity, but with variations within it, to the present day, is at bottom the consequence of the rise of the idea of science and therefore the Renaissance itself. But the triumph of the idea of science was not an easy one, it had to meet the opposition of a number of powerful counter-ideas before it was accepted. The conflict between the idea of progress and the theory of perfectibility on the one hand and the cyclical theory of history, the doctrine of uniformitarianism (that human nature never changes), and the idea of decline on the other is but the first stage of a controversy which reached its height and was resolved with the victory of science in the seventeenth century. These ideas however are both English and continental in scope, and are not confined to any particular type of intellectual activity but are found in all fields of Renaissance endeavour. Although these were not new ideas – their origins being deep in classical structure, they were in the Renaissance recombined into new intellectual constructions.

Revived from late classical antiquity and locked together in the Renaissance mind, the idea of progress and the cyclical theory of history, reinforced when necessary by the doctrine of uniformitarianism and the concept of perfectibility, were welded together to form the idea of science as the basis of a continuously expanded future of an ever expanding modernity to which there could be no end. The impact of religion had an important role to play.

## Questions

### Renaissance: the idea

1 What was the impact of the Renaissance on world history?
2 Account for the varied interpretations of the Renaissance.
3 Discuss the radical innovation of humanism in the Renaissance.
4 Write a critical review of Plato's work *The Republic*.
5 Why has autocracy been a favourite form of government over the past thousand years?

### Dignity of man and humanism

1 Account for the importance of creativity in the Renaissance.
2 What is meant by 'the dignity of man'?
3 Assess the impact of the revival of Platonism.
4 Define humanism.
5 Account for the links between the humanists and the Renaissance.

### Renaissance historiography

1 Why was the concept of modernity so important in Renaissance thought?
2 Why did the potential of the idea of history and the cyclical theory of history have to await for recognition and use until the Renaissance?

**Further reading**

Burckhardt, J., *The Civilisation of the Renaissance in Italy*, Harper & Row, New York, 1956.

Gottschalk, Louise, *Foundations of the Modern World* (1300–1775), George Allen & Unwin, London, 1969.

# 4
# Reformation

## The creation and disintegration of Christendom

The barbarian invasion of Rome and the collapse of the Empire had an important result in the history of European religion. The Christian Church of the West, after the collapse of the Roman Empire, was the only unifying force left in Western Europe. Modelled on the lines of the Imperial administration, with its dioceses and provinces corresponding to Roman divisions, it was able to maintain its cohesion while the Empire crumbled. It was, therefore, the main bastion of order and administration, able to take charge of cities and regions. This ability, together with its unique spiritual authority, was to make the Church the most influential power in preserving the past and refashioning the future. It was this which both enhanced the power of the Bishop of Rome and ensured the predominantly Roman character of Medieval Western Christianity.

Two of the most important factors determining the course of the development of religion in Europe during the Medieval period were the enhancement of the status of the Church which followed the collapse of Rome, on the one hand, and on the other, the rise of Islam in the seventh century and the growth of Moslem political power and cultural influence in the Mediterranean region. During the early Medieval period – from the tenth to twelfth centuries – the focus of European culture was no longer in Greece and Italy but in the North West, especially in France during the latter part of the period from the twelfth century to the fifteenth century, with the decline of Islamic influence in the Western Mediterranean, Italy regaining some of its former cultural importance.

The ideal of a Roman empire was revived by the crowning in 800 of Charlemagne, Emperor of the Holy Roman Empire, in St Peter's at Rome. The idea of a Roman empire had thus been revived; it was, however, beyond the ability of Charlemagne's successors to give it political reality in the highly fragmented state of feudal Europe. Although the theory of Empire persisted there was no effective emperor, with the possible exception of the Pope. Only an international body like the Church could transcend local boundaries and the Pope alone was able to make his voice heard throughout Christendom. It was this fact which lay at the root of the predominantly Roman character of Western European Christianity during the medieval period.

**Papal Christianity**, dominant in Europe from the fifth century, was territorial, authoritarian and priestly. The monasteries were a benefit to modern Christianity as they were centres of learning and culture and their function in keeping scholarship alive in the Dark Ages, the period of unenlightenment from the fifth century AD to about 1000 AD, was paramount. They were also centres of missionary activity from which monks went forth into new areas to establish new monasteries and to Christianize the surrounding territories.

Any person born during the medieval period in Europe, unless he or she were a Jew, would find him or her so far as religious life was concerned, required to believe certain propositions about the world in which he or she lived. These included beliefs that the world was created by a single, absolutely powerful divine being who had created all things *ex nihilo*, and that the human race was in a chronic condition of rebellion against this omnipotent deity, and was deserving of eternal torment. It is easy to assume that there were universally accepted religious beliefs in medieval Europe. However there was a degree of scepticism, intellectual unrest and outright disregard for religious practice. There were a number of movements of dissent which occurred from time to time and in various places, but most characteristically in the cities. Surprisingly in view of the power of the Church and the very harsh penalties for religious deviation, there were many widespread expressions of alternative religious ideas and practices.

In addition during the medieval period an alienation occurred between the Church of the Latin West and that of the Greek East. There were and are basic differences of emphasis. The Western Christian view of man lays stress on his original guilt and the Eastern Church emphasizes man's potential goodness. Western theology tends towards a dualism of matter and spirit, whereas the East holds to the idea of the unity of matter and spirit or at least their interdependence. In keeping with the West's emphasis on the guilt of man and his prime need being for justification, it is the idea of Christ as the victim, the sacrifice to God, which eradicates man's sin which is emphasized; whereas in the East it is the idea of Christ as victor over the forces of evil which is more strongly emphasized. When ecclesiastical structure comes into consideration, the Western Church is characterized by a monarchical authoritarian system, i.e. authority with a recognized focus, namely the papacy; whereas in the East, authority is vested in the whole congregation of the faithful and there is no single visible head, no authoritarian individual who is regarded as Christ's vicar. This shows itself in another way in the strong sense of identification with the community which is characteristic of the Eastern Church, whereas Western Christendom has tended to emphasize the individual.

In the later middle ages increasing nationalism and the assertion of power by temporal rulers weakened the united structure of the papacy and the Holy Roman Empire. With the attack on central authority came a greater boldness in dissident criticism of the Church, exemplified by John Wycliffe in England.

By the sixteenth century the Church no longer had the power to override national interests; in this weakened state it was unable to resist the inevitable fragmentation caused by the Reformation.

# Reformation

The unity and therefore the essence of medieval Europe was shattered early in the sixteenth century by two not unrelated events: the Reformation and the rise of the nation state. The unity of Christendom, which, if one ignores the Orthodox Churches, was a reality in the Middle Ages, was now destroyed by the movement unleashed by **Martin Luther**; the authority of the Emperor, never much more than a myth, could not be upheld even in theory now that states were becoming so integrated and differentiated and their princes were acquiring so much power.

Luther's doctrine was based on the priesthood of every Christian and on emphasis on the authority of the Bible. He was strongly in favour of the constituted authority of the prince, whose power he claimed was directly delegated by God. He justified persecution of those who did not share his own religious beliefs and defended the right of a ruler to enforce religious uniformity on purely secular grounds. He adhered to the Pauline doctrine that all men are equal in the sight of God, although it was not until the eighteenth century that this idea became widespread. Like the great thinkers before him – Augustine and Aquinas – Luther worked from the assumption that the will of God was the ultimate social and political authority.

The Reformation and the influence of Luther led to the secularization of the concept of revolution, previously inextricably associated with divine authority. This authority was strengthened by the fact that, under Luther, it extended as far as combatting the overall power of the Church itself. Luther saw the use of secular power as a temporary emergency based on wider principles. Its purpose was to defend those who were the defenders of true religion by maintaining a system of law within which they could preach in favour of a purified doctrine. Luther taught, therefore, a medieval doctrine of passive resistance to the ruler, the agent appointed by God to punish wrongdoers.

Luther began his movement primarily in order to reform the Church from its gross abuses, and the famous 95 theses nailed to the door of the Church at Wittenberg in 1517 were not primarily theological but moral complaints dealing with the actual behaviour of the clergy rather than Church beliefs.

Luther was a predestinarian (a believer in the act of God preordaining every event from eternity) and determinist (a believer that all acts, choices and events are the inevitable consequence of antecedent causes), but he was also a conservative and soon became alarmed about the position taken by many extremists once the Reformation was under way. He had really wanted the Church to reform itself, but when he alienated Rome he had perforce to rely more and more on the secular powers which finally resulted in the state–church form, i.e. a state-controlled episcopalianism which flourished in Germany.

**John Calvin**, the French theologian, provided in his *Institutions of the Christian Religion* the first logical definition and justification of Protestantism, thus becoming the intellectual leader of the Reformation as the older Martin Luther was its emotional instigator. The distinctive doctrine of Calvinism was in its dogma of predestination which stated that God had unutterably destined some souls to salvation to whom 'efficaceous grace and the gift of perseverance' is granted, and eternal damnation to others.

Calvinism's greatest influence outside the Church was the result of belief that to labour industriously was one of God's commands. This changed the medieval notions of the blessedness of poverty and the wickedness of usury, proclaimed that men should shun luxury and be thrifty and yet implied that financial success was a mark of God's favour. It was thus related to the rise of capitalism either as cause or effect. Max Weber, the German sociologist, believed that Calvinism was a powerful incentive to, or even cause of, the rise of capitalism. Weber perceived that certain features of Calvinism, most glaringly its encouragement to accumulate worldly goods, suited the interests of capitalism. Conversely, Marx and the Englishman, R. H. Tawney asserted that Calvinism was a result of developing capitalism, being its ideological justification.

Calvin went a stage further than Luther, in more favourable political circumstances regarding the secularization of the concept of revolution. Having achieved political authority within the state of Geneva – his area of ministry – he reinforced the message of obedience with the overwhelming weight of the consciousness of the consequences of opposing the actions of God's elect. The Calvinist state was one in which revolution simply could not exist. But a state that had Calvinists within it, but which was not Calvinist in religion, could not but be called into question. The authority of the people, vested in what Calvin called the 'inferior magistrates' was held to be supreme in religious and hence secular matters. Sanction was given to the people to resist a ruler in the name of true religion provided that their claim to authority was voiced in an orderly manner. From this it was a short step to the much more extreme and influential formulation of another strand in the concept of revolution propounded by Knox and Buchanan in Scotland and the Huguenots in France.

The Calvinist tradition of authority passed down the centuries and was used by many governments to excuse or fortify their actions. For example, this tradition was upheld in the English Civil War which was fought in the name of the people, represented by the Parliament against the King.

Calvinists and Jesuits alike in the sixteenth century stood for the ideal of a Church state which, by the very tenacity and ferocity of their quarrels they ensured should succumb before the one alternative neither of them wanted, a state Church.

Like Luther, Calvin was opposed to the idea of undermining the influence of the sovereign ruler, and Calvin particularly advocated passive obedience to the ruler, whom he considered 'the Vicar of God'. However, Calvin's followers rejected his theory of passive obedience when they found themselves in opposition on spiritual grounds to state policies. This occurred in Scotland where in the sixteenth century John Knox, faced with a Catholic monarchy, justified resistance to maintain the Protestant faith. Nevertheless, the divine right of kings reigned supreme.

## Questions

### Medieval Europe

1 Why was medieval Europe politically strong?
2 Assess the important factors which determined the course of the development of religion in Europe during the medieval period.
3 Comment on the links between political and intellectual influence.
4 Discuss the alienation between the Church of the Latin West and that of the Greek East.
5 Account for the decline in the united structure of the Papacy and the Holy Roman Empire.
6 Critically appraise the role of Luther in the Reformation.
7 In what ways did Calvin become the intellectual leader of the Reformation?
8 Compare and contrast the work of Luther and Calvin.

# 5
# Ideas on political duties and responsibilities

## The Divine Right of Kings

This is the oldest of all theories of state origin, and goes much beyond the general notion that all power comes from God. It holds that monarchy is the only legitimate form of government and that the order of succession by primogeniture is divinely appointed, so that there can be no question as to who is the 'rightful' king. The king's authority is absolute and unlimited and he is only answerable to God for the uses he makes of it. The subject owes the king implicit obedience and has, under no circumstance, any right of resistance. Its recommendations were, first, that it put the civil ruler on a level with or above the ecclesiastical authority which had always claimed in a special degree to be divinely appointed. Second, succession to the throne remained fixed and certain, so that it removed one of the possible causes of civil strife. Third, it gave a religious flavour to the allegiance to the king in which the developing nationalism of the time tended to express itself.

The Protestant Reformation destroyed the supremacy of the Church in spiritual matters, while divine law was no longer regarded as above temporal law. In the sixteenth century it became a justification of the *status quo* in a time of unrest and civil wars. This became more extreme in the next century with the assertion of the king's power to govern without any restrictions. This met with increasing questioning by the king's subjects and led to the execution of Charles I in 1649 and the uprising which deposed James II in 1688. In the nineteenth and twentieth centuries the last Emperor of Germany and Czar of Russia claimed to rule by divine right and demanded passive obedience from their subjects.

## Machiavelli

Machiavellianism has historically come to mean that effectiveness alone counts in politics; political actions should not be restricted by considerations of morality of good or evil. In this sense Machiavellianism existed before Machiavelli and is as old as politics itself. The view that the struggle for political power should be excepted from the usual norms of ethical behaviour was widely recognized in the ancient world.

The common denominator of all Machiavellian attitudes was doubt that successful action was compatible with living according to a strictly moral code. The work of Machiavelli most often quoted is *The Prince*, dedicated to Machia relli's patron, Duke Lorenzo di Piero de Medici. It is a short analysis of how to rule an Italian state successfully in the late middle ages. Machiavelli's claim to fame comes from apparently cynical and 'cool' advice he offers to any potential Italian political leader in *The Prince*, and his name has become synonymous with highly manipulative and cynical political activity of a self-seeking nature, especially when totally devoid of general principles. This is actually an unfair view of a man quite dedicated to the welfare of his native city state, and whose other works are an outstanding plea for Italian unity, which aim was indeed the inspiration of *The Prince* itself. Machiavelli has contributed to what can be described as a theory of force, accepting the principle that the essence of a state is power. Broadly it is the belief that political events are determined largely by the struggle for power, to the exclusion of other considerations. Thus *The Prince*, written at a time when civil wars and foreign invasions were frequent, suggested that if the ruler of a state wished to remain ruler he had to acquire as much power as possible. Otherwise the right to rule would pass to a person able to employ power effectively, both to become ruler and remain one. He believed that if law and order were to be maintained, a state would recognize no limitation on its authority. Thus he banished ethical considerations from the art and practice of politics, believing that considerations of national unity, security and interest should take precedence over religious dogma. The grimmest aspects of power politics distinguished by Machiavelli were practised by the Americans and Russians during the earliest parts of the Cold War after 1945. *The Prince* was an early example of a book of rules concerning inter-state relationships.

Where *The Prince* deals with monarchies or absolute governments, his work *The Discourses* is mainly concerned with the expansion of the Roman Republic and is a solid study of early Italian political history. He reflects on the character of Roman constitutional government as described by Livy and tries to ascertain what the rule of law ideally should be. He rejects Aristotle's division of governments into three good and three bad forms, and proposes as an ideal a form of mixed government. Machiavelli argues that in mixed government the separate classes will through institutions of representation limit each other's power and so contribute to the liberty of all. This defence of limited government as a necessary condition of liberty is an invaluable tradition which has lasted down to the present time. He finds that dissent and opposition might be necessary to the whole idea of a state in which liberty can be preserved. Lastly in *The Discourses* he emphasizes the importance of the rule of law as superseding faction and private vengeance and explores the constitution that might be necessary to uphold it. A constitution with established institutions is defended partly as a guarantee against usurpation. Both books show equally the qualities for which Machiavelli has been especially known, such as indifference to the use of immoral means for political purposes, and the belief that government depends largely on force and craft. What does not appear in *The Prince* is his genuine enthusiasm for popular government of the sort exemplified in the Roman Republic, but which he believed to be impracticable in Italy when he wrote.

Machiavelli writes almost wholly of the mechanics of government, of the means by which states may be made strong, of the policies by which they can expand their power, and of the errors that led to their decay or overthrow. Political and military measures are almost the sole objects of his interest, and he divorces these almost wholly from religious, moral and social considerations, except as the latter effect political expedients. The purpose of politics is to preserve and increase political power itself, and the standard by which he judges it is its success or otherwise in doing this. Whether a policy is cruel or faultless or lawless he treats for the most part as a matter of indifference though he is well aware that such qualities may react upon its political success. Ultimately Machiavelli abstracts politics from other considerations and writes of it as if it were an end in itself. The closest analogy to Machiavelli's separation of political expedience from morality is probably to be found in some parts of Aristotle's *Politics* where he considers the preservation of states without reference to their goodness or badness. To many political theorists the test of morality is best exemplified by the social contract.

## Social contract

The notion of social contract, although particularly influential in the seventeenth and eighteenth centuries, has its origins in the ancient Greek system of government. The term refers to the act by which men are assumed to establish a communally agreed form of social organization. This act has been given various characteristics by the numerous theorists who have described it. They may refer to the establishment of society prior to the inauguration of government, or alternatively to the state and society having arisen concurrently. In the first case, the social contract is often thought of as a pact that all men make with each other as equals, while in the latter case it may be a less egalitarian agreement by which the rulers and the ruled are differentiated and their various rights and obligations made explicit.

The idea was chiefly used as a tool for criticizing established, traditional authority when the modern nation states were breaking away from Christendom and seeking both autonomy and just internal constitutions. Its chief exponents were Hobbes, who argued that the social contract created mutual obligations which did not exist prior to the constituted state; Locke, who argued that moral principles and obligations existed before the creation of the state, so that men could change the state if it failed to uphold these principles; and Rousseau, who devoted a famous work to the subject. His work, *The Social Contract*, can be read either as a celebration of liberty and the rights of men, which condemns all forms of absolute or arbitrary government, or as a recipe for the abolition of human liberties and the absorption of the individual into a sovereign collective. It seemed to Rousseau to follow that he whose will conflicts with the general will is in conflict with himself. The condition of society is one in which all rights are alienated to the sovereign power.

Rousseau's whole argument depended upon the fact that a community of citizens is unique and coeval with its members; they neither make it nor have rights against it. Such a community is an 'association' not an 'aggregation', a moral and collective personality. The general will represents a unique fact about a community; namely that it has a collective good which is not the same thing as the private interests of its members. Rousseau moved freely back and forth between his own **theory of the general will** and the indefeasible individual rights which ostensibly he had abandoned. Since Rousseau believed as a matter of course that social well-being itself dictates some liberty of individual choice and action, wherever he meets this sort of case he sets it down as a limitation upon the general will. Logically it is not the case, if liberty itself is one of the things that the general good requires. On the other hand, Rousseau was quite capable of arguing that because there are no indefeasible rights in defiance of the general good, there are no individual rights at all. This again was a logical confusion unless one argues, as Rousseau certainly did not mean to do, that all liberty is contrary to the social good. The truth is that the general will is so abstract that it justifies no inference at all about the extent to which individuals might be left alone in society to 'do their own thing'.

In Rousseau's intention, the theory of the general will greatly diminished the importance of government. Sovereignty belongs to the people as a corporate body while government is merely an agent having delegated powers which can be withdrawn or modified as the will of the people dictates. Government has no vested right whatever, such as Locke's theory of the contract had left to it, but has merely the status of a committee. Rousseau conceived this to exclude any form of representative government, since the sovereignty of the people cannot be represented. Rousseau argued strongly that the only free government is therefore a direct democracy in which the citizens can actually be present in town-meeting. For his time perhaps, Rousseau was too much of a romantic.

## Romanticism

Initially, this was a term for a movement in the arts which spread into politics. In terms of political ideas it represented an anti-intellectual movement. It was against the rationalism (the belief that it was possible to obtain by reason alone a knowledge of the nature of what exists) and empiricism (the thesis that all knowledge of matters of fact as distinct from that of purely logical relations between concepts was based on experience) of the period of the Enlightenment or Age of Reason. During the Age of Reason increasing scientific knowledge gave rise to the development of empiricists, naturalist and materialist doctrines and strong opposition to clericalism. Romanticism was best characterized by its idealist celebration of the self, by its respect for the transcendental and by its conviction of the power of the imagination and of the supreme value of art.

Through Rousseau, romanticism was to recast the social contract vision as one of the state of nature; Herder connected it with nationalist philosophy; Coleridge linked it with cultural conservatism, and Shelley argued that it invoked utopian socialist ideals. It became a fundamental ingredient of modern thought which cannot be summarized in any single doctrine.

The nationalist side of romanticism became an attitude of mind which pervaded many of the arts and much of nineteenth-century scholarship. Music was composed and history written in a consciously, even self consciously, nationalist vein. Added justification was given to the essentially political movements for national unity and independence which created the German and Italian nation states and destroyed the Habsburg and Ottoman Empires.

It was Hegel who, though not a conscious nationalist, brought the contemporary threads together to produce a consistent philosophy suitable for the nation state. He who gave the state and nation the mystical, almost divine power – the ultimate conclusion of Rousseau's concept of the general will. In thus stressing the supremacy of the state he laid the foundations for the development of totalitarian nationalism in which the individual was subordinated to the state. To some extent this was the antithesis of idealism.

What was unclear at Hegel's time of writing was that certain characteristics of romanticism could lead to attitudes harmful to political and social relationships.

## Idealism

The basis of the theory of idealism was that metaphysically the sole matters that existed were ideas or mental entities so that the whole structure of reality had to be understood as a conscious entity. Kant maintained that the world as known before the imprint of the knower was based on the guarantee of practical reason. The succeeding view of the sovereignty of moral law had profound political influence in giving a rational basis for universalism (the belief in universal valid principles of government and individual rights usually founded in the doctrine of universal human nature) and natural law (a system of law binding on men by virtue of their nature alone and independently of all convention or positive law).

Moral and political idealism was the pursuit of, and unwillingness to revoke ideals of conduct even when present reality conflicted with them and even when future realization seemed unlikely or impossible. In thinking about relations between states, idealists were often contrasted with realists, the former seeing international relations in terms of moral precepts, justice, trust and obligation, the latter seeing them only in terms of power.

Idealism had some features in common with romanticism. Its two philosophies were: first, **anti-materialism**, the belief that the spiritual or ideal was the supreme reality or that it was just as real and important as the reality of the empiricist, humanist and rationalist; second: **collectivism**, which placed the Church, state and society higher than the individual and stressed the importance of duties rather than rights. It did not conceive that the individual might have an automatic right to pursue self-aggrandisement since he existed for the development of spiritual ends. Many observers see close affinity between the concepts of idealism, romanticism and utilitarianism.

## Utilitarianism

Basically, the political and ethical theory of the utilitarians states that the criterion of all individual and political action should be the greatest happiness of the greatest number. This political philosophy was propounded by Jeremy Bentham and James Mill who believed that what made utility in the widest sense was the test of the rightness of political and moral action. What was good was pleasure or happiness; what was bad was pain. If one acted on this basis of self interest (pursuing what one believed to be one's own happiness) then what one did would automatically be for the general good.

The serious failing of this thesis was that it made no distinction between the quality of one pleasure and another, and that Bentham failed to see that the law might not be framed and administered by men as benevolent as himself.

Mill accepted Bentham's position in general but seeing its failings emphasized that self-interest was an inadequate basis for utilitarianism and suggested that one should take as the real criterion of good the social consequences of the act. Bentham also argued that some pleasures ranked higher than others and held that those of the intellect were superior to those of the senses. Not only was the social factor emphasized but emphasis was also placed on the nature of the act.

Mill's son, John Stuart, expounded on utilitarian ideals in his book *Utilitarianism* published in 1869, and he introduced quantitative and qualitative distinctions in pleasures, feeling that the original doctrine was too narrow in principle. In emphasizing the importance of principles of a more emotionally satisfying character he never officially forsook the principle of utility.

According to Mill, the theory of **utilitarianism** rests on two premises. First, the merits of an action lie in its consequences and not in the motive or character from which it sprang. Second, the consequences have to be assessed in terms of happiness, later identified in terms of pleasure and pain. Hegelians in particular argued that utilitarianism was founded on a mistaken and unduly individualistic view of human nature.

Some aspects of Benthamite thinking had a pervading influence on political developments, particularly in nineteenth-century Britain. Bentham advocated legal and political reform, still absent in his lifetime (1748–1832), and argued vehemently that all men wanted to maximize their enjoyment, and should therefore have the right to vote, not on grounds of any 'natural rights' but because their interests could then be fairly represented.

One of the key aspects of utilitarianism in the development of political ideas was that it represented the complete establishment of the primacy of the idea of purpose over the idea of law. The law had to be regarded as an instrument subserving a purpose. The only rights were legal rights and these had to be given or withheld by the law simply on considerations of utility, meaning by that conduciveness to the greatest happiness.

The doctrine was a powerful intellectual weapon in the campaign against abuses. Vested interests, established privileges, prescriptive rights of individuals or groups which ran counter to the general welfare, antiquated institutions which had no justification except long existence – all these things were tried by the test of utility, and if they did not meet the test they were to be swept away.

So, utilitarians were in the van of the reform movements that, to a greater or lesser degree, affected the legal system, the Church, local government and many other spheres of public life. There was a wide field in which the results of applying the principle of utility were obvious and unquestionable. But beyond that, when the abuses had been swept away and the question arose of the positive policies to be adopted, there was plenty of scope for differences of opinion about the application of the fundamental utilitarian principles.

Utilitarians in the quest for happiness believed the state had to intervene only to forbid certain classes of actions which were clearly detrimental to the happiness of other people. This was what the criminal law was for. Beyond that, however, the state had to interfere as little as possible and the positive steps in the pursuit of happiness had to be left to the initiative of individuals. This point of view was dominant in the movement, and utilitarianism became associated, particularly in the economic field, with a belief in the utmost possible limitation of state control, in free trade and free enterprise generally, in freedom of contract, in all the things in fact which nowadays are associated with the term *laissez faire*.

From the other side it has been argued that most people are not very good judges of what will produce their own happiness. Over the last century it has been argued that the *laissez faire* idea underestimates the extent to which individuals by pursuing their own happiness may lessen or destroy the happiness of other people. Utilitarians were opposed to the principles behind the republics.

## Republic

'Republic' can have various meanings – it can be a form of government in which people or their elected representatives possess the supreme power, a political or national unit possessing such a form of government, or any community or group that resembles a political republic in that its members or elements exhibit a general equality and shared interests. Historically, the distinction between republic and monarchy has corresponded to two rival theories of political obligation, one based on an idea of consent, the other on an idea of obedience. The Frenchman, Jean Bodin, wrote a major political text *The Republic* during the French religious wars of the sixteenth century and his aim was to strengthen the central authority so seriously weakened by these wars. The central point of Bodin's argument is his assertion that the sovereign has complete authority to alter and create law; and there remains then little restriction on his power.

Plato's great work, *The Republic*, remains one of the most important studies of political literature. The main ideas expounded by Plato in this work were that each citizen should perform the task in the state to which his abilities best suit him and the communal way of life. Although this austere and rigid political system was in certain respects a reflection of contemporary Spartan life, Plato admits that such an organization represents the ideal and is hardly attainable with far from ideal nature. Philosophers in Plato's view could not be induced to become kings nor kings to be philosophers. Plato firmly believed that in a state which did not attain perfection, the element of change had to be taken into account. Plato based his arguments on theoretical assumptions derived from his interpretation of human nature.

Plato's ideal state in *The Republic* has often been compared with modern totalitarian states, but it differs from them in a number of respects, not least in that tighter restrictions are placed on the governors than on the governed. It is true that Plato appears to put the interests of the state or community above those of the individual, to the point where individual identity might also be supposed to disappear. It is the hospitality of democracy to a variety of different ideas that constitutes one of the main charges in his condemnation of democracy in *The Republic* though he is equally critical about the oligarch's obsession with wealth and property. His chief objection to the pluralistic society is that it leaves open the possibility of its members making the wrong choices.

Plato's ideals in relation to the republic have passed down through the generations. Republics have no hereditary heads of state.

## Autocracy

An autocracy is government by an individual with unrestricted authority. The execution of policies is generally arbitrary since the power of the ruler is not subject to any regularized check within society. However, an absolute ruler may govern according to ancient traditions and customs and government is then no longer arbitrary. According to contemporary Islamic ideas the head of the umna (Islamic community) is expected to have absolute executive power but to be a 'just despot', which might be regarded as a contradiction in terms. His despotism is of a special and conditional sort. He is expected to be elected by the entire community and to be pious and learned, and the community has the right to remove him from office if he ceased to be 'just'.

Most theorists of this doctrine held that true autocracy requires the concentration of power in a single person, and not for example, in a party (a group of people organized together to further a common political aim), or caucus (the influencing of government by secret, semi-secret or exclusive organizations within the officially recognized party political system). Although parties may rule in a manner that admits no limitation by law, their multiple agency serves partly to restrict their power. There are, however, marked similarities between party government in the USSR since the revolution and the supposedly autocratic government of the czars which preceded it, and in a sense the second might be called autocratic, as indeed might the first.

## Questions

1 Assess the strengths and weaknesses of the doctrine of divine right of kings.

2   What was the impact of idealism on seventeenth- and eighteenth-century political thought?
3   Examine the appeal of romanticism.
4   Describe the work of Hegel.
5   Compare and contrast Bentham's and Mill's views of utilitarianism.
6   Why were utilitarians the vanguard of the reform movements?
7   What aspects of utilitarianism appealed to the early Socialists?
8   Examine the reasons for the misuse of the term 'Machiavellianism'.
9   Assess the value of the work *The Prince* to historical thought, and compare with *The Discourses*.
10   What is meant by the notion of the social contract?
11   Compare and contrast the views of Rousseau and Hobbes.

## Further reading

Charvet, J., *Social problem in the Philosophy of Rousseau*, Cambridge University Press, 1974.
Cranston, M., ed, *The Social Contract by Jean Jacques Rousseau*, Penguin, London, 1968.
Oakeshott, M., *Hobbes on Civil Association*, Blackwell, Oxford, 1975.
Sorell, Tom, *Hobbes*, Routledge and Kegan Paul, London, 1986.
Spragens, T., *Politics of Motion: the world of Thomas Hobbes*, Croom Helm, London, 1973.

# Part 2  Modern Political Ideas and Assumptions

# 6
# Sovereignty, constitutions and liberties

## Political sovereignty – power and authority

Since the Second World War there have been changes in the political environment which have given increased opportunities to nations to pursue independent policies. The creation of many new states, the widespread recognition of their independence, and their equal status in a world organization, have helped to support sovereign independence and equality in international relations. Thus non-alignment is more practical than it would have been previously, and a system of non-alignment is relevant to the political and strategic circumstances of the post-war world.

The rise of sovereign states goes back to the eleventh or twelfth centuries and was accompanied by the rise of new social groups. City burghers, secular state officials and medium sized landowners acquired some of the power which in previous centuries had been monopolized by great landowners. These new social groups often supported the monarchs, and were frequently welcomed as allies, or manipulated as political instruments by them. The groups continued to have conflicting interests, yet also were increasingly linked by a common loyalty. Horizontal links between the subjects grew strong, in addition to the vertical links between ruler, feudal superior and inferior. The interests and wishes of the people began to form part of the basis of legitimacy of government.

It is unclear actually what is meant by sovereignty, and the concept seems to focus disputes in political science and philosophy. External sovereignty is an attribute which political bodies possess in relation to other such bodies. There are many theories of external sovereignty; perhaps the most important distinction among them is between those which regard sovereignty in instrumental terms (e.g. as an institution existing in order to protect a society from internal and external violence); and those which see it in expressive terms, as the 'realization' or embodiment of social and political order. Hobbes's theory appertains to the instrumental view.

To understand sovereignty one should first try to conceive the condition of man without it. Hobbes believed that security lay in a kind of social contract, first, between men, to set up the sovereign who will command and protect them, and, perhaps, derivatively between each man severally and the sovereign power under which he placed himself and on whom he conferred the power to enforce the contract with his fellows. Sovereignty may be embodied in one man or in an assembly of men, but once established, it has absolute authority in making law, and can be rejected by the subject only by an act of rebellion which, in breaking the contract which confers supreme entitlement on the sovereign, must always amount to injustice.

The **state of nature**, i.e. the state of man outside society, in Hobbes's view must be thought of, not as a state which precedes the institution of sovereignty, but as a state which will certainly succeed upon its dissolution. It is also a state in which sovereigns exist in relation to each other, since here too there is no overriding sovereign whose command has the force of laws. The complete absence, in Hobbes's view, of any power that will enforce rights in a state of nature confers an absolute obligation on the subject to obey the sovereign in return for whatever rights the sovereign may guarantee. It seems then that there can be no justification for civil disobedience. Hobbes goes on to argue that there are real limits imposed on the legitimacy of state action by that natural law which, without the state, could never be upheld.

**Internal sovereignty** is an attribute possessed by a political body in relation to a society that falls under its government. Sovereignty lies in supreme command over a civil society, and it has a *de jure* (legal) aspect as well as a *de facto* (coercive) aspect. Legal sovereignty vests in that person, office or body whose decisions cannot legally be challenged in court. Coercive sovereignty vests in that person, office or body which controls the powers exerted and enforced in the name of government.

In Britain the Queen has legal sovereign powers in Parliament, whereas all decisions of an executive nature are made by the Cabinet. Owing to constitutional pressure coercive sovereignty can only be exercised in accordance with the law, and all exercises of political power are ultimately the responsibility of parliamentary scrutiny. This convergence of the legal and the coercive seems to be the ideal of internal sovereignty. It is a uniting of power and legal authority.

The constitution of the Soviet Union leaves the question of legal sovereignty undetermined. Article 2 states that it is supposed to vest all power in the people, but at the same time affirms the leading role of the Communist Party in Article 6, in such a way as to imply that both legal and coercive power vest in the Party. The situation is equally enigmatic in so far as the United States' constitution is concerned. This seems incompatible with the fact that the constitution can be amended and with the fact that, unless some body can enforce the constitution, it is without coercive power. Once a body, e.g. a legislature, has legal sovereignty there is clearly no limit to its legislative competence. It can be challenged by no one and is not bound by its own decisions. The British Parliament conforms to this rule, whereas the United States Congress does not, since its legislative powers are limited by the constitution, the interpretation of which, however, constantly changes as Congress presses up against its previously defined limits. While the concept of sovereignty might still be thought to be useful in describing the workings of the United Kingdom constitution, its application to modern states such as the United States and the USSR is in both cases problematic.

In contemporary social theory, the important component in the exercise of government authority is legitimacy, the rightful rule or exercise of power based on some principle jointly accepted by the ruler and the ruled. One of the most important questions in political thought concerns the relation of power to authority.

Power is a matter of degree. It may be based on consent or on coercion – thus it can be conferred, delegated, shared and limited. One can therefore distinguish between power with authority, power with common belief in its authority, and naked power such as that exercised by a lawless gang. Politics can be seem as an attempt to translate the third into the second: to eliminate from public life all powers that do not have the sanction of a public acceptance of their authority. Even with no political process there may still be a process of legitimation whereby the naked power of the ruler attempts to represent itself as sanctioned by right. Naked power is weaker than the same power publicly accepted and so this process can still be seen as a pursuit of power. Only if there is an objective authority to be gained can the pursuit of authority be seen as something other than the pursuit of power. Power is an indisputable fact and easily understood as such – and the important feature of every institution lies in its transformation, limitation and rationalization of power.

Power can be exercised through influence or control – but the sense of power as we have been discussing must be distinguished from the legal sense where it denotes not *de facto* ability but *de jure* permission. Powers conferred by law are permissions to do things without legal sanction. Persons who exercise such powers can be legally restrained only from exercising them *ultra vires*, i.e. beyond the powers granted, in which case they are not exercising them.

In all cases authority must be distinguished from power, being a relation *de jure* and not necessarily *de facto*: authority is a right to act rather than a power to act. It may be accompanied by power and so upheld, or be without power, and so ignored. One of the most important powers that uphold authority is the power of people's belief in it: thus, in a sense, authority can create its own power and this gives rise to a disposition to use the two terms as though they were synonymous.

Hobbes argues that the contract is between subjects, to appoint and obey a sovereign; in accepting the sovereign's protection, the subject implicitly contracts with all other members of society to obey him. Obedience is circumscribed by natural law, i.e. by a system of rights that cannot be alienated under the terms of the contract.

Locke similarly argued that sovereign power is not a party to the contract but at best its result; the contract is between the members of society, who mutually forswear certain freedoms that they enjoy in a state of nature for the benefit of the security provided by society. But the terms of the contract do not permit the alienation of certain inalienable natural rights. Locke wished to oppose absolutism in the name of limited government, and foresaw the objection that absolute government might be precisely for what it had been contracted.

**Political obligation** can be seen as the obligation of a citizen towards the state or the subject towards the sovereign. The expression is sometimes used to denote the reverse obligation from sovereign to subject or the reciprocal obligation between the two. The definition is rough since some theories of political obligation deny that there can be obligation towards a state, but admit the possibility of obligation towards society; others deny even that, and argue that political obligation is held neither towards the state nor towards society, nor towards any other abstraction or office, but towards each member of society individually. Sovereignty is closely associated with democracy and representative government.

## Democracy

Democracy is government by the people. The historians and philosophers of the Aegean world invented the term, situated it within a larger political vocabulary, again of their own invention, and provided a mode of political analysis that enjoyed authority well into modern times. Greek political institutions did not survive, but Greek political theory did. The Greek achievement was not a capacity for institution building, but a means for developing modes of analysis that survived even when filtered through Roman and Christian experience. The Greek preoccupation with order is apparent throughout; so also is the overwhelming and perpetual fear of tyranny. Governments are inherently unstable and one has to search for the least vulnerable form. The decision to vest authority – in an individual, a small group, the multitude – is recognized to be the significant political act. Stability and justice are the desired ends. Herodotus, the Greek philosopher, saw that equality before the law was promised by democracy. But he believed that if that good might be obtained from monarchy, with the added advantage of stability, there was no doubting its superior claim.

Plato maintained that as long as there were extremes of wealth and poverty there could be no just society. Democracy by definition must always be government by and for the many. The poor who lack birth and property will always control a democracy. Unlike the great Athenian orator, Pericles, Plato excluded the possibility that a just state can exist in which all citizens participate and he explicitly denied the Periclean ideal. Democracy Plato accepts as the best of the lawless states, but the least desirable of the law-abiding. If moderation is the quality hoped for it comes only from combining the best in monarchy, aristocracy and law-abiding democracy.

Aristotle, Plato's pupil, while interested in reflecting on the ideal state, showed a great propensity to study actual conditions by analysing the constitutions of a large number of existing states. He dwelt on the class character of the political societies he surveyed. Farmers in an agricultural society with a democratic constitution may concern themselves little with public affairs preferring to leave such matters in the hands of wealthier men who have the leisure to attend to public business. In this case citizens choose not to make use of their authority for as long as they think themselves well governed. Aristotle clearly considered this kind of democracy better than one that saw large urban populations involving themselves in the daily management of their affairs; such democratic rule generally opened the way to demagogues and almost invariably ended in some form of tyranny. In Aristotle's view, how to unite an intelligent administration with the power of the citizens was the problem that democracy had always to contend with. He hoped for a state that would combine the best features of democracy and oligarchy: this he called a polity or constitutional government. He was concerned to emphasize the relation between the constitution of the state and the character of its citizens. Polybius, a Greek philosopher a century later, sought to show how the Roman constitution survived due to being associated with the Consulate representing the monarchical principle, the Senate the aristocratic and the popular assemblies the democratic. In checking each other's authority these powers prevent disintegration and disorder and were self-regulating in their activity. Cicero believed the state, a *res publica*, an affair of the people, existed to give the people justice and derives its authority from them. Though it never represented itself as democratic the Roman republic was proud of its popular instruments of government and took care to protect its fame as lawgiver. The Roman Empire never enjoyed an equivalent success to republican Rome.

With the barbarian invasions and the destruction of Roman political authority, local rule asserted itself. In the feudal situation that developed, older concepts of citizenship became increasingly irrelevant. Democracy has no place in a society increasingly supportive of a value system that emphasized stability and custom. The world was a divine creation; man's obligation was neither to control it, nor to make it over.

For new democratic ideas to develop it was necessary that medieval attitudes be set aside, that man perceive himself in a new way, and aspire to new political roles. Such perceptions began to be common in England and France after the Reformation; events in both countries were to have marked influence elsewhere. The disintegration of an earlier religious unity produced marked disquietude as did rapid economic changes, with large social dislocations flowing from them. For Hobbes in the seventeenth century, the state was a human convention, created by man to satisfy a basic need, a release from the fear that existed when he could depend on no protection other than that provided by his own brute strength. Man in Hobbes's view, created the state to avoid perpetual war, and his questions were simply: shall sovereignty rest with one, with a few or with the multitude? On utilitarian grounds, Hobbes established the advantages of monarchy over democracy.

John Locke emerged as the political philosopher of the late seventeenth century. He was concerned with developing a rationale for political authority. Locke believed that man endowed with reason wished to enter a social contract with his fellow men to give up personal rights to interpret the laws of nature in return for a communal guarantee that his rights of life, liberty and property will be maintained. Locke did not believe, as Hobbes had, that authority once established can never be broken; the community is always free to remake its constitution. While accepting that monarchy is the original form of government, he refuses to accept Hobbes's view that it is the best. As for oligarchy, it tends to favour the interests of a few, to the disadvantage of the many. Democracy offers the only adequate solution for a just rule. Locke argues that the legislative power ought to be one in which delegates are controlled by popular election. Locke accepted the fact that monarchy would continue. His main concern was that the monarch should not have the supreme legislative power.

These ideas were valuable in the eighteenth century but they did not create democratic government. In England they provided a defence for the Glorious Revolution and a rationale for the legislative supremacy that developed under the Hanoverian kings. In France they provided an additional incentive for comparing the 'free' institutions of Great Britain with the more despotic institutions of the Bourbon monarchy. For example, Montesquieu in his *Spirit of the Laws* (*De L'esprit des Lois* 1748) dwells on what he assumes to be the uniqueness of the British Constitution – its separation of the executive, legislative and judicial powers and its balancing of these powers, one against the other. Yet it was left to Rousseau to produce what could be described as a theory of democracy via the concept of citizenship, i.e. the awareness of interests in common that creates the bond between men. Rousseau was keen to prevent inequality among men, in the general will of the people.

After 1776 and even more after 1789, talk of democracy increased, but examples were no longer borrowed from Greece in the time of Pericles. The greatness of the American political experiment or the horrors of the Revolution in France, depending on the point of view taken, were the new subjects of major political discourse.

The American colonists in the eighteenth century saw themselves as maintaining a tradition of opposition that had already shown its strength in the mother country. Their hostility was to certain types of government, based on corruption, that threatened traditional liberties. The power of a few office-holders and members of Parliament was endangering the freedom of the many. Despotic government for the colonists at least seemed a real possibility. The colonists disputed Parliament's claim to authority over them. While members of Parliament might claim that the colonists were as much represented in Westminster as 90 per cent of the people of Britain who did not vote, American pamphleteers criticized this notion of 'virtual representation'. In England, where representation was traditionally by 'interests' the idea of personal (or individual) representation was unknown. The Americans saw no one in Parliament at Westminster who represented their 'interests' who stood to lose or gain in the way they would, through new taxation. The idea of 'virtual representation' was condemned, and support grew for the principle that a man could be bound only by his own assent or by that of a representative for whom he had voted. Increasingly, Americans came to define a constitution as a 'set of fundamental rules' that even the legislature was forbidden to alter. These rules they insisted ought to be instituted by delegates elected by the people, and could be altered only by procedures that involved the people. The nascent idea of federalism existed in American eyes that sovereignty might be limited; and an authority might have full power in one sphere and none in another. Paine saw America's cause as the cause of all mankind, and wanted a distinction between kings and subjects, and the need for a final separation between colonies and the mother country. Paine saw any alternative as a perpetuation of royal tyranny. For Paine the word 're-public' meant the public good, or the good of the whole.

By the late 1780s Americans were referring to their governments as democracies of a new kind, 'democratic republics' or representative democracies. Madison in defending the constitution was keen to establish a non-tyrannical republic and do away with minority 'factions'.

In France the *Declaration of the Rights of Man* of 1789 maintained that all sovereignty rested in the nation and that the aim of all political association was to preserve the natural rights of man, that no group and no individual might exercise authority that did not emanate from the nation. All citizens had the right to participate personally, or through their representatives, in the making of law and in voting on matters relating to taxes. Every man was presumed innocent until judged guilty. Punishments had to be established by law, freedoms of speech and press were guaranteed. No one could be disturbed for his opinions, even in matters of religion, provided that he did not trouble public order as established by law. Ultimately, citizens possessed rights that could not be trespassed on. The sovereignty of the people was simplicity declared and with it the principle that there would be one law for all, with public office open to citizens on the basis of their abilities.

By the turn of the century, groups argued about the sovereignty of the people. Popular sovereignty was pitted against the old order with its royal, aristocratic, inegalitarian traditions. Basic rights to liberty, equality, security and property were constantly reiterated, so also was the notion that sovereignty lay with 'citizenry as a whole' and that the right to vote ought to be extended generally to male citizens.

Bentham established support of universal male suffrage and the secret ballot. The only good government was derived from the people, the interest of the people needed to be the same as the interest of the government. The right and proper aim of government was the greatest happiness of the greatest number and this could not be legislated for. There was an explicit preference for individual over collective action. John Stuart Mill, influenced by Benthamite thinking, looked for reform of government that would bring the 'most virtuous and best instructed' to the top in a position to give the lead to others. After the Reform Act of 1832, Mill went out of his way to remind his readers that popular government meant not so much that the people govern as that they are in a position to choose their governors.

The democratic theorist, Alexis de Tocqueville, maintained that the tyranny of public opinion could prove more burdensome than the tyranny of any monarch. Democracy in his view did not guarantee efficient government; but did provide freedom for the pursuit of one's own interest, subject always to the tyranny that comes from the majority insisting that its values and ideas should be safeguarded. Democratic societies have a taste for easy success and present enjoyment; this is their strength and their weakness. Equality, de Tocqueville insisted, tends to isolate men to cause them to concentrate on themselves only and gives them an inordinate desire for material goods and comfort. De Tocqueville was not clearly favourable to democracy.

Towards the end of the century, liberalism moved increasingly in a collectivist direction and lost its earlier hostility to socialist experimentation. It was almost possible to believe that representative institutions had indeed resolved the political and social problems of industrial society. Marx in accepting the industrial system, in insisting that social inequalities could be overcome through a rational organization of society, laid the basis for a doctrine that gained new adherents late in the nineteenth century. Eduard Bernstein believed socialism could only come about through democracy.

He and the Fabians believed socialism was a continuation and a fulfilment of industrialism and of democracy. Conversely Georges Sorel believed democracy was weakening the ardour of the working classes.

So long as democracy was a political movement making its way, so long as there were classes to be enfranchized, constitutions to be written, partisans of popular rule were disposed to be fairly uncritical of democracy. By the twentieth century, people became cynical about democracy. They believed that political movements that insisted on instituting complex democratic mechanisms – reconsiderations of legislation, referendum, proportional representation and the like – dwelt on quite secondary matters.

One of the early twentieth-century exponents of democracy was Woodrow Wilson, the President of the United States 1913–20 – who in the post-World War I period pledged a League of Nations, of peace-loving states, the institution of a permanent organization to which only democratic states would be admitted. Through persons like Wilson, democracy became a word of common usage in a way that it had never been previously. Democracy in another form appealed to Lenin. This was seen in the Communist Party, a centralized party, of professional revolutionaries which accomplished what social democracy had never been able to achieve in the West – absolute control, through party instruments of government and a highly centralized bureaucracy of the whole of the state's power. Lenin achieved this in the name of democracy – not the bourgeois democracy of parliaments, but the proletarian democracy of soviets.

Joseph Schumpeter in the 1930s and 1940s argued that the classical theory of democracy did not describe the political situation as we know it. He believed the democratic method to be that institutional arrangement for arriving at political decisions in which individuals acquired the power to decide by means of a competitive struggle for the people's vote. Modern democracy was the product of capitalism. If capitalism were to disappear and be replaced by socialism, democracy's institutions would remain. Central to the survival of democracy was the agreement of the vast majority of people in all classes to abide by the rules of the democratic game. The American, Robert Dahl, argued in the 1950s that the possibility of majority rule on any specific policy was negligible. Constitutional forms were not a principal device for protecting one group in society against another. The American Constitution survived because it was frequently altered to fit a changing social balance of power. Bargaining made the American political process work.

Eric Weil argued that constitutional regimes involve a set of judicial institutions independent of political authority and generally provide for a method whereby political leadership may be altered by the citizens' vote. Democracy is the best form of government in a healthy society as it has the best chance of bringing good men to major positions. Reasonable discussion has to lie at the base of any stable democracy. Parliamentary institutions are no guarantee against tyranny, nor can universal suffrage be held to provide any defence. The basis of democracy is an administration capable of acting rationally and keeping the confidence of the electors. Electors have to be prepared to accept the judgement of those who are qualified to know.

## Representative democracy: government and representation

In the modern world, democracy implies **representative government.** Universal suffrage is expressed by voting for representatives who then are responsible for making and supervising the administration of public policy. The direct participation of voters in the making of public policy (as in the referendum and initiative process) is relatively infrequent and, among the best governed countries, it is most often found in Switzerland and in several states of the United States. In most cases it is the voters who elect representatives and it is the representatives who govern.

To expound universal suffrage and representative government, however, is still to leave a lot unsaid. Citizens of all communist states, and of many manifestly authoritarian states enjoy the formalities of universal suffrage and representative government. One has to separate real democracy from sham democracy. Representative democracy in the United States occurred partly because there were too many people to participate directly in policy making and partly because the older citizens correctly understood that continued direct democracy threatened their control of local government. By instituting elections and by delegating policy making to elected representatives (a town council, for example) the chances of continued control by the more influential citizens was much improved. The writers of the US Constitution also knew that by providing for the indirect election of the president and members of the Senate (qualified citizens voted for electors who in turn selected these public officials), they were most likely to prevent policy making from failing into the hands of the 'irresponsible' elements in society (meaning the socio-economic classes).

Strictly speaking the United States and other contemporary democracies are republican governments in which citizens participate in policy making through elected representatives.

The ancient Greeks well understood that the election of public officials almost invariably worked against true democracy. At the height of Athenian democracy, public officials were selected from among all the citizens by lot and were quickly rotated with other citizens through public office. To institute elections meant to disqualify many citizens from equal access to public office. The more articulate, the more personally appealing, the better organizers, and the richer citizens inevitably had (and have) superior advantages in an election contest. For the ancient Greeks and for many other political thinkers in more recent times, elections and representative democracy invariably lead to government by the few and rule by a self-interested oligarchy.

To overcome the obstacle of achieving a high level of continuous governmental involvement in mass societies, representative democracy has emerged as an adaptation which meets the needs of modern nation states. Governments of representative democracies have to be derived from public opinion, be answerable to it and operate through the machinery charged with continuous assessment of governmental objectives and work. This entails regular elections and the existence of institutionalized checks and balances.

In representative democracy, the only widespread form of democracy in practice, political decision making is done by a small number of people elected by the whole electorate. Two problems lead critics sometimes to challenge the 'democracy' claim of representative democracy. The first is that the vagaries of electoral laws and voting patterns may well result in the control of the legislative assembly lying in the hands of a group representing very much less than a majority of the population. It is common in the United Kingdom, for example, for a government to be formed by a party which, though having a majority of members of the House of Commons, was supported at the polls by perhaps only a third of the total electorate. Nonetheless because of party structure and discipline, this highly 'unrepresentative' group may be able to force the passage of laws bitterly disliked by a majority of the population for the whole term of a parliament. The second point relates to the whole doctrine of representation. There are really only two models of how the mass of individuals can be represented by a few people. One, usually called the 'delegate' model, involves the elected member being instructed by those he represents exactly how he should vote in the legislative assembly. In this way, the majority of preferences of each constituency are dirctly transmitted to the assembly, and the mass of the population can be said in some sense to have their views turned into law. The other model, most ably and famously defended by Edmund Burke in his addresses to his own constituents in eighteenth-century Britain, rejects the idea of binding delegation. Instead the representative is seen as chosen for his qualities, and perhaps for the general principles on which he stands for election. Once chosen, however, he is a free agent, entitled to cast his legislative vote as he believes best, regardless of the opinion of his constitutents. At best this latter model is what is practised in actual representative democracies. In fact the usual system does not even give the voter the chance of selecting persons who will at least stand by their own convictions. Instead most systems operate with tight party discipline and in a political system where only those nominated by major political parties can be elected. Thus the voters are in fact choosing among rival party teams, and the character of the person they elect is largely irrelevant. Exactly who is being represented and exactly how democratic representative democracy actually is, can therefore sometimes be in doubt.

Within many representative democracies the referendum is a method of referring a question or set of questions to the people directly, as opposed to allowing them to be settled by the people's representatives in the legislature.

## Representation

Representation is the process whereby the interests of the governed are 'represented' to those who govern them, for example, through parliamentary institutions. The House of Commons in Britain makes real the principle of representation and elected representatives (members of Parliament) are the personsification of this ideal.

Two definitions shed most light on the idea of representation. First, a person, or a group of people, is said to be representative or typical of a larger group or community. Such a person or group is identified as representative because it reflects the characteristics of the larger group.

Second the word can denote the function of an agent or delegate. A representative in this sense acts to safeguard and promote the interests of an individual or group. Spokesmen of interest groups act as representatives when they are consulted by government departments or royal commissions.

Technically representation simply means a system in which interests or beliefs of many are represented, are argued for, given audience before, some decision making body by only one or a few people working on behalf of the many. In parliamentary terms, representation refers to the constitutional system for electing members of the legislative body who will work for the interests of those who elected them and for whom they are representative. In other political contexts representation may mean the mass, or some governing elite, choosing a few people, from the many not normally allowed access to decision-making, to come to meetings in order to pass on the views of those they represent. It does not follow, either in theory or in practice, that representatives have any share in the making of decisions. Thus even though opportunities for manipulation and difficulties of coherent and consistent decision making in mass meetings are rife, to transfer decision making to a limited number of people – while keeping them in significant contact with the larger group – can give rise to problems. Some forms of representation, however, flawed, is inevitable in contemporary industrialized societies.

A representative is bound by a double duty, that towards the institution in which he sits, and that towards the electorate. Neither duty is the result of a promise, but each must be upheld in obedience to the constitution under which the representative holds office. Thus representation is a conventional relation, mediated by conventions and rules, while delegation (the relation between an officer and an electorate when the electorate has instructed him to convey certain requests and commands to another body) and mandation (the relation between an officer and an electorate, when the electorate has instructed him to convey certain requests and commands to another body), are both natural relations, founded in obligations undertaken by the appointee. Ultimately the representative must be not just influenced, but in some crucial sense controlled by those whose interest he represents – otherwise he will represent the state to its subjects, but not the subjects to the state. Edmund Burke went a stage further by suggesting that the representative should be controlled by the party.

## The machinery of democracy according to Burke

Burke believed that in any state parties were essential to the preservation of freedom. He refuted the view that they were vicious aberrations from normal political life. Party divisions, whether they were for good or evil, were things inseparable from free government. Party was an ever present political practice to which recourse might be had in exceptional circumstances.

Burke conceived of the **party** as a temporary expedient, a means of resolving problems within a static political system. He did not think of party in the context of a developing constitution, nor as a dynamic force affecting the development of the British Constitution. If the British political system were in need of reform, then reforming endeavours had to be directed towards restoring the constitution to its basic principles, not towards changing the nature of the constitution itself. Party was, therefore, a profoundly conservative force. The idea that the British political system might move towards a two-party system of government was entirely absent from Burke's mind. The restoration of the constitution which Burke envisaged was to be achieved not through the institutionalization of party conflict but by bringing virtuous men into government through the agency of party and thus by ending, not prolonging, any political partisanship. Party was Burke's method for annihilating conflict and, as such, was not capable of political change or constitutional development in his political theory.

Burke did neglect the organizational side of party. He never seriously entertained the prospect that a party ought to seek to augment its numbers in the lower house, preferring to rely upon the goodwill of other groups. In an intellectual and political climate which accepted the assumption that political power stemmed from property and not from people, it was impossible for Burke to conceive of a ministerial party independent of the king resting upon a parliamentary majority, representing the body of the nation.

It was not merely political institutions that needed changing. Indeed the institutions ought not to be tampered with. It was the men who needed to be changed and party was the vehicle by which this change would be effected. Burke continually underlined how acting in unison strengthened a man's principles and stiffened him sufficiently to resist the temptations of court emoluments. Party was made for man's weakness, for without it he was too weak and vulnerable to maintain correct political principles in the world. Party enabled him to develop his political and moral capacities to the full. A breakdown in man's public responsibility and a lapse in his moral control would be remedied by party, because it is rooted in man and designed to further the standards of his public activities.

Party for Burke was a means of placing at the disposal of the state attributes of the aristocracy. Politics and thus party started and stopped with the aristocracy. Because he wished to maintain the unity of their order, Burke did not believe it to be the business of politicians to legislate on contentious issues. Their business was to preserve the constitution by safeguarding its principles. Political action for Burke meant the removal of abuse, not the implementation of a programme; the restoration of a theoretically ideal constitution, not a series of humanitarian reforms. For Burke the programme of a party was to be found in its history, not in its plans for the future.

The function of government was to preserve the state and its institutions. Necessary adjustments, adaptations and changes might occur, but ultimately existing institutions had to survive. The state had a right to perpetuate itself and its institutions. The monarch's emergency and discretionary powers had to be exercised upon public principles and national grounds, which could best be done by placing the exercise of these powers in the hands of ministers. Burke had a high conception of the art of politics and saw it as a process which required the exercise of all the great qualities of the human mind, whose aim was to secure the confidence of the governed as a step towards pursuing the interest and desire of common prosperity. How this was to be achieved was the problem of statesmanship. Essentially Burke believed that government ought to be in the hands of the aristocracy rather than in the hands of the people. Burke argued that the sober conduct of business, to say nothing of the independence of parliament, might be severely compromised if government had constantly to pay attention to popular opinion. Yet perhaps ambiguously in view of these elitist views, he maintained consistently that a minister had to come to power on public and national rather than on private grounds. Burke believed in a standard of judgement whose criterion was how far parliament was able to maintain its historic character. Anything which weakened the essential characteristics of parliament, such as its control over its own membership, its necessary connection with the opinions of the people, had to be illegal.

The representative system was not primarily a mechanism for registering the opinions of the country. It was first and foremost the arena for reconciling different interests in the state. Although political power must be exercised for the good of the people, it ought to be exercised neither by them nor under their surveillance. He believed that representatives of the people must not act purely from local or from sectional considerations but upon a very enlarged view of things. Burke was more concerned to represent the best interests of the people rather than their opinions. He thought of radicals as unreliable, treacherous men who had no stake in the country, whose rantings threatened the principle that political power should be closely related to the ownership of property. It was the abuse and the excesses of royal influence that Burke proposed to remove, not the influence of the crown in politics. Burke did not envisage a political system in which the crown counted for nothing. It was the consequences rather than the principle of parliamentary reform which Burke abhorred.

He maintained that government should exist for the good of the people but not that it should be controlled by the people. His firm belief that government and party should rest upon public principles did not mean that the people should be consulted constantly.

### Freedom

There are many problems in defining **freedom**. Not only are there many meanings of freedom, but the same definition may be accepted by many groups who will interpret it differently according to their own political beliefs and culture. It is endorsed by so many political persuasions that it tends to lose some of its value in meaningful communication. The idea of a free society is purely a value judgement. If someone believes that a particular society offers freedom it is because it is free in those things which are valued most. The last problem is probably the most relevant to the contemporary world, i.e. freedom is situational in time and place. The concept is subject to new interpretations and modifications as conditions and circumstances change.

One can view freedom in a negative and positive way. Thomas Hobbes defined freedom 'as the absence of opposition' and suggested that liberty of the individual depended on 'the silence of the law'. Negative freedom infers that the state permits the maximum scope for the individual to do what he or she wants. In the eighteenth century, freedom and rights were seen by political philosophers such as John Locke in terms of establishing certain claims by the individual against the state. Man was seen as naturally good, being ruled by the artificial creation of government, which interfered with individual activities. Individualism results in licence or anarchy, when the state does not have the power to enforce any rules. Groups can thrive through having too much freedom, so there have to be restrictions on freedom in all states whether 'democratic' or 'non-democratic' in the interests of safety and national security as defined by the government. An individual is free to act, think, write or speak provided he does not break the law. Restrictions are sometimes placed on the freedom of worship for political considerations, as in the Soviet Union. Most countries impose restrictions by means of laws relating to libel, slander and sedition. Limitations may exist on the facilities for obtaining and publishing information. States have been known regularly to restrict the right of certain persons to move freely within their borders or to go abroad.

Both justice and freedom are very apposite to the concept of equality – which can be interpreted as equal concern and respect for all people as individuals. The concept of equality includes the political principle of 'one person – one vote', efforts to reduce inequality through laws and policies by ending discriminatory treatment of minorities, women or racial and religious groups, and reducing inequalities of income and wealth.

Marx maintained that the right of man to freedom was based not on the union of man with man but on the separation of man from man. He was concerned particularly with the right of man to property which was the right to enjoy possessions and to dispose of the same arbitrarily (without regard for other men) irrespective of society's reaction. This formed the basis of civil society.

Marxist–Leninist philosophy treats freedom and necessity as a dialectic unit. Freedom is considered to consist not in man's complete independence from natural and social laws, but in the cognition, understanding and utilization of such laws by him. But the laws operate objectively, i.e. interdependently of man's will, so that necessity is primary, while freedom is secondary. Thus necessity is viewed as inexorable only if it is unknown, while the knowledge of necessity enables man to be a master over it. Engels pointed out that freedom is the appreciation of necessity.

The liberal position was expounded, at about the same time as Marx was explaining his ideas, by J. S. Mill in *On Liberty* in 1859. Simply expressed, this finds freedom in the power of the individual to assert himself against the state. The power of the state is enshrined in law, so that the measure of the freedom of the individual is not the lenience, but the scope, of the law that governs him. A further embellishment of the liberal view construes such freedom as itself the aim of the law, which should not merely permit these areas of untrammelled choice but also maximize them. The thought was given impetus by Locke, who also emphasized that licence is a freedom that is exercised only at risk to another's freedom: to forbid it is not to lower but to increase the sum total of individual liberty.

In a reply to Mill, Sir James Fitzjames Stephen expounded the conservative position in 1873. Emphasis is placed on the value of freedom which is only for someone who can also value the activities which are permitted by it. Men have values as a result of their perception of themselves as belonging to a social order; if freedom is to be preserved social order must be preserved as its necessary precondition.

The welfare socialist view differs from either the liberal or conservative position, in that it pays attention to the conditions for positive freedom. If men are to be free in the positive sense of possessing power to fulfil their natures, they must suffer whatever constraints are necessary to organize their labour and ensure a satisfactory distribution of its product.

Hegel took a more individualistic approach by arguing that freedom consists, in the last analysis, not in the power to oppose the state, but in the disposition to obey it.

In all the theories, freedom is seen as a rational agent which has autonomy, values, and long term aims and projects. The problem of freedom thus raises complex problems of human nature, focusing on the tenability or otherwise of individualism, with a pluralist political development.


## Pluralism

**Pluralism** is a political sociological theory of society as several autonomous but interdependent groups having equal power. Institutional arrangements are made for the distribution of political power in which no particular political, ideological, cultural or ethnic group is dominant. Such a situation normally involves competition between rival interest groups out of which the plural society arises. The main exponents of this view were G. W. Leibnitz and W. James.

Pluralism therefore is any view which is in opposition to monism and perhaps also to dualism and arguing for a multiplicity of basic things, processes, concepts or explanations. **Monism** is the doctrine that reality consists of only one basic substance or element, such as mind or matter, and is the attempt to explain anything in terms of one principle only. The best known proponent of monism was Hegel – in particular of its idealistic version regarding ideas as the essence of all phenomena.

A pluralist democracy is the political outcome of a liberal ideal of freedom. Governments in the Western world, of all persuasions generally, zealously upheld notions of freedom of the individual against the state and against the tyranny of public opinion. The main threats come from diffuse power structures such as bureaucracies and from totalitarian societies which brand plural socictics as anti-social and immoral. Totalitarianism is the antithesis of pluralism which tolerates heterodoxy and accepts that there is a multitude of competing political truths. Tolerance is found in conjunction with pluralism, as political tolerance rests on the view that there can be no conclusive proof or disproof of the truth of political ideas.

The pluralist system is decentralized, advances in policy depending heavily on bargaining. The system aims to reach compromises rather than to discover political truth or the 'right' policy. The advantage of pluralist theory is that it suggests that the political system is all-inclusive and operates on the basis of consensus, which ensures that everyone's interests are taken into account, and everyone attains satisfaction. Group competition for the achievement of political goals is a vital concept of pluralism.

The American, Robert Dahl, analysed pluralist theory and spoke of multiple centres of power, none of which is or can be wholly sovereign. He maintained that a basic problem of modern political systems was the degree of differential participation existing from group to group. Dahl saw pluralism as encouraging centres of power on a local rather than on a national scale, which could be argued in terms of community power.

## Liberalism

The liberal is concerned with aspects of freedom that have come to be important since the Renaissance and Reformation. The causes of their emergence in the West are as much cultural and intellectual, as they are social and economic.

The liberal views of freedom started in a part of the world deeply affected by Greek philosophy, by Roman conceptions of law, and by a religion affirming the closeness of man's relations with God. The liberal idea of freedom, though it emerged in a society deeply influenced by Greek philosophy, Roman law and Christianity, is not to be found in ancient Greece or Rome or in Christian countries before the Reformation. The modern or liberal idea emerges with the attribution of rights of the mere individual against those in authority over him. It is admitted that these rights are not to be exercised to the injury of others, or that in practice not everyone can exercise them, or that their universal exercise is a gradual achievement.

The liberal idea of freedom arose slowly with the rise of the modern state and the gradual acceptance of religious diversity in a part of the world where the church was a unique institution and personal faith of peculiar value.

The modern state, as no political community before it, is both highly centralized and highly populated; its authority is extensive and pervasive. Conversely in the old empires supreme authority, though extensive, was not pervasive, for most people most of the time were not directly affected by it. Supreme authority in the Greek and Italian city states was close to the persons over whom it was exercised. In the modern state the holders of supreme authority are not personally known to the vast majority of the citizens; but there are large numbers of state officials and the citizen has more to do with them than ever before. He rarely sees in person the men in authority but he sees pictures of them and reads or hears their words repeatedly.

The state, even when it is federal, is a tightly knit organization in which everyone's rights and duties are clearly defined. It is also quickly changing. To do what is expected it must be highly adaptable and have elaborate and precise rules for the guidance of its officers. It could not be adaptable unless procedures, powers and obligations inside it were carefully defined. In a modern state the rights and obligations of the citizen are also well defined. He has a variety of social roles, and his rights or duties in them are defined not only by custom but also by statute and contract. He is ordinarily more mobile socially and geographically than his ancestors were. Even in the most authoritarian or 'illiberal' of modern states, men and women have a variety of rights and duties that they share with everyone or with most people. Increased mobility is associated with two developments: with the rise of the modern state and with the emergence of an elaborate legal system.

The authority of the modern state is 'impersonal' in the sense that the persons who exercise it are not concerned with the persons subject to it as unique individuals but rather as belonging to some category or other. Though the private citizen often lacks a remedy against official abuses of power, lesser officials are more strictly responsible to greater ones. There is also a sharper distinction made between rights and duties attached to particular occupations or social roles and more general ones. The citizen is at least encouraged to look upon himself as a citizen. Even though he has little remedy against abuses of public authority this is not officially admitted. The official claim is that his rights are well defined and adequately protected.

The modern state also claims to be democratic. It did not do so in the sixteenth and seventeenth centuries. The modern state in its early days was a monarchy or oligarchy. It was much less centralized than it became later, and its authority much less pervasive. As that authority increased, as local autonomies lessened or survived only within limits defined by the central power, as the individual found himself more and more controlled by that power, his desire to control it grew stronger. This desire arose first among the wealthy but spread in time to other classes. In Britain the powers of the king and of Parliament increased together, long before Parliament became democratic. In France, when the French equivalent of the British Parliament was revived and reformed at the Revolution, the popularly elected legislature was reduced to impotence by the group of extreme radicals.

Political theory has had a bias towards democracy from the time that the modern state arose and long before it became democratic. It has held that the legitimacy of government derives from the consent of the governed. Locke spoke of the rights which men have, and argued that governments are obliged to protect these rights, and that subjects have the right to resist or remove governments when they fail in this duty. Conversely, Marx later argued that rights (on which Locke based his views) could only be exercised effectively by the wealthy and the educated.

## Toleration

John Stuart Mill was the first political theorist to analyse tolerance. He believed liberty for all required that neither the few nor the many dominate completely, but that each have its due. This could be accomplished only if all points of view could be heard in public. Tolerance of all views, the freedom of speech, must be guaranteed so that the most rational ideas would be accepted by all. This tolerance and the rational acceptance of argument meant to ensure that the powerful do not convince by dint of their power alone. In Mill's revision of classical liberalism, tolerance was its chief social virtue. A decent life for all could best be protected in a society in which every interest is allowed expression and access to power. In modern liberalism, tolerance is the keynote, with emphasis on self restraint on the part of the better established, more powerful groups. Nevertheless, the tolerance supposedly characteristic of Western governments has not been tested. A free society given flexibility in political opinion can hope for peaceful evolution, rather than revolution, in its political and social development. In normal times and given the civilizing influence of tolerance, such lack of ideological unity is on the whole to be recommended. Unfortunately in a world racked by the tensions of conflicting doctrines, flexibility may lead to a lack of direction and therefore to uncertainty. Democracy cannot work if tolerance of other men's ideas and respect for other men's lives are not instilled into the mind of society. So important has this element become that it has even been suggested that it is the fundamental difference between democracy and authoritarianism.

The concept of tolerance started as the idea that a man's religious beliefs were his own personal concern and not a proper sphere for interference by the state. Such a belief was first expressed in a forcible way by Locke in his *Letter concerning Toleration* published in 1689. In this book, Locke argued the essential separation between religious and civil spheres, between faith and coercion. Force, he argued, was ineffective, for it could only make a man say he accepted a belief; it could not change his soul.

At the same time that Locke was defending toleration in theory, his political allies, the Whigs, were introducing the idea in practice by their Act of Toleration (1689). Under Voltaire's influence the idea gained credence in France. It was not too long before the principle was taken out of its religious context and transferred to the realm of politics and law. Respect for a person's religious views became respect for his political opinions; respect for his political opinions became concern for his happiness and very life. Humanitarianism and religious tolerance were born of the humanism of the sixteenth century and nurtured in the Protestant communities of Europe. The practice of religious toleration frequently asserted itself because governments of communities found it more convenient, rather than from conviction of its being morally desirable. Henry IV of France, the first monarch to tolerate opposing religious ideas in his realm, issued the famous Edict of Nantes in 1598 because France had suffered so much from the internecine religious wars and only by a period of religious peace could be expected to recover. Liberty of conscience, closely linked with the whole principle of freedom of thought and with humanitarianism, blossomed in the eighteenth century. Fraternity, one of the bases of the French Revolution implied the acceptance that other people have a right to live different lives or hold different opinions. A group of people who are pursuing one way of life and who happen to be in a majority must not use their weight of numbers to force the minority to renounce their individual beliefs or practices. If the majority act in a tolerant way the minority must resign themselves to accepting the decisions of the majority.

Liberty and tolerance are justifiable in a political context only if they are mutual. In practice, however, it is recognized that recourse to repressive measures is itself dangerous; it can become a habit. Liberty of conscience can be hard to express in such conditions.

## Liberty of conscience

In Europe in the Middle Ages two ideas were widely accepted: that salvation or union with God in an afterlife depended not just on leading a good life, but on holding certain beliefs about God and his relations to man; and that there is a church, a community of the faithful, having sole authority from God to teach the beliefs necessary to salvation. At the Reformation the first of these ideas – that salvation depends on holding certain beliefs – was not challenged and the second only partly so. Luther rejected the authority of the Pope and of other ecclesiastical superiors who disagreed with him; and he taught that every Christian must interpret for himself the Scriptures containing the truths necessary to salvation. Yet he proved in the end unwilling to admit that avowed Christians whose interpretations of the Scriptures differed widely from his own should be allowed to propagate their beliefs.

With the passing of time, belief in toleration grew stronger. Governments learned by experience that they were more likely to provoke disorder by trying to establish uniformity of religious belief by force than by allowing diversity. Religious conflict strengthened and spread the belief that 'faith' is more important and it made people keener to associate for the defence and propagation of beliefs that they cared deeply about. These beliefs were at first mostly religious, but they came in time to be much more than merely religious or ceased altogether to be so. Beliefs about how men should live and society be organized had long been associated with beliefs about God and his purposes for man. As the association between these two kinds of belief weakened and for many people was quite severed, beliefs about man, morals and society still kept something of the 'sacred' character of religious beliefs. The idea that faith is important can be used to justify either persecution and indoctrination or toleration and freedom of speech. It was used at first much more for the first purpose than the second, and at the present time is still used widely for both purposes.

## The argument for religious freedom

Years of controversy and long and painful experience were needed to bring home to men two lessons: that domestic peace and security do not depend on people having the same, or even broadly similar, religious beliefs, and that persecution is unlikely to bring about uniformity of belief. The first lesson disposes those who learn it to accept liberty of conscience on political grounds: let people hold and publish what religious opinions they choose, since the attempt to impose religious uniformity endangers the peace more than does religious diversity. The second lesson disposes them to accept it on religious and moral grounds. Let individuals hold and publish what religious opinions they choose since forbidding them to do so will not ensure that they accept with sincerity the opinions of those who impose the sanctions.

Locke believed that the proper business of civil government was to protect and promote men's interests. 'Though everyone has the right to try to persuade others to hold beliefs which they think are true and important, nobody has the right to use force to that end. No man deserves punishment at the hands of other men, unless he has offended some man, unless he has invaded his rights.' All societies distinguish between enforceable promises (contracts) and promises that are not enforceable.

## The rights of man and government by consent

The doctrine of social contract was first used to support the claims of religious minorities or of churches and sects anxious to assert their independence from the civil power. The doctrine has egalitarian and libertarian implications for it postulates an individual with rights and wants prior to the setting up of government whose proper business is to protect the rights and supply the wants. The state of nature is a condition of rough equality. Great inequalities arise only with the rise of government and yet the social rules that government is established to enforce it are in everyone's interest.

It was not until the latter part of the eighteenth century that political writers had much to say about three rights which since that time have been subjects of continual controversy: the right to vote at free elections, the right to form associations to promote shared purposes and beliefs of all kinds, and freedom of the press. In the seventeenth century the supremely important beliefs were religious, and so argument turned on the right to associate for religious purposes. In the next century other beliefs and association for other purposes came to seem no less important.

In the eighteenth century there was more concern for freedom of the press than for freedom of association and the right to vote. Freedom of association for other than religious purposes mattered more in Great Britain where there was already a partly elected legislature, than in countries like France, though even in Britain it was not widely and strongly upheld until the demand arose for extending the franchise. Freedom of association and the right to vote came to seem important when leaders arose who had or aspired to have a large following. Such leaders wanted to 'politicize' the people or some broad section of them, to draw them into political activities, into organized bodies making demands on government. Freedom of association still can be greatly prized where there is neither democracy nor a widespread demand for it. Anti-democratic liberalism especially on the European continent took the form of attacks on the doctrines of Rousseau, proclaiming the sovereignty of the people, having in mind not representative assemblies elected by universal suffrage but political communities small enough for all adult men to come together to make laws and major decisions of policy. His notion of a social contract was rejected as unhistorical and unnecessary. Hume and Bentham argued that there was no need for one if we wanted to show that men have interests, and 'therefore also claims or rights that governments ought to promote or secure, to postulate a deliberate setting up of government; to achieve these ends'. If there are rules, rights and obligations common to all men everywhere, this is only because their wants and conditions are everywhere in important respects the same, so that everywhere experience teaches them that the rules, which are in everyone's interest, should be generally observed, the claims are ones that everyone makes and the duties are ones from which no one is exempted.

## Man as a social being

The idea that man is essentially a social being, not only because his distinctively human capacities and needs are developed in social intercourse but also because their exercise and satisfaction consist in social intercourse, goes back to the time of Aristotle. Rousseau maintained that man, whose ability to reason is developed as he learns to live with other men, cannot be free outside society nor independent within it. To be free he must be rational and able to make deliberate choices, he must have capacities that he acquires only in society; and to be independent, to be able to do without others, he must be without the needs that he requires in acquiring these capacities. In other words, he must be unsocial.

For Kant, the freedom that consists in obedience to self-imposed laws belongs to a sphere with which the state is not directly affected. In his view, the business of the state is to make and enforce laws in the common interest; and its concern is that men should keep the law and not that they should keep it from the right motive. Implicit in the idea of moral freedom is that being free consists in more than just having desires and not being prevented from satisfying them, that it involves having a will, being able to make decisions.

Hegel improved on Rousseau in believing that man's ideas about himself, his purposes as distinct from his mere appetites, are related to the social order he belongs to. His ability to reason, to form purposes, and to make decisions, is developed in the process of acquiring a cultural inheritance, a process that involves coming to have standards and to accept rules.

The state as Hegel conceives it, is both an effect and a condition of this greater understanding and control. It is a social order in its most rational aspect; for it is through its laws and policies that men express most clearly and effectively their aspirations both for the individual and the community. Hegel puts forward four theses of which liberals since his day have taken large account. Only as a creature educated by social intercourse and having purposes and ideals that are meaningless outside a social context, does man come to conceive and to cherish the rights and opportunities that he dignifies by the name of freedom. A long course of social and cultural evolution has gone to formulating these rights and opportunities and to inquiry into their social and political conditions. This formulation and inquiry are closely related to the emergence of the modern state and the effective maintenance of these rights and opportunities requires a legal order such as in a state.

The liberal often takes pride in being suspicious of the state. The price of freedom is eternal vigilance and the liberal is, or claims to be, vigilant for freedom, presumably against those well placed to threaten it, who for the most part either hold public office or belong to organized bodies controlling or aspiring to control those who hold it. What he or she is suspicious of is not so much the idea of the state as the state as it actually is, but of a party or group that controls the state or aspires to do so.

## Freedom, equality and the state

The desire to secure to the unprivileged rights held to be essential or to constitute freedom has been a strong motive behind reforms that have greatly increased the power of the state. This power has increased at the expense of the privileged in the obvious sense that it has deprived them of powers they used to have.

To the liberal the reforms aimed at ensuring that everyone regardless of wealth and social status can effectively exercise the rights that constitute freedom, do more for the unprivileged than the privileged; for, in his or her eyes, the advantages of the privileged consist above all in their being better able to exercise these rights. Even the society that prides itself in being liberal is to some extent illiberal. Most groups inside it are willing to sacrifice their own freedom to other advantages or to resist reforms enlarging the freedom of others. Reforms aimed at extending freedom have had two effects often regarded as dangerous to freedom: the increased power of the state and more intense competition. The rise of the state has brought with it inequalities of power greater than any known before and this rise has been to a considerable extent an effect of reforms aimed at extending freedom.

Suspicion of the powerful and centralized state has been strong in the West among all classes ever since that state emerged. To the liberal there are three questions about the state in relation to freedom that are supremely important. To what extent does securing the essential freedoms to everyone require the control by public authority of what people do? To what extent must this control, to be effective, be centralized over large areas and populations? How can it be contrived that the great inequalities of power inseparable from a centralized and many-sided control of the activities of vast numbers of people do not curtail the freedoms the control is meant to secure?

The indifference to the state of many of the early socialists meant that they took little notice of two questions of great concern to liberals: what legal rights must the citizen have, if he is to be free, and how can the rulers of large communities be made responsible to their subjects? Where indifference to the state turned to hostility, it often brought with it contempt for the legal rights that meant so much to the liberal. Suspicion of the state and faith in it have been and still are socialist, just as they have been and still are liberal.

## Human rights

**Human rights** is a term of recent origin signifying all privileges and immunities possessed by human beings in a civil social order. They are rights and privileges held to belong to everyone regardless of any legal provision that may or may not exist for him or her in the legal system, simply because a human being may not be forbidden certain things by any government. It is often difficult to distinguish human rights from various concepts of natural rights. In the United States the term was first made popular by President Woodrow Wilson, and was later employed repeatedly by President Franklin D. Roosevelt. It assumed international significance with the *Universal Declaration of Human Rights* promulgated by the United Nations Organization. In the *Declaration* the term comprises a lengthy list of privileges, immunities and conditions considered desirable by the states subscribing to the *Declaration*. Some of these human rights are unenforceable in non-democratic countries. Critics of the *Declaration* believe it confuses right with desire and that if an alleged right has no sanction or authority for appeal, it cannot accurately be categorized as a true right. Because of its vagueness it is a term of small value when questions of conflicting aspirations and privileges arise. Everyone may appeal to 'human rights'; but courts of law necessarily refer to established concepts of natural, constitutional, statutory or customary law, rather than to undefined human immunities and privileges.

The *European Declaration of Human Rights* is actually enforceable because it forms the legal basis for the European Court of Human Rights to which citizens of subscribing nations may bring cases against their own governments. Cases to the European Court have varied from complaints against court martial procedures in the Netherlands Army, restrictions on press freedom in English cases arising from contempt of court orders, to the validity of corporal punishment in Scottish schools, and the access to lawyers of suspected terrorists.

Philosophically all these lists and institutions derive from a long developed notion of natural rights. **Natural law** is seen variously as God's will for the world, moral principles innate in the structure of the universe, the principles of rational self-interest or the necessary elements logically underlying any legal system. There could only be one correct way of organizing a political system, or of acting in case of moral doubt on a political issue. How these natural laws governed political society and determined the grounds of political obligation, and the balance of power between the state and the individual was rather harder to discover. The natural law tradition fell under attacks by sceptics like Hume and philosophical radicals like Bentham. Their inability to discover a foundation for natural law led them to resort to human psychological drives as the foundation of political principles culminating in the utilitarianism so pervasive today. Natural rights are those human rights or entitlements which are held to stem from natural law, whatever definition may be given to the latter concept. One can divide natural rights into two broad kinds, as they are encountered in legal and political theory. One group consists of those rights, seldom specified, that a man would hold, even if he could not enforce them, in the theoretical state of nature; rights, that is, that are fixed by divine law or by the very nature of man and the universe. These have often been taken over by various Declarations of Human Rights, and include those such as the right to life, to property, to family life, general rights to do anything one wants, in total freedom, so long as one's exercise of those rights does not hurt or deprive others of their rights. The second group consists of the more procedural rights that most legal systems find logically necessary if they are to be fair and efficient, as characterized by the English doctrine of natural justice. Whatever natural rights are, they are held to exist independently of what any government does or says, and are not to be capable of being legitimately overridden by any government, however often they may be ignored in practice.

What can be legitimately demanded from the state?

Authority and loyalty determine what the state may demand of its people; human rights sum up what people may legitimately demand of their state. Authority and loyalty define personal duties toward the government; and if one performs such duties one should not expect to be thanked for it. The same applies to rights.

Throughout the centuries, many writers, from Cicero and Saint Augustine to Saint Thomas Aquinas and to great liberals like John Locke and John Stuart Mill, have held that certain rights are natural. By this they have meant that certain rights are in-born. The concept of natural rights does have an operational meaning. Natural behaviour is probable behaviour. It is likely to occur whenever it is not prevented by 'artificial' obstacles, that is, by obstacles that are less probable and that can be maintained only by special efforts or arrangements. Natural rights are rights that people are likely to claim whenever not specifically restrained from doing so and likely to claim again as soon as the restraint ceases.

A human right can never be sold or signed away. In the two centuries since the American and French Revolutions, the demand for human rights has spread around the world. Britain has had a Bill of Rights for nearly 300 years dealing with legal procedures that safeguard individuals against the abuse of power by the government. The first ten amendments to the United States' Constitution encompasses a Bill of Rights. In the German Federal Republic, similar rights are embodied in the country's Basic Law. The constitutions of most countries, including the Soviet Union, contain some provisions of this kind.

Many of the early measures on human rights are negative in character. They state what governments may not do to individuals. They may not mutilate or torture them, or kill or imprison them without due legal process, or deny them equal protection of the law. They may not stifle their freedom of speech or stop them from worshipping according to conscience or force them to worship against their will. The limits and margins of these rights vary with time and place, but their core is the same in many countries.

In the twentieth century, demands for positive human rights have come to the forefront. It is not enough to treat all people equally before the law. The right to life, it is now argued, implies the right to food and shelter and medical help when needed. Freedom of speech implies the freedom to read; it implies the right to knowledge and education. Generally the absence of restraint is useless without the presence of opportunity and the knowledge and capacity to act.

All human rights and freedom thus have their positive aspects; and when these are not automatically supplied by social and economic life, people turn increasingly to their governments for them. It is one thing to promise human rights and another to deliver them.

The main political rights in Western democracies are the right to vote, the right to communicate one's ideas of a political nature; the right to organize political groups; the right to lobby, or to campaign for political causes; and the right to run for political office.

The traditional Western emphasis on individual liberties and political rights has encountered objections and scepticism from the socialist and developing countries. Marxists, for example, stress that equality is also an important human value and they regard the liberal notions of individual rights as a 'bourgeois illusion'. They point to the substantial inequality in income, quality of life, and power that exists in many capitalist societies. The gulf between the 'haves' and the 'have-nots' is often very wide in these societies. The socialist governments, therefore, contend that the Western conception of human rights merely promises to give everyone an equal chance to be unequal, e.g. to become richer than his or her neighbour. Furthermore, according to them, this promise of equal opportunity is in reality a myth because power, wealth and expertise are concentrated in the hands of a few. This concentration gives the elite control over the masses, and it allows a minority to exploit the majority. Finally, communist officials argue that the interests of society must override the rights of individuals.

The governments of developing countries also question the relevance and motivation of the Western conception of human rights. Their officials often feel that Western governments are trying to impose values derived from the European liberal tradition on other cultures. Western ideas such as the freedom of speech and of the press are not very meaningful to a person who is illiterate, unemployed or starving. Officials of Third World countries tend to associate human rights with the social and economic conditions of their citizens rather than with the Western values of personal and political freedom. They put a higher premium on a person's right to be employed and to receive adequate food, shelter, education and medical care. According to them, a decent standard of living is at least equally as important as, and perhaps even more important than, civil liberties and political rights. One should realize, however, that the Third World leaders sometimes use the need for economic development merely as an excuse for suppressing their political opposition.

Strictly speaking, food, housing, education, health care and employment represent basic human needs. They are thus better understood as ingredients essential to human dignity than as human rights as traditionally defined by the Westerners. Yet in relation to common usage and to existing international covenants, human rights is the term used rather than human needs or conditions for human dignity.

Various governments tend to disagree about the question of whether groups have certain rights. The developing and socialist governments have criticized the Western democracies for defining human rights exclusively as rights enjoyed by individuals. They charge that Westerners tend to ignore the rights of groups such as classes, nations and races. In their view the liberal democracies have paid too little attention to concerns about class exploitation, national self-determination and racial discrimination. The satisfaction of so-called positive rights does not necessarily require active government intervention. These rights could be enhanced by certain kinds of government inaction. The moral difference between a positive and a negative right does not lie in the duty to do something (commission) and the duty to do nothing (omission). The determination of what is 'moral' or 'right' depends on actual circumstances and consequences. The general inaction of the United States government to the widespread deprivation of social and economic rights abroad has aroused considerable scepticism among the Third World countries. Some foreign observers feel that human rights, defined primarily in terms of civil liberties and political rights, are merely intended by Americans to be a convenient way for Washington to condemn Moscow's repression of Soviet dissidents. Nevertheless, within the last ten years many Americans, and people in other democratic countries, have come to realize that where there is poverty (lack of economic development) there cannot be full political participation and freedom; and where there is political oppression there will also be economic exploitation.

In assessing the spread of human rights one can study political rights and civil liberties. **Political rights** are defined primarily in terms of electoral democracy, that is in terms of citizens' right to select their representatives and of political parties to vie for power in free elections. Civil liberties are taken to be people's immunity from arbitrary governmental power. They include such things as the freedom of expression and movement, the protection of due process of law, and personal security from torture, arbitrary imprisonment and summary execution. The citizens of Western liberal democracies generally can enjoy these rights and liberties. The term liberal democracy is used to distinguish Western countries from communist or socialist countries, which call themselves social democracies or people's democracies. The ideology of the latter countries emphasizes egalitarianism, the dictatorship of the proletariat, and governmental economic planning.

Most West European countries are free, as are the United States and the former British dominions which have inherited not only many of Britain's political institutions, but also its traditions of political tolerance and freedom. The Soviet Union and communist countries in general do not permit their citizens to have the right to elect their government officials in free elections with a genuine choice between the candidates. They also do not enjoy the same freedoms of opinion, expression and movement that are widely taken for granted in the Western liberal democracies. The Third World countries also generally have an abysmal record on political rights and civil liberties. Many of these countries are ruled by military juntas or authoritarian strongmen who are not accountable to the people by means of elections.

What conditions tend to promote or to impede the development of liberal democratic values and institutions such as regular and free elections, mass political parties, universal suffrage, due process of law, and individual freedoms of thought, expression and movement? Social and political dislocations caused by rapid economic growth tend to reduce a government's observance of human rights as traditionally defined by the Western democracies. The development of liberal democratic institutions usually occurs in societies with high levels of communication, urbanization and per capita income. Thus a certain minimal level of socioeconomic development is necessary in order for liberal democratic values and institutions to take hold in a country, and a rapid rate of socioeconomic change is detrimental to the growth of these values and institutions. The social and political structures of traditional societies are usually too fragile and inflexible to cope with rapid change. A minimal level of socioeconomic development is necessary to promote civil liberties and political rights. Yet this level cannot be quickly attained except by increasing the tempo of modernization, which appears to have precisely the effect of undermining these values as well as political stability. The moral dilemma is further exacerbated because any deliberate attempt to slow down modernization and to delay improving the quality of living of the people would be an injustice. The higher one's education, the more likely one is to believe in democratic values and to support democratic principles.

## Patterns of political behaviour

In the last two decades the behavioural revolution has overtaken Western political science. One of the advantages of behaviourism has been its concentration on the political system as such. The most lasting effect of the behaviourist approach is the attempt to see politics as a system. Behaviourists are less interested in the effects of class and privilege inside certain political systems than in the central question to them of power distribution, and Weber's maxim of '*verstehen*' or understanding.

Most political issues in a modern state do not have a clear 'national interest' solution, but rather a range of alternatives which often benefit some but impose costs on other members of the society. The best illustration of this is in a developed country which has problems of planning new forms of transportation or of preserving run-down segments of the economy to stave off local unemployment. Except in a few cases, it is difficult to conceive of a national interest that has not been reached by debate or conflict between specific interests inside the polity. **Power** is an amorphous concept but when allied to the act of decision making it takes on an active role. Similarly the belief that political systems are in a constant state of change or 'development' provides a necessary dynamic strain to the static nature of political theorizing.

Max Weber, one of the 'founding fathers' of sociology and an exponent of political sociology, maintained that man can 'understand' or attempt to 'understand' his own intentions through introspection and he may interpret the motives of other men's conduct in terms of their professed or ascribed intentions. A state, in Weberian terminology, was a human community that successfully claimed the monopoly of the legitimate use of physical force, within a given territory. Power (*macht*) and the state dependent on it (*machstaat*) feature heavily in Weber's writing on the nature of politics.

Behaviourism has inexact definitions and can be said to mean any of the following overlapping terms: the study of political behaviour as a way of understanding the nature of politics; the development of a value-free political science; the elaboration of quantitative and other analytical methods to make for exactitude in the study of politics; the creation of a 'science' of politics which would be as rigorous as the natural sciences; and lastly the establishment of a comprehensive explanatory theory of political systems and political behaviour. Interests in political behaviour will survive as long as an interest in political arrangements remains. Most aspects of the theory of political behaviour have contributed greatly to our understanding of the political process. The ethical base of political action is one aspect of political science and behaviourism which will receive future attention.

## Behaviourism

It is sometimes said that Aristotle and Hobbes were the political theorists who developed a study of **behaviourism**. Yet the distinction between the private world of the individual's own consciousness and the public world, which all could observe, was alien to the Greeks. Indeed there is a sense in which the Greeks had no concept of consciousness, in that they did not link together phenomena such as pains, dreams, remembering, action and reasoning as exemplifying different modes of individual consciousness. The concept of consciousness was largely a product of individualism, of the various movements such as Stoicism, Epicureanism and Christianity, which supplied types of conceptual schemes that were very different from those which were appropriate to the shared life of the city states. The coordinating concept of individual consciousness was not made explicit until it found expression in the systems of Saint Augustine and Descartes. Although Aristotle was the first to approach the study of human beings in an objective and systematic way, his doctrine of form and matter was incompatible with the materialism espoused by many behaviourists and in his psychology he was an explicit critic of the mechanists of his day. Aristotle held that a living thing is a 'body with a soul', 'soul' designating the self-originated tendency of living things to persist towards an end. He accused mechanists such as Democritus and Empedocles of the mistake of concluding from the fact that the soul is the cause of movement, that it is itself moved. Aristotle maintained that the soul moves the body by means of a purpose of some sort, that is thought. Thinking is not a sort of motion any more than desire or sensation are.

There would be more plausibility in attempting to trace behaviourism back to Hobbes than to Aristotle. To start with, Hobbes was one of the great thinkers of individualism and wrote at a time when the private world of the individual was both recognized and valued – and threatened by tendencies towards absolutism. Hobbes not only extolled introspection as the appropriate method for investigating mankind, he also pointed to the unreliability of inferences made on the basis of the observation of others. Nevertheless, there are underlying assumptions common to the views of Hobbes and modern behaviourists which are deeply embedded in modern thought. Hobbes believed there was some reliable method for advancing knowledge. He was one of the many men of the post Renaissance period who believed that the knowledge of nature was available to anyone who was prepared to master the appropriate method. Hobbes was convinced that knowledge meant power. His psychology and politics were constructed with a very practical end in view – the preservation of peace – and he thought that there was no hope for England in the throes of civil war unless those who had some influence on the course of events could be persuaded to accept the logic of his views concerning man and civil society. This practical concern underlying his theorizing was later supported by Marxists.

A more explicit link between Hobbes and the behaviourists was his materialism, and his attempt to extrapolate the contents and laws of Galileo's mechanics to the human sphere. Thus he analysed 'endeavours', infinitely small motions, in the medium between the object of sense and the brain and he had recourse to them also to explain how movements coming from outside bodies are passed through the body so that they eventually lead to the gross movements observable in desire and aversion.

Descartes was more well known than Hobbes in relation to the dualism of mind and matter which he postulated. Descartes maintained that the human body, which was regarded as functioning mechanically right up to the level of instinctive behaviour and simple habits, becomes a fit subject for objective study. On the other hand, mind, by which Descartes meant mainly the higher thought processes and the will, could only be studied introspectively. Descartes's dualism involved the assumption that the behaviour of the body below the level of willed action could be explained mechanically.

The psychological theory of Descartes and the empiricists which developed *pari passu* with the philosophical theory about the grounds and acquisition of knowledge had two main features. First it maintained that the experience, thought and consequent action of an individual is caused from without. The environment causes simple ideas (Locke) or impressions (Hume) to arise in the individual. Second, a theory of meaning developed which has come to be known as **logical empiricism**. This maintained that only those terms are strictly meaningful that can be studied by reference to what can be observed.

It came as little surprise that behaviourists contributed little in the way of theory to the understanding of behaviour, for basically most of them were not interested in explaining behaviour or even learning for that matter. They were interested in conditioning. Behaviourists tend to think that the form of description and explanation applicable at the lowest level of reflex behaviour can be extrapolated to explain the much more complex phenomena at higher levels. Historically, behaviourism was a salutary corrective pushed to inordinate extremes.

## Questions

### Political

1 Why has the term 'sovereignty' so many varied meanings?
2 Critically appraise Hobbes's, Rousseau's and Locke's views of sovereignty.
3 Compare and contrast sovereignty in democratic and totalitarian states.
4 Discuss the links between sovereignty and power.
5 Define political obligation.

### Democracy

1 How democratic is democracy?
2 Compare and contrast Plato's and Aristotle's views.
3 Account for the differing emphasis of Hobbes and Locke towards democracy.
4 What is 'the general will'?

5   Analyse the French and American revolutionaries' attitudes to revolutions.
6   What are the pros and cons of Thucydides's and Herodotus's views of democracy?

## Representative democracy/government and representation

1   Why is representation an important feature of liberal democracy?
2   Account for critics challenging the 'democracy' claim of representative democracy.
3   What are the duties of a representative?

## Representation and the machinery of democracy

1   Account for Edmund Burke's concern with the concept of democracy.
2   What reasons can be adduced for Burke being viewed as the first propagandist of party?
3   Why did Burke believe political power should correspond to property and not to opinion?

## Freedom

1   What are the positive and negative approaches towards freedom?
2   Why was Marx so concerned with issues of freedom?
3   Analyse the liberal and welfare-socialist views of freedom.

## Pluralism

1   Outline the impact of pluralism on a democratic society.
2   Prepare a critique of Dahl's theory.

## Liberalism

1   Write a critique of the liberal views of freedom.
2   In what aspects are the authorities of modern states considered to be impersonal?
3   How does the modern state claim to be democratic?
4   Write an essay on the liberty of conscience.
5   Prepare a set of arguments against religious freedom.
6   Compare and contrast Kant's and Hegel's views of man as a social being.
7   Examine the reasons why the liberal is suspicious of the state, and why the radicals resent such a view.

## Human rights

1   Critically appraise the various definitions of human rights.
2   What can be legitimately demanded from the state?
3   Account for early measures on human rights being negative in character.

4 Why do the governments of developing countries question the relevance and motivation of the Western conception of human rights?

**Patterns of political behaviour**

1 Under what circumstances can a person understand his or her own intentions through introspection?
2 Why has behaviourism no exact definitions?

**Further reading**

Birch, A. H., *Representative and Responsible Government*, George Allen & Unwin, London, 1966.
Drucker, H. M., *The Political Uses of Ideology*, Macmillan, London, 1977.
Ely, J. H., *Democracy and Distrust*, Harvard University Press, Cambridge, Mass. 1981.
Finer, S. E., (intro.), *Five Constitutions*, Penguin, London, 1979.
Hinsley, F. H., *Sovereignty*, G. A. Watts & Co., London, 1966.
Holden, B., *The Nature of Democracy*, Nelson, London, 1974.
Macpherson, C. B., *Democratic Theory*, Clarendon Press, Oxford, 1973.
Manuel, F. E. (ed.), *Utopias and Utopian Thought*, Beacon Press, Boston, 1966.
O'Gorman, F., *Edmund Burke: His Political Philosophy*, George Allen & Unwin, London, 1973.
Quinton, A. (ed.), *Political Philosophy*, Oxford University Press, Oxford, 1982.
Savastano, L., *Contemporary British Conservatism*, Holborn Publishing Co., London, 1951.
Simmons, A. J., *Moral Principles and Political Obligations*, Princeton University Press, New Jersey, 1979.
Wass, D., *Government and the Governed*, Routledge & Kegan Paul, London, 1984.

# 7
# Capitalism and communism

**Capitalism** is an economic system based on the private ownership of the means of production, distribution and exchange, characterized by the freedom of capitalists to operate or manage their property for profit in competitive conditions. It is known as private and free enterprise. The term was popularized with a critical connotation by socialist thinkers of the nineteenth century. It was first used in France by J. J. C. Blanc in 1839 and a decade later in Germany by Marx and Engels; and was first employed by an English writer, W. M. Thackeray, in 1854 in *The Newcomes*.

To Marxists it is a socioeconomic formation which evolved from decaying feudalism and is bound to be succeeded by socialism. Although in their view capitalism in its early stages performs a useful historical function, it degenerates into a grossly unjust system embodying the existence of two antagonistic social classes – the bourgeoisie and the proletariat – the exploitation of the latter by the former in the form of surplus value, and the intense class struggle. Under capitalism, Marx believed that the bourgeoisie reinforced its dominant position in the economy by all possible social and political means.

**Communism** is a political movement, based upon the writings of Marx, that considers history in terms of class conflict and revolutionary struggle, resulting eventually in the victory of the proletariat and the establishment of a socialist order based on public ownership of the means of production. Communists advocate a classless society in which private ownership has been abolished and the means of production and subsistence belong to the community.

Although the idea of communism can be traced back to ancient times, the term was first introduced in secret French revolutionary societies between 1834 and 1839 and was derived from the French communes or small village communities which appeared in the Middle Ages. The term was first used in France in 1841 to denote the proletarian and militant versions of socialism, while in England it appeared first in 1843 in the *New Age*, a London-based weekly review, where it was popularized by the advocates of Owenism, a doctrine based on the communal ownership of the means of production, social justice, equality, universal civic education and cooperation among different social classes. Marx and Engels used the designation communism, in the *Communist Manifesto* (1848) to distinguish their socialism from the utopian socialism of the earlier French and English theorists. The latter views exemplified idealistic socialism divorced from reality and impossible to achieve in practice, and embraced theories of the socialist transformation of society in peaceful, evolutionary ways without the need for revolutionary social violence.

Apart from the stated definition, other meanings have been attributed to communism. It is another name for Marxism, i.e. the complete system of philosophical, political, economic and sociological concepts, critiques, theories and prescriptions for the demise of capitalism and the creation of a communist society. It has also been used as a vague general description of the social system after the overthrow of capitalism which will consist of two stages: the lower phase of communism (also called socialism) and the higher phase of communism (also called simply communism or 'full communism'). Communism is a totalitarian system of government noted for the supremacy of the state over the individual based on the monoparty system of all power exercised by the Communist Party, as contrasted with Western parliamentary democracy. Since the Second World War, communism has been seen as an extremist militant ideology and associated with policies pursued by the communist regimes, especially those of China and the USSR in the international scene, resorting to subversion, terrorism and aggressive wars designed ultimately to destroy capitalism. Communism, to an even greater extent than capitalism, has evoked strong emotional responses and attitudes in its favour and in opposition to it.

In countries where communism is practised and where it is seen as a coherent theory, stress is laid on the party as an elite, to be kept select by periodical purges, peaceable or violent. The Communist Party forms, in effect, an oligarchy or aristocracy in whose hands all real power rests. The Communist Party, and indeed other revolutionary parties, have at times been compared to Plato's ideal rulers, occasionally by way of commendation but more often as grounds for condemnation both of Plato and the parties. Parallels, however, are not very close. The Communist Party resembles Plato's Guardians in that it is a select body of rulers based on a philosophical theory which they are all supposed to master. They are also supposed to exercise a certain degree of personal self denial, but this has been shown to be more in theory than practice. Within the Party there is an hierarchical situation which is highly secretive – such as the means by which members rise to the top – and this state of affairs in particular would have been anathema to Platonic thought.

## Elites and class interest groups

An **elite** is a superior or privileged group noted for special qualities such as race, birth, wealth, education, occupational status or achievement – whatever is regarded as important in a particular society or organization. Some adhere to a more specialized meaning, and distinguish government by an elite – that is by a class that is chosen for the purpose, say by some ruling party – from government by a ruling class, which obtains its powers by prescription. In Marxist sociology, the term has a depreciative meaning usually applied to the ruling class and separated from the majority of the population, especially the working class. Historical materialism treats the historical development as a process of struggle for power between the old and new elites, representing different social classes or interests. Each socialist country has its own elite, i.e. the top hierarchy in the party and state apparatus enjoying a good deal of power and privileges. Additionally there are technocrats, and talented and successful professionals, such as top architects, engineers, scientists, writers, actors and so on.

The supporters of elitism argue that different persons are essentially unequal owing to racial, ethnic or class origin or background. Marxism is strongly opposed to elitism as it is in conflict with equality and social justice as well as being embraced by the propertied and ruling classes as a convenient justification for the domination of the oppressed masses. Yet elitism is implicitly subscribed to in the socialist countries, too. Power is basically exercised by the Communist Party, to the exclusion of other political parties. In fact, crucial decisions are made exclusively by the Party's top elite, generally known as the Politburo, removed from the rank and file of the party membership and even more so from the rest of the population. Many people argue that elites are inevitable. All organizations, including the organization of a democracy, generate both kinds of elite, the one dominating politics and the other society. In all developed societies there is a plurality of competing elites, which rise to eminence through the several systems of control. Politics is only one such system, others include management, trade union organizations, military organizations and cultural and educational institutions.

Those concerned with the development of elites are interested in the whole range of class consciousness issues. These issues can be seen in two ways, to denote either the individual's sense of himself or herself as belonging to a social class or those features of the individual's outlook and understanding which are to be explained by membership of a social class. An offshoot is class identity, which can be manifest in loyalty to one's own class and hostility to, or suspicion towards, members of another. In considering membership of a social class one has to take into account the precise nature of class consciousness and explain such things as social aspiration (the desire to change one's class, when this does not seem to be primarily a desire to change one's material condition), snobbery (whether normal or inverse) and the relative absence of class consciousness in the United States (as contrasted with the United Kingdom) despite very great differences of material wealth and despite the economic relations characteristic of capitalism.

The doctrine of elitism is diametrically opposed to the social doctrine of **egalitarianism**, postulating a political and economic system which would ensure complete or reasonable equality of all the members of society with respect to legal status, human rights, property ownership, income and other significant conditions of life. The doctrine is based on the premise that people are essentially equal, that their needs are similar and that, for the sake of social justice and maximum social welfare, the state should ensure the equality of opportunity and living conditions for its citizens. In general the scope for the implementation of egalitarianism is limited in a capitalist society, owing to the unequal distribution of (private) property, the existence of non-labour incomes, sensitivity to vested interests and individualism. Although the popular view of communism implies complete equality, most leading Marxist thinkers as well as communist policy makers reject its validity or advisability in practice. Marx himself recognized that one person was superior to another, physically or mentally or both. Lenin as well as Stalin opposed the extreme form of egalitarianism advocated by left communists. It has been widely accepted officially in the socialist countries that under socialism differentiation in occupational status and income is inevitable. In the social interest, egalitarianism is vaguely assumed to be achieved under full communism, but even so, distribution will not be totally uniform, rather 'according to needs'. Indeed there is often realization among workers that they constitute a distinct and fraternal social class, both nationally and internationally, and separate from the rest of society. Workers often have pride in their belonging to the largest class, united by common problems, and a struggle for a just cause; and subscribe to the conviction that the interests of the proletariat are irreconcilably opposed to those of the bourgeoisie, against which the workers must unite and fight to ensure social justice and to achieve a classless society.

However, one of the cornerstones of Marxist ideology has been the class struggle (in its extreme form also known as class war), explaining the course of history in terms of the struggle between conflicting social classes in antagonistic socioeconomic formations (slavery, feudalism and especially capitalism). Capitalist rule and exploitation is opposed by the oppressed class in two spheres – economic (a struggle for the improvement of the conditions of work and a change in the principle governing the distribution of the fruits of labour) and political (a struggle for the seizure and maintenance of political power).

Further stages in the development of class consciousness among the working class are the Hegelian concepts of class 'in itself' and class 'for itself' adapted and used in classical Marxist terminology. The former concept indicates the earlier stage of development of class consciousness, when workers become aware of their grievances against capitalists. If they take any action, it is directed against individual employers, not capitalists as a class. In the class 'for itself' stage, workers become conscious of their class identity (as the proletariat) and of the unbridgeable antagonism that divides them from the class of capitalists (the bougeoisie). The latter stage is reached as a result of the development of capitalism and corresponding social injustices, when the proletariat increases in size, develops a revolutionary theory, organizes national trade unions and communist parties, strengthens the bonds of solidarity, accumulates experience in the class struggle and prepares for a proletarian revolution.

Class antagonism can be the result of inherent hostility between social classes. In the Marxist view it existed and exists in all antagonistic, socioeconomic formations, such as slavery, feudalism and capitalism and between the 'haves' and 'have-nots' of the means of production. The 'haves' (masters, feudal lords, capitalists) impose their will upon and exploit the 'have-nots' (slaves, serfs, proletarians). Such antagonism can be hidden or open, but generally expresses itself in the latter case through the class struggle, which may lead to a proletarian revolution.

Conversely non-Marxists imply or advocate class cooperation, i.e. collaboration and harmony between different social classes. This situation is opposed by revolutionary Marxists, as antagonistic socioeconomic formations (slavery, feudalism and especially capitalism) exist and they view it as a betrayal and a postponement of the inevitable revolution. Those who support cooperation are thought to be guilty of opportunism and revisionism. In the communist doctrine cooperation is admissable only as a temporary tactic in the exceptional circumstance of a people's war against fascism, national liberation movements against imperialism, and possibly, in a bourgeois-democratic revolution, paving the way for a proletarian revolution.

However complex and at times contradictory it may be to construct class models, politics require them. Though not all parties have a class base, most do, and all societies have at least one political party which is clearly supported because it offers special policies in the interest of one class rather than another. Some political parties, conservative and liberal, claim as part of their ideology to be classless or to regard class as irrelevant, but this does not necessarily mean that voting support or policies are any less class-oriented. Although Marx adopts a definition of classes in terms of their position there is a tendency in Marxist writing to dramatize history by speaking of whole classes as though they move upwards or downwards through the social and economic hierarchy. This is perhaps true of individual members of a class, but it can never be true of the class. Nevertheless, many struggles are seen in terms of class, and thus what some may describe as a 'struggle for control of the means of communication', others regard as a conflict between propaganda and impartiality. The Marxian notion that existence determines consciousness and the relation between social position and ideology cannot easily be maintained.

## Communism

It is not easy to construct a communist society, as Marx well understood, in a world of competing nation-states – at least a communist society that is communist in fact as well as in name. Nor is it easy to build communism in a world where, in fact, there are as many kinds of communism as there are communist states with different cultural backgrounds at different stages of economic, political and social development, and with different views of what represents the best interests of humanity, both at home and abroad. If there are as many kinds of communism as there are states that fly the communist banner, it is clear that all of them cannot legitimately claim to be the orthodox followers of Marx.

History is filled with examples of noble ends poorly served by inappropriate or corrupted means. In politics, especially revolutionary politics, no one is innocent. But if it is true that even humanity's notable accomplishments inevitably fall short of its ideals, it also is true that, without ideals, nothing notable is accomplished. Greater social justice for all is likely to continue to be the principal ideal of the large majority of mankind, whatever the ideological banner unfurled above its head. In part, because of the very ambiguity of their meaning, Marxism and communism are likely to remain an inspiration to those revolutionaries and reformers who seek to build a new Golden Age. Marx, along with Darwin and Freud, is one of the three most important thinkers of the modern world, a world that has as its most distinguishing mark political and ideological conflict.

Each of these three giants of modern thought says something about the world about us, something about the societies we live in and something about ourselves. Each of them explains, from a different perspective, why division and conflict have written such a large part of the history of the human race. Each one viewed his intellectual insights as a major contribution to modern science, a contribution that would raise understanding above religious dogma, unlock the mysteries of human development and behaviour, and reveal themselves and the world they have made as they really are, or as they apparently are.

It is possible that neither Darwin nor Freud nor Marx were right, even partly right. They had a monumental impact on the modern world. What Darwin does for biology, and Freud does for psychology, Marx does for politics. Darwin explains how we got here in terms of organic evolution through species' adaptation and natural selection. Freud explains our dreams, thoughts, and behaviour in terms of the compulsive drives that are rooted deep in our unconscious. Marx explains our social and political relationships in terms of the material needs that are fundamental to human existence. These ideas paint a comprehensive picture of the generalities and details of the human condition.

These thinkers individually regard their discoveries as an extension of the scientific inquiry that came before them, and that prepared their particular field of research for a major breakthrough in human understanding. What was necessary to the breakthrough was the discovery of some driving dynamic of development, some compelling force that operates independently of our personal will. Thus each one, in his own way, adopts a notion of determinism, whether biological, psychological or economic, the forces that structure his body, behaviour and social relationships. They are impersonal forces that are largely beyond control, if not entirely beyond understanding. The problems of nationalism and international conflict – of national community and world community – are still a challenge to society's understanding and leadership.

## Questions

1 In what circumstances can the development of capitalism lead to communism?
2 Are the claims made by communists often overambitious?
3 Compare and contrast the role of elites under the two ideologies.

## Elites and class interest groups

1 What is an elite?
2 Account for the development of elites in the range of class consciousness issues.
3 Compare and contrast elitism and egalitarianism.
4 Discuss the various interpretations of class and causes of antagonism.
5 Assess the reasons for class cooperation.
6 Examine the role of class models.

## Communism

1  Assess Marx's impact on either theoretical or revolutionary communist issues.
2  Analyse Darwinian, Freudian and Marxian attitudes on political issues.

## Further reading

Carew Hunt, R. N., *The Theory and Practice of Communism*, Bles, London, 1957.

Cornwall, John, *Modern capitalism: its growth and transformation*, Martin Robertson, London, 1977.

Lichtheim, George, *Marxism an historical critical study*, Routledge and Kegan Paul, London, 1961.

McLellan, D., *Marx: the first 100 years*, Fontana, London, 1983.

Milibard, Ralph, *State in Capitalist Society*, Weidenfeld & Nicholson, London, 1969.

Wilczynski, Jozef, *An Encyclopaedic Dictionary of Marxism, Socialism and Fascism*, Macmillan, London, 1981.

# 8
# The realities of political theories within capitalist and communist states

## Marxism

Marx, one of the most important thinkers of the modern world, sought to explain social and political relationships in terms of the material needs that are fundamental to human existence. One of Marx's early concerns was the alienation of individuals from their neighbours and the society in which they lived. Marx was concerned about the psychological consequences of surplus value, the worker being separated from an important part of the value that he produces, and this in turn being used to exploit and oppress the worker, depriving him of the full satisfaction that derives from controlling the total result of his creative energies. **Alienation** in his view was inherent in the human condition prior to the inception of communism. Physical needs forced people into an economic dependency which contradicted desires for freedom and autonomy. From views on alienation, Marx soon turned to the evils of society and politics and to the possibility of revolution as a remedy for them. For the rest of his life he was an ardent revolutionary. Even many lost revolutions won his sympathy; but unlike some recent revolutionaries he never willingly urged people to risk their lives in uprisings he knew to be hopeless. Above all else, he wanted to be the theorist of a successful revolution, one that would produce more fundamental changes than any that had gone before.

Marx's immediate objective was **democratic socialism**. The most apparent political consequences of Marxism might be called authoritarian socialism. Marx's own focus was on the economic characteristics and political consequences of classical liberalism. He was a deep exponent of **determinism** – the notion that the general patterns of what we do and think are determined, or shaped by forces and circumstances beyond our control (and typically, even beyond our conscious awareness of their existence). Specifically, he was a **dialectic determinist** – the dialectic referring in part to the interrelationships of all phenomena, so that any particular phenomenon can be understood only in terms of its more general context. One cannot understand the characteristics of capitalism without understanding its initial development in the context of feudalism and mercantilism. Nor in Marx's opinion could one understand the behaviour of the proletariat without reference to its peasant origins or to the demands and interests of the bourgeoisie. From the perspectives of the dialectic, the more complete (or scientific) knowledge is the knowledge of phenomena as they interact with other phenomena. Thus each man defines himself only as he interacts with nature and with the social reality around him.

Marx viewed dialectical relationships as inevitably antagonistic relationships. History could only be properly understood as the working out of tensions and contradictions between nature and man, ever more efficient means of production, competing social classes and opposing ideologies. At any point in time it is possible to identify a specific characteristic of social life as a thesis (for example, feudalism and economic restraint) which is eventually confronted by an antithesis (capitalism and free trade) with the contradictions generated by the clash of thesis and antithesis. This can lead to a synthesis of the best attributes of each. Socialism enables man to enjoy the efficiency of production developed by capitalism, but in the context of the social harmony and stability that characterized feudalism.

Marx distinguished his thought from the ideas of the utopian socialists (including in the nineteenth century the ideas of Saint-Simon, Charles Fourier and Robert Owen) by maintaining that they had an undialectical view of history. This meant in fact that the utopians had failed to recognize the inevitability of capitalism and failed to understand that capitalism was a positive stage in historical development and a definite benefit to mankind. For Marx, the capitalists had developed technology and organized the means of production with immense ingenuity and unparalleled efficiency. But this was achieved at the price of immense inequality, poverty and want. Thus there was something economically and morally wrong in a society where the few who did not perform manual labour enjoyed most of the wealth that was produced by manual labour.

Humanity's development would thus lead from the small, classless, and propertyless communities of primitive communism (men living in hordes or tribes that knew neither social classes nor private property in land or in persons), through a sequence of property based and class-divided social systems to a future worldwide community of economic abundance. Once this situation had been achieved, people could aim at the full and free development of all the potentialities and powers of every individual.

As technology progressed from muscle power to machine power a new middle class of merchants, business owners and capitalists would rise in power and prestige and eventually take the leadership of society away from the nobility. The new ruling class would consist of burghers or bourgeois who collectively make up the bourgeoisie. Within the bourgeoisie (or middle class) the rich and super-rich would make up the top layers of bankers, large factory owners and the like – the big bourgeoisie. Beneath them would be their far more numerous, far less affluent colleagues, the petty bourgeoisie, who shared much of the outlook of the richer business people, but, alas, neither their security, nor their prestige.

In Marx's image of the world, these wage earners were the chosen people or the chosen class of destiny. They owned no significant property in land, machines or major tools and thus no substantial means of production – their kind became known as proletarians and their class as the proletariat. Being propertyless, the proletariat in Marx's opinion had to be international in its point of view. The interests of the workers in all countries were the same: better wages and working conditions in the short run, but, beyond that, a rise to political power, the overthrow of the old order of property and privilege and the establishment of a new society.

Within each country the effects of merciless competition would inevitably turn most members of the middle class and peasantry into proletarians. In each country workers would seize power. During a transitional period they would exercise a dictatorship of the proletariat, by the vast majority and in the interests of the vast majority. Since the proletarians were internationalist by nature, the countries they now ruled would all cooperate in a fraternal community of socialist nations. This state of socialism would still know scarcity, social classes, and the state. But these too would soon pass. Technology would have progressed under capitalism, and this progress would be accelerated in the socialist stage. Soon, therefore, an economy of abundance would usher in the next stage – communism – and with it the stateless and classless future of mankind.

Thus, with these injustices the state would still be needed, to guard against external threats from surviving capitalist countries and to enforce its own laws and partly unjust distribution of incomes and opportunities even against members of the proletariat and the working population. Only after this socialist stage had accomplished its task could one enter the more highly developed stage of communism. In that exalted stage, in Marx's view, most goods and services would be so abundant that they would not have to be distributed by being priced and sold unit by unit. In the distant communist economy of abundance, each person would work according to his or her ability; but at last the individual would take according to his or her needs. Marx's notion was that most consumer goods would become so abundant that the question of allocation would become irrelevant. Nations would disappear, allocation problems would vanish, and there would be a single, unified mankind.

Marx, however, did overlook certain issues. His principles of socialism – payment according to amount of work – also applied to the international division of labour among socialist countries. A rich socialist nation like the USSR, well equipped with skills, capital and improved land, will expect to be paid for its exports in accordance with their value, even if they go to a poorer, socialist country. Such a country could be China, which lacking skills and equipment, could produce only exports of much lesser value even if they should require greater human effort to produce. Thus, contrary to Marxian views, there was a likelihood that a significant degree of inequality and potential injustice would persist among socialist countries. If their states and armed forces have the task of defending these unequal socialist patterns of distribution at home and abroad, they may also have to defend them against each other.

Marx in the great body of his writings had little to say about the characteristics of socialism and much less to say about communism. His attention was focused on capitalism – he sought to describe the way capitalism had developed and the way it worked or failed to work. He overlooked the intensity of nationalist and patriotic sentiment which compromised class solidarity along economic lines and the extension of the suffrage and popular democracy. His whole energies were directed to seeing capitalist society splitting into two classes, ultimately leading to catastrophic depression. Subsequent political thinkers have been hard pressed to explain how the socialist revolution could develop in the context of an underdeveloped capitalist society, where the major classes were peasants and landowners instead of proletarians and an urban bourgeoisie.

## Socialism

Like communism, socialism can mean a variety of different things, not because of ambiguity or vagueness but because it is a concept that operates in several different ideological vocabularies.

It is a politicoeconomic system where the state controls, and may legally own, the basic means of production. In so controlling industrial and sometimes agricultural plant, the aim is to produce what is needed by the society without regard to what may be most profitable to produce. All versions of socialism expect to produce an egalitarian society, one in which all are cared for by society, with no need either for poverty, or the relief of poverty by private charity.

It arose as a reaction to the dehumanizing and brutalizing impact of the industrial revolution and to the economic doctrine of *laissez faire* associated with it. The progenitors of socialism believed that the policy of *laissez faire* was the cause of poverty with its wasteful use of economic resources and its unwillingness to provide a living wage for workers and welfare for the poor. A substitute for *laissez faire* would be a policy of social cooperation, economic planning and community welfare.

The term first appears in the ideas of *Robert Owen*, the English industrialist and philanthropist, who believed the doctrine of *laissez faire* caused men to act selfishly rather than for the good of the community. He would educate people to the idea of cooperation and unselfish community action. In this way planned cooperative communities would come into being. Living wages would be paid to workers and social benefits such as housing, hospitals and educational institutions for all would be promoted. Owen sought to accomplish his ideas in Scotland and the United States. Although these ventures failed, his ideals spread as the basis for the cooperative movement. In 1844, textile workers in Rochdale, England gave cooperative principles a special twist by using shared, democratic principles in organizing purchases of food. This was the beginning of the powerful and worldwide consumer cooperative movement.

On the European continent, followers of Henri de Saint Simon and Francois Fourier were called socialist. St Simon believed that captains of industry should be enlightened to bring his new society into being. Planning would promote productivity and eliminate wasteful competition. Fourier wished to establish small, self-sufficient, non-political communities called phalanx. Its members would have diverse interests and abilities. They would share in the work of the community in accordance with their interests. The fruits of the labour would be shared in accordance with the work done. With the publication in 1848 of the *Communist Manifesto* by Karl Marx and Frederick Engels, socialism entered a new and essentially modern phase. The *Manifesto* as a political pamphlet predicted that the old order would perish in revolution and a new politicoeconomic order would replace it. This would be accomplished by the working class by means of its own effort. The new ruling class, the dictatorship of the proletariat, would continue until the last vestige of the old order had been eliminated. With this, true freedom would be the right of all. The *Manifesto* indicated a certain programme industrially advanced countries probably would follow. Included in that programme was public ownership of the means of production, including land, credit facilities, transport and communication. Agricultural and industrial expansion by the state would be planned to eliminate the difference between the country and the city. A graduated income tax and inheritance tax would eliminate economic differences. Education would be provided for all.

These principles became the central elements for the new socialist programmes. With the publication of the *Manifesto*, the socialist movement became egalitarian, political and democratic in intention. The aim of freedom would be achieved by the establishment of economic, social and political equality. Whereas liberals emphasized liberty as the essence of democracy, socialists emphasized equality. The *Manifesto* called on workers to organize for self-help into a political force; and as a result, social democratic parties sprang into existence in a number of Western European countries.

Marx soon joined with other intellectuals to form the first of what were to be many Socialist Internationals. These were attempts to create a worldwide organization of socialists – who by definition were distrustful of nationalist manifestations – to coordinate and to inform the actions of individual socialist groups. The First International (1864–76) broke up over the quarrels between anarchists (see Chapter 9) and Marxian socialists (based on the theoretical writings of Karl Marx and centred around the concepts of the class struggle and historical inevitability). The Second International was formed 1875 and in 1923 was fused with the International Working Union of Socialist Parties to form the Labour and Socialist International, which after 1945 became the present Socialist International. The Third International (the Comintern) was an organization founded by Lenin to bring about world revolution and it was soon under the hegemony of the Russian Communist Party.

It was during the timespan of the Second International that socialist theoreticians began to question some of Marx's conclusions. Eduard Bernstein, the German intellectual, believed the working class, far from being pauperized, actually was improving its condition under capitalism. Bernstein questioned the validity of Marx's judgement that class war and revolution were inevitable. He did not repudiate socialism as an ideal, but believed that it should be sought in a democratic and evolutionary way.

About the same time other evolutionary socialist movements came into being. In England, intellectuals including Sidney and Beatrice Webb, George Bernard Shaw and H. G. Wells joined to form the Fabian Society (1884) to promote democratic socialist ideals. They saw in gradual and non-violent reform the best method for the attainment of socialist goals. Agitation by these intellectuals was a factor of some importance in causing the British Labour Party to adopt socialism as a party programme in 1918.

Suspicion of political bureaucracy caused some socialists to urge the adoption of a programme by which workers would organize and operate industrial plants directly. These would be united in guilds (relying on democratic changes in the workplace particularly) for cooperation and would be regional and nationwide in scope. Leaders for a time in this thought were the English socialists, G. D. H. Cole and Harold Laski.

The First World War and the establishment of a communist state in Russia brought on a crisis for socialists. They had believed that war could not come, for socialist workers would refuse to fight or to produce for the war machine. Some socialists believed the failure was owing to an excessive decentralization of socialist parties. Instead of a single, strong international party, there had been numerous national parties. Such socialists were sympathetic then to the attempt of Russian communists to build a highly centralized Third International. However, the subordination of the International to Russian foreign policy aims and the repressive nature of the communist dictatorship in Russia soon caused second thoughts. Socialist parties split into revolutionary and evolutionary parties, the former, supported by Russia, the latter most prominent in the democratic West.

In the last two decades, the experience of a number of Western democracies with political intervention in and control over economic affairs, and the establishment of wide-ranging social welfare programmes, have caused socialists to question portions of their programmes. Nationalization, long considered the essence of socialism, no longer appears so often as a major aim. What remains then is the underlying commitment to egalitarian ideals and collective political action. Public planning and control or guidance of the economy for the achievement of an essentially egalitarian society in which freedom of choice and the right of self-expression are open to all may be said to comprise the central theme of socialism today.

The basic varieties of socialism today can be arranged by means of a system based on how much control of the economy, and just how much equality are seen as necessary or desirable. To some extent this converges with the more broadly used left/right syndrome, on which, for example, the British Labour Party is only mildly left or socialist, and the Communist Parties of Western Europe are very far to the left and very 'socialist'. An alternative principle for differentiation would be the extent to which a basically Marxist 'economic determinist' view is taken, as opposed simply to a fairly untheoretical demand for a more just and equal society, with more state impact on the economy. In this sense, the German Socialist Party (SPD), the earliest in Europe, started far to the left and became less socialist, more 'right wing' in the late 1950s when it officially gave up Marxism and became a reformist party acceptable even to the conservative CSU–CDU in the grand coalition government of 1965–9.

Socialism is principally a doctrine about the political implications of economic organization. Socialist parties differ widely indeed in the degree to which they aspire, or contrive, to remove the power of private capital to determine the organization of society, as they do in their assessments of the appropriate political format in which they undertake this task. What they have in common is an aversion to economic privileges unrelated to the discharge of current social functions, and a hostility to permitting the shaping and reshaping of society to be determined by the logic of a process of private economic appropriation.

The main pressure towards socialism has always come from the experience of discontent at the character of an existing society. This is particularly clear in the case of reformist socialism in conditions of free political association and is perhaps disputable in the case of the revolutionary triumphs of socialism. The potential for socialist revolution may be far higher in a country with relatively quiescent domestic class conflict than it is in one in which class hatred has reached a murderous intensity. A socialist society aspires to distribute labour tasks and opportunities and effective entitlements to economic goods on the basis of egalitarian communal membership; and it hopes to succeed in doing so without militating against the productivity of labour and the resulting range and scale of effective economic entitlements.

## Stalinism

Joseph Stalin is best remembered in the annals of the history of contemporary political theory for his long standing row with Trotsky, one of the leaders in the revolutionary success of the Bolsheviks in Russia. A clear message of the irreconcilable differences between Trotsky and Stalin was their attitude toward the proper role of the **Communist International** (Third International or Comintern) founded in Moscow in 1919. The purpose of the various Internationals was to bring together workers from all countries in order to advance the cause of socialism. Trotsky viewed the Comintern as a vehicle for coordinating revolutionary activity throughout the world – or the institutional expression of his concept of 'permanent revolution'. In opposition to Trotsky's position, Stalin sought to subordinate the Comintern to Soviet national interests. Stalinism represented an extreme suspicion of revolutionary adventure at home or abroad. Stalin wished to make his country a bastion of socialism, a model of socialist development that would inspire socialists throughout the world. Thus in the 1930s, Stalin collectivized agricultural production and initiated the first of a series of Five Year Plans designed to make the Soviet Union an industrial and military power. These programmes coincided with Stalin's liquidation of opposition elements in the party and state bureaucracy, and made obvious his commitment to rapid economic development. Stalin maintained that capitalist encirclement threatened the security of the Soviet Union and intensified as the socialist state advanced toward communism. Instead of withering away, the state consequently had been and would continue to be strengthened.

Today, Stalinism denotes an extreme bureaucratic centralization of political power in the hands of a single leader who dominates both the party and the state; the ideology becomes a dogma that stifles dissent. He constantly criticized working class leaders in the West as lackeys of the bourgeoisie. He was a great exploiter of ideology – he did not wish to persuade others but to corner them, to put them in a position where they dared not disagree openly or refuse to do what Stalin demanded. He delighted in treating his opponents in this way, wanting to humiliate or crush them, and not to win them over.

The process of **'de-Stalinization'** which began with Khrushchev's 'secret speech' to the 20th Party Congress in 1956 and the repudiation of 'the errors of the personality cult' weakened the Soviet Union's authority in the international communist movement, strengthened the polycentric tendencies in it, and raised the question of Stalinism's role in Soviet history. The attempts to dissociate Stalinism from Marxism–Leninism as the basis of ideological legitimacy, both internally and externally, during the 'de-Stalinization' period were minimized after the fall of Khrushchev in 1964. Later developments in the Soviet Union have underlined the durability of the Stalinist legacy and the continuous impact of his rule on Soviet institutions and on communist orthodoxy. In connection with the latter view the thought continues to present difficulties to a certain kind of historical materialist, since Stalinism seems to imply that history is made by individuals, rather than by 'material forces' which project them into eminence. Many observers suggest that Stalinism in some form is practised today in Rumania and North Korea.

## Leninism

In 1898 the Russian Social Democratic Labour Party was formed in Minsk – an illegal creation in Czarist Russia; but five years later it split on the question of when the socialist revolution should come to Russia. The Mensheviks, or members of the minority faction, accepted the necessity of a prolonged period of capitalist development in Russia prior to any formation of a socialist creed, as a viable alternative. They called for the organization of a loosely structured and mass-based political party. The Bolsheviks, or members of the majority faction, argued instead that the socialist revolution need not be postponed and that its arrival could be hastened by the organization of a highly centralized and disciplined core of professional revolutionaries.

The political and ideological leader of the Bolsheviks was Vladimir Ilyich Lenin (born Ulyanov). In a pamphlet published in 1902 Lenin urged the organization of the kind of tightly knit revolutionary party that in fact came to characterize the Bolsheviks, who were to adopt the 'communist' label after the Russian Revolution in 1917.

For Lenin, the revolutionary party was likely to be most effective if it was composed not of workers but of intellectuals dedicated to pursuing the interests of the working class. That such a party was essential was made clear by the repressive autocracy of the Czarist state which prohibited working class organization. The socialist revolution, in Lenin's eyes was inevitable only if the party made it so. For Marx, the socialist revolution was a largely impersonal process propelled by the contradictions in capitalist economic development. Lenin substituted the personal intervention of the Leninist party for the objective forces of Marx's history. In the process of turning Marxism upside down, Lenin insisted that the socialist revolution was inevitably violent and an abrupt departure from the past.

In 1916, Lenin published *Imperialism: The Highest Stage of Capitalism* in which he elaborated Marx's earlier argument that monopoly capitalism inevitably attempts to ensure its further development by absorbing foreign territories and exploiting their resources and native peoples. In this sense, domestic and international politics were to be explained primarily in terms of underlying economic interest. Lenin stated that the advanced capitalist nations had temporarily postponed catastrophic economic crises by finding new markets in the underdeveloped countries of the world. Imperialist expansion had enabled the bourgeoisie to buy off its indigenous proletariat through the distribution of some of the profits expropriated from foreign and less class conscious workers.

The revolution was likely to occur in the weakest link in the chain of European capitalism. The least developed of the capitalist states, Russia was also the least advanced in the imperialist race for foreign markets. Its proletariat was consequently more susceptible to revolutionary mobilization, and in alliance with the Russian peasantry and led by the Bolshevik party, the Russian working class could be the first to inaugurate a socialist regime.

## Trotskyism

Along with Lenin, Leon Trotsky (1879–1940, born Lev Bronstein) was the essential leader in the revolutionary success of the Bolsheviks in Russia and the Red Army's subsequent victory over the counter-revolutionary Whites during the Russian Civil War 1918–20.

However, Trotsky believed that instead of his converting to Leninism, Lenin had adopted his views on socialist revolution. Stalinist and post-Stalinist history in the Soviet Union have denied that Trotsky was anything other than a traitor to the Russian Revolution.

Ideologically it was Trotsky who explained how revolution in backward Russia could result in socialism, but socialism on a necessarily international scale of political and economic change. Trotsky's doctrine of **'permanent revolution'** held that the revolution could succeed and sustain its socialist ambitions only if it were extended beyond the borders of Russia, eventually overwhelming the forces of capitalism elsewhere in Europe. After the Bolsheviks seizure of power, Trotsky believed that news of their success would be an important catalyst in eliminating the false consciousness of workers in the more advanced capitalist countries.

The failure of the communist revolutionary efforts in Europe in 1918 and shortly thereafter induced Trotsky to argue that the international proletarian revolution was only temporarily postponed and that continuous efforts should be undertaken to raise the revolutionary consciousness of the workers. Trotsky then itemized a second dimension to the principles of permanent revolution, that of 'telescoped revolution'. In Bolshevik Russia, the foundations of socialism could be laid even while the state encouraged the economic development and cultural transformation that elsewhere had resulted from capitalism and the efforts of an enterprising bourgeoisie. He maintained that while the working class was being enlarged and socially educated through state sponsored industrialization, agricultural production should be collectivized, to hasten the development of a socialist spirit among the peasantry. For Trotsky the New Economic Policy's failure to collectivize the peasantry, and its encouragement of the bourgeois spirit among the entrepreneurs, represented a setback in the development of socialism in Russia.

Trotsky believed by the late 1920s that the revolution had been betrayed. Socialism in his country was impossible in as far as it was not supported by working-class revolutions elsewhere in Europe. Socialist development was hindered in so far as political power was concentrated in the hands of a narrow state bureaucracy which intensified the exploitation of the working class. Because of these views and because of his failure to win the intraparty struggle with Stalin after Lenin's death in 1924, Trotsky was exiled from the Soviet Union in 1929 and assassinated in Mexico in 1940.

Today, Trotskyite intellectuals are found in many parts of the world – and they vehemently argue that the Soviet Union is not really a socialist state, nor are its communist allies, and they remain committed to the organization of proletarian revolution wherever such an opportunity occurs, for advancing the cause of socialism and ultimately, communism.

## Titoism

It was no coincidence that the most serious challenge to Stalinism came initially from Yugoslavia, where Tito's partisans, operating against the German occupation of Yugoslavia after 1941, succeeded in capturing power without the aid of the Soviet Army. Elsewhere in communist Eastern Europe, the presence of Soviet military power ensured the communist leaders' subordination to Moscow and Stalin, at least until Stalin's death in 1953. The case of Yugoslavia was very different. From his vantage point after the Second World War, Marshal Tito (born Josip Broz) believed that the opportunities for communist revolution were not limited to the zone of operations of the Soviet Army and that many of the countries of Europe were vulnerable to the forces of indigenous communism. Tito believed power could be seized through superior military organization, competent political leadership and civil war. But Tito's implicit variation on Trotsky's permanent revolution met with the conservative opposition of Stalin, who was content to consolidate the Soviet Union's control over Eastern Europe. The founding of the **Communist Information Bureau (Cominform)** in 1947 represented a modest victory in the Tito supporters' struggle against Stalin's revolutionary position. Tito's initial call in Cominform was for violent confrontation with the institutions of the bourgeois state – but this was a failure. Yugoslavia was then expelled from the Cominform; and all the communist parties vented their wrath on the renegade Tito who was accused of collaborating with the Germans during the war and insituting a fascist state in Yugoslavia.

The political, diplomatic and economic isolation that suddenly descended on Yugoslavia forced a major shift in Tito's policies, especially as the threat of a Soviet military invasion loomed on the Yugoslav horizon. The United States gave immediate support to Yugoslavia, which assured the survival of Titoism, which came to denote the very opposite of what it initially stood for – revolutionary adventurism.

Titoism gave rise to a non-aligned foreign policy that does not consistently support the position or interests of either the communist or non-communist states. Yugoslav communism represents a relatively non-coercive style of communist government. It is a federal state with planning and other administrative functions distributed among the six states which are defined along the lines of culture and language. The state itself, contrary to the views of Stalin on the matter, has begun the process of withering away, although the Communist Party remains as a general guide to policy choices – but more through education than command. Worker participation in factory management is also allowed, which represents a relatively humanistic approach to industrial organization that approximates to the original spirit of Marxism. Bureaucratic control of citizen life is also being lessened. Titoism was as revolutionary in the European context as a variant of Leninist orthodoxy, as was Castroism in Latin America.

## Castroism

Fidel Castro, the leader of Cuba since 1959, came from a wealthy background. He initially became a leader of the Cuban liberals who were opposed to the dictatorship of Fulgencio Batista. Batista's authoritarian and corrupt regime enjoyed substantial support from the United States government. Business interests in the United States had been deeply involved in the Cuban economy and in Cuba politics since 1898.

Castro initially tried to seize power in 1953 but was captured and imprisoned. Released under amnesty he went to Mexico and organized the 26th July Movement, which received political and economic support from prominent Cuban exiles also hostile to the Batista regime. Castro's declared intent was to raise a popular revolt against Batista that would return Cuba to democratic and constitutional government, restoring civil liberties.

In 1956 an armed uprising, planned to coincide with the amphibious landing of Castro and eighty armed men in South West Oriente province, failed to materialize and few escaped Batista's men except Fidel, his brother-in-law Raoul, and Che Guevara, a medical doctor born in Argentina. This small band of intellectuals and urban-oriented revolutionaries took refuge in the mountains of Sierra Maestra and began to cultivate the support of local peasants.

Like Mao, Castro was forced by initial defeat to rethink his strategy for revolution, and what emerged was a programme of agarian reform coupled with the tactics of guerrilla warfare. Batista's inability to root out guerrillas enhanced their popular appeal – which incurred Batista's wrath by way of a campaign of terror. Castro's guerrilla army never numbered more than 2000 and its victorious entry into Havana in 1959 was the result more of Batista's accumulated weaknesses than of the guerrilla's military capabilities.

The Castro movement initiated the collectivization cf Cuban agriculture and nationalized all domestic and foreign-owned industries and business enterprises. By the 1970s and through rigorous economic planning, Castro's charismatic leadership and Soviet economic aid, the Cuban population had made important gains in housing, welfare and education. All this development was at the expense of gaining the hostility of the government of the United States. Castro purged the Communist Party's top leadership, and assumed control over the party, whose militants were then infiltrated into the critical centres of Cuban government and society. Anxious to demonstrate its time honoured commitment to revolution the Soviet Union proved willing to subsidize the struggling Cuban economy.

That Castroism represented a unique ideological and political phenomenon was also suggested by the revolutionary ideology that eventually emerged from the Cuban revolution, especially as elaborated by Che Guevara and Regis Debray – the latter a young French intellectual who became a confidant of Castro and his close associates. To the constant embarrassment of the Soviet Union which remained committed to the extension of its diplomatic and economic influence rather than to revolutionary adventure, Castroism became identified with peasant-based revolution throughout Latin America.

It was believed that millions of impoverished Latin American peasants were ready to revolt and that the prime instrument of peasant revolution was the presence of armed guerrillas who progressively enlarged their scope of military activity against the existing government. Contrary to Leninist, Maoist, and Vietnamese communist principles, the political arm of the revolution was to be subordinated to the military and it was events in the countryside (as determined by the military) rather than in the city that were ultimately to determine the success of revolution.

But Castroism seriously overestimated the revolutionary potential of Castroite guerrillas and peasants elsewhere in Latin America. It also underestimated the effectiveness of counterinsurgency techniques developed in Latin America (with the help of military equipment and training from the United States) after Castro's revolution in Cuba. Guevara was eventually defeated, captured and killed in Bolivia in 1967 and thereafter direct Cuban involvement in Latin American revolutionary politics significantly declined. The overthrow of the Somoza regime in Nicaragua in 1979 was the result of revolutionary forces with Nicaragua, and not Castroite adventurism.

The role of Cuban military advisers and armed forces in various African countries (especially in Angola since 1975) and Cuba's geographic position as a staging area for the export of military equipment and personnel in the Caribbean, kept alive the popular identification of Castroism with communist revolution abroad. Cuba was heavily dependent on the Soviet Union for economic and political support. Thus Cuban mercenaries played the role of proxies for Soviet big power politics – a relatively inexpensive way for Cuba to service its economic and political debts to the Soviet Union. The Soviet Union has been concerned in recent years about the increasing independence of thought which has been developing in its European communist parties.

## Eurocommunism

The term **Eurocommunism** was first used in 1967 by the Yugoslav journalist, Frane Barbieri. It implies a liberal version of communism accepted by the leading Western European Communist parties since the mid-1970s, in their conviction that only this form of communism has an electoral chance of success and of implementation in the democratic West. Many communists wish to adopt communist ideas according to the needs of their own countries rather than to accept universal blueprints. In November 1975, the French and Italian Communist Parties issued a joint declaration on the subject. The leading exponents of Eurocommunism at its birth were Georges Marchais, Enrico Berlinguer and Santiago Carrillo, leaders of the French, Italian and Spanish Communist Parties respectively.

Democratization and the humanization of communism could be achieved by:

- the plurality of political parties and the abandonment of the idea of the dictatorship of the proletariat;
- democratic elections and the democratic parliamentary road to socialism and communism;
- the right to the existence and activities of opposition parties;
- the guarantee of civil liberties – the freedom of thought, expression, religion, the press assembly, association, demonstration and of foreign travel.

Eurocommunists have reserved the right of selective criticism of the policies pursued by the communist regimes in the socialist countries, and in particular Eurocommunists regard the Soviet and Chinese policies as reflective of the early and crude stage of communism.

The Soviet Union denounces Eurocommunism as **revisionism**, i.e. opposition to Marxism from within Marxism itself. Over the last decade Eurocommunists have been notable for their frequent denunciation of Soviet foreign and domestic policies and their respect for those political institutions which are denounced in the Soviet Union as bourgeois democracy, i.e. institutions in which power will always vest in the bourgeoisie or its agents.

In spite of Soviet hostility, Eurocommunism has gained a considerable following, especially among those who have wished to take advantage of the common political institutions and law-making capacity of the European Common Market in order to advance the condition of the working class throughout its member states. There have been communist members in the governments of Italy, France, Spain and Greece and the European Parliament.

Attitudes to Eurocommunists vary, and the 'dovish' or traditional view discussed so far is not held by a considerable number of hawks. They do not automatically assume that the West European Communist Parties have already developed a type of communism that is radically divergent from that in force throughout the Soviet Union and Eastern Europe. Nor do they believe that it implies the arrival of a new political phenomenon arising out of Western tradition. The hawks argue that while there have indeed been variations in doctrine and attitudes towards Soviet hegemony of the international communist movement, such subtle departure from orthodoxy cannot lead to their being dignified as a wholly new political category, indigenous to Western Europe, unlinked to the communist past and experience in the Soviet sphere. They question that Eurocommunism implies a pan-Western European movement, a uniformity of ideological and political development among the various communist parties. There are continuing substantial differences between the various communist parties, not only between North and South (the 'major' and 'minor') groupings, but between the Latin organizations themselves. Certainly the Spanish Communist Party in the 1970s, particularly under its then leader,

Santiago Carrillo, exhibited a political fluidity that could have developed into a new kind of communism. Yet his apparent liberality was not infectious, certainly not so in the rest of the Iberian Peninsula, nor in France, and not even in Italy.

Despite electoral reverses in the 1980s in France, Spain and Italy, the Southern European communist parties are large and well organized. They have had significant electoral support which despite the current setbacks could grow. Some have aspirations, not entirely unfounded, of participation in government. In addition they maintain control over sizeable sectors of the labour movement and other strategic non-governmental sectors (including the media), which accord them considerable extra-parliamentary leverage over their societies. The leadership of these parties has been in the forefront of change both domestically and in their relationship towards the Soviet Union.

If there is to be a resurgence of this new communist phenomena then it will manifest itself most markedly in these parties, according to the opinions of most political analysts. If it does not, then it is unlikely that it will be present elsewhere in Western Europe, in the smaller and weaker parties. One such party is the British Communist Party which, although miniscule electorally, has a significant influence within the powerful British trade union movement. The Party remains a political and industrial force. It has made overtures for greater collaboration with the Labour Party – a collaboration which the dominant left wing within the Labour Party apparatus does not appear to resist as strenuously as did its social democratic predecessors. In the late 1970s the Party changed – both domestically and in its relations with the Soviet Union, a process resulting in the departure of some of its Stalinist militants.

The lure of gaining votes in the democracies has posed dilemmas. The French communists and certain members of the Italian Communist Party have officially repudiated the dictatorship of the proletariat – and with it Marxism itself. On these strange developments, and any similar ones in future, could be based the coffin of Eurocommunism. It could end in social democracy or revert back to some form of Leninism. In the first case it would cease to be communist and in the second it will no longer be Euro. Recent elections in West European states suggest that the communist vote is, and seems destined to remain, a protest vote rather than a vote for government. The protest vote is attracted because communists are thought to stand for everything which social democrats do not. At the time of writing, Eurocommunists deny their drift to social democracy and of course the suggestion that self-preservation may put them back on the Leninist road.

The Soviet rejection of Eurocommunism has been rather feeble compared with their traditional denunciation of other deviationist policies, such as Titoism. It expresses the fear that the Soviet Party's remaining authority in its struggle with China and other 'splitters' of the world communist movement will be eroded with great consequences for the uncertain stability of Eastern Europe. The Soviets fear the Eurocommunists' freedom to criticize the Soviet system without the inhibitions of office. They are aware that socialism with a human face is more attractive than socialism with a Russian face.

The West European communist parties' links with Moscow have been weakened – not cut; and Moscow still provides funds to the Eurocommunists. The commitment to parliamentary democracy of Eurocommunists is ambiguous. For example, the freedom of political parties, from far left to far right, to function outside the framework of socialism, and to seek office with a mandate to replace socialism is not clearly stated. Given their ideological affinity and the continuing thrust of their foreign policy, the West European parties remain a net advantage to the Soviet Union. While it may be possible to exploit the changes that have occurred, and by skilful diplomacy to divide them further from the Soviet Union, their increased strength remains an important net disadvantage to the West.

## Questions

### Marxism and Stalinism

1 What did Marx mean by 'alienation and dialectical relationships'?
2 Was Marx's image of the world realistic?
3 In Marx's views what were the pros and cons of capitalism?
4 Account for the Stalinist view of history.
5 Why did de-Stalinization occur?

### Socialism

1 Were the ideas inherent in Owenism born ahead of their time?
2 What were the socialist principles enunciated in the 1848 *Manifesto*?
3 Critically appraise the basic varieties of socialism in democracies today.
4 Examine the main pressures towards socialism.

### Titoism, Leninism and Trotskyism

1 What was unique about Tito's attitude to communism?
2 Examine the role of non-alignment.
3 Account for Lenin's desire for an intellectual revolution.
4 Discuss Lenin's cynicism towards imperialism.
5 Is 'permanent revolution' a possibility?
6 Why did Trotsky split with Stalin?

### Castroism

1 Why has Castroism appealed to Third World nations?
2 Why is Castroism a unique ideological and political phenomenon?

### Eurocommunism

1 Analyse the dilemmas inherent in Eurocommunist belief.
2 Compare and contrast the 'dovish' and 'hawkish' views toward Eurocommunism.

3  Consider why France, Italy and Spain have well developed Euro-communist parties.

## Further reading

Acton, H. B., *What Marx Really Said*, Macdonald, London, 1967.
Bottomore, T. (ed.), *A Dictionary of Marxist Thought*, Blackwell, Oxford, 1983.
Bottomore, T., *Political Sociology*, Hutchinson, London, 1979.
Carew Hunt, R. N., *The Theory and Practice of Communism*, Geoffrey Bles, London, 1957.
Childs, D. (ed.), *The Changing Face of Western Communism*, Croom Helm, London, 1980.
Cohen, A. S., *Theories of Revolution, An Introduction*, T. Nelson & Sons Ltd, London, 1975.
Collins, H., *Marxism and Law*, Clarendon Press, Oxford, 1982.
Deakin, F. W., Shukman, H. and Willetts, H. T., *A History of World Communism*, Weidenfeld & Nicholson, London, 1975.
Djilas, M., *The New Class*, Thames & Hudson, London, 1958.
Drucker, H. M., *The Political Uses of Ideology*, Macmillan, London, 1977.
Duncan, G., *Marx and Hill*, Cambridge University Press, 1973.
Dunn, J., *Politics of Socialism*, Cambridge University Press, 1984.
Fine, B., *Democracy and the Rule of Law*, Pluto Press, London, 1984.
Godson, R. and Haseler, S., *Eurocommunism*, St Martins Press, New York, 1978.
Grimes, A. P. and Horwitz, R. H., *Modern Political Ideologies*, Oxford University Press, 1959.
Hallas, D., *Trotsky's Marxism*, Pluto Press, London, 1979.
Lenin, V. I., *The State and Revolution*, Progress Publishers, Moscow, 1972.
Lichtheim, G., *Marxism: An Historical and Critical Study*, Routledge and Kegan Paul, London, 1961.
McLellan, D. (ed.), *Marx the first 100 years*, Frances Pinter, London, 1983.
Seliger, M., *The Marxist Conception of Ideology: a Critical Essay*, Cambridge University Press, 1977.
Steele, J., *The Limits of Soviet Power*, Penguin, London, 1984.
Taylor, A. J. P., *Marx, Engels, Communist Manifesto*, Penguin, London, 1979.
Thomas, D., *Political Ideas*, Pelican, London, 1982.
Urban, G. R. (ed.), *Eurocommunism, its Roots and Future in Italy and Elsewhere*, Temple Smith, London, 1978.

# 9
# Anarchism and extremism

Anarchism is often viewed as synonymous with extremism, and, while in many ways this is correct, it is sometimes inappropriate in the context of contemporary politics. Life without government is anarchy. The very word 'anarchy' is emotive, yet many aspects of society are conducted without government, albeit in an orderly manner. It is not chaos, but in many ways the orderly self-regulation of social affairs. Nevertheless, an effective anarchist group is never going to be anything like the size of a nation or a country, as we think of them today. Anarchists believe social interaction on a national scale would be impossible without government. More to the point they think that it is unnecessary.

The literal meaning of the word anarchy – absence of authority, is less menacing and expresses the central view of anarchists that in spite of the relationship between social interaction and government, the latter is an absolute evil.

Theories of anarchism originated after the triumph of secular and scientific thought in the Enlightenment (an eighteenth-century philosophical movement stressing the importance of reason and the critical reappraisal of existing ideas and social institutions), and were concurrent with the development of the sophisticated apparatus of the modern state. The modern fathers of anarchist theory concluded that once authority in all its forms had been abolished – they equated the idea of God and that of authority – society could be refashioned on a new moral basis and human nature, no longer degraded by subjection or corruption by authority, would come to fruition.

The doctrine of anarchism does not advocate anarchy in the popular sense of the word. What it does reject is the power apparatus of the modern state. He who wields political power abuses it, he who is controlled by political power has his individuality stifled. Primarily anarchists wish to weaken and diffuse institutionalized power – the bureaucracy, police and the law. Bureaucracy means the exercise of power by distant impersonalized control, and the priority for the 'expert' over the individual. The function of the police, as the anarchist sees it, is not so much the maintenance of law and order as the preservation of state power. The legal code which the police are employed to uphold is no more sacrosanct. For the anarchist the law is only a complex attempt to justify the very system they reject.

There is often a tendency for democratic theory to spill over into anarchism. Anarchism emphasizes individual autonomy like many theories of democracy, but unlike the latter, it focuses clearly on the tension between individual autonomy and the power of the people as a whole – and if necessary rejects the power of the people. When democrats emphasize the individual at the expense of the people there is, then, an affinity with anarchism. Anarchism completely rejects state power, even if such power is exercised by the people. Some varieties of anarchism concentrate on small groups – and their autonomy – rather than on individuals. Such versions have some apparent affinities with pluralism, but the closest connections are with varieties of the 'new democratic theory'.

The apparent distant relationship between democratic theory and anarchism ties in with the two contradictory stereotypes which historically anarchists have suffered from at regular intervals: they are either described as 'bomb-throwing lunatics' or 'muddle-headed utopian dreamers'. Neither image is accurate. While individuals have attempted acts of violence and revenge, anarchism frequently has been a minority social movement infused with ideals. Anarchists have condemned war, violence, industrial exploitation, political repression, educational regimentation, religious superstition and economic and political imperialism.

The rapid development of anarchism was both its strength and its weakness. The advance of technology put raw materials in the hands of many who were unfitted to use them politically, but who lacked the will to live and to build and were prepared to face destruction as martyrs in the cause of 'the idea'. Anarchists never made a successful revolution. Their political theories are full of flaws and mistaken assumptions. Any sympathy for the anarchist cause has been swamped by mass violence and terrorism endemic in the thoughts of other anarchists.

In practice, anarchists have shown themselves opposed to what the majority of people in the twentieth century have regarded as essential for political and social progress – namely the political party. Collective hatred of the state by anarchists means that agreement among them is unanimous that in the new society human beings will live in extreme simplicity and frugality and will be happy to dismiss the technical achievements of the industrial age – in some respects a conservative approach. Much anarchist thinking is based on a romantic backward-looking version of an idealized past society of artisans and peasants and on a total rejection of the realities of twentieth-century social and economic organization. Certain types of anarchists are extremely individualistic, rejecting all conventions and restrictions. Anarchist doctrine in another way is not new – for the idea of a morality without obligations or sanctions has been as attractive as that of a society without government or governed – and these will have followers in the future. The student riots of the late 1960s and the terrorist movements of a decade later provided examples of the younger generations' anarchistic ideal which provoked the same reaction from governments – symptoms of international conspiracy to subvert the existing order as the anarchist movements of the other generation in the late nineteenth century had done. This point of view shows how contemporary revolutionaries, like their predecessors, are torn between their belief in cooperation and peaceful communal living on the one hand and their belief in direct violent action on the other.

At the time of writing, the violent element in anarchist theory holds sway – all part of the aspect of a late twentieth-century counterculture. Anarchists' views on decentralization and communality have been overshadowed on a vast scale by the techniques of terrorism which are still regarded, in many ways mistakenly, as characteristic of anarchism. Thus a challenge is offered to basic assumptions of a liberal society.

Several issues have to be borne in mind when making judgements about anarchism. Contrary to popular belief, anarchism is not a dramatic doctrine. A major restructuring of society into primitive communes is sheer utopia. The individualistic tone of anarchist thinking can act as an important regulator on more realistic social thought. Anarchism has never had much support except in the modified form of syndicalism (a form of socialism which stresses the class struggle and the achievement of socialism by means of industrial action, such as the strike and sabotage rather than via political methods). Anarchists are quick to resort to direct action and civil disobedience, opposing the idea of representation and believing, like syndicalists, that individual freedom could not be guaranteed if the state was all powerful, even if it were socialist.

Classical anarchism as part of the wider socialist movement was originally inspired by the mutualist and federalist ideas of Proudhon. Proudhon adopted an essentially cooperative approach to socialism, but insisted that the power of capital and of the state were synonymous and that the proletariat could not free itself by means of the use of state power. These views were propagated by Bakunin under whose leadership anarchism became a rival of Marxist socialism at international level. Unlike Proudhon, however, Bakunin advocated the violent and revolutionary expropriation of capitalist (landed) property, leading to a form of collectivism. Bakunin's successor, Kropotkin, emphasized the importance of mutual aid as a factor in social evolution. He was mainly responsible for developing the theory of **anarchist communism** according to which everything belongs to everyone. Superficially there is the view that Marxists and anarchist communists agree about the end (a classless, stateless society) but differ about the means to that end. At a deeper level the disagreement is about the nature of the state, its relationship to society and to capital, and how politics as a form of alienation may be transcended.

Anarchists' supreme political ideal is individual freedom: with the concomitant adjuncts of equality, cooperation and solidarity. Freedom is specified in contrast to authority. For Bakunin the term denotes both freedom from oppression by the external world, attained by means of knowledge, and freedom to act in conformity with one's own judgements. Anarchists are thus able to argue that the abolition of authority will be as beneficial for the oppressors as for the oppressed.

The goal of anarchism is to eliminate dependence and oppression. The abolition of authority would result in freedom which in turn will promote individual happiness. Although anarchism, like liberalism, focuses on the individual, anarchists conceive of individualism as self-fulfilment within society, not as the withdrawal and self-differentiation which liberals emphasize and which ultimately rests on wealth. Individual fulfilment is achieved through creative work, while cooperation was to be the basis of anarchist society.

Criticism of anarchist theory rests primarily on its utopian ideals especially in relation to morality. With regard to criminals and disruptive elements, Godwin suggested expulsion, while Bakunin believed in starvation for anti-social individuals. Another criticism of anarchism is that leadership is a natural phenomenon which cannot be abolished. Yet it is the sense of control over one's own destiny, which can never be achieved under authority, which anarchist society would promote.

The strongest and most publicized criticism of anarchism concerns its exponents' willingness to use violent methods. Godwin argued for the force of moral persuasion, while Proudhon promoted propaganda plus passive resistance to government. The greatest proponent of the ethics of violence was Georges Sorel, the anarcho-syndicalist. He believed middle class violence was pervasive but disguised and justified by reference to God and the state, whereas proletarian violence was purely and simply an act of war, justified by the brutal nature of state violence. Sorel argued that violence was educative, pure and virtuous.

Anarchists do offer a defence of violence. First, violence merits violence in that whoever uses violence deserves, in some absolute moral sense, retaliation, and that violence in self-defence against violent attack, duress or coercion is permissible. Second, it is suggested that the ends justify the means, and that violence even against a symbolic victim is justified by its consequence and the ideality of the revolutionary's goal. Third, the state creates a self-justifying moral ideology which includes the sanctity of life, so that the state can condemn *a priori* any move towards revolutionary change. Generally violence is associated more with anarchists than Marxists – yet in both there are strong revolutionary ideals.

In stark contrast in envisaging a homely life devoted to unsophisticated activity and filled with simple pleasures, anarchism belongs to the 'primitive tradition' of Western culture and springs from the philosophical concept of the inherent and radical goodness of human nature. Indirectly modern anarchism has been influenced by the primitivistic strain in the thought of Jean Jacques Rousseau, who sceptically and critically regarded Western civilization as a sad deviation from natural conditions of existence.

Modern thinkers influenced by anarchism, e.g. Nozick, are usually of a liberal persuasion and are therefore more tolerant towards private property, on account of the interference in freedom that its abolition seems to imply. The views of Hegel are antithetical – that true human nature requires the state, not only as means to its security but as the highest expression of its freedom, with ownership of private property being a vital ingredient of the state scheme.

Anarchism has often been associated with the term **extremism**, particularly in relation to intolerance towards all views other than its own and to the adoption of means to political ends which disregard accepted standards of conduct and disregard for liberty and human rights of others. The antithesis of anarchist thought has been the development of fascist thought.

## Questions

1 Examine the reasons behind anarchists' hatred of the power apparatus of the modern state.
2 Why do anarchists suffer from contradictions in their thinking?
3 Outline the validity of the view that there are myths in anarchist thinking.
4 Account for the hold of anarchist thought among intellectuals.

## Further reading

Callaghan, J., *British Trotskyism Theory and Practice*, Basil Blackwell, Oxford, 1984.
Calvert, J., *Revolution*, Macmillan, London, 1970.
Hartman, T. and Mitchell, J., *A World Atlas of Military History, 1945–84*, Leo Cooper, London, 1984.
Hyams, E., *A Dictionary of Modern Revolution*, Allen Lane, London, 1973.
Joll, J, *Anarchism*, Methuen, London, 1969.
Kedward, R., *The Anarchists: The men who shocked an era*, British Publishing Corporation, London, 1971.
Perlin, T. M. (ed.), *Contemporary Anarchism*, Transaction Books, New Jersey, 1979.
Perlmutter, A., *Modern Authoritarianism*, Yale University Press, Yale, 1981.
Revel, J-F., *The Totalitarian Temptation*, Pelican, London, 1978.
Ritter, A., *Anarchism: Theoretical Analysis*, Cambridge University Press, 1980.
Thomson, D. (ed.), *Political Ideas*, Pelican, London, 1982.
Wheatcroft, A., *World Atlas of Revolutions*, Hamish Hamilton, London, 1983.

# 10
# Fascism

Specifically **fascism** was born in the Fascist Movement formed in 1919, which Mussolini led to power in Italy (1922–45). The Italian word, *fascismo*, is derived from the *fasces*, the bundle of rods with a projecting axe, which was carried before the Consuls as the insignia of state authority in ancient Rome.

As an example of theoretical analysis of international relations, fascism in all its variants stated simply that might makes right, and that powerful nation states should rightfully dictate to weaker nation states. Fascism has always been policy orientated, advocating the growth and enhancement of national power. Under national socialism, the German variant of which was called nazism, the entire industrial and productive capacity of the nation state and all the energies of its population were to be devoted to strengthening the state. The national leader was deified, and the military glorified. Territorial expansion was considered proof of the superiority of the system. Nazism was a similar authoritarian movement to the falange in Franco's Spain, the Iron Guard in Antonescu's Roumania, and Sir Oswald Mosley's British Union of Fascists.

Small and unimportant, the movement began with hardly any programme or platform. It stressed action, mouthed vague slogans and talked of law and order, while using lawless methods. Mussolini – an ex-socialist turned nationalist – drew his ideas from Sorel, Marx, Pareto, Nietzsche and D'Annunzio. However he had no clear goals, except to acquire power for himself and his handful of followers. Some years later he was to describe himself as an 'aristocrat and democrat revolutionist and reactionary, proletarian and anti-proletarian, pacifist and anti-pacifist' in short, all things to all men. Aided in part by the inability of his opponents to reconcile their differences, his strategy – a mixture of ruthlessness, violence and propaganda – succeeded. After 1925, fascism, now the official designation of the former *fasci di combattimento*, established a one-party dictatorship. Only then did it begin to elaborate a political philosophy and work out an economic state structure.

Mussolini's rather inchoate theories were amplified and more precisely defined into the official philosophy of fascism by others, notably Giovanni Gentile, one of Italy's foremost Hegelian philosophers, who explained that fascism opposed liberalism not because it wanted authority instead of liberty. Rather, fascism substituted a real and concrete freedom for the abstract and false freedom of liberalism. Fascist freedom was derived from the attempt to unite state and individual into a collective entity. The fascists then turned to the social and economic structure of Italian society, which they elaborated into the 'corporate state'. The organization of Italy's economy represented an attempt to introduce an integrated socioeconomic order and to do away with old class differences.

Having endowed the state with a mystical personality, while at the same time subordinating each individual to it, and having reorganized the economic structure, the fascists reduced the powers of parliament. Finally, in 1939, it was replaced by the Chamber of Fasces and Corporations, the last effort to erase completely the remaining vestiges of nineteenth-century liberal government. Representation was transferred from the individual to the group: politically the *fasces*, or party nuclei; economically the corporations representing the nation's economic interests. Each Italian thus became part of a group in a hierarchically structured society. The new fascist structure developed parallel to the old *statuto*, or constitution of the pre-fascist Italian state. The *statuto*, which gave the king the authority to appoint and dismiss the prime minister, was never abbrogated. Superseded and set aside it retained the strength of law to become operational once again should the situation require it. The survival of this constitutional charter distinguished fascism from other totalitarian states.

The common traits were strongly nationalist, violently anti-communist and anti-Marxist. Mussolini's followers hated liberalism, democracy and parliamentary parties, which they sought to replace by a new authoritarian state in which there would be only one party, their own, with a monopoly of power and a single leader with charismatic qualities and dictatorial powers. They shared a cult of violence and action, planned to seize power, exalted war, and with their uniforms, ranks, salutes and rallies gave their activities a paramilitary character. In political campaigns, they relied heavily on mass propaganda and terrorism. Once in power they used the power of the state to liquidate their rivals without regard for the law. Racism and anti-semitism were strongly marked features of some fascist movements, for example the German, but not all (e.g. the Italian). The movement appealed to people who resented the outcome of the First World War and who felt threatened by inflation, depression and the spectre of revolution.

Fascism was the product of the First World War and the social upheaval and economic depression which followed. It was discredited by the total defeat of the fascist states in the Second World War. Since 1945, a number of neo-fascist parties have appeared in Europe, though without achieving any real success. These movements embody, or seem to embody, a revival of the ideas and methods of post-1945 fascism, especially in France, and as the Movimento Sociale Italiano in Italy.

Just as military defeat can lay part of the foundations for fascist strength, it is the typical end of the fascist state. While the basis of fascist strength, especially in Europe, was in the middle classes (fearful of the upward mobility of the lower classes), fascism came to power with the support of members of the old aristocracy. Their defeat, along with the military catastrophies wrought by fascist leaders, helped to pave the way for more enlightened political elites, committed to the principles and norms of more egalitarian and democratic ideologies.

The anti-communist and anti-liberal stance of fascist movements has made the fights against fascism a rallying point for left and liberal causes. The label 'fascist' may often be applied very loosely to denote almost any doctrine which conflicts with left–liberal ideology. The term conveys no very clear idea, a fact which perhaps explains its popularity. The fact that it is a term used almost always in a pejorative fashion, has made the task of distinguishing its meaning still more difficult. During the years immediately preceding the Second World War, Soviet leaders and the Soviet press consistently referred to Hitler's Germany as fascist. This description was undoubtedly correct. Yet in the 1970s Soviet leaders and the Soviet press have stigmatized the present West German government as fascist – a description which is as false as it is alarming. What do the German governments of 1940 and 1970 have in common, what is it that makes them fascist? The only substantial common factor is that both governments were German.

Therefore as a political conception it is often misunderstood. Diverse intellectual influences have converged to challenge fascism. Surprisingly, fascism has had the ability to win massive popular support for ideas that are expressly anti-egalitarian. Wilhelm Reich, a twentieth-century Austrian psychoanalyst, criticized fascism, and communism which he called 'red fascism', for their coercive nature and saw them both as expressions of the same warped instincts and as inherently exploitative of the masses' propensity to submit to external control. Fascist leaders, notably Mussolini, advocated regeneration through conquest and perpetual struggle, and spoke in speeches seething with imagery, of the need to overcome degeneracy and impotence, to make sacrifices for the nation and to connect to the great 'dynamo' of fascism. The ultimate doctrine of fascism contains little that is specific, beyond an appeal to action – it is, one might say, the form of an ideology, but without specific content other than can be provided by admiration towards the leader. It is clear from what has just been stated that there is no completely satisfactory definition of fascism.

What is clearer than the definition is the artistic background of fascism. There has always been a very powerful link between the arts and fascism. Many influential poets, novelists, artists, sculptors, photographers and musicians have been associated with fascism in one way or another. Many have been associated with fascism since their youth and others have never publicly repudiated their commitment. Men and women unconnected with politics were associated with fascist movements. This fact was a valuable asset to fascist parties. There was a connection between music and fascism. Wagner made a major contribution to an exotic and exaggerated Teutonic romantic nationalism. The link between poetry, literature and fascism is even stronger. Names such as D'Annunzio, Pound, Lawrence, Marinetti, Benn, Celine, Eliot, Wyndham Lewis and Yeats are all linked with fascism and not all of these were fascists. Their works were of comfort to fascists and were used by fascist propagandists. Fascism's structured society appealed greatly to those who had lost enthusiasm in the motivation which affected intellectual activity and creative composition in the early twentieth century. Fascism was believed not only to satisfy basic human urges but also to approach problems from a sharper and more intellectual viewpoint. This view was based on the combination of intellectual arrogance and belief in earthy or primitive values. The fascists interpreted the arts with greater physical contact – music, photography, drawing, sculpture – for these could reach a wider and less literate audience. Music (and sculpture) reached a wide audience and the fascist laid great emphasis on, for example, the importance of 'relevant' music. The experiences of Speer, whose rise to power began through his skills as an architect, are eloquent testimony to the value attached to work which could lend itself to fascist interpretation. Fascist journals employed skilful artists and cartoonists. Photography, both as an art form and as an adjunct to political use, reached new heights under the fascist regimes. Leni Riefenstahl, the director of the films of the Nazi rallies at Nuremberg, played a vital part in the establishment of nazism as a vital force in Germany. Contributions of artists to the rise of fascism and its grip on the popular imagination were considerable and helped the derivative and imitative qualities of fascism to grow. Extremist politics are directly related to unprincipled behaviour; but it must not be forgotten there are many political principles which have to be considered.

## Questions

1  What was the appeal of fascism in the inter-war period?
2  Account for Mussolini's initial success as a fascist leader.
3  Why were economic issues closely related to fascist principles?
4  Describe fascist culture.

## Further reading

Felice, R. de, *Fascism: An Informal Introduction to its theory and practice*, Transaction Books, New Jersey, 1976.
Grimes, A. P. and Horwitz, R. H., *Modern Political Ideologies*, Oxford University Press, 1959.
Hayes, P. M., *Fascism*, George Allen & Unwin, London, 1973.
Kitchen, M., *Fascism*, Macmillan, London, 1976.
Lunn, K. and Thurlow, R. C. (eds), *British Fascism*, Croom Helm, London, 1980.
Seton-Watson, H., *Nations and States*, Methuen, London, 1977.
Thomson, D. (ed.), *Political Ideas*, Pelican, London, 1982.
Walker, M., *The National Front*, Fontana, London, 1978.
Wilkinson, P., *The New Fascists*, Grant McIntyre, London, 1981.

# 11
# Principles and ideals in politics

## Morality

A recurrent problem in politics of all countries is the moral responsibility of individuals for taking part in large organizations that do things that they as individuals would not do.

Increasingly people in democratic countries may have to decide whether it is enough for citizens to carry out unquestioningly whatever orders their government may give or whether they should pursue a more active interest in what the government does – in the actual means, methods and results of its policies. Such a profound decision may take years to reach.

In short, individuals and small groups are often merely small cogs in the large machines of bigger interest groups or national governments. There is a moral interdependence between individuals and the large organizations they compose. Man's most fateful decisions, therefore, will not be technological but political. They will deal with changes in patterns of communication, obedience, criticism and responsibility among people.

Morality is an important issue in all spheres where the actions of one person have consequences in the lives of others, but where the relation between the two is mediated by an office or a role. Thus a judge who condemns someone to punishment in accordance with the law is not normally thought to be acting in *propria persona*, but rather as the holder of an office. A judge is not normally criticized in moral terms unless he exceeds that office, i.e. acts *ultra vires*, may be condemning someone of proven innocence in order to settle a private account. How could war be conducted, unemployment created, or people left homeless or propertyless, if there were not some way of exonerating the politician whose actions initiate these things from the responsibility that might otherwise attach to them? If politicians could never carry out this exoneration then most of them would have to be condemned as immoral.

In this regard the concept of political virtue is important. Each kind of state generates and is generated by a character in its citizens, and each political virtue will correspond to its own political order. Aristotle, and particularly Plato, believed that the ideal state is itself conceived on the model of a human character. These views have declined in modern times and questions of constitution tend to be discussed in terms of such abstractions as freedom, right and distribution, rather than in terms of the quality of individual experience with which they are conjoined. There are other opinions that take the Platonic view as dangerous in its imputation of a political significance to every aspect of personal life.

The Roman orator and statesman, Cicero, also believed in political virtue. The highest human virtue resides in the possession and employment of knowledge in practical affairs: philosophy provides the knowledge, while rhetoric makes it effective. The individual virtue generated by their union defines also an ideal of political order: a constitutional republic in which not force but persuasion is the instrument of power and where monarchy aristocracy and democracy are combined in a stable equilibrium. Machiavelli, no doubt taking account of Cicero's views, proposed as an ideal a form of mixed government, which is monarchical, aristocratic and democratic at one and the same time. He emphasized the importance of the rule of law as superseding faction and private vengeance, and he argued that each constitution had its own peculiar virtue and that the value of a political arrangement cannot be discussed without reference to the human character that is engendered by it.

Thus Aristotle, Cicero and Machiavelli argued that moral virtues express themselves in the political sphere, but in a manner that shows flexibility to the needs of politics. The politician is like a soldier: although the activity in which he is engaged may require him to harm people, there are only some things which a virtuous character will tolerate. Moreover, there are forms of virtue which find their highest expression in the political sphere. It may also be part of virtue to accept the probability of political expediency and to adapt one's conduct to them, for what the just, wise and courageous man will do depends partly on the circumstances in which he is required to do it.

Even more important than political virtue is the nature of moral judgement, when one is discussing morality and politics. Moral judgement is an expression of value where the object is a human act or character. According to one popular view given substance by the eighteenth-century German philosopher, Immanuel Kant, moral judgement takes the form of commitment to universal and exceptionless laws, governing the behaviour of all rational beings as such, irrespective of circumstances, consequences and roles. This view would not countenance the distinction between spheres of personal responsibility and political expediency, but at best allow that expediency may sometimes place the agent in a dilemma. According to a rival view – that of Aristotle – moral judgement concerns itself not with universal rules of conduct but with the specification of the dispositions of character that we all have reason to admire (the virtues).

It is clear that political ideals are not independent of moral values and that even a moderate who thought of all politics on the model of conciliation, must recognize that some courses of action are ruled out as morally impossible, and that some forces ought to be, not conciliated but confronted. Thus the imposition of any form of government also implies the preparedness to use force; it could even be, as Machiavelli suggested, that a rule of law can be achieved only through violence.

There has to be a distinction between moral and immoral procedure in politics. Lenin's 'revolutionary morality' – which concerns itself only with ends, never with means – abolishes that distinction. Hence it is not surprising if arguments from natural justice and human rights leave it unmoved, since these concern essentially the way things are done. The more or less universal horror at terrorism suggests that the sense of moral and immoral procedure is deeply seated in the ordinary conscience and whether there can be a morality without it is open to doubt. In the twentieth century the development of nationalism has been closely associated with questions relating to political morality and ethics as well as to terrorism.

## Nationalism

The concept of **nation** does not refer to common historical, ethnic, linguistic or religious background alone. It is based on the people's feelings. Do they feel that they belong to the same group and share the same visions of the future? This feeling is nationalism. People with similar background have sometimes chosen to form separate states as, for example, the United States and Canada. It is not uncommon for one state to challenge the legitimacy of another state on the grounds that the latter does not actually represent its nation. The problem with feelings is that they are subjective and difficult to measure. Governments often proclaim rather than de- monstrate people's feelings about belonging to a nation. Their positions often reflect attempts to extend or legitimize the authority of the states they represent, or to deny to others the right of such assertion. Questions about the national status of different peoples and about the legitimacy of different governments provide the basis for many disputes between states. The ideology of nationalism exalts the nation state as the ideal form of political organization with an overriding claim on the loyalty of its citizens. Both Burke and Rousseau contributed to the idea of nationalism, but Burke's adherents thought that aristocracies and wars would have to be preserved; whereas Rousseau's followers hoped to abolish them. The con- flict between these two basic views of politics played a part in the wars and revolutions of the early nineteenth century.

Developing first in Western Europe with the consolidation of nation states, nationalism brought about the reorganization of Europe in the nineteenth and twentieth centuries – the unification of Germany and Italy, the break up of the Habsburg and Ottoman Empires; and has been a prime force in the political awakening of Asia and Africa. People identified themselves as members of a nation state. Nationalism superseded loyalty to and identification with the more parochial groups, such as the village, the guild, the region, or a religious sect.

In nineteenth-century Europe, nationalism formed one of the dynamic elements of romanticism which marked the transformation of the intel- lectual's self image from objective to subjective; the intellectual ceased to be an acknowledged part of the world, passing from social being to outcast. It was chiefly an artistic and cultural movement.

In the first half of the nineteenth century, nationalism was associated with democracy, liberalism and the demand for civil and constitutional liberties. Its greatest prophet, Mazzini gave a generous interpretation of the 'principle of nationality' seeing the individual nations as subdivisions of a larger world society which ought to live together in peace.

By the end of the nineteenth century, nationalism had assumed aggressive, intolerant forms identified with military and trade rivalries, national expansion at the expense of other peoples, and imperialism. This century it became the essential element in fascism and other totalitarian movements, as well as a moving force in the rebellion of colonial peoples and in the resistance of nations and national minorities threatened with subjugation by more powerful states.

The chief motive behind nationalism has been to find some binding force between people that is stronger than any revocable agreement to be governed, wider than any merely personal affection and sufficiently public to lend itself to the foundation of political institutions and laws. Modern nationalism is often decried on account, for example, of its attempt to found political obligation in purely social allegiances, or its alleged irrationalism, or its opposition to universalist doctrines such as international socialism, human rights and the moral law of Kant, or its basic belligerence or imperialism.

Patriotism is often contrasted with nationalism in relation to its settlement of attachment, and respect for political institutions and laws, whereas nationalism is an ideology of national superiority, and an attachment to race, language or custom. Patriotism is seen as a beneficial alternative to nationalism, a sentiment which fills the gap between obligations incurred and obedience required, without recourse to the desires for national integrity. Yet although both terms are used loosely they are clearly compatible.

At a personal level, will and morale, character and leadership are important elements in a statesman's sociopolitical strength, while the degree of integration adds a significant dimension to sociopolitical strength as well. Degree of integration can refer to the sense of belonging and identification of any particular statesman's people. This often translates into nationalism at a state level. In many ways the degree of integration contributes to will and morale, to character and acceptance of a particular leader. Increased senses of nationalism are apt to cause increasing conflicts of values as the latter part of the twentieth century progresses. Those who practise extreme nationalism are becoming common and they identify totally with their nation. Though extremist nationalists are willing to sacrifice themselves for their country, their nationalism is a form of egotism written large.

Governments today are engaged in widespread activities, and as a result, the governmental sector has become bigger, and a larger part of human life has been politicized. As government becomes more important to it, as more and more of society's goods and services become subject to allocation through the political process, a people wish to associate with a state that its members call their own – staffed by their own kind, administered in their own language and run in terms compatible with their basic culture. They want it to be their state, in a sense, regardless of whether the state is democratic or not.

Thus, despite the rival claims of class war on the one hand and internationalism on the other, nationalism as a mass emotion has been the most powerful political force in the history of the modern world.

## Internationalism

This is the doctrine that political activity should define its objectives not in terms of the constitution, history or geographical boundaries of any particular nation, but in terms of a universal human condition.

Examples of internationalist doctrines include Marxism (in its classical form see Chapter 8) which thought of all political activity in terms of an international class struggle. In this view, the proletariat is sometimes held to be the only class that is truly international, having been stripped of every asset that would attach its interests to a particular nation, territory, sovereign, or other object of localized political allegiance. International socialism thus was the form of socialism advocated in the *Communist Manifesto* which regards its aims as universal and recognizes no national boundaries, seeking the emancipation of the proletariat everywhere from bondage imposed upon it by private property in the form of capitalism. The doctrine of internationalism was also evident in the political theory of Kant, who saw the aim of politics as the abolition of national jurisdictions and the adoption of a single body of objectively determined and universally applicable law. Lastly the doctrine is seen in the medieval conception of natural law which associated an internationalist theory of the human condition with a defence of the international jurisdiction of the church. This medieval conception, however, did precede the widespread nationalism against which internationalism is in part a reaction.

## Internationalism and ethics

Historically the place of ethics in international relations has assumed that policy makers have a choice between posing as 'realists' or 'moralists' and that ethical constraints are in a sense voluntary or optional.

Many people believe that one cannot apply ethical principles in international politics. Commitments to self-interest or ethical principles have to most observers appeared incompatible.

Both moralists and realists assert that there is a choice between following policies of self-interest or of principle. The moralists imply that the pursuit of self-interest at the expense of principle leads to amoral diplomatic and military behaviour. The realists reply by declaring that self-interest, when prudently pursued, is ethically justifiable in itself, and that the pursuit of ideals only causes great ideological crusades which end in tragedy.

Continued progress in technical and economic development has made it possible for policy decisions to have ever-greater consequences, good and bad, on the lives of ordinary citizens. And as nation states become more interdependent, the decisions made by one government to protect its interests can have considerable negative impact on the affairs of other societies. Policy makers are in a unique position to make decisions that will have adverse consequences on their own citizens and people all over the world. Decisions taken to implement great moral principles may lead to disastrous consequences just as easily as decisions made in the light of selfish interests.

One way of relating ethical considerations to policy making is to conceive of ethics as a combination of cultural, psychological and ideological value structures which inhibit consideration of all possible policy alternatives in a given situation. If one looks at the decision to drop the atomic bombs on Japan in 1945, one can draw certain conclusions. As the technical means of destruction in wartime have grown, so has tolerance for destructiveness. Were a nuclear war to break out in our own era, policy makers would still make the same kinds of calculations as they did in deciding to drop atomic bombs. Military advisers would likely regard their problems from a professional and technical point of view, quite immune from considerations of individual suffering. It remains for civilian policy makers to inject, if they are capable or strong enough, ethical and moral factors in the use of the instruments of violence-and to reject certain alternatives offered by their military advisers on the ground that they are ethically reprehensible or politcally impracticable. The decisions were exceptional rather than typical, taken by policy makers in circumstances of acute tension of total war. While on hindsight other alternatives might have been possible, the alternatives that were considered would probably have involved even greater suffering.

Some of the decisions to undertake acts with horrendous consequences are made ultimately by individuals with supreme authority where their perceptions of reality, prejudice and personal ethical orientations are clearly revealed. Others, like most foreign policy decisions, are the products of lengthy consultation among many governmental organizations and individual specialists. It has to be stated that the decision to drop the atomic bomb, or even to make a loan offer to an underdeveloped country, is the result of complicated negotiations among various agencies in government. It is much less likely to display the value orientations of any single policy maker.

Policy makers are responsible for pursuing and protecting collective objectives and in this capacity cannot always follow the dictates of their conscience. If they honestly disagree with a course of action they can resign as one means of protest – though in totalitarian governments such a course of action can lead to imprisonment or even liquidation. Despite the effect of role factors on policy making, it should not be assumed that state behaviour is necessarily less ethical than private behaviour. Given the difficult situations with which officials have to deal, their behaviour is frequently no less moral than that of private citizens.

Some policy objectives are honourable in terms of ethical content. Such long range goals as 'peace', 'the rule of law', 'justice', 'international stability', 'socialist solidarity' and 'freedom' are ethically desirable to their proponents, and moreover the proponents often are convinced that these are also great human objectives, endowed with ethical value to which all good people aspire. The problem of course is that what may seem perfectly just and legitimate as a goal to one government may seem just the opposite to another. To the United States, a world of free, independent states, regulating their relations according to law is eminently just and ethical. A communist views this order as representative of American world domination, slavery under capitalism, and an international law that perpetuates inequalities between states, and economic exploitation of underdeveloped countries by imperialists. Observed in this light, the goals seem hardly just and ethical. Whether or not these goals are ethical depends very much from which position they are being viewed. Rules which appear under slogans as 'free trade' and 'no interference in internal affairs' relate to action taken by governments to influence the behaviour of other states. They establish the distinctions between legitimate and illegitimate means of utilizing a state's capabilities.

The moralists, however, fail to observe the restraints imposed on the policy maker by conditions abroad over which he has no control; they also neglect the possibility that strict observance of rules and commitments might lead to catastrophic consequences. They often fail to see that policy makers are cast in a situation where all the alternatives are actually unpleasant. The realists who say that policy makers' behaviour is, or should be, dictated only by 'reasons of state', fail to observe the role of ethical limitations in ruling out what may be more expedient alternatives. Moreover, in focusing on behaviour in crisis situations, the realists fail to acknowledge thousands of transactions between states in which diplomatic positions conform rigidly to the principles of international law and the Charter of the United Nations. If in some situations all possible courses of action are ethically reprehensible, in many others, self-interest and ethical behaviour are highly compatible.

Because governments advocate and justify their actions in terms of long range goals and doctrines, the average interested citizen will judge his or her government's daily behaviour according to these pronouncements. Diplomatic rhetoric and appeals to general principles and popular sentiments make communications easier between governments and domestic and foreign audiences. Statements of principles also evoke popular enthusiasm for policies because they are held to be inherently righteous, while technical discourses on foreign policies are more than likely to create apathy. When governments are groping to find an adequate course of action in a difficult set of circumstances, they often hide their uncertainty under the veil of vague principles. Thus government leaders often speak in two voices to different audiences. To their own people, and often to their allies, they express themselves in terms of moral purposes, ultimate values and the importance of observing the 'rules of the game'. Among themselves they discuss the preservation and pursuit of various objectives, deterrents, bargaining strategies and complex technical transactions. In situations where a state's objectives, interests and values are threatened or frustrated, high sounding platitudes and general principles do not often serve as realistic guides to action. No foreign policy or indeed domestic policy is conducted exclusively by deducing actions from vague moral principles. It is easy for a government to forswear the use and threat of force in its relations with other states. No government admits that it is anything but peace-loving. Despite their rhetoric, policy makers have to choose constantly between courses of action that represent conflicting values and often feel compelled to accept not the 'best' solution, but the one that requires the least sacrifice of direct interests and values. When governments are not deeply involved in a critical situation, they can afford to proclaim fidelity to ultimate purposes and commonly recognized rules, but when they are in the middle of conflict, vague principles such as those in the United Nations Charter may not help very much nor does the regular misuse of the term 'peace'.

## Peace and ethics

Aggressiveness and hostility have always marked man's behaviour. History indeed could be read as the progressively successful pursuit of the technology and waging of war.

A sophisticated appreciation of peace arises in the classical period of Greek thought. Plato, though writing of the ideal state, recognizes the desirability of peace. He first describes a society on a marginal level of existence without government or strife. When this is rejected for lack of human amenities, Plato recasts the republic in Spartan-like terms so as to control the internal aggression of human appetite in a world of scarcity. Its simplicity makes it unappealing to an external aggressor and if attacked it can always secure allies by letting them have the spoils. But Plato is too pessimistic to conceive of a world of such republics and even expects human appetite to ensure the corruption of the best state for the appetites are bound to engender a class struggle when the rulers inevitably make mistakes.

Aristotle too seems to regard war as inevitable, but wants basic ethical and educational focus to be on the pursuits and virtues of peace rather than on those of war and on the arts of leisure rather than those of business. Aristotle argued that military training ought to be directed towards defence alone; its purpose to prevent enslavement of the citizens by conquerors. The end of a just war is always peace.

The view of a single world community overriding distinctions between Greek and barbarian, slave and master, man and woman, remained a powerful ingredient in the history of ideas of peace. It was to some extent, at least in so far as civil peace was guaranteed through a centralized authority, exhibited in the *pax romana* and it was given a Christian statement by Saint Paul. The Roman Stoics searched for tranquility and peace of soul. War, anger, hatred and killing are renounced not so much out of compassion for the suffering they entail, but because they interfere with the individual's capacity to respond to God.

Christian pacifism could also be turned toward humanitarian responsibility. Yet historically Christianity generally compromised its pacifist commitments. The idea of *pax romana* – of civil peace secured under a strong central authority – was inherited by the Church as it entered reciprocal relations with civil government and control. The issue became not that of outlawing war but of distinguishing just from unjust wars.

As the theoretical vision of a unified Europe was shattered and with the emergence of national states and the revival of Roman law (which strengthened the secular at the expense of religious power) it became evident that there was no arbiter to legislate a war's justification. A search was begun for a new kind of authority to fill the vacuum. The choice lay between alternatives: that of a Machiavelli or a Hobbes, in which individual sovereigns, owing allegiance only to might, would entail an unending series of wars; or that of a Grotius, which projected Roman law on to relations between nations. Grotius combines the *jus gentium*, the laws and customs common to all peoples, with *jus inter gentes*, the traditional laws governing relations between peoples or nations. It was left to those writing in the context of an eighteenth-century belief in the perfectability of man to conceive of the elimination of war itself and to challenge the morality of any use of force.

Hobbes regarded human nature when left to itself as egotistic, greedy and aggressive without limit. This is for Hobbes not a moral reproach since in his view the laws of human behaviour are derived from more general laws of bodies in motion; human beings being a particular sort of object, and that 'artifical body' the state an extension of human behaviour under the pressure of needs and the rational search to satisfy them. Even in an instituted civil society, stability is threatened by the omnipresent causes of quarrel: competition which makes men war for gain; diffidence which makes men war for safety; and glory which makes them war for reputation.

Kant takes the next and obvious step: mechanisms similar to those that lead men to form civil societies are also at work encouraging nations to form federations. In his view the state aims not at happiness but at justice. The ideal of peace in a modern sense could not even have arisen until the rise of the republics. Kant maintains that the practical side of diplomacy – given the will – would support the establishment of perpetual peace. For example, when at war nations must seek to minimize the hatred and bitterness which would make final conciliation difficult; when at peace they must avoid undertaking provocative or bellicose diplomacy. They must cultivate those hospitable attitudes and increase those commercial and cultural activities which transcend national boundaries. Kant foresaw a time when the irrationality of war would also become generally apparent; and peace which would be no more truce between powers, no temporary secession of hostilities, but a way of civilized life, would become so rooted that appeal to violence would be inconceivable. The plan of nature with its laws of human and social development does not guarantee peace as inevitable but as sufficiently feasible to make its pursuit reasonable and obligatory.

Jeremy Bentham, with greater faith in legal reform, refashioned these attitudes into concrete proposals for international peace. Bentham's test of an institution by use of the view of the greatest happiness of the greatest number would have been unacceptable to Kant, but both were equally committed to a federation of nations. Thus international law has as its objective the securing of the common good for all nations. It aims not merely at minimizing evils during times of war, but has a positive task of maximizing benefits across international boundaries. Most wars, according to Bentham, are caused by passion or ambition and in either case the remedy lies basically in an appeal to reason, supplemented in the first instance by justice and in the second by self-interest (wars are not compatible with enlightened self-interest). Bentham distinguishes between two functions of international institutions: a court without coercive powers beyond those of justice and an international legislature supported by public sections.

Strictly speaking the geographically bounded sovereignty of a nation is unbreachable; domestic injustice, civil strife and most rampant abuse of nationals by their own governments cannot legally be touched.

Hegel moved toward such a super state, building on Kant's dynamics of historical growth but in large measure destroying the pacific conclusions.

Throughout history each nation emerges as a self-contained moral institution without obligations of any sort to other nations. Thus right certifies right, and war is a legitimate expression of the dominant power of the moment; but war is more than that – it is a force for the good of the state since it discourages internal dissent and corruption and fosters the spirituality of patriotism. Hegel lent support to rising nationalism, justifying at the same time the need for a strong military hierarchy in society.

Karl Marx too saw war as a special form, part of an exploitative class society under given conditions of production. Hence war cannot be eliminated and genuine peace secured until a world of socialism based on unleashed productive power has eliminated exploitation.

The twentieth century has brought with it violence of unprecedented intensity and scope. Earlier wars, although centrally important, were isolated phenomena; now even the quality of peacetime life has been modified by the demands and anxieties of undeclared wars, cold wars and military reparations. The religious tradition of the idea of peace had its strong and radical statements in Tolstoy and Gandhi. Theologians such as Maritain and Muste denied the justice of any war, while Freud, Einstein and Russell deepened the insights of Hobbes and Kant. Tolstoy, for example, believed men can change attitudes, and violence can be replaced by love if only the obstacles created by the iniquitous socioeconomic structure of society are terminated.

Like Tolstoy, Gandhi saw in industrialization and the concentration of power sources for the destruction of the moral individual. He wanted a moral reawakening that required a return to the simplicity and asceticism of peasant life. Internationalism would come, but only after future member states had achieved some measure of self-reliance and self-respect. This future federation must be founded not on compromise, but on the forging of genuinely common interests, the peace it serves is a transhistorical and cosmic force.

Bertrand Russell viewed (like Hegel) human nature as self interested, aggressive and fearful. Yet self interest was not always aggressive and passions could be channeled constructively by social institutions. Fear to Russell produced the three concomitants of conflict: the fear of nature, the fear of others, and modern social institutions, and above all governments aggravating fears and institutionalized aggression.

Einstein, a convinced pacifist believed governments institutionalized aggressiveness and were bent on a cataclysmic course. Freud added psychological observations to Einstein's pacifism. Conflicts of interest were invariably won by the strong; and court decisions and common law reflected the interest of the strong. In the evolution of culture it became popular to think in the mid-twentieth century of the progressive control of instinct by intelligence and the internalization of aggression.

War is the grossest affront to cultural achievement and the psychical attitudes which this achievement has bred; the pacifists commitment is thus grounded deeply into an intellectual and emotional repudiation of war.

Nevertheless for the most part modern warfare has only a remote and indirect connection with an individual's hostility either as a cause of war or an outlet for aggression; thus the fostering of good will, love and sublimation is an abysmally inadequate remedy.

War and peace are complex not only by virtue of the variety of their causes, but their multiple connections with the whole fabric of human life. Wars will not be prevented until the problems of poverty, population and pollution have been eliminated. War is a possible outgrowth of all the phenomena of conflict that permeate life today, and has led nearly one-third of the nations of the world, to consider themselves to be non-aligned or neutral.

## Non-alignment

There is often confusion over the differences among such terms as neutrality, neutralism and non-alignment. They all signify the same type of foreign policy orientation, where a state will not commit its military capabilities, and sometimes its diplomatic support, to the purposes of another state. Unwillingness to commit military capabilities to others' purposes is the hallmark of **non-alignment** as a foreign policy strategy, but there are some variations in the circumstances by which a state adopts a non-aligned policy. It is here that neutrality and neutralism have distinct meanings.

**Neutrality** refers to the legal status of a state during hostilities. Under the international laws of neutrality, a non-belligerent in wartime has certain rights and obligations not extended to the belligerents. These rules state, for example, that a neutral may not permit use of its territory as a base for military operations by one of the belligerents, may not furnish military assistance to the belligerents, and may enjoy free passage of its non-military goods on the open seas and, under certain conditions, through blockades instigated by belligerent powers. A **neutralized** state is one which must observe these rules during conflict but which, during peace, must also refrain from making military alliances with other states. The major differences between a neutralized state and a non-aligned state is that the former has achieved its position by virtue of the actions of others, whereas the latter chooses its orientation by itself and has no guarantee that its position will be honoured by others. A state is often neutralized when the great powers agree to guarantee its non-aligned position through a multilateral treaty.

Under neutralization treaties, the state in question binds itself not to allow foreign troops on its soil or in any way to compromise its status by making military agreements or giving military privileges to other states on its own territory. In turn the guaranteeing powers undertake not to violate the territorial integrity or rights of the neutral in both wartime and peace. A state may perform functions of value to the major powers, and it is understood that these functions can only be carried out if all nations observe its neutrality. For instance, Swiss diplomatic establishments have frequently taken over minimal tasks of communication and representation for countries that have severed diplomatic relations.

The most common form of non-alignment today is found among those states which on their own initiative and without the guarantee of other states, refuse to commit themselves militarily to the goals and objectives of the major powers. Though they lend diplomatic support to blocs or bloc leaders on particular issues, they refrain from siding diplomatically with any bloc on all issues. Their roles are independent in the system as a whole although within regions they might well be aligned militarily, ideologically and economically. The non-aligned states of Western Europe – for example Ireland, Sweden and Finland – are usually sympathetic to Western diplomatic or economic projects but do not formally join these except when the project or organizations contain no conditions that might compromise their non-alignment. They try to remain uninvolved in the major bloc conflicts, though on occasion they promote plans for non-violent settlements. The non-aligned countries in the underdeveloped areas similarly avoid formal commitments to blocs but they show a greater inclination to distrust the major Western powers, criticize publicly the actions of any state, and give vocal support to bloc actions when they are deemed in their own interests.

In the present international context, non-alignment strategies are military. Nations that consider themselves non-aligned do, in fact, create temporary blocs and diplomatic coalitions. They have certain common interests such as supporting anticolonial movements and organizing attempts to obtain better terms of trade from industrialized nations. In international forums such as the United Nations, and at conferences, non-aligned nations combine to increase their influence *vis à vis* the industrialized nations and bloc leaders. Some non-aligned states have sought to create regional military alliances. Non-alignment thus appears more as an orientation toward East–West bloc conflicts than as a true strategy toward all issues in the system or in regions.

Non-alignment orientations can be linked to a number of domestic considerations and pressures. Some political units have adopted this orientation as a means of obtaining maximum economic concessions from both blocs, recognizing that to make permanent military arrangements with one bloc would close off the other as a possible source of supply, markets and foreign aid. Thus, to be non-aligned is to maximize opportunities to meet domestic economic needs, while minimizing dependencies.

Non-alignment can also increase the diplomatic influence of those which adopt it as a foreign policy strategy. As independent states, non-aligned nations have room to manoeuvre and may be able to influence the behaviour and actions of both superpower blocs. A strategy of non-alignment is particularly well suited to the domestic political conditions and needs of underdeveloped countries. To many African and Asian nationalist leaders, non-alignment foreign policy strategies express and emphasize the independence of their countries. They find that it pays political dividends at home and abroad not to give any impression of making military or ideological commitments to their former colonial overlords or to states that might compromise their independence in the future.

Non-alignment in order to defend independence and secure economic and social needs can usually be expected to succeed if the state in question is geographically distant from the main areas of international conflict. Successful non-alignment is also basically a problem of credibility – convincing other states that the strategy is actually advantageous to their own interests. The non-aligned state must avoid any kind of military engagements with third parties, in order to safeguard its position. The general condition of politics within a non-aligned country is also important. All political groupings in any such country have to be seen by the outside world to be pro non-alignment, as is the case in Sweden, Ireland and Finland. For an orientation of non-alignment to be respected by others, there must be a favourable political stability in the non-aligned country so that conditions that might attract outside intervention or subversion do not develop. In times of great international conflict or widespread war, however, most nations gravitate either voluntarily or through coercion toward alliances.

Non-alignment is a multifaceted objective that is variously interpreted in the capitals of the Third World. To some countries, non-alignment implies tilting one way or another in the East–West conflict; to others, it implies viewing both the East and West with mistrust and caution. Occasionally states which have no clear claim to external sociopolitical appeal through ideology, religion, human rights, or the like, sometimes seek to enhance their stature by claiming to be leading spokesmen for other concepts of international appeal. India and Yugoslavia both did this with non-alignment and both states acquired sociopolitical strength and prestige that they had not previously had. Thus today, the non-aligned movement can be categorized into three groups, the pro-Soviet radicals, the pro-Western conservatives and the legitimately non-aligned nations. Legitimacy and illegitimacy in a political sense is closely linked with morality and ethics in the development of international politics and to understand this more closely one needs to look at the interrelationship between law and politics.

## Questions

### Nationalism, internationalism and morality

1  In the contemporary world, can nations afford to adopt moral principles in their external policies?
2  Account for the Greek and Roman people's obsession with virtue.
3  What are the distinctions between moral and immoral procedure in politics?
4  Were the founders of internationalist doctrine too ambitious?
5  What potential dangers are posed by the practice of nationalism?

### Internationalism, ethics and morality

1  Can a fair comparison be made between internationalism and ethical issues?
2  Does ethics have a permanent role to play in relations between the great powers?
3  Assess the freedoms held by policy makers in making decisions.
4  Compare and contrast the moral principles inherent in foreign or domestic policy making.
5  Are rules of the game always ethical?

### Peace and ethics

1  Assess the Greeks' sophisticated appreciation of peace.

2  Discuss Hobbes's view of human nature.
3  Were Bentham's views of international peace too sophisticated for the times in which he was living?
4  Why were Tolstoy and Gandhi concerned with 'moral reawakening' in connection with the desire for permanent peace?

## Non-alignment

1  Examine the reasons for the contemporary interest in issues of non-alignment.
2  Can nations be truly neutral in the world?
3  Account for the interest towards non-alignment being shown by Third World countries.

## Further reading

Grimes, A. P. and Horwitz, R. H., *Modern Political Ideologies*, Oxford University Press, London, 1959.

# Part 3   Political Activities

# 12
# Law and politics

## The reign of law

The codification of the common law of Rome was made at the very end of the Roman Empire. From 529 to 534 a commission of jurists at the command of the Emperor Justinian made collections of imperial laws (the Codex), and of opinions of republican and imperial jurisconsults (the Digest). It also compiled a textbook for the use of students of law (the Institutes). Collectively these became known as the *Corpus Juris Civilis* which played a leading role in the great revival of the Roman law from 1100–1300 in the reception of the modern age, and in the medieval-modern development of legal science. Mixed views are held on the legacy of Roman law. One finds no democracy in the jurisconsults' treatment of the power or authority of the emperor; even free men could be tortured and deprived of a fair trial when suspected of treason; punishments for crime were cruel; and the Roman courts and judges were readier to help the rich than the poor. Medieval and modern supporters of the royal authority and absolutism have found inspiration in Roman legal thought. They deduced from the Roman laws on treason that it was just to deny the rules of fair trial to heretics as well as traitors; and thus they helped create the medieval papal and the modern Spanish inquisitions. Nevertheless, medieval and modern thinkers have also found inspiration in the Roman laws dealing with the fundamental rights of the individual and with 'constitutionalism'. Like all legal systems the Roman law naturally dealt chiefly with problems associated with rights in material things, or with the protection of free men from crimes and injuries to their property rights. Yet there was a real concern for human rights.

Customs and laws arose that were common to all peoples, the *jus gentium*, a kind of international law which regulated the relations of peoples or states with each other in such matters as war and peace, slavery, commercial relations and the rights of men belonging to one state who lived as foreigners in another state. Also in the *jus gentium* were those principles of natural reason which approved the right of each society, people or state to wage war in defence of its safety, which inspired men to revere the gods and obey their fatherland and their parents, and which demanded equity or natural reason in men's handling of problems of relations between their states. As a result of this, in the Middle Ages and in modern times the doctrine has arisen that if the *jus gentium* is an aspect of the law of nature, the state itself is natural, not a necessary convention or lesser evil as in Stoic thought.

In the Middle Ages, lawyers accepted both the presumption and limitations of Roman law. By the mid-thirteenth century the papal inquisition applied to heretics the Roman law on treason, for its was assumed that the accused could be guilty of the highest treason of all, namely, treason to God and the faith. Although the papal inquisition was never established in England in the Tudor period, men accused of treason suffered a similar kind of treatment.

Separation of Church and State was not recognized. The public law affected the private law and private rights. All ideas of private law, however much of direct interest to individuals and their rights, had to be subordinated to the public law and the state. Such views of public law played a significant role in the rise of modern states in the medieval period, and in nationalism. In the twelfth century, urged on by advisers trained in the Roman law at Bologna, Frederick Barbarossa, German king and emperor, tried to make the medieval empire truly Roman, calling it the Holy (sacrum) Roman Empire, thus challenging the Holy Roman Church and the superior authority claimed by the pope. By the mid-thirteenth century despite the brilliance of Frederick II, the church triumphed over the empire. The pope was the true emperor, the Holy Roman Church was the true heir of the Roman Empire. Indeed, the church had become a great state, with its own public law taken largely from ancient Rome.

By the mid-thirteenth century, students of Roman law were saying that England and France were sovereign realms, and that the king who recognized no superior was the emperor in his kingdom. Each kingdom became an empire in itself; it was also an independent, sovereign state, governed by the principles of public law. So by public law the king enjoyed extraordinary powers when enemies threatened the safety of the people and the 'state of the realm'. In times of national emergency it was both the duty and public right of the king to make use of the right of eminent domain and to levy taxes to pay for the costs of defending the realm. Nevertheless, 'right of state' and 'reason of state' gave an able monarch the public right to demand consent. Both the royal authority and the state thus began to overcome old feudal rights.

From the thirteenth century on, despite the threat of privileged nobles and communities and despite civil and religious wars of the early modern age, the public law and the state gradually became predominant. Further, the Roman principle that the public law gave the ruler and the state control over religion, priests and churches, reached its climax when Henry VIII declared in effect that the imperial crown and empire of England were completely independent of the Holy Roman Church. Thus the modern national state, an empire in itself, had appeared.

**Common law** is a category of the jurisprudence of every legal system that has reached a certain level of complexity. The term indicates a body of rules which is contrasted with some other body of rules belonging to the same legal system but having a special character. In the terminology of Roman law, which has been more influential than that of any other legal system, the expression *jus commune* occurs principally in two such contrasts. All nations governed by laws and customs use partly law which is peculiar to themselves and partly law common to all mankind. Yet students of law can distinguish between those rules of Roman law which applied to citizens generally and those which were restricted to a particular group. The first of these conceptions of *jus commune* may be regarded as the parent of the continental common law, and the second of the English common law. By the end of its classical period (roughly the first two centuries AD) the remedies of Roman law were available to all free residents of the empire without regard to whether they were Roman citizens or not. However, the Germanic tribes which formed the barbarian successor states after the collapse of the Roman empire in the West held to the personal principle in legal matters.

Allowance must be made for the appearance in the early Middle Ages of ideas about law and government which had not existed in antiquity, and yet which, by their gradual incorporation into common modes of thought, had an important influence upon the political philosophy of Western Europe. Some of these ideas may have been in some peculiar sense Germanic; at least they belonged to the Germanic peoples. The ideas of the Germanic people about law were broadly similar to those of other barbarous peoples with a tribal organization and a semi-nomadic habit of life. They developed in contact with the vestiges of Roman law and all under the stress of political and economic circumstances which were much alike in all parts of Western Europe.

Throughout the changes which changed law from tribal practice to personal attribute, and from the latter to local custom, the conception was retained that the law belongs to a people or a folk. The **folk** as a communal body was perhaps more truly conceived to be made by their law, much as a living body might be identified with its principle of organization. The law was not supposed to be made by anyone, either an individual or a people. It was imagined to be as permanent and as unchangeable as anything in nature. Although everyone in the middle ages believed in the reality of natural law, this belief by no means exhausted the reverence in which law was held. Literally all law was felt to be eternally valid and in some degree sacred, as the providence of God was conceived to be a universally present force which touched men's lives even in their most trifling details. Law was identified with right and equity and human and divine laws were conceived to be cohesive.

Thus there was an overwhelming conviction that the law belonged to the people whom it governed and was evident by their observance of it, or in case of doubt, by the statement of some body properly constituted to determine what the law was. The belief that law belongs to the people and is applied or modified with their approval and consent is universally accepted. The belief was, however, very vague, so far as the procedure of government was concerned. It implied no definite apparatus of representation and was in fact centuries old before medieval constitutionalism took form in such bodies as the parliaments that appeared in the twelfth and thirteenth centuries.

From the fifteenth century doubts as to what constituted the common law were resolved by reference to the 'common opinion of the doctors'. It was gradually recognized that the justification for regarding this law as the common law of Europe was not so much its formal authority as the law of the Holy Roman Empire as its substantial superiority and comprehensive character compared with any possible rival. It was said to be a universal law not by reason of the empire but by the empire of reason, and its doctrines came to be regarded as 'reason in writing'. As such it was the only secular system of law to be taught in European universities, side by side with the canon law of the universal church. To distinguish it from the latter it was called the civil law.

The movement by which the **civil law** superseded the local laws and became in fact accepted as the common law of all the countries of Europe, except England and Scandinavia, is known as the reception. It took different forms and occurred at different times. The civil law was received as common law throughout Europe out of a mixture of motives. In the political field, it expressed the idea of the state, superior to feudal groupings and local interests. From the economic point of view it provided the elements of a commercial law especially with regard to contracts, which was urgently required by the rising merchant class, but which the local customs lacked. Lastly, from the jurisprudential point of view, it asserted itself as soon as there reappeared theoretical reflection of legal subjects.

In England the situation was very different. After the Norman Conquest, William I began to impose a centralized structure of government and his policy of strengthening the administrative organs in the control of the king against the local institutions was continued by his successors, especially Henry II in the twelfth century. The evident superiority of its justice naturally increased the popularity of the king's court and resulted in its splitting into three. The substance of the common law was created by the judges of these three courts: King's Bench, Common Pleas, and Exchequer. The term 'common law' used to describe the law of the king's courts was taken over from the exponents of canon laws of the church.

Until the middle of the fourteenth century, while the common law was fairly flexible, the judges of the king's court had adopted a free and accommodating attitude towards parliamentary legislation. They looked on statutes as merely settling the details of the common law and did not regard them as a distinct source of law. Thereafter, they made a sharp distinction between legislation and adjudication and interpreted statutes strictly so as to interfere as little as possible with the ancient usages which constituted the common law. In the fourteenth and fifteenth centuries, the law of the king's courts became increasingly rigid and technical. The judges no longer included ecclesiastics, who could contribute an experience of other legal systems. The bench consisted entirely of secular judges appointed by the king from the ranks of practising barristers.

The very technicality which enabled the common law to resist the influence of the civil law, together with the possibility of tampering with its juries, led to growing dissatisfaction with the common law courts among litigants. They petitioned the king's council for remedies outside those of the common law. These petitions were dealt with by the Chancellor who dispensed a discretionary equity which softened the effects of the now rigid common law. The Court of Chancery gradually established itself as having a jurisdiction parallel to that of the common law courts and as administering a body of rules which were collectively known as 'equity' and which became over time almost as rigid as those of the common law. Equity never constituted a complete system in itself.

## Justice

Various conflicting definitions or interpretations of justice have been given depending on the nature of the society or the political viewpoints prevailing at the time. A broad definition of **justice** can be the perception of fairness or rightness in the application of rules and laws; the settling of disputes or the distribution of resources, benefits, and punishments between people.

Four main approaches to justice are:

- *merit and worth* This is typical of a Western type of market economy, i.e. the idea of treating people according to their deserts, achievements or ability.
- *need* Socialists in particular argue that the requirements of the poor should be satisfied at the expense of the rich.
- *established rights* Common in traditional, feudal or hierarchical societies when emphasis is placed on prescriptive rights. Everyone is allocated by birth, ability or luck, to a certain station or social position which carries rights and obligations.
- *impartial or fair application of the law* Lawyers in the main associate justice with the impartial application of the law. A tendentious issue is the extent to which cruel or bad laws ought to be obeyed.

Many persons regard justice as the enjoyment of human rights protected by national laws. Human or basic rights are the basic conditions necessary to enable one to develop and use human qualities to the full, irrespective of belief, nationality and class. Human rights of a normal or standard kind are endorsed in the UN Charter and in the Helsinki Accord of 1975, which tries to use international sanctions in order to compel respect for human rights in states not given to upholding them. The problems facing the defender of human rights are threefold – is the doctrine that there are natural rights defensible?; which rights are natural and which merely local?; can a natural right always override a conventional right which conflicts with or denies it?

Justice, in the Platonic view, is the interest of those with power. Aristotle considered justice to be at the core of political philosophy. He distinguished between distributive and commutative justice, the first being concerned with the distribution of goods among a class, the second with the treatment of the individual in particular transactions. Nowadays people tend to have two applications of a single idea. To some extent the differing interpretations of justice, freedom and human rights, along with the controversy in many countries as to the extent to which the state should be allowed to impinge on the life of the individual, can be summed up in the contrasting views of Nozick and Rawls, two current influential thinkers in this area.

Contemporary use of the term 'social justice' makes considerable use of the distributive conceptions, while in regulating actions between people, the commutative conception – justice as right or desert – seems to be prevalent. Many of the problems arise because the two may enter into conflict. Those who take patterns of distribution as their model include the American political philosopher, John Rawls. They maintain that those who act unjustly, by taking what they have no right to take, in order to bring about social justice through redistribution, are correct. This of course is provided perhaps that they dignify themselves with the title of sovereign and redistribute in the name of the state.

The principles of justice that Rawls sets forth are those that free and rational persons would accept in an initial position of equality. In this hypothetical situation, which corresponds to the state of nature in social contract theory, no one knows his place in society, his class, position or social status, his fortune in the distribution of natural assets and abilities; his intelligence, strength and the like; or even his conception of the good. Thus deliberating behind a veil of ignorance, men determine their rights and duties. Rawls believes that utilitarianism has been the dominant systematic moral view for the past two centuries.

Justice is the first virtue of social institutions, as truth is of systems of thought. The public conception of justice is a society in which everyone accepts and knows that others accept the same principles of justice, and the basic social institutions generally satisfy and are generally known to satisfy these principles. Once the conception of justice is on hand, however, the ideas of respect and of human dignity can be given a more definite meaning. Among other things, respect for persons is shown by treating them in ways that they can see to be justified. Furthermore, it is manifest in the content of the principles to which we appeal. Thus to respect persons is to recognize that they possess an inviolability founded on justice that even the welfare of society as a whole cannot override. It is to affirm that the loss of freedom for some is not made right by a greater welfare enjoyed by others.

Rawls has his critics, notably his fellow American, Robert Nozick also a philosopher, who argues against the supposed emphasis on the end state of a transaction at the expense of the rights that are upheld and abused in the course of a transaction. Nozick regards the respect for individual rights as the central idea in justice, and he might resolve the issue of those who act unjustly only to find himself condoning distributions of goods so unequal as to be very oddly described as just. Nozick argues that any theory of distributive justice is bound to do violence to the more defensible idea of the just transaction. Thus he is opposed to certain socialist ideas of redistribution and in favour of certain ideas of private property.

His argument is essentially liberal – proceeding by arguing that everyone should be free to do what he has a right to do, but not to interfere with the rights of others. Appositely in today's world, all political order is a *prima facie* interference with a natural right to pursue one's own ends; and therefore such order can only be justified if it can also be shown to contribute to the upholding of individual rights. His arguments rekindle a debate that has long existed between those who think of justice in terms of patterns of distribution and those who think of it in terms of transaction. His views are contested because they are based on an unargued individualism concerning human nature and human rights, which attempts to detach the individual from the history and social arrangement which has formed him.

The important questions seem to be: is justice primarily the attribute of an act, of a person, or of a state of affairs?; is justice a forward-looking or a backward-looking conception?; is justice a constitutive or a procedural concept?; can equals be treated equally?; is there, in other words, natural justice and if so, does that solve the question, why be just? In all these questions the problem of the objectivity of justice is paramount.

There is a further problem suggested by them – the nature of the 'sentiment of justice'. David Hume, the eighteenth century Scottish philosopher, argued that the principal sentiments involved in political order were sympathy and benevolence. He regarded the sentiment and idea of justice as ultimately derived from them. Justice he believed required the establishment and defence of private rights, principal among which was the right of private property, for which he gave a classic utilitarian defence. Is there a real fact of human nature here, or could that sentiment be educated away? It always seems as though political systems that override the sense of justice thereby render themselves precarious. This issue has been prevalent in many countries in the twentieth century and it could be that a sense of justice is at the root of sentiments of allegiance to a genuine conception of political obligation. In discussions about peace which have achieved prominence in recent years, positive peace is seen as implying the growth of a reformed society where features of structured violence have largely been removed and a high degree of social justice has been created. Looking to the future, in order to achieve economic welfare and social justice, a world development authority would have to be created to aim to achieve a more equitable system of distribution of the world's resources. Such a development would depend on the goodwill of the nations of the world, many of which have differing perceptions of justice.

## Political activity and the judiciary

The last two decades have been times of upheaval in the field of judicial politics. New ideas challenged old assumptions. A central issue has been the role of political factors, primarily judges' personal policy preferences, in judicial decisions. The courts have to be seen by the state to operate outside the 'normal' flow of the policy making process through the legislative and executive branches.

The judiciary is the branch of the central authority in a state concerned with the administration of justice. The powers and role of the judiciary will vary from country to country but there will always be some, albeit indirect, significance both in the doctrines used by judges to interpret the law and in the *ex cathedra* statements of individual judges. The scope for **judicial review** (the method whereby a superior judicial body may decide whether an executive or legislative action is constitutional – most frequently used when a court decides that an act of the legislative is unconstitutional and hence void) in the policy making process will be greatest where there is a written constitution with ambiguous provisions. However, even in systems such as the British legal system where the judges are traditionally reticent about their law making as opposed to law finding functions, there may be great scope for judicial policy making and for judicial intervention in the political arena. Thus in the United Kingdom in the 1960s, the field of administrative law was elaborated by a series of judicial initiatives and the courts have found themselves in conflict with governments of all parties over the interpretation of statutes.

The recruitment pattern of the judiciary is of political interest because it has frequently been assumed by critics that the law has an individualistic and conservative bias which, when combined with a socially unrepresentative judiciary, militates against collectivist policies. Because of the danger of corruption and undue or improper influence on the judiciary, most democracies make it difficult to remove judges, although where they are elected they may be subjected to recall and are therefore subjected also to direct political constraints.

In the United Kingdom the doctrine of parliamentary supremacy prevents disputes over the interpretation of written or unwritten constitutions from occurring. In one-party states the settlement of disputes is secured by party fiat; in theocracies the priesthood regard themselves as the sole interpreters of the law and hence of its constitutionality. Judicial review is found in many federal states where it is used to adjudicate on constitutional disputes regarding the division of central and local powers. Not only is it important in the United States, but also in West Germany, Australia, India and Canada. Sometimes the expression 'judicial review' is used more widely to mean the judicial review of the exercise of any power of government, including the executive power, as expressed, for example, through administrative decisions. This is clearly both possible and also necessary if there are to be constitutional guarantees of individual rights.

The idea of judicial independence can be difficult to achieve since it requires that the power that appoints a judge must also be prepared to yield to him. By an accident of the United Kingdom's constitution the House of Lords is both a legislating body and also the highest court of appeal; but by convention, its two functions are kept separate. Judicial independence might exist *de jure* – it may be specified in a written document which purports to describe the constitution – but not exist *de facto*, say because a judge is removed from office whenever his decision displeases the executive. However, it may be that judicial independence is a necessary condition for the rule of law, and for a genuine constitution, in which case it could be said that, without it, the distinction between the *de jure* and the *de facto* is resolved. Law does not determine the outcome of any issue but only the will of those in power. Moreover, no constitution can guarantee rights if the citizen cannot contend for those rights in open court and no citizen can contend for his rights against the executive power if the judge of his case is always identified with the executive power.

Much independent discussion takes place on the extent to which this 'judicial legislation' is, or should be, permitted. Some esteem it, on the conservative ground that judges tend to be freer from impetuous reformism than politicians and usually have a better grasp of the effects of legislation on the lives of ordinary citizens. Others oppose it as an obstacle to reform and perhaps also as an instrument of class hegemony. Class interests of the judiciary are nowadays a frequent object of political comment. The judges in Western democracies belong inevitably to the professional classes. Opposition to their independence often comes from those who see this independence as simply an indefinite permission given to a particular class to advance itself behind the shield of law. Moreover, law itself is only the rewriting in terms of positive rights of those relations of power which determine the ascendancy of the bourgeoisie.

Thus the vital question is how is independence to be secured without also dissolving the organic relations between the various powers of government? Aspects of judicial independence that are generally accepted are promotion of judges on advice from the existing judiciary; no retroactive legislation; acceptance of the doctrine of precedent (that judicial proceedings, previous decisions by superior courts are binding); established judicial procedure that is not subject to constant executive and administrative review; and the possibility of judicial review. A judge in some people's view makes the law and to others he elaborates its implications.

## International politics and international law

States have the choice of holding the future of other states to ransom by threat of superior force or submitting to collective means for making international decisions and for enforcing compliance. The latter is international law which has been practised with varying degrees of enthusiasm and performance for over three centuries. In a well ordered society there is a complex legal system with specific organs for making, adjudicating and enforcing laws. The state has the authority to call individuals to account for their behaviour relative to the law. Laws are made on their behalf, they can be called to court against their will, and legal regulations are enforced whether an individual likes them or not.

The international system is not so well ordered. Since only the nation state is sovereign, it is not subject to the decisions of external institutions in the way citizens are to the institutions of their societies. No legislative body exists above the state, no international court has the capacity to compel its behaviour, and there are few organs to execute international regulations. The debate among scholars is within the realm of jurisprudence (science of law), within which countless interpretations have been offered. Two theoretical interpretations differ vastly: positivism and neorealism. **Positivism** understands the law to be a system of rules (norms) that specify the rights and obligations governing the external behaviour of states. Positive theory holds law to have a consensual basis – that is, states become subject to rules only by voluntary consent. At the other end of the theoretical spectrum is the **neorealist** school. This interpretation denies that rules are at the centre of a legal order, and argues instead that policy and values are the foci. This theory is said to be policy oriented and value oriented. Thus international law is not a system of rules, but a constitutive process of authoritative decision. The law is what the policies of the contributors make it. If a government prefers the neorealist interpretation of international law, it will shun the reliability of formal agreements and justify its behaviour on the claim that its value objectives are superior to those of its adversary, that its foreign policies most clearly approximate the goals of human dignity than do those of someone else. In this way declarations of foreign policy become international law. No government accepts either view of the law exclusively. In fact for most powerful states the choice of legal interpretations depends on the facts at hand. A safe rule of thumb emerges: governments will seek to maximize their rights (neo-realist interpretation) and minimize their obligations (positivism), but they will attempt to minimize their adversaries' rights (positivism), and maximize their adversaries' obligations (neorealism). When governments have genuine concerns for legal interaction they will speak as positivist, but when they have politicized concerns for the law, they will come forth as neorealists.

The authoritative statement of the sources of international law is found in Article 38 of the Statute of the International Court of Justice, the permanent judicial organ of the United Nations. The statute lists the sources as international conventions (treaties) in force between parties, international customary rules, general principles of international law and such subsidiary sources as prior judicial decisions and the writings of highly qualified publicists.

Treaties, bilateral and multilateral, are the most logical primary source. Whether a convention be one of codification (merely formalizing in codes practices already accepted through custom) or of a legislative character (creating new rights and obligations), it represents the maximum explicit consent of signatories. Custom, until recently the largest component of positive law, is the practice of states. It is generally held that usage becomes an international legal norm when it has been repeated over a period of time by several states, when they have generally acquiesced in such behaviour by one another and when governments begin to act in certain ways out of a sense of legal obligation. General principles of international law are less clearly defined, but there are some principles that can be readily identified. Many of the amenities of international relations are general principles that arise out of the theory of sovereignty. Other general principles emerge from the necessity for sovereign equality, including the principle of legal equality and the expectation of fair treatment of one another's nationals.

**The sanctions of international law**

Any form of law has as its incentive a variety of normative utilitarian and coercive sanctions. Governments do not generally regard reciprocal behaviour as mutually beneficial and are often sensitive to international pressures. They wish to avoid reprisals and embarrassing declarations and resolutions brought on by improper behaviour, except where perceived needs exceed the risk of external criticism. States also rarely enter into formal international agreements unless they intend to benefit, and unless they intend to comply with them. Nor do they acquiesce in custom over the long run without anticipating benefits. Coercive sanction takes over where all else fails. Among the coercive measures that states utilize are a vast array of forceful and non-forceful acts. Non-forceful acts are referred to as retorsions, which are reciprocal, punitive acts, and often referred to an non-forceful acts of retaliation. Retaliatory acts that are responses to forceful violations and that themselves involve actions that would otherwise be considered illegal are called reprisals.

The ultimate sanction in international relations is war. War is a political instrument, not always undertaken to destroy, but to deprive the target state of the ability and will further to violate normal behaviour. Traditionally, responses to illegal behaviour have been left to aggrieved states. Indeed international law includes a doctrine of self-help which permits each state to launch punitive responses to illegal or other noxious acts.

The principle of 'all against one' – the entire world against the aggressor – is termed **collective security**. This differs from **self-help**, which is a doctrine of unilateral action, and from collective **self-defence**, which is an alliance arrangement by which a few states agree that an attack upon one shall be considered an attack upon all. Means of collective sanction through the United Nations include not only enforcement measures, but also diplomatic intervention, economic sanctions and peacekeeping operations.

Much of the conduct of states is regulated by legal means. The law of the high seas is highly developed, though laden with modern complications, and there are developed principles for international exchange of fugitives through extradition; and a host of relatively non-political functions is regulated by international conventions.

**International law** provides effective restraints upon states. Compliance is a function of several factors, among them: the subject matter that law seeks to regulate; changes in the motives and needs of governments; the ability of states to violate the law without serious threat of sanctions; and the importance of the outcome of an event. The decision as to whether one will be 'law-abiding' is a decision for the state's political apparatus. A state's compliance with legal obligations is a function of the degree to which issues are politicized and the state's ability to behave in a lawless manner without serious threat of adverse consequences.

International law consists of norms of varying political levels. On some subjects states readily recognize the utility of collective regulation, especially where the subject matter is relatively mechanical and depoliticized. This level of law, referred to as the law of reciprocity, is a network of treaties and customs through which governments acknowledge reciprocal benefit. Compliance is predictable.

As the subject matter of the law becomes more politicized, states are less willing to enter into formal regulation or do so with loopholes for escape from apparent constraints. In this area, called the law of community, governments are generally less willing to sacrifice their sovereign liberties. The law of the political framework consists of the legal norms governing the ultimate power relations of states. This is the most politicized level of international relations; hence the pertinent law is extremely primitive.

### Areas of urgency in international law

No issue is more vital to the global political context than prevention of aggression, serious disruption of important international transactions and massive destruction and death.

Even in the presence of general agreement on a definition, collective security is not likely to serve as an effective deterrent or remedy. Individual or multinational responses are much more likely for the foreseeable future to be the act of choice.

Arms control and disarmament are matters that touch directly upon the political context and are, therefore, so sensitive to national governments as to be submitted rarely and only partially to effective legal control. In eras of instability and of vastly changed economic relations, modern weaponry has become not only a coveted prize of governments, but a major instrument of international trade. As a result, while super-powers negotiate limitations on strategic nuclear arms, they are busily and enthusiastically supplying other governments, many of them unstable, with conventional arms at the same level of sophistication as those with which their own forces are equipped.

The commencement of the new international economic order has called for a comprehensive legal order. The industrializing countries call for a legal order that limits the political activities of the transnational corporations, ensures the transfer of technology, protects agricultural and semi-finished products from dangerous variations in international prices, protects natural resources from foreign exploitation, removes political strings from intergovernmental aid and places restrictions on foreign direct investment. For their part, the industrialized states call for protections against nationalization of property by host governments, assurances of controlled increases in the prices of natural resources, guarantees against repudiation of contracts to purchase industrial produce, and guarantees of a steady export flow of raw materials.

Aggression is not the exclusive province of national governments. In recent years the frequency of terrorist violence by national and transnational extremist groups has become a common element in political activity. While most of it occurs internally and is, therefore, solely within the domestic jurisdiction of the state, there are a number of international considerations. Many acts of terrorism have occurred against foreign nationals, as in many cases in which foreign businessmen have been shot by Italian and Latin American terrorists. Prevention, apprehension and conviction are the responsibilities of national governments, and international substitutes for ineffectual national actions do not yet exist. Furthermore, some terrorist acts have occurred on the territories of third parties, the most notable the massacre of Israeli athletes by Arab terrorists at the 1972 Olympic Games in West Germany.

Many terrorists have sought protective refuge in countries where they are aliens, but which fail to prosecute them under domestic jurisdiction or to return them to their national governments or to the governments of territories from which they have fled. In the absence of extradition treaties or of formal international obligations to do otherwise, these governments are free from all pressure save moral persuasion to bring law to bear upon terrorists. A special case in point is the form of terrorism called skyjacking, in which a commercial aircraft crew is commanded by armed terrorists to divert the craft to an unintended destination, usually a foreign one where the individuals will be free from prosecution. The absence of established norms compelling national governments to act on behalf of the international community in the legal prosecution of such terrorists contributes to the frequency of the act.

Although most theories and radical findings subordinate domestic law to international law, there are several that endorse the superiority of national law and jurisdiction. Until states agree on the extent to which national jurisdiction is subordinated to or defined by international law, there will be little opportunity for international organs to pursue international criminals into protective jurisdictions. Furthermore, only under certain regional codes of law does international jurisdiction address itself to individuals rather than to governments. These twin problems of jurisdiction, the place of the individual in international law and the relationship of international jurisdiction to national jurisdiction, are major obstacles to a more effective international legal order.

Diverse outlooks toward contemporary international law exist because four fundamental bases of Western legal order no longer enjoy universal validity. It is no longer accepted that there is a fundamental distinction between law on the one hand and ideology and politics on the other. There has been a breakdown in the practical distinction between war and peace, and the mere conviction of the desirability of peace. Our revolutionary international system does not accept the sanctity of the coexistence of independent, territorially discrete states. Finally it is no longer universally held that governments are able to undertake mutually binding obligations through consent and voluntary compliance. These issues have deteriorated because we live in a multicultural world which the West no longer dominates. Nevertheless, though multiculturalism will continue to mark the international system, there is encouraging evidence that material interdependence, especially among states of equivalent power, fosters the growth of positive legal principles. In addition as friendships and enmities change, some bilateral law may cease to be observed among new enemies; but new law may arise among new friends who have new-found mutual interests. On social, political and economic grounds, international law is intrinsic to transformation and modernization of the international system, even though the 'law of the political context' has remained primitive so far. The whole interrelationship between law and politics is constantly changing and affects developments ranging from crises to the birth of alternative political systems in many countries.

## Questions

### The reign of law

1 What was achieved by the codification of the common law of Rome?
2 Write an essay on common law.
3 Examine the Germanic ideal of the law as belonging to the folk (nation).
4 Assess the importance of the reception.
5 Give reasons for the judges of the king's court adopting a free and accommodating attitude toward parliamentary legislation.

### Justice

1 Examine the close relationship between rights and justice.
2 Critically appraise Rawls's theory of justice.
3 Account for Nozick's differences of opinion with Rawls.

4   Describe the 'sentiment of justice'.

## Political activity and the judiciary

1   Why is the role of the judiciary closely linked with political issues?
2   Examine the problems surrounding the achievement of judicial independence.
3   How can independence be secured without dissolving organic relations between various powers of government?

## International politics and the international legal system

1   Account for the chaos of the international system.
2   Discuss the various interpretations of international law.
3   What are the strengths of bilateral and multilateral treaties?
4   What is meant by the sanction of international law?
5   Critically appraise areas of urgency in international law.
6   Why do governments have a need to commit aggression?
7   Analyse the diverse outlooks towards contemporary international law.

## Further reading

Jones, W. S., *The Logic of International Relations*, Little Brown & Co., Boston, 1985.
Papp, D. S., *Contemporary International Relations*, Macmillan, London, 1984.
Rawls, J., *A Theory of Justice*, Harvard University Press, 1971.

# 13
# Culture, change and welfare

## Culture

It is commonplace of modern thought that culture is always in a state of transformation, that the complex of arts, institutions, and ideas by which any society lives has been built up gradually through a long process of development that is still going on. This idea of culture entered modern thought as an inheritance taken over more or less intact from certain thinkers of classical antiquity; but the classical versions of it were like culture itself the products of an evolutionary process.

In Greek thought there was admiration for the unparalleled achievements of an age of heroes – which included individual feats of skill and strength as well as the general level of power, wealth, and military organization. By circa 700 BC it was probably the pressure of external events which more than anything else led to the ultimate abandonment of such views of the past. The period witnessed the opening of all the Mediterranean to Greek trade and colonization, the diffusion of the art of writing, the invention of coinage, the first written constitutions, extensive reorganization of political and social structures over much of Greece, and important developments in technology, mathematics and the fine arts.

By circa 440 BC, the development of technology grew within the context of the struggle which men, like all other animals, had to wage for survival. For example, the various social virtues (reverence, piety, and justice) were a set of techniques devised to secure a peaceful communal existence. The civic technology was viewed as one in whose development all men participated and as the product of man's capacities directed toward the satisfaction of material needs.

Plato contrasted the culture of his contemporaries with culture at an entirely different stage of technological and material development to show that not technological superiority but the possession of philosophical and political wisdom was the criterion to be used in determining which culture is better for man. In the *Republic* the contrasting culture is that of a simple state in which a rudimentary division of labour and exchange of services satisfies man's essential needs. In the *Laws* it is primitive pastoral society (peopled by the survivors of one of the cataclysms which occur periodically through human history) which has retained from the period prior to the cataclysm certain rudimentary arts (weaving and pottery) and social institutions (the patriarchal family) but lost all the rest. Plato clearly suggests that the rudimentary technologies of this pastoral society and of the simple state in the *Republic* are more conducive to virtue and happiness than the more advanced technology of his own day.

Political progress was so intimately bound up with technological progress in ancient Greece; but by the end of the fourth century, Greece's control over its own destiny had passed out of its own hands and the most that the educated class could hope for politically was to maintain the social *status quo* against the threat of internal revolution. The coming of Roman domination in the second century BC only intensified this trend in Greek thought and Roman historical thought, in so far as it did not simply reflect Greek ideas but was dominated by retrospective admiration for its own race of heroes: the plain-living, self-denying warriors and statesmen of the early republic.

## Culture and civilization in modern times

Both culture and civilization derive their original meaning from Latin: from *culture*, which referred to the cultivation of the soil, and from *civis*, which referred to the status of citizenship. *Civis* denoted not only the fact of Roman citizenship but also its superiority over the primitive conditions of the foreigner or barbarian. The words 'culture' and 'civilization' did not gain approval in European thought until the second half of the eighteenth century. Yet even by this time such philosophers as the German, von Herder, were concerned about the indeterminate nature of the word 'culture'.

Distinctions between 'culture' and 'civilization' have also been abundant. In some cases, man's spiritual development has been identified with culture, in others with civilization; the same is true of man's control over nature and his external social relations. Frequently, man's moral development and the improvement of his material conditions or refinements of social manners have been viewed as opposing rather than reinforcing tendencies. Then again culture has been treated as a particular component or stage of civilization, a sort of subculture within a 'superculture'; at other times culture has been considered the more generic term, while civilization has been confined to the culture of cities. A distinction commonly made is in terms of modes of development, according to which **civilization** (defined as techniques) is a continuous and cumulative process, susceptible to generalizing methods and capable of universal diffusion, whereas **culture** (defined as creativity) occurring sporadically, is not susceptible to these methods and not transferable.

Two distinguishable approaches can be made with regard to ideas on the content of culture: those which essentially constitute a critique of modern civilization, stressing its cultural fragmentation, and those which conceive of culture as an integral whole. At times both positions have been held concurrently, the critique of disunity being in fact a plea for unity. The French political philosopher, Diderot, argued that modern civilization imposed its pattern on men unlike the original cultures which grew out of men's needs. Rousseau and Herder indicted their age. Rousseau maintained men had lost their sense of identity; they became estranged from themselves and from each other. In place of the bonds of organic community relations there arose rivalry and competition on the one hand and conflicting interests on the other. Herder maintained that the human machine had lost its zest to function, as a result of so much in the arts, in industry, in war and civil life being mechanized. Both commented on the ills of the age as including alienation, acquisitiveness, and colonialism.

Marx, in the nineteenth century, also commented on alienation, and cultural development (see Chapter 8). In relation to the latter, Marx believed that the sum total of the relations of production constitutes the economic structure of society – the real foundation on which rise legal and political superstructures and to which correspond definite forms of social consciousness. In addition to his descriptive theory of sociocultural development, Marx advanced a prescriptive doctrine, intended to meet the problem of alienation. The alienation theme linked Marx most intimately with the romantics, but whereas Marx sought the cure of man's alienation in the future, the romantics reverted to the past, finding that man had taken the wrong turn by seeking liberation from a traditional order of society.

## The performance of government in a cultural framework

The performance of government relates to both the present and the future. It must aim at attaining as much as possible of each of the many values that people now desire, and it must keep the pursuit of all these values as compatible as possible. But it must also preserve and enhance the capacity to seek new values in the future and to attain these, too. Serving these three tasks governments must often work for subtle configurations of values that are not easily spelled out, but that people can sometimes recognize by intuition. People then speak of the quality of a political system or of the quality of life in a society. There are two qualities which go to the make up of a culture: namely, the quality of leaders and of ordinary people. A more profound test of the quality of a political system was stressed by Pericles in ancient Greece and by John Stuart Mill in nineteenth-century England. It consists in the kinds of individuals who grow up under it and in the kind of persons it elevates to leadership. Clearly in all countries the personalities of leaders will vary as they succeed one another over the course of time. But the personalities and actions of Britain's prime ministers and cabinet ministers since 1945, such as Attlee, Churchill, Macmillan, Wilson and Thatcher say something about the quality of British politics since the war. Another test for the quality of a political system is in the types of personality and behaviour it produces among ordinary men and women. How many crimes are committed? How many persons suffer from race discrimination? What is the modal personality which accounts for so much of what is called 'national character'? And the quality of life is determined as much or more by the presence of good things as by the absence of bad ones – how many people volunteer to help those in need?

Taken together, all these qualitative aspects of a political system add up to the political culture underlying a country or a people. In particular, in the second half of the twentieth century, the culture of a people means the collection of all its traditions and habits, particularly those transmitted by parents to children and by children to each other. It includes their common stock of images and perceptions of the world in which they live. It thus includes their views of what is practical and possible and what is not; what is beautiful and what is ugly; what is good and what is bad; what is right and what is wrong.

People who are used to submitting to their environment will readily submit to rulers, foreign or native, and may feel frightened and bewildered when faced with the task of ruling themselves. People accustomed to working along with their environment in constant two-way communication also may favour compromise and decisions by unanimity even at the cost of much delay; they may dislike quick decisions by majority rule. This trait, common among many of the emerging peoples in Asia and Africa, often has exasperated Western economic development experts. People taught to master nature will resort more readily to power and manipulation. They will seek quick decisions overriding all doubt and obstacles, disregarding the needs of dissenting opinions, minorities and the less obvious consequences of their actions. Those who have learnt to work with nature may learn from their dialogue with nature the art of working through dialogues with their fellow people. Likewise, people's basic view of the relative importance of the past, the present and the future will shape their attitudes towards economic growth. Finally, if a people tends to regard its members as equals its politics will be different from that of a people which tends to divide its members into superiors and subordinates. Political culture is related to the frequency and probability of various kinds of political behaviour and not to their rigid determination. Britain has had its great forward thinking reformers; Germany and Japan have had their democrats, and the United States has produced its share of conservatives and conservationists. Nevertheless, the different political cultures of these countries can be seen in the record of their past behaviour and will not soon disappear completely from their future actions.

All societies, institutions and groups have at least one system of culture and ideology and sometimes more than one. Culture here means a more or less wide network of standardized customs and regular behaviour or ways of doing things. These differ in their forms and particulars from society to society and often between different sections (for instance, classes and religious groups) within them. All institutions have cultures; so too do clubs, factories, churches and voluntary associations, and indeed families.

**Ideology** refers to such things as religious beliefs and practices, myths, values, moral codes and norms, that is, the general ideas and attitudes which serve to endorse certain forms of behaviour and frown on others.

Thus cultures and ideologies are bound up in the politics of any group and cultural conflicts between groups constitute part of the politics of some societies. Cultures and ideologies form part of the broadly common 'language' of shared behaviour, meanings and understandings which make interaction possible within a group or society. They both embody and help to shape the ways in which resources (human and other) are used and distributed. And, in the final analysis, conflicts between cultures and ideologies in societies turn out to be conflicts between different ways of doing things, or of wanting things to be done, that is, different ways of the use and distribution of resources. This in turn can be related to the political welfare of a country.

## Welfare

Welfare, politically, is closely associated with freedom, and is often considered in the context of converting non-liberal societies to a liberal scale of values. It is a disputed concept meant to describe the flourishing or happiness of human beings. Many political philosophers have argued that the individual may not be better off simply for having what he or she prefers, and that, although values are preferences, not all preferences are values. Some of our preferences we regard as reflections of our own constitution – as mere preferences that we are under no obligation to justify when challenged. Values on the other hand have an authority greater than that, and indeed we learn to perceive and understand the world in terms of them. A value seems to have not only strength, like a preference, but also 'depth', a quality whereby it brings order to experience by determining the interpretation of experience.

The welfare state is a political system assuming state responsibility for the protection and promotion of the social security and welfare of its citizens by universal medical care, insurance against sickness and unemployment, retirement pensions, family allowances, public housing, etc., on a 'cradle to grave' basis. Social insurance was introduced in Germany in the 1880s, and in Britain before 1914, but a comprehensive scheme (and the term 'welfare state') was first adopted by the British Labour government of 1945–50. Similar provision is made by the state in many other countries, e.g. in Western Europe and New Zealand. Critics of the welfare state assert that its beneficiaries become less industrious and self-reliant and that the element of personal choice is so restricted and that state control is more enhanced so as to create a modern version of serfdom.

**Welfarism** is seen as a vague, and often pejorative political reference to the principles behind the welfare state. It does no more than indicate that the person so characterized believes that the state should take responsibility for the financial security of those in society unable to manage on their own resources. The development of a welfare state is seen as a sign of political and social change in a country.

## Political change

The ability to undergo and absorb change is a characteristic of Western society. The West's knowledge of the past suggests that this change normally is inherent in the democratic political process; within several hundred years, Western political life has been thoroughly transformed. In the rest of the world until recently, however, unchanging traditionalist societies have prevailed. These societies are beginning to feel the impact of modernizing influences. The underdeveloped states find themselves in a traditional status moving from their past toward the Western present.

Because change is a new experience for these states it is painful and disruptive. Their achievement of modernization, comparable to that of the Western world, cannot be taken for granted. The problem of political alteration is thus very important.

The process of change and modernization is everywhere under way to some degree in the 170 states of the world community. These countries are so differently situated and constituted that there is no simple explanation of this process nor accurate generalizations about its results.

Developing states, however, do have some common characteristics – they are agricultural with the typical family engaged in subsistence farming. They have little technology, low productivity and almost no innovation or invention. Political power and social prestige depend mainly upon land ownership and are thus hereditary. An oligarchy of the largest landowners rules, which generally opposes the development of commerce or industry. The hierarchical society stresses the family and clan as the principal instruments of political socialization, as well as the conservators of prevailing cultural and religious values. Custom affords the main guide to social behaviour.

To achieve modernity, therefore, substantial changes are necessary throughout societies. First of all the people, generally divided into numerous local and tribal communities, must be imbued with a strong sense of common nationalism – the ideology providing the strongest force for modernization. Thus the people need to be brought to identify with the new nation, which is organized into a modern state. Government must be formalized, with the base of political authority being a rational rather than a traditional one. Popular participation needs to be introduced into the political process. Political power and political roles as well as offices of government have to be organized upon a functional basis.

Forces for change in any society have a number of dimensions. The first relates to the disposition to change. Some societies are highly inventive and innovative. They are accustomed to change and receptive to it as is the United States. Other societies have existed for long periods with almost imperceptible change; examples of communities so impervious are ancient China and India. Second, the rate and extent of change are highly variable. Although the amount of alteration observable within recent decades in most African or Asian countries is impressive, actually it has been most rapid and extensive in such developed countries as the United States and West Germany. A third dimension relates to the means by which change is effected. These may be peaceful or violent, expected or unexpected, continuous or discontinuous, and so on. Their nature has much to do with the stability of a political system.

**Revolution** signifies complete and drastic change. In the political realm it connotes the forcible overthrow of an established government, usually with widespread popular participation. Revolutions are monumental events – they mark not only a breach in the legal continuity of government, but also transformation of its political institutions, examples are the English (1688), American (1776), French (1789), Mexican (1910), Chinese (1912), and Russian (1917).

These political changes, or attempted ones, may be accompanied by some degree of internal violence. A common occurrence in many countries, the *coup d'etat*, is the alteration of government by forcibly ousting a few men at the top and their replacement by others, or a major change in the basis of government authority; examples are Nigeria (1966), Greece (1967), and Pakistan (1977).

By no means all efforts at political change by force and violence are successful, nor do they necessarily aim at a complete overturn of government – they may seek only a change of policy. The confusion of terms in this area results not only from the variety of such uprisings but also disagreement over how to define or distinguish them. Some would describe an unsuccessful attempt at revolution, as in Hungary, 1956, with the term 'revolt'. Germany provides the term *putsch* to describe an unsuccessful coup or insurrection as Hitler's Munich Beer Hall *Putsch* in 1923. A rebellion is ordinarily a fairly spontaneous and short lived resistance to government authority, e.g. the Irish Easter Rebellion, 1916. Of particular importance in the contemporary era is the widespread incidence of guerrilla warfare. Guerrilla war consists of irregular and limited hostilities conducted by small groups against conventional military forces of an established government or a foreign invader. Such warfare must be fought in areas where the guerrillas can obtain substantial support, supplies and sanctuary. Today few efforts at guerrilla warfare can be successful without foreign supplies of arms, but these are now rarely unavailable. Guerrilla tactics were used with some success by the Americans against the British in the Revolutionary War 1775–81, but ultimately failed for the Boers against the British in 1899–1902. Guerrilla war succeeded against the Germans in Yugoslavia 1941–4, and against the French in Algeria 1954–61, but failed for the Hukbalahap in the Philippines 1946–55 and for Che Guevara in Bolivia, 1967. Still more serious dislocations result when political change follows a major conflict between political groups or regions from within the same state – civil war – usually bitterly fought, prolonged and destructive as in the United States 1861–5, Spain 1936–9 and Nigeria 1966–70. The form of extremist action most glorified as well as despised is undoubtedly political terrorism (see Chapter 23).

International war and foreign intervention also have been important means of bringing about significant change within states. Since the mid-seventeenth century, the character of many modern, especially European, states has been substantially altered by war and territorial occupation (sometimes followed by annexation). Modern warfare is an extremely expensive method of producing political change, whether to victor or vanquished, as are other methods involving violence. However, many wars have had positive results; national histories offer numerous examples, for virtually every state commemorates a war of national liberation.

Colonialism has effected substantial change in large areas of Africa, the Middle East and Asia. Colonialism is the imposition of rule over an alien people and their subordination to the ruling power. The term has long been separated from colonization, which involves the settlement of territory by emigrants from the controlling state. The result of colonialism was a mixture of loss and gain on both sides for these primitive societies were no more pure and free from evil than were the colonizing powers ruthlessly exploitive and destructive. Yet colonialism had two obvious consequences. First, colonial rule altered at least partially the existing traditional society.

By bringing public order, education, communication and transportation, urbanization, occupational specialization and sanitation, for example, it introduced elements of modernization. Second, under colonialism a new indigenous elite emerged that began to react against both traditional and colonial rule. The colonial experience thus stimulated nationalism and the demand for independence. Adoption and innovation are quite common means for producing change. In the Western world the exchange of thoughts, ideas and opinions is widespread and takes place rapidly. Developmental change is the common process observable in democratic systems. It is indeed the means by which democracy itself has been extended. This kind of change is peaceful and orderly effected within the framework of constitutional rules.

The new states have definitely accepted modernization and development as their objective. But they have before them two major models, typified by the United States and the USSR. These models differ not only in their political ethos and system, but also in the means and manner by which they achieved their development.

The developed states of the Western world emerged historically from feudalism to commercial capitalism and are parliamentary democracies.

The states of the European communist world have been dominated by the example and power of the Soviet Union and China – they are increasingly urban but still have a substantial peasantry on the land. Although displaying considerable diversity, economies are based on all-encompassing government ownership and control of means of production. Government is controlled by a highly bureaucratic communist party elite as a dictatorship. The underdeveloped states are characterized by important urban concentrations but most of the population is on the land. Economies are mixed and the political systems mainly populistic-democratic in form, but oligarchic in fact and thus highly unstable (see Chapter 20).

## Alternative political systems

The major political entity today, the modern state, is itself a historic and not a logical fact. It was preceded by and grew out of the earlier stages of political organization: the ancient empires, the Greek city-communities, the Roman republic and empire and the medieval political order. The modern state emerged during an age of absolutism with its form of government monarchical. After the eighteenth century, some states became republics, vesting sovereign powers in the citizenry as a whole and the direction of public affairs in non-hereditary hands. For a time differences between republican and monarchical states seemed their most distinguishing feature, yet by 1945 the incidence of monarchy had become rare, and had generally ceased to be a significant characteristic of the states' essential nature. Today most states are republics. Along with their predecessors the new states, emerging in great numbers this century, took the form of nation-states.

From ancient times observers perceived a basic threefold classification of governments as by the one, the few or the many. Aristotle developed refinements upon these distinctions, discerning three types of lawful constitutional forms: monarchy, aristocracy and polity (modern democracy), each with its lawless counterpart: tyranny, oligarchy and ochlocracy (mob rule). But as all modern governments are conducted by the few, the most important difference in political systems lies in how these few obtain and exercise power, whether they are accountable to the populace and in what ways. A classification for political systems can focus narrowly on some features of the political process – on what political systems do and how they do it. Yet even among states with structural and philosophical similarities there can be large differences; for actions of all governments are circumscribed by realities of geography, economic development, historic and cultural traditions, technological skills, quality of leadership, foreign relations and many other factors. Yet there are many similarities – all governments must maintain their own stability and internal order, defend themselves against foreign enemies, determine the needs of their citizens and priorities for fulfilling them, implement policies and recruit leaders, etc. Thus one can have political democracy, e.g. a regime of civilian rule through representative institutions in the matrix of public liberties. There has to be an acceptance of legitimacy and authority of government and a belief that it is reasonably honest, competent and receptive to popular needs. There has to be freedom to criticize and offer alternative policies. Sets of ideals are invaluable. Countries that qualify are Australia, Austria, Belgium, Canada, Denmark, Finland, France, West Germany, Iceland, India, Ireland, Israel, Italy, Japan, Luxemburg, Netherlands, New Zealand, Norway, Sweden, Switzerland, the United Kingdom and the United States of America.

Political development in most states is insufficient to achieve democracy, despite the well-intentioned efforts of some to reach it. In many cases, a tutelary democracy exists, that is, civilian rule with representative institutions and public liberties essentially, but with qualifications. The executive commonly identifies with a dominant party and authority is substantial. Its leadership is committed to the idea of democracy and works steadily to widen it – but there has to be a competent, stable and honest political elite. Such states include Bahamas, Barbados, Botswana, Colombia, the Gambia, Greece, Jamaica, Malaysia, Malta, Mauritius, Mexico, Papua New Guinea, Portugal, Spain, Trinidad and Tobago and Turkey. Some states with great promise have fallen by the wayside – Chile, Cyprus, Lebanon, Ghana, Philippines, Surinam and Uruguay. Some states are on the periphery of tutelary democracy – South Africa has a largely democratic government for its white population, but authoritarian rule for its black.

Modernizing oligarchies can include most of the new and underdeveloped states, which are governed by authoritarian regimes based upon concentrated authority rather than on representative institutions. Civil rights are generally curtailed, and such oligarchies are concentrated in emergent states, including half the countries of Asia and the Middle East, and three-quarters of those in Africa and Latin America. Examples include, Cameroon, Ivory Coast, Indonesia, Burma, South Korea, Thailand, Dominican Republic, Panama, Morocco, Sudan, Tunisia, Kiribati, Maldives, Seychelles, St Lucia, St Vincent, Solomon Islands, Tuvalu, Vanuatu.

Traditional oligarchy is likely to be chosen only in rare instances by leaders of new states and is a possibility where leadership is unsuccessful in achieving progress, disenchanted with modern secular government, or proposes to continue national life by sustaining or reviving traditional beliefs and practices. It inclines towards established traditions and political arrangements rather than some fixed situation. It is government by an absolute monarch, without constitution, legislature or political parties – and includes Bahrain, Bhutan, Brunei, Kuwait, Nepal, Oman, Qatar, Saudi Arabia, United Arab Emirates, the Yemen, and perhaps Haiti, Pakistan and Iran.

Totalitarian oligarchy describes a political system that goes beyond traditional dictatorship, a rule by a small elite, dominant in all spheres of life, based on doctrine and ideology and founded on mass support. Some are rigid totalitarian states – Albania, China, Cuba, East Germany, Kampuchea, North Korea, Vietnam and the USSR. By contrast, Poland, Yugoslavia and Hungary have displayed some degrees of liberalization. Other states – Bulgaria, Czechoslovakia, Romania, Laos and Mongolia – range somewhere in between. Only a few of the new states are totalitarian oligarchies and nowhere as a result of free popular choice. Political crises can occur in oligarchies as well as in democracies.

## Political crises

A **crisis** is a condition of extreme instability. Thus in a political context it is a time when elements of a political system are in an unstable state, and liable to change their relationships to each other, and to the system or their own state. Thus a controversial policy proposal, an external threat to the security of the system, a decline in political resources, a challenge to the legitimacy of the political authorities may all constitute a political crisis. A crisis may not lead to change, but it can be overcome and the situation returned to its former state.

Often in political circles there is reference to crisis management. This was a phrase coined after the Cuban Missiles Crisis of October 1962 by Robert McNamara, then United States Secretary of Defence, who remarked: 'There is no longer any such thing as strategy, only crisis management'. The term implies a somewhat mechanistic view of the relations between states as a system which needs to be managed by its chief members so that crises in their relations with one another may be prevented from turning into courses which could only lead to mutual destruction. In a blunt way, diplomatic relations reveal their meaning and potential only in crisis, and all foreign policy is focused on surviving crises.

In today's world, the crisis of the state does exist; the nation-state is a vulnerable entity and ill-suited to perform its traditional functions. Although some states may perform better than others, the kind of weakness displayed can, in principle, be located generally. The incidence of crisis is uneven, and in some types of state regime – notably those with an authoritarian or dictatorial bent – the symptoms can be masked or suppressed, but that reservation merely serves to postpone crisis not eliminate it. The points of vulnerability or crises are often unrelated to one another.

By definition, wars involve massive, organized violence. On the other hand, interventions and crises may or may not involve physical combat. Crises are periods of intense international tension that can result in wars. An intervention is an involvement by some third party government in a dispute that did not initially or directly concern it. Interventions can vary in nature and scale. They can take the form of direct participation in another country's civil war or covert activities such as bribing its politicians. Wars, interventions and crises often overlap, and are all subcategories of the broader concept of international conflict.

A precise history of the word 'crisis' does not exist. The end of the *ancien régime* in the Western world was hastened by three great revolutions: the American, the French and the industrial. Their impact on many observers was that of precipitous, even calamitous, change: in a word, crisis.

Although earlier centuries had experienced frequent economic disturbances, it was only during the period following the great revolutions that economists undertook a preliminary analysis of what is today known as 'the business cycle'. Crisis in economic terms was seen as only a transitory occurrence, and that after it had passed the economy would return to a state of equilibrium. The exception to this interpretation was provided by Marx, who saw in economic crises one of the characteristic features of the prevailing capitalistic system which he considered of enormous significance. In Marx's view, capitalism having harnessed productive forces and turned them to its own ends must go on to develop those forces beyond its power to contain them, so that the production relations of capitalism begin to fetter the productive forces. Finally, the fetters burst asunder, along with all the social and political superstructure that rests on them. Socialists differ as to the extent of their belief in such crises, and as to the precise explanation offered for their occurrence. Yet, in whatever opinion they hold, in all versions of the theory the crisis is supposed to be inevitable, either because it is of the essence of capitalism to foster growth beyond the limits that can be contained by it, or because capitalism generates social oppositions that can only exacerbate over a period of time.

The converse of the crisis of capitalism is one of socialism, a term used by defenders of capitalism (or of a mixed economy) in order to point to the apparent facts that, first, the predicted internal collapse of capitalism has not occurred (perhaps because production relations have bent in conciliatory directions, perhaps because productive forces have not continued to grow at an accelerating rate); and, second, that in those societies called socialist there seems to be no satisfactory rate of growth, but rather a constant tendency to overproduction of some essential goods, and underproduction of others.

The Swiss historian, Jakob Burckhardt, appears to be the only outstanding thinker who accepted the gambit of a theory of crisis. Three forces make up the fabric of history: state, religion and culture. Burckhardt contended that these slow and lasting mutual influences and interactions are accompanied by certain phenomena which provoke an acceleration of the historical process. He calls them historical crises. He believed early migratory movements and invasions are important because they provoke a clash between old cultures and young ethnic forces. He believed there was a healthy barbarism just as there is a negative and destructive one. Thus in exhausted civilizations a crisis may bring greatness. Burckhardt discusses wars as elements of crises. He classes wars as genuine crises which produce a sudden acceleration of the historical process in a terrifying manner. Developments which might have extended over centuries in normal circumstances, are completed in a matter of weeks.

Crises may be regarded as authentic signs of vitality, and as a proof of growth. All spiritual growth takes place by leaps and bounds both in the individual and in the community. Crises can both fertilize and annihilate human thought.

Economic and political crises are most easily detected, perhaps because they affect the lives of more people more directly and more brutally than intellectual or emotional changes. More often than not, economic crises can only be properly understood in retrospect. Political upheavals on the other hand seem less opaque and less difficult to group under the heading of crisis. Political crises may be more readily recognizable because they have a great degree of visibility; their protagonists attract the limelight in history and provoke a more complete documentation both of the actual events and of the motives behind them.

Wars must be counted among the most important causes of historical crises. Wars may by themselves indicate a turning point in history, and great battles are engagements in which the survival of this or that power was at stake. Yet wars spark crises in still another way. They release economic, social and moral forces of unforeseen power and dimensions which often make any return to the *status quo* impossible.

Future historians may well see the two world wars with their social and economic concomitants as wave movements in the great transformation that is taking place at all corners of the earth. A consciousness has emerged which is learning, or trying to learn, a way of life that can accommodate the antithesis of crisis. We are beginning to wonder whether our destiny is to live under conditions of permanent crisis throughout any predictable future.

In the age of technology, crises have become international in scope. International crises are situations of acute tension or instability. They can and do sometimes involve economic and political relations, but generally the focus is on the situations which have threatened military escalation. In some situations such as the Cuban Missiles Crisis, actual combat was averted. In other situations, however, the crises developed into fully-fledged wars. The 1982 conflict between Argentina and Britain over the Falkland Islands is an example of a crisis escalating into hostility.

There are three approaches to research on international crises. One is known as the event interaction approach. This approach focuses on the exchange of actions between the states involved in a crises. In this approach, a crisis refers to both a real prelude to war and an averted approach to war and in some way it is a change of state in the flow of international political actions. Patterns through the study of interaction can be determined which lead to the escalation or de-escalation of conflicts.

The decision making approach is often another way of studying international crises. Instead of looking at events representing governmental interactions, this approach stresses the value of the decision makers' perceptions. A crisis can be distinguished from normal situations by the officials' perception of a high degree of foreign threat, a feeling of urgency about the situation, and a sense of surprise over its occurrence. In combination, the pressures created by high threat, short response time and surprise can produce unsound policies. In a crisis situation, officials may be apt to make less rational or belligerent decisions.

A third approach is known as the mediated stimulus response approach. This approach tries to combine the event interaction and decision making perspectives.

Just as great powers are more likely to fight wars and undertake interventions, so they are likely to get involved in international crises. The stronger and larger states tend to feel that they have more foreign interests to protect and they are more able and willing to undertake militant actions to protect these interests. The Middle East is the most unstable part of the world – thus in recent years it has experienced, proportionately, the largest number of wars, interventions and crises. Arms races, trade wars, competition for colonies and threats and counter-threats during crises all tend to excite or increase the belligerence of one's opponent.

Public opinion in a crisis situation is generally permissive. It tends to lag and support government policies rather than to lead and constrain these policies. To the extent that public opinion is a factor in the formulation of foreign policy, it is perhaps more likely that it acts as an inducement rather than as a constraint on officials. In other words, given the rally-around-the-flag syndrome, national leaders may find it tempting to exploit crisis developments in the hope of enhancing their domestic popularity. A bellicose foreign policy, especially if perceived as successful, can boost the standing of a national leader in the opinion polls. The Cuban Missiles Crisis was a rare situation in which domestic public opinion was possibly a major factor in determining the administration's policy response. Ordinarily, mass attitudes do not substantially limit public officials' flexibility in choosing or formulating policies.

Of the attributes of crisis, the time dimension may be the most important. The process of formulating foreign policy in all nations, democratic and authoritarian, share at least one characteristic: in crisis situations, statesmen are denied the luxury of decision making in leisure. The capacity to respond with weapons of almost incalculable speed of delivery and destructiveness has created one of the crucial paradoxies of the nuclear age: the very decisions which, because of their potentially awesome consequences, should be made with the greatest deliberation, may have to be made under the most urgent pressure of time. The common use during crises of threats with built-in deadlines – as well as the rapid delivery time of modern weapons – is likely to increase the stress under which the recipient must operate. High stress tends to result in distorted perceptions of time. Finally, when decision time is short, the ability to estimate the probable outcomes, the costs and benefits of each policy option is likely to be reduced, and concern for short-run consequences of decisions increases. Thus, to some extent decisions made under stress may be more likely to violate some of the premises about calculated decision making processes that underlie nuclear deterrence. Extreme stress may increase the likelihood of reflexive behaviour and concomitantly decrease the probability of cautious and calculated policies; for example the crisis which led to World

War 1 – a classic example of war through escalation – showed how weapons, time and stress can affect decision making. The Cuban Missiles Crisis is a similar example. Comparison of the decision process in 1914 and 1962 underscores the importance, in a crisis, of the ability to lengthen decision time. Although the weapons available to the protagonists of 1962 were incalculably greater in destructive capacity than those available to World War 1 combatants, those weapons also permitted a more flexible approach to strategic and diplomatic manoeuvres. Decision makers in Moscow and Washington apparently understood that in crises, weapon systems must be used to communicate both threat and reassurance. Aware not only of the frightful costs of miscalculation, failures in communication or panic, but also of the consequences of reducing options to war or total surrender, they appear not to have lost sight of the need to consider the consequences of their decisions for the adversary.

For a crisis to prevail, four sets of circumstances have to be apparent – high priority goals of an actor must be threatened; a limited amount of time is available before action must be taken; the situation must be for the most part unanticipated; and the situation must not escalate into armed conflict. Although quantitative evidence shows that crisis escalation to warfare has become less frequent, possibly because of the increased cost of war, crises nevertheless must be viewed as a special stage in the relationships between international actors. They are in a classic sense manifestations of a condition of neither war nor peace. John Foster Dulles' concept of 'brinkmanship' offers a most useful description of crisis; it is the art of being willing to move closer to the brink of war than one's potential opponent. The more skilled an actor is in practising brinkmanship the more successful he will be in resolving crises to his advantage. Crises may in this light be viewed as situations in which one's resolve and intent are communicated to potential opponents. Negotiation by crisis is an extremely risky way to achieve one's objectives.

International actors, and states in particular, continue to be willing to engineer crisis situations in efforts to achieve their objectives. In the west, some analysts have developed a degree of confidence in man's ability to 'manage' crisis. **Crisis management** has become a major conceptual tool, for example in the United States. Basing its appeal on the assumption that war and violence are not, in the end, rational or cost-effective responses to disagreements between international actors, crisis management theorists have developed techniques of bargaining, signalling and non-verbal communications that, they hope, will prevent actors from taking the portentous last step into war and violence. Little evidence suggests that their methods have been successful. Indeed by wrongly assuring decision makers that their lines of logic are clearly evident to others and by incorrectly persuading decision makers that a particular action will send an unambiguous signal to others, crisis management techniques may have precipitated the transition of some situations from crisis to war and violence. Ideological crises continue to exert an attraction of prime political significance in an age of enlightenment, emancipation, universal technological development and secularization.

Many of the world's contemporary ideological panaceas and ideas have witnessed economic, political and social crises.

## Questions

### Culture and welfare

1 Does culture always have to be in a state of transformation to be effective?
2 Analyse the links between political and technological progress.
3 What are the distinctions which can be made between 'culture' and 'civilization'?
4 Is it possible to measure a political culture?
5 Compare the Platonic and Burkean approaches to political change.
6 In what circumstances is welfare linked to freedom?

### Political change

1 Compare and contrast the abilities to undergo and absorb change.
2 Analyse the stability in terms of change of developed states.
3 Critically appraise the importance of modernization.
4 Outline the relationship between revolution and violence.
5 Write an essay on the pros and cons of colonialism.
6 What is the appeal of oligarchical government?

### Political crises

1 Are there any unique features about political crises?
2 Do some governments need to practise crisis management to survive?
3 Account for variations between democracies and totalitarian regimes in approaches to political crises.

### Further reading

Chan, S., *International Relations in Perspective: The Pursuit of Security, Welfare and Justice*, Macmillan, New York, 1984.
Holsti, K. J., *International Politics*, Oxford University Press, 1974.
Mackenzie, W. J. M., *Politics and Social Science*, Penguin, London, 1967.
Miller, S. T., *Society and State 1750–1950*, Macdonald & Evans, Plymouth, 1979.
Papp, D. S., *Contemporary International Relations*, Macmillan, New York, 1984.
Rawls, J., *A Theory of Justice*, Harvard University Press, 1971.
Rodee, C. C., Christol, C. Q., Anderson, T. J., and Greene, T. H., *Introduction to Political Science*, McGraw Hill & Co., New York, 1983.
Runciman, W. G., *Social Science and Political Theory*, Cambridge University Press, 1965.

# 14
# Contemporary ideological panaceas

All doctrines are in effect ideologies, with close interrelationships. Ideologies are articulated sets of ideals, ends and purposes which help members of the system to interpret the past, explain the present and offer a vision for the future. It is the pattern of ideas developed by specific social circumstances: all societies generate their own ideologies, a total, all embracing and systematic explanatory system and plan for political action; a set of ideas formulated into a precise political programme, and to some a fervently held but impractical formula for a political utopia. Ideologies which can most clearly be described as panaceas are those whose exponents believe that they possess the key to political harmony. Man is endowed by nature with the capacity for thought, and either by choice or force of circumstance cannot help but formulate ideas, attitudes and beliefs about the society in which he lives. For the great bulk of mankind these thoughts are crude, perhaps barely consciously held. For many, a set of untidy ideas linked together in the mind because no single set of doctrines seems to provide a completely satisfying explanation of social relationships or guide to action. Others follow a cohesive ideology about the way to political salvation – coinciding with a decline of the apocalyptic beliefs of Western industrial societies.

## Class conflict

Many ideas familiar to us at the present time appear first among the Greeks. It is among them that one finds the first clear formulation of the idea of social conflict and of the struggle between the classes for economic benefits, and the first clear appreciation of the pervasive influence of this on political movements.

Marx predicted that under capitalism an increasing polarization of society increased exploitation of the worker and even sharper conflict between the working and upper classes, leading ultimately to the social revolution. Great emphasis was placed on polarization whereby a social or political group was divided on a political or religious issue into two diametrically opposed subgroups with fewer and fewer members of the group remaining indifferent or holding an intermediate position.

Social development for the West has, however, belied Marx's prediction. Real wages of the working class have risen, the working class has gained

increasing social and political rights, and class conflict, though not eliminated, has become regulated, i.e. subject to legal rules and institutionally
isolated, so that there is little carry-over from industrial conflicts into other
areas of life.

Nevertheless, there is some truth in the idea of class struggle. It is the
sudden radical changes in the political, social and economic structure of
society that form the subject of revolutionary theories. These are concerned
not with mere changes of rulers ('palace revolutions'), but with changes of
ruling classes, of the methods of administration and of social institutions,
with the revolutionary passions and actions which lead to these changes,
and with their consequences. As long as the supply of good things in the
world is limited there will always be the possibility of a conflict over the
division of the wealth available at any one time. There is also the possibility
that any particular group may combine to advance its interests against
those of some other group: in doing that it will doubtless develop some
degree of group loyalty, a sentiment that does not always tend to make the
members of the group more clear-sighted in seeing where their individual
interests really lie. In the period in which modern industry grew up it was
natural that many of those concerned should be most conscious of the
conflict between the employer and the wage-earner.

Other forms of class conflict do exist. When people are thinking of increasing their share of the available wealth the conflict can just as well be
horizontal as vertical, between different industries as much as between
different ranks in the same industry. This could be happening at the present
time, even though old loyalties may obscure it from the eyes of those most
concerned. Conflicts between agricultural and manufacturing interests have
been familiar in many countries. Ultimately, and indeed inevitably, everyone's interests are opposed to those of everyone else.

Marx often called ideology in this context **'false consciousness'**, 'determined' by social conditions or **'social existence'**. Nevertheless, Marxian
theory was in line with the class interests of the proletariat, and therefore a
theory that the proletariat would gradually come to accept as it learned to
recognize its class interests. The proletariat was in one respect a uniquely
privileged class: the beliefs about society and the course of social change
that favour its interests are true beliefs. It is a condition of proletarians
recognizing the real interests of their own class that they should hold these
beliefs. It is their destiny to be the only class that understands the course
of social change and rises above false consciousness.

Although the working classes in capitalist countries are exhorted to
struggle to unseat the bourgeoisie from their favoured positions, the collapse of capitalism is believed in the long run to be inevitable: in theory
because of the inevitability of the historical forces at work; in practice
because of the inner contradiction from which the capitalist system suffers.
Marx emphasized that capitalism is based on a fundamental anomaly that
would eventually lead to the collapse of the whole structure. This anomaly
is the combination of private ownership and profit-seeking with the socially
interconnected network of its mode of operation. Marx ultimately believed
that it was the overriding function of the working class to assume control.

In the post Second World War era class conflict has had three major
impacts in different parts of the world. In Western Europe – Britain, France

and Italy – communists have secured influential positions in trade unions, whence they have on occasions fermented strikes in these countries. People's democracies in Eastern Europe, Asia and Africa have achieved victories for the working classes. Globally the class war is epitomized by the communist states acting out the role of the working class and the capitalist countries the bourgeoisie. To loyal communists the fortunes of the world's workers were dependent on the strength of the Soviet Union. Parties looked to Moscow for support and Moscow in its turn expected loyalty, even obedience from the **'fraternal parties'**.

Social divisions do generate bitter hatred but perhaps not in the ideal mould as exemplified by Marx. Marxian doctrine presupposes a rigid demarcation unaffected by social mobility or charitable legislation which in practice advanced industrialized countries have enjoyed. The destruction of the bourgeoisie in the communist countries has been followed rapidly by the elevation of Party members to privileged positions and enhanced standards of living – a **New Class** established.

Where classes are highly exclusive society tends to change slowly. Where classes are less exclusive, society tends to change quickly and people are aware that it does change. Social change, social mobility and awareness of social change tend to reinforce one another. As social mobility increases, the idea gradually takes hold that it is for every man to make his own place in society. People come to believe that institutions do, or ought to, help men to get what they want. Egalitarian and liberal doctrines gain in popularity, and the conviction grows that the established order favours some classes unduly compared with others. People become more sharply aware that the interests and the beliefs of classes differ and are often incompatible. It is then that there arise acute class conflicts. They arise largely because people come to accept principles whose realization requires that classes should disappear.

The struggle between free societies and totalitarian societies is the dominant issue of political conflict in our time. The struggle between freedom and totalitarianism occurs within societies as well as between them. Totalitarianism rests on many ideas, one of which is that conflict can and should be eliminated. Pluralism of free societies is based on recognition and acceptance of social conflict. In a free society, conflict may have lost some intensity, but it will not disappear, as freedom in society means one recognizes the justice and creativity of diversity, difference and conflict.

## Social reform

Reformism can be best defined as a policy of social and economic reform by gradual stages rather than by revolutionary change. The term has been applied in particular to the social aspects of reform and to the tendency within the socialist movement to abandon the idea of revolutionary violence and to rely instead on the slow transformation of social institutions through democratic means. Reformism found its expression in Britain in **Fabianism** – the Fabian Society being founded in 1884 largely on the initiative of George Bernard Shaw and Sidney and Beatrice Webb preaching the 'inevitability of gradualness'. Fabianism had a profound impact on society inculcating a belief in pragmatic reform of social conditions rather than those of doctrinal socialism – on the thinking and action of the Labour Party. Fabians rejected the doctrine of economic laissez-faire and stressed the need for state action to ensure greater equality (egalitarianism) and the elimination of poverty. By accepting a constitutional approach they helped to make socialist ideas respectable in Britain. A mode of approach to social questions based on socialist ideas was established. In France, **réformisme** gained credence. In Germany, **revisionism** developed, and in Russia '**economism**' began to be viewed favourably by the state. It was generally only in countries with parliamentary suffrage that the constitutional framework favoured such a gradualist approach.

Fundamentally, revisionism was a concept denoting a critical reinterpretation of Marxist theories and/or a doctrinal deviation from the official ideological position among communist factions, parties and states. In communist polemics the relationship of revisionism to orthodoxy appears to be a secular counterpart to that of heresy to religious dogma. The term dates from the 1890s, when the German Social Democrat, Eduard Bernstein, attempted to modify Marxist ideas in the light of historical experience. In the communist world it became a term of abuse for any attempt to revise official interpretations of the Marxist doctrine. It has been developed particularly since the emergence of communist polycentrism. After the 20th Congress of the Soviet Communist Party in 1956, which undermined Party infallibility by admitting Stalin's errors, revisionism became a label used to denounce the ideas, policies and general ideological positions of the opposing Communist Parties, all of which claimed to be orthodox. These parties considered their own doctrinal innovations to be the creative development of Marxism–Leninism or its application to local conditions.

Khrushchev's speech at the 20th Congress showed to a rather startled world and to the Kremlinologists that the dictatorial Stalinist control of all other parties and the stern Leninist acceptance of the need to resort to violence were to be thrown to the winds and the creeds of the different roads to Socialism and peaceful coexistence set in their place. Despite the Hungarian uprising rather undermining this view, Khrushchev's softer line was welcomed by many. The Chinese, however, denounced what they considered to be betrayal of established Leninist doctrine, and have maintained a high degree of tension since that time, indulging in a walk out at the World Communist Party Congress in Bucharest in 1960; clashing with the Soviet Union along their common border in the late 1960s and adopting a cold indifference to the Russians interspersed with charges and counter charges of hegemonism and revisionism in the 1970s.

The expected realization of government and Party control was one of the many attractions of replacing revolution by reform. For example, in 1968 the Czechs followed through this position to its logical conclusion. Under the leadership of Alexander Dubček a whole series of reforms was planned, both economic and political, in order to provide 'socialism with a human face'. An action programme was devised which recognized that the social revolution had entered a new 'epoch of non-antagonistic relations' and that consequently there was a 'need to develop, shape and create a political system that would correspond to the new situation'. The Party 'decisively condemns the attempts to set individual classes and groups of socialist society against each other, and it will remove every cause creating tensions among them.' The Soviet leaders considered the Czechs 'dangerously adventuresome' and crushed the Dubček regime and the reform movement by military intervention with the help of their satellite countries. The more open minded Dubček, who had replaced Stalinist Antonin Novotny in January, was placed in a series of minor posts including that of Ambassador to Turkey and a clerk in the Forestry Department. His successor was the conservative, Gustav Husak, who reimposed censorship and abjured the ideas of the reformists in favour of so called normalization. The reformists were decried as 'revisionist' or 'counter-revolutionary', and this showed to the world that Moscow resented independent attitudes to communism.

**Polycentrism** – the process of splintering of a unitary organization or movement into independent centres of power, with reference to communism, meant not just the breakdown of what was once regarded as the political monolith under Stalin, but to the emergence of independent Communist Parties in general. The process started with the Soviet–Yugoslav dispute, which produced in Yugoslavia the first communist state no longer dominated by the ideological authority of Moscow, and keen to take greater account of local conditions in its political line.

These dichotomies within international communism resulted not only in some communist states like Albania and Romania taking a maverick position on many issues, and some parties like the Italian and Dutch insisting on their autonomy, but also in providing a point of ideological attraction like Maoism or Castroism – the former shifting the focus of revolutionary struggle from the town to the countryside, or urban workers to the peasantry; and the latter instead of waiting for Marxist–Leninist conditions for the revolution to mature, proposed to create them by starting guerrilla movements which would develop from insurrectional foci and eventually conquer the whole Latin American continent.

The Sino-Soviet dispute to some extent polarized the world communist movement, providing at the same time the opportunity for neutralism to be adopted by other countries to the dispute. In some respects this extended the possibilities for the political autonomy of the national parties, in other respects it had limited possibilities in the need for support from one or other of the powerful antagonists. This need for support and the demand for solidarity among Communist Parties has not prevented the diversification of communist ideology and the evolution of national communist parties as was shown in statements made by the French, Italian and other national parties at the Conference of European Communist Parties held in Berlin in 1976. Although these national parties stressed their independence from the USSR, they have given no hint of any weakening of Leninist democratic centralism, which constitutes a fundamental constraint on the evolution of national Communist Parties. It is supposed to combine free political discussion in the Party and free election of its leaders with strict hierarchical discipline in the execution of decisions reached by democratic methods. In effect, democratic centralism has come to signify the method of autocratic or oligarchic control of the party through its central committee or bureaucratic hierarchy.

Reformism became the hallmark of the **Socialist International**. The establishment of the **Communist International** reflected the split in the labour movement between the evolutionary and the revolutionary attitudes towards democracy and Marxism. The British Communist Party's reformist policies are not perceived as a threat in Moscow. Their current programme foresees a more collaborative relationship, a closer drawing together with the left wing element in the Labour Party which is firmly rejected by some elements in the trade unions. Yet the British Labour Party has never embraced Marxism; while the further evolution of the socialist movement produced a growing differentiation between moderate and radical elements. The latter have tended to prefer the socialist, the former a social democratic label. In some countries, like Italy and Japan, and more recently Britain, this division led to the establishment of separate socialist and social democratic parties. In others it tended to create a growing gap between the moderate and left wing groups in labour and socialist movements.

As **Eurocommunists** have shown the Communist Party can operate through institutions that exist in many capitalist countries, namely parliament and trade unions. Depending on electoral strength, they can be a parliamentary force in their own right, or alternatively they can collaborate with other left wing groups.

At the present time, violence can be renounced by a number of parties in the belief that more could be done for the cause and in practical terms for ordinary people economic rather than military competition with capitalist states.

If the amelioration of the working class is not to be by violent revolution then whole ranges of techniques for effecting reform are available. Social reform highlights one of the panaceas of ideology – the exponents of which believe they possess the magic key to political harmony.

## New Left

No vigorous alternative to the intellectual refuge of communism was forthcoming until the 1960s. Czechoslovakia and Hungary indicated not only the desire (as we have seen) for social reform, but also the betrayal of the revolutionary tradition by the moderate tactics of the Communist Parties as they moved hesitantly towards a new utopian doctrine. In 1968, the New Left seized public attention by a series of dramatic outbursts in both the USA and Europe. The New Left are clusters of small groups, usually youthful in age, but often led by ex-communists, sometimes quarrelling with each other, but sharing a common hatred of modern, industrial society. Alienation from the regimentation of industrial society has led this New Left to recognize its intellectual roots in the early writings of Marx where he emphasized the social problem of alienation. The theory of alienation holds that capitalism 'has divorced us all in our work from any meaningful perception of its product, even of man's very place in nature'.

The ideas the New Left groups emphasize in turn have been dependent on the circumstances in which they have originated and worked. There are anarchists, also Trotskyists, supporters of a revolutionary tradition founded by Stalin's most distinguished opponent. The other political giant in the Marxist revolutionary tradition is Maoism. Inspiration derives from

Mao's practical achievements in creating a society which appears to accord top priority to the interests of the working class and gives due recognition to honest toil. The New Left movement has thrown up its own personalities – a group of brilliant young men of both intellectual power and practical revolutionary experience who have become cult figures especially among students with the phrase 'Che lives and so does Fanon'. Guevara struggled for the Latin American peon, Fanon for the African peasant, Cleaver for the American ghetto Negro, but in reality their messages were universal, directed to the oppressed wherever they might live.

Marcuse on the other hand was on the philosophizing, intellectual wing of the New Left and believed capitalist democratic society to be as oppressive as fascism. He believed that because 'the purblind indoctrinated masses were unconscious of their condition, tolerance was a positive danger, indeed a consciously administered opium of the masses. Tolerance must not be tolerated, and the whole structure must be overthrown'.

The basis of New Left ideology is the belief in the utter degradation, corruption and oppression of virtually every established political regime of whatever complexion. Modern society is ordered for the benefit of an elite, whether viewed primarily in political, economic, social or racial terms. Association with the New Left has provided an outlet for frustrated intellectual youth. The zenith for the New Left was the May rebellion in France in 1968. France was paralysed by strikes and the country was brought to the brink of full scale revolution. The initiative and influence of the university students was the most notable feature. No effective organization existed, student protest being remarkable for its spontaneity.

Orthodox communism and the New Left were uncomfortable bedfellows. For if there is something that a communist really must have it is discipline and rules. His Marxism is a scientific, rational doctrine. Conversely, the New Left is often irrational, violent and intolerant, but it is also speculative and imaginative. This is often how people view such a political tendency as the New Left which emerged in the 1950s through disenchantment with the Old Left which stood for egalitarianism against inequalities of reform (or revolution) as opposed to tradition; or radicalism against Conservatism; economic intervention as a challenge to *laissez-faire*; and internationalism the antithesis of patriotism. The emergence of the New Left contributed even more to the confusion and shifts in meaning of terms left and right. The perception of politics as a spectrum became more difficult and a definition of the 'left' in terms of traditional and consistent attitudes even more so.

The New Left's idealism became more vague and utopian and it has favoured direct action, initially in its Gandhian non violent form such as 'sit-downs'. However, the radicalization of the New Left tended to make it move towards more extreme forms: for some a temporary phase from which they turned to more conventional politics, for others a road towards violent forms of action, such as terrorism.

In Britain the New Left originated in 1956 with the double trauma of Hungary and Suez. Khrushchev's denunciation of Stalin at the 20th Party Congress in 1956 shook many members of the British Communist Party who began to publish *The New Reasoner* (a journal of socialist humanism): **Humanism**, a term which signifies that a doctrine is more concerned with man than with something other than man; while at the same time a group of non-communist academic radicals produced the *Universities and Left Review*. The merger of the two resulted in the publication of the *New Left Review* the first official organ of the New Left. In the USA, the New Left started in the early 1960s with the Civil Rights Movement and became more militant with the escalation of the Vietnam war after 1964.

The New Left therefore was essentially a student movement which became more violent – in the USA starting with the radicalization of the Students for Democratic Society, and leading to the emergence of the Weathermen terrorist group; in France to the civil unrest in May 1968; in West Germany from the student unrest in universities to the actions of Baader-Meinhof terrorist groups; and similarly in Japan from the Zengakuren student politics to the terrorism of the Red Army faction Rengo Shekigun.

The 1960s were the heyday for the New Left. By the 1970s it was a youth movement whose successes were limited, while its violent tactics had produced a middle class and working class reaction. Its radicals turned to work in established political organizations and institutions.

Over the past five years, changes have occurred. The utopian ideal is still prevalent but more concern is being shown for 'coalition politics' than with violence, and there has been an increasing convergence again with the ideas of the Old Left.

Some influence of Hannah Arendt seems to have pervaded into New Left thinking – by the contrast of the rule of ideology with the rule of law. In a polity governed by law, the government cannot have total power over the citizens, while the citizen is protected from the arbitrary exercise of power. Cohn Bendit and Marcuse, the prophets of brief risings, called for a total revolution with society being recreated on the basis of a new system of values possessed by the young and disenfranchised. As the symptoms of the disease recurred, so old medicines were brought out.

Like many social theories, the New Left has a notion of ideology which suits its general outlook on political action. What seemed politically relevant to the New Left in the 1960s has turned, to some extent, to ideological myths by the 1980s.

## Racialism

Racialism emphasizes differences between groups, defined ethnically, and places its trust for human progress in segregation and domination. Racialism is a social ideology – making judgements about groups in terms of supposed relative human worth. Racialism is the belief that differences between races are mere social and political arrangements and that racial superiority is rewarded by social and political privilege.

It is similar to nationalism in trying to reach an identification with a cohesive group. Just as the nationalist searches for a cultural means of distinction such as language, so the racialist seeks to emphasize distinguishing physical features like colour.

The Frenchman, Count Gobineau, the German, Richard Wagner, and the Englishman, H. S. Chamberlain, placed emphasis on a hierarchy within the white race. Gobineau argued for a correlation between the fortunes of civilization and the division of mankind into races; the Aryans were leading mankind to an unsurpassed level of civilization. Wagner believed in the greatness of the German hero spirit and as a result propagated racialist views. Chamberlain wrote about racialist ideology.

Racialism is dogmatic, illogical and inaccurate; at its simplest form it is prejudice; put into positive operation this becomes discrimination; the need to retain distinctive characteristics leads to segregation; while genocide is the ultimate outcome.

Prejudice is when people express for a group a dislike unfounded on accurate factual knowledge. Discrimination involves distinctive treatment of people of different races in a mixed population.

Inflexible adherence to apartheid has led to a totalitarian exercise of power. Racialism as well as extensive roots in modern society, surrounding the general thesis that the world is divided into the rich ex-imperialist countries and the poor, underdeveloped, coloured ex-colonies: a global racial schism.

Britain has been noted in the past for its toleration of minority groups whether they be racial, national or religious and occupies a special position as mother of the multiracial Commonwealth. The incidence of racially induced violence has been limited, the riots in Notting Hill, London, and Nottingham in 1958 being the only serious outbursts until the recent troubles in Brixton, the St Paul's area of Bristol and the Toxteth district of Liverpool in 1980 and 1981 which erroneously have been attributed solely to racial matters. It is, however, very difficult to get all racial groups to live harmoniously together; and indeed in the broader term, few people would wish all racial differences to be levelled out.

The 1980s, so far, more than any other decade this century have shown that toleration and justice must prevail if human misery is not to be overshadowed by racialist ideology. No individual can change his race, even though he may avoid nationalist persecution by adopting the language and customs of the aggressive group. Nowadays racialism is synonymous with actions which discriminate, in most cases adversely, with population minorities. Increasingly the term racialism is becoming interchangeable both with racial prejudice – in its usual hostile connotation covering attitudes hastily or unreasonably formed to the detriment of those deemed racially alien – and also with racism.

Hitherto this last label has maintained a valuably distinctive application to ideology. There it covers particularly those systematic doctrines about the central significance of racial inequality that constituted a major, though still underestimated theme in Western thought from at least 1850 until 1945.

At first supported by scientists these ideas were soon linked with **Social Darwinism**. This was the application of the concept of evolution to the historical development of human societies which laid particular emphasis on 'the struggle for existence' and 'the survival of the fittest'. Though not rooted in Darwinism (the idea preceded publication of the *Origin of Species* such theories had a great popular vogue in the late nineteenth and early twentieth centuries when they were applied to the rivalries of the great powers and provided a pseudo-biological justification for power politics, imperialism and war.

The ethos of imperialism centres on the extension of the power of a state through the acquisition, usually by conquest of other territories, the subjugation of their inhabitants to an alien rule imposed on them by force, and their economic and financial exploitation by the imperial power. As a development from the older term 'empire' the word 'imperialism' was adopted by the advocates of a major effort led by Joseph Chamberlain in the 1890s to develop and extend the British Empire. The word rapidly became associated with the contest between rival European powers to secure colonies and spheres of influence in Africa and elsewhere, a contest which dominated international politics from the 1880s to 1914 and caused this period to be named the **Age of Imperialism**. Both British and continental imperialists justified their policies by claiming that they were extending the benefits of 'civilization' based upon the racial, material and cultural superiority of the white races to the inferior peoples of backward lands. Colonialism became a form of imperialism based on maintaining a sharp and fundamental distinction between the ruling nation and the subordinate populations. Such an arrangement arises most naturally in relation to a remote territory with a population of a conspicuously different physique and culture. These, however, are not necessary conditions – witness Nazi colonialism in Eastern Europe, bolstered up by a pseudo-racialism based on fictitious racial differences. Colonialism has always entailed unequal rights.

Decolonization has been the process whereby a metropolitan country has given up its authority over its dependent territories and granted them the status of sovereign states. Controversy has reigned over whether real independence has been achieved or only neo-colonialism. This is the formal juridicial independence accompanied by a *de facto* domination and exploitation by foreign nationals, together with the retention of many features of the traditional colonial situation – namely, narrow economic specialization, cultural and educational inferiority. Cultural imperialism has a strong racial bias, and is the use of political and economic power to exalt and spread the values and habits of a foreign culture at the expense of a native culture. Opposed to all these issues are anti-colonialism and anti-imperialism, used to describe any movements, e.g. various African national movements, aiming at ending the subordination of a people to colonial rule.

In Europe, anti-semitism characterized the main racist views of the last hundred years; an adherence to views or practices directed against the interests, legal rights, religious practices or lives of Jews. The term, anti-semitism, was coined by Ernest Renan in the 1870s but the theories for its justification have changed from religious to racial, from nationalist to class conflict. Since the Holocaust (Final Solution) or Nazi extermination programme of the Second World War, the burden of guilt and the fear of being associated in any way with the views which led to that catastrophe have been a potent force in European politics, leading in many countries to legislation against the incitement to racial hatred, and internationally inclining the countries of Western Europe and the USA towards the side of Israel. Anti-semitism is still a potent force in East European political life and, under the guise of hostility to Zionism, in Arab states.

Landmarks in the literature of racist determinism (the world or nature subject to causal law, that, every event in it has a cause) are de Gobineau's *Essay on the Inequality of the Human Races* (1853–5) and Chamberlain's *Foundations of the 19th Century* (1899). The theory and practice of Nazism (a term formed from the abbreviation for National Socialist German Workers' Party), a political movement founded in 1919 and taken over by Adolf Hitler, marked a culmination. Its special characteristics were belief in the racial superiority of the Aryan race and specifically of its best exemplar, the German people, a .'master race' (Herrenvolk) with an inalienable claim to lebensraum (living space), at the expense of so-called inferior races in Central and Eastern Europe. Even now the tradition's basic maxim of virtuous purity and vicious blending, though biologically discredited, remains embedded in much popular thinking about race.

## Right

The term **'right'** has been applied to a range of views at the other end of the political spectrum from the 'left'. The five elements – nationalism, racialism, militarism, anti-communism, anti-democracy – form the bare bones of fascism, but what has been lacking has been the breath to give the bare bones life – there have been no charismatic leaders, no idealistic goal to attract youth. An essential condition for the resurgence of fascism must be its conquest of youth – and this has not occurred. **Fascism** was descredited by the total defeat of the Fascist states in the Second World War. A number of neo-Fascist parties have appeared in Europe since 1945, though without achieving any real success, notably in France and the Movimento Sociale Italiano in Italy. They have embodied or sought to embody a revival of the ideas and methods of pre-1945 Fascism. Neo-Fascism can be considered as an ideological–religious cult movement. Italy was one European country where a neo-Fascist mass party seemed to have some chance of making real headway in the 1970s. Success was unevenly distributed and can largely be attributed to local circumstances, and an ability to exploit the political and economic difficulties of the country to the full. By the mid-1970s the leaders of the extreme right lost their valuable links with their former protectors in the security forces when leading plotters were arrested and the initiative in political violence switched to groups on the far left.

In Britain, the neo-Fascist movement which made some progress towards creating an effective mass party with at least a chance of winning some leverage was the **National Front**. Like the Italian neo-Fascists, the National Front has tried to develop a two-track strategy. On the one hand it has followed a policy of presenting itself as a respectable political party appealing by argument and peaceful persuasion for the support of the British electorate. On the other, its leadership has been deeply imbued with Nazi ideas, even though they are no longer affiliated with more blatantly Nazi movements, such as Colin Jordan's British National Socialist Movement. The National Front sees the new immigrant communities as the major enemy of the British race and way of life and has desired the compulsory repatriation of all immigrants.

The National Front was formed in 1967 out of a merger of the League of Empire Loyalists, the majority of the Racial Preservation Society, the British National Party and John Tyndall's Greater Britain Movement, which Tyndall had formed in 1964 as a splinter from the British National Party. Although personal squabbles and splits among the National Front hierarchy have plagued the movement, many conditions in Britain in the mid-1970s seemed to be propitious for a big push by the National Front for public support. Severe economic recession was hitting hardest at areas with heavy concentrations of immigrants among their populations, worsening housing situations and severely over-strained educational, health and social welfare services. They also exploited the growing unpopularity of British membership of the Common Market by demanding British withdrawal.

After achieving more support at elections in the mid-1970s, the National Front suffered political failure at the 1979 general election. The mass media rapidly established the facts about the National Front's leader's Nazi past and doctrines, and conveyed these clearly to the public. Both the major political parties took steps to equip themselves with a policy on immigration.

Notably the movement was plagued by schisms and leadership struggles – which diverted energies, disrupted organization and continuity, and created an image of disarray and weakness which tended to destroy its credibility as a political force. Members were dismissed from the executive after abortive attempts to dismiss the leader, and membership slumped. A major split occurred in 1980 when Tyndall set up the New National Front. Other Fascist propaganda organizations active in the 1970s were the **British League of Rights** affiliated to the fascist World Anti-Communist League, specializing in low-key racist propaganda, and the **League of Saint George**, founded in 1974, serving as an umbrella organization for British fascist groups.

Links have developed over the past two decades between neo-Fascist groups in Europe and the New Right in America. Across the Atlantic there has been a broad grouping of political tendencies, organizations and individual publicists united in their common opposition to international communism and the internal communist conspiracy.

Most prominent is the **John Birch Society**, founded in 1958, which although losing public attention still remains influential locally, especially in the West and South-West where it provides a medium for anti-semitism and vilification of Black Americans. Another group, the **Minutemen**, favoured violent action.

The Radical Right differs from the old extreme Right of Nazism and Fascism in being strongly anti-racist, though it is heavily infiltrated by anti-semitic and anti-Negro extremists of this kind, traditionally associated with the Ku Klux Klan. This is a secret society in the USA, violently hostile to Negroes, Catholics, Jews and other 'aliens'. Although officially disbanded in 1869, its influence has survived to the present day. In the 1960s it not only intensified its intimidation of Negroes but also terrorized white activists in the Civil Rights Movement, resorting to murder in some cases. Its influence has become more widespread in recent years with the extension of the New Right, but has also been weakened as a result of being openly challenged by Black Power which advocates a rejection of integration as a solution to the race problem.

It was not only in Europe and the USA that fascistic movements, so long written off for dead, began to surface again. In Japan, the military imperial mutation of fascism was still alive in the minds of a tiny fanatical cult on the extreme right. In South Africa, a powerful fascistic secret society, the Afrikaner Broederbond, formed in 1918, has penetrated, and now tries to manipulate, the government, the armed forces and every important institution in the state.

Even in Europe, where the majority of explicitly fascist or Nazi groups are concentrated and where there are strong memories of fascist rule and traditions, these movements remain tiny and politically marginal. Yet they have managed to intensify their racist propaganda and attacks on immigrant communities and have become increasingly bold in both physical intimidation and terrorist attacks against immigrant Jewish and left-wing targets.

Prolonged economic crisis and an inability of democratic government to deal with it; a heightened fear of communism, external or internal; a sense of national impotence or humiliation, and a charismatic leader might recreate the conditions for fascist resurgence.

The latest manifestation is the 'new right', a term to denote the rise of right wing conservative-style parties and governments in the 1980s: United Kingdom, United States and West Germany.

## Questions

1  Why have measures towards social reform in many communist states caused so much concern to the USSR?
2  Assess the impact of Khrushchev's speech to the 20th Party Congress in 1956.
3  Describe developments in class conflict since 1945.
4  What are the main political dangers resulting from racialism?
5  Account for the controversies surrounding decolonization.
6  How is racialism related to anti-semitism?
7  Describe the various forms of class conflict.
8  Assess the impact of class conflict in Western Europe.
9  Why has the New Left never really been of any great importance as a contemporary ideology?
10  Discuss the ideological and practical implications of the New Right.

## Further reading

Cantor, N. F., *The Age of Protest: Dissent and Rebellion in 20th Century*, Hawthorn Books Inc., USA, 1971.
Cranston, M. (ed), *The New Left*, Bodley Head, 1973.
Crouch, Colin and Alessandro, Pizzorno, *The Resurgence of Class Conflict in Western Europe since 1968*, Macmillan, 1970.
Dahrendorf, Ralf, *Class Conflict in an Industrial Society*, Routledge & Kegan Paul, 1959.

Deakin, F. W., Shukman, H., and Willets, H. T., *A History of World Communism*, Weidenfeld & Nicholson, 1975.

Deakin, N., *Colour, Citizenship and British Society*, Panther, 1970.

Deutscher, Isaac, *Marxism in Our Time*, Cape, 1974.

Drucker, H. M., *The Political Uses of Ideology*, Macmillan, 1974.

Duncan, G., *Marx and Mill: Two Views of Social Conflict and Social Harmony*, Cambridge University Press, 1974.

Field, G. C., *Political Theory*, Methuen, 1976.

Fleming, Marie, *The Anarchist Way to Socialism*, Croom Helm, London, 1974.

Grimes, A. P., and Horwitz, R. H., *Modern Political Ideologies*, Oxford University Press, 1959.

Heater, D., *Contemporary Political Ideas*, Longman, 1975.

Horowitz, D., *Imperialism and Revolution*, Penguin, 1972.

Kitchen, M., *Fascism*, Macmillan, 1976.

Mason, P., *Race Relations*, Oxford University Press, 1970.

McInnes, N., *The Western Marxists*, Macmillan, 1972.

Parekh, B., *Contemporary Political Thinkers*, Martin Robertson, 1982.

Plamenatz, J., *Ideology*, Macmillan, 1971.

Segal, R., *The Race War*, Penguin, 1966.

Seliger, M., *The Marxist Conception of Ideology*, Cambridge University Press, 1978.

Seliger, M., *Ideology and Politics*, George Allen & Unwin, 1976.

Wilkinson, P., *The New Fascists*, Grant McIntyre, 1981.

Woolf, S. J., *Fascism in Europe*, Methuen, 1978.

# 15
# Ideas unique to the contemporary world

## Managerialism

In 1943, James Burnham in his work *The Managerial Revolution* argued that both capitalist and communist societies were being replaced by a new managerial society. The 'managers' were going to form a new class in the modern industrial age and acquire such influence that they were taking over effective control. Burnham believed that capitalist and communist states instead of becoming increasingly different and hostile were converging as the managers – technocrats and top executives – rendered established ideologies obsolete. Thus the ex-Trotskyite, Burnham, predicted the rise of a new social class, the managers, which would supplant the old capitalist class. His theory was weakened by a lack of clarification of the term 'managers'. They loosely covered production managers, administrative engineers (excluding financial executives of corporations), government bureau heads and the like.

A theory more in vogue was that espoused in the 1930s and 1940s by Berle and Means in the United States. They believed in parallel changes within the modern corporation from the owner to the professional manager, and from ownership to control associated with the decline of the importance of private property in contemporary capitalism.

## Scientism

This term covers the methods and principles of science, and the mental attitude of scientists. **Scientism** is both the application of, or belief in, the scientific method and the uncritical application of scientific or quasi-scientific methods to inappropriate fields of study or investigation. The characteristic inductive methods of the natural sciences are the only source of genuine factual knowledge and they alone can yield true knowledge about man and society. This contrasts with dualism which insists that the human and social subject matter of history and the social sciences can be investigated only by a method involving the intuition of human states of mind, that is proprietory to these disciplines. It is opposed primarily on the grounds that it gives a false sense of knowledge in a state of actual ignorance. Its acceptability is seen mainly in terms of progress. J. T. Bury in 1920 argued that the entry of the concept of the idea of progress into the realm of human values was part of the scientific revolution and the consequent secularization of thought that occurred in the post-Reformation world. Kant maintained that if the accumulation of scientific knowledge enabled us to master our fate then, since this accumulation was progressive, the human condition had to improve under its influence. It has often been said since Kant's time that belief in progress involves a confusion between ends and means. Science which has enabled mankind to improve the means, has always stood in need of the guidance of the ends. Knowledge of the ends has rested on those enduring values which have defined the invariable aspirations of human nature.

As social scientists have extended the boundaries of their understanding, so political thinking has shifted its focus from all-embracing theories to the possibility and desirability of detailed social engineering. The immense potential of human reason has been vividly demonstrated by the incredible strides made in this century by the natural sciences, even though the political lessons to be drawn from these advances have been ambivalent. Scientific knowledge has always meant control; but where control over nature means more prosperity, control over man means less freedom. In political terms, science both generates progress and freedom and strengthens authority and bureaucracy. The basic political danger is the technical ease with which governments can now control and manipulate a population and the unavoidable surrender of decision making to the scientifically proficient 'expert'.

Science is not a panacea and yet under appropriate political control it can improve the quality of life for many. Politicians, civil servants and citizens have had to adapt to the new scientific age, learn to exploit the values of the new knowledge and techniques and guard against the dangers. Science – the pursuit of absolute truth and understanding – has not been able entirely to escape totalitarian control. In the late 1940s, Stalin felt competent to use Marxist principles to judge the hypotheses of the Soviet biologist, Lysenko, which showed that scientific activity could be controlled in order to shape future society.

Technology and science have now forced mankind, by virtual global miniaturization, into greater interdependence than ever before in history, and yet politically we now live in an era of fragmentation with a rapid multiplication of the number of independent units.

## Technocracy

Rule by technicians as an ideal acquired support in the nineteenth century, particularly from the French political theorists – Saint-Simon and Comte. The theory was developed by the American, W. H. Smyth. He maintained that under the separation of ownership from control, real power was vested increasingly in those able to control the means of production. The chief among these were **technicians** with the knowledge to operate the complex machinery of modern production.

When one considers technocracy it reveals a paradox of the modern technological society. The society creates problems so complex that they can be handled only by those with specialist skill and intricate knowledge, and at the same time it produces people who are in general more highly educated and inquiring than previous generations. It centralizes decision making but spreads the desire to make decisions. Faced with this predicament it is difficult for democracy to satisfy both the need for great efficiency and the need for wider participation. In many ways democracy and technocracy are incompatible: democracy is government by the good sense of the common man; technocracy is government by the dictates of scientific knowledge. The common man is ignorant in an age in which knowledge is power. The growth of massive, supranational industrial businesses with personnel and wealth in excess of some nation-states raises the spectre of considerable political power being exercised by people outside the whole government apparatus altogether.

The root political issue with which the development of science and technology has faced mankind is the role of the expert. Scientific knowledge is expanding at such a rate that it is virtually impracticable to think in terms of any individual combining both political and scientific expertise. The danger is that the technocrat can achieve power, immense political power, without responsibility. To many social scientists merits offset the dangers of the ideology of technocracy. The supposed benefits are twofold. First there is efficiency with decisions being placed in the hands of those with the technical expertise. By this argument, politics is equated with efficiency and efficiency with technical knowledge. Second, if matters are left in the capable hands of the expert, the wasteful bitterness of ideological conflict will be avoided. It is the use of technology that is good or evil and problems have to be met by established priorities. Decisions about how the results of technology are to be used are political questions because they are questions about ends. The power of the technocrats is identified with the rise of economic planning, strategic thinking in defence matters, and the expansion of science and research. In contemporary industrial society, while the role of the expert has been enlarged, it is doubted whether rule by technicians can supplant the political order.

## Political socialization

Political ideas are diffused through a society as the opinions, attitudes and beliefs of its citizens, which can be acquired by indoctrination. **Socialization** is the process of communicating a culture or subculture to an individual. Ideas can be picked up from relatives, friends, business associates or individuals. In democracies, particularly, opinions can be gleaned from the media which helps to determine political orientations. Individuals can learn political orientations through intentional teaching or through overtly political experiences such as when they observe the actions of the political system.

The civic culture is transmitted by a complex process that includes training in many social institutions – family, peer group (people of approximately equal standing in the large society to which they belong), school, work place, as well as in the political system itself. Such influences give an individual a predisposition to certain political stances. Family influence is pervasive as it operates intensively and continuously over a long period of time. Political sociologists maintain that attitudes are acquired through environmental influences, of which the family is the most significant. Education is connected with a person's socioeconomic status. The more highly educated and socially secure a person, the more likelihood there is of participation in effective political activity. Adults unconsciously are moulded by their childhood experiences; and they should be conscious of each others opinions and recognize their prejudices.

A particular person's orientations towards politics can be partially explained in terms of his or her personality or character, the political culture in which he or she operates, his or her own political socialization, personal experience and circumstances, in fact the impact of the entire environment on his or her life. Political socialization is the continuous learning process by which individuals through information and experience come to understand their duties, rights and role in society and identify with the political system. It is also the process by which values, attitudes, beliefs and customs are passed on from one generation to the next and by which these are altered in the process. Political socialization is one of the main facets making up political culture and this concept implies that the functioning of a political system can only be fully understood if values or orientations to politics are appreciated.

If people are socialized politically into the traditional rules and practices of a society, this does not necessarily reinforce the *status quo*, inhibiting change or progress. Political socialization may, owing to the two-way process of communication of ideas or 'feedback', introduce new ideas and alter accepted ones. Changes in attitudes and customs caused by this process are eventually reflected in changes in the political system. The organizers of strikes and the fomentors of strife in any society usually are politically socialized.

## Strife and strikes

Strikes are stoppages of work by organized labour directed towards the improvement of working or social conditions. Strikes are weapons of the working classes developed during and after the industrial revolution in the nineteenth century.

A strike may assume different forms: simple (when workers merely do not turn up for work); passive sit-in (when they turn up but do not work); and picketed (when they prevent strike breakers from entering their workplace). With respect to its purposes, any strike may be either purely economic (wages, penalty rates, hours of work, membership and physical conditions of work) or political (protest against government policies or social conditions). As to the extent of strikes, they may be single (affecting one trade union), multiple (several unions, including a sympathy strike) or a general strike.

**Strife** has become widespread in the democracies in the industrial spheres since 1945. Methods have been sought to alleviate this problem through worker participation, a form of industrial democracy. Two views exist on the question of participation and its desirability. One is that improved communication between government and governed is both more to be desired and more practical in a large modern state than any attempt to achieve total participation. The other is the belief that apathy is an essential ingredient for democracy. This belief is grounded in the assumption that the engagement of the great bulk of the populace in political activity would result in one of two unfortunate conditions: eiher inefficiency and instability; or the surrender of power to an authoritarian regime because the mass of the people do not want political responsibility.

A representational system is a necessary concomitant of the modern nation-state. Direct participation in the running of the state is possible only on the level of the Greek *polis*. The major problem of the indirect representational form of democracy is how to ensure that the elected representative truly reflects the views and interests of his or her constituents. How does one improve the tenet of political democracy? In Europe industrial managers are only just learning to consult with their workers. The economic emphasis in industrial democracy provides a firm foundation for political democracy; for by participating in the affairs of their workplace people become practised in the arts of democracy and more confident in their ability to play a participatory role generally.

Four different approaches exist towards the issue of industrial democracy: first, the idea of collective bargaining which presupposes a considerable degree of trade union independence from state or managerial control, and is essentially a process by which employees take part in decisions that affect their working lives; second, workers' participation in management; third, schemes for co-ownership by workers, employers and investors; and last, the most radical of all, is the programme of the New Left for complete workers' control in the belief that capitalism and democracy are utterly incompatible. Some measure of cooperation between employers and employees has been achieved in Britain and France in recent years.

To interpret politics in Britain as a conflict between classes in the twentieth century is certainly not too wide of the mark. Until the General Strike there were significant industrial upheavals, which were quickly stopped by the governments, while at the same time they had an open determination to maintain the *status quo*. In this period of social and political conflict, the established authorities were noticeably dominant and kept organized trade unionism comparatively acquiescent for several decades.

In the decades either side of the Second World War, and helped by favourable economic circumstances, the British political system avoided the collapse and revolution which characterized other major powers. It gained a reputation for flexibility, resilience and tolerance. The obverse side of this was an inheritance of much dead wood from the past – old, comparatively unreformed institutions; old, unchallenged attitudes and unreformed social structures. The political system had become steadily more and more out of line with economic and social realities. The cushioning effect of great economic prosperity based on empire had long postponed admission of the underlying weaknesses. When these finally began to show in the 1960s with underinvestment, unemployment and serious errors of planning and administration, the inertia of the political system was revealed. Thus the British political system, long praised for its adaptability and stability in a period of favourable economic circumstances, now shows the very opposite quality, that of an inability to change in unfavourable economic and social conditions which may therefore subject it to very testing strains. Yet, periodic outbursts of industrial unrest at industrial relations legislation and against government incomes policies and unemployment indicates that the working class have been far from docile in Britain.

When one looks at the Soviet Union, tensions can also be perceived. There is a tendency, even where economic classes have been abolished, for social class distinctions which arise with advantages of wealth, education, social position and career opportunities to be passed on to children. Food shortages, unsatisfactory working conditions and lack of institutional structures capable of dealing with complaints that arise – for Soviet trade unions do not regard organizing and negotiating in industrial disputes as part of their role – give rise to tensions which may sometimes result in petitions to politicians, or even strikes. Recently, efforts to form free trade unions have been ruthlessly suppressed. These unions would have been prepared to campaign for better pay and conditions and workers' rights.

Concerns about the environment can lead to a social awareness at times almost as militant and strife laden as the industrial scene.

## Environmentalism .

**Environmentalism** is basically concern for the environment, for natural resources, natural beauty, and for the character of cities and towns, when elevated into a political pursuit. The doctrine was enunciated by Hippocrates in the fifth century BC and has reached its peak in the late twentieth century. Modern workers tend to acknowledge the importance of the natural environment, but see it operating through a complex network of psychological, social and economic channels which may dampen or accentuate different properties of the environment for different groups, or for the same group at different points in time.

Politically, environmentalism refers to a situation in which economic growth is regarded as much less important than the protection of standards often referred to as 'the quality of life'. In practice, environmentalists tend to be in favour of pollution controls, even if these reduce economic productivity, and against developing extractive industries. They also oppose nuclear power as a major safety hazard, and in general are enemies of large scale industrial expansion. As a political force, environmentalism has had some moderate successes. In New Zealand and West Germany, for example, there are organized parties, the former called the Values Party, the latter the Green Party, both of which names give an indication of the sort of political position they have adopted. In Britain the Ecology Party fought in many constituencies in the 1979 and 1983 general elections. In 1986 it changed its name to the Green Party.

Although a concern for such values in itself does not really constitute an organized set of policies for governing a society, many other policies which have a psychological rather than logical link to the central concern are espoused. Thus policies like industrial democracy, liberalization of laws on private morality, and often a considerable degree of pacifism, are associated politically with the main ecological protection thrust. At its most fervent, environmentalism becomes a considered economic-technological policy of opposition to economic growth and commitment to a much simpler and less materially affluent socioeconomic system, through well argued fears of depletion of world resources. There are several important international and national pressure groups such as the Club of Rome and the Sierra Lodge which may influence government policy rather more than the more widely-based political parties.

The term **ecology**, originally used by Ernst Haeckel in 1873 to denote the branch of biology which deals with the interrelationship between organism and environment, has been adopted by political movements. These are sometimes romantic in temperament, anti-industrial, with liberal or socialist leanings in matters of property and law. They favour strict legal control over every activity that can in any way alter the balance of nature, or reduce or pollute natural resources. Often the underlying idea here is one of justice: the earth is held in trust by those who at present occupy it, and cannot be appropriated for their sole use without violating the rights of succeeding generations. In the United States, however, where a majority of people seem to favour strict environmental laws, major support for ecology movements comes also from well to do conservative elements. The movements are sometimes opposed by those on the left as catering for the leisure and aesthetic interests of the affluent at the expense of the productive activity which provides employment to the rest.

**Environmental groups** fall within the organizational category of voluntary organizations – formal groups in which individuals freely associate, without commercial motive, to further some common purpose. This clearly distinguishes them from commercial and statutory organizations. The movement consists of a number of environmental groups, the organizational embodiment of the movement, and the attentive public: those people who, though they do not belong to any of the groups, share their values. The attentive public for the environmental movement would include the readership of various environmental magazines, students of environmental studies in schools, colleges and universities, sympathetic members of the design and land use professions, and the many people who, through their personal convictions, behaviour and life styles, express their concern for the environment. Environmental groups are only one indicator of the wider social movement. Other indicators include the degree of sympathy expressed by non-environmental organizations, the burgeoning of environmental literature and the coverage of the environment in the news media.

Groups may be the creation of movements and vice versa. **The Green** (formerly Ecology) **Party** is a clear example of a group that has arisen out of the contemporary environmental movement giving political expression to unease at the economic and conservation policies of established parties. However, it also seems that formal groups can exist without a social movement. There are certainly examples of organized groups in British society that enjoy minimal support beyond their own membership. Examples include extremist groups totally opposed to the prevailing order, those with very specialized or obscure objectives and those promoting thoroughly unpopular causes. Though environmental groups currently enjoy the support of a large attentive public, this has not always been the case. Many predate contemporary concern for the environment and indeed their publicity and campaigning efforts have helped to awaken and enlarge that concern. It has only been during the course of this century that a recognizable sense has emerged that the preservation of historic buildings, wildlife and natural beauty should be ensured deliberately rather than left to chance.

The post-war period has seen a widening of the environmental movement with control of both national and local groups firmly in the hands of the professional and managerial classes, though often with considerable lower middle-class support. Some of the new groups are concerned with a different and broader range of issues such as the finiteness of resources, the dangers of global pollution and the adverse consequences of economic growth. Many environmental groups begin by challenging fundamental tenets of government policy or dominant social values. To win public acceptance or government recognition, they must wage public and parliamentary campaigns.

Organization renders available the diffuse energy and enthusiasm of the environmental movement as tangible political resources. But particular organizational forms place specific constraints on the use of these resources. The form adopted by many environmental groups is an oligarchy of a few leaders plus many supporters. This has advantages and disadvantages. By concentrating a group's resources and decision making, it ensures the maximum tactical manoeuvreability in dealing with the centralized organs of government and the media. But members are regarded primarily as a passive source of income rather than as active agents in securing environmental change and thus are not encouraged to play a part in the group's affairs. In general, environmental groups offer their ordinary members little scope for participation in lobbying and campaigning. As a consequence, the mass following of environmental groups remains a largely untapped political resource.

Environmental groups deploy their political resources through the channels available to them to express their views. Different political channels are used for different functions. Links with administrative agencies are necessary for groups wishing to influence the way in which environmental programmes and policies are implemented. Access to senior civil servants and ministers is vital for involvement in the formative stages of policy making and the allocation of resources. Support in parliament is important for amending and sometimes initiating legislation and putting pressure on ministers. Access to the media is crucial for bringing issues to the attention of government and parliament and in demonstrating and sustaining a group's public support. None of these channels is mutually exclusive.

Government has been an active agent in Britain establishing many new consultative procedures, funding environmental groups, even promoting the creation of such groups. Yet governments in the West hold sway over groups, because it is only through close contact with government departments that groups can acquire the advance intelligence and much of the information necessary to develop their criticisms of the course of official policy.

In the main, environmental groups have less influence with government than the major economic interest groups. They have fewer political resources and lack powerful sanctions. Unlike these other groups, they are not of central importance to the effective performance of government, the economy or various sectors of production.

Ultimately among the wider public in the Western world, concern for the environment has to an extent been supplanted by the more immediate material and physical concerns of finding security in employment and housing, devising long-term solutions to ailing economies, and combating social disorder, violence and crime. There is anxiety not only over the world economy, but over the failure of arms limitation and the growth of international tension.

## Questions

### Managerialism, scientism and socialization

1   Has a managerial revolution occurred?
2   Account for the increasing acceptability of scientism.
3   What has been the impact of technology and science on political developments?
4   Do all groups of people benefit from political socialization?

### Strife and strikes

1   Why have strife and strikes become an accepted form of activity in democracies?
2   Account for the complexities inherent in an industrial democracy.
3   Describe the role of trade unions in a democracy.

### Environmentalism and ecology

1   Can political activity aspire to truly environmentalist beliefs?
2   Discuss the tradition of voluntary support for environmental groups.
3   How do environmental groups deploy political resources?
4   Why have some environmental groups less influence with government than major economic interest groups?

### Further reading

Barker, R., *Political Ideas in Modern Britain*, Methuen, London, 1978.
Beloff, M., *Tide of Collectivism – can it be turned?*, Conservative Political Centre, London, 1978.
Crespigny, A. de and Cronin, J. (eds), *Ideologies of Politics*, Oxford University Press, 1975.

Flackes, W. D., *Northern Ireland: A Political Directory*, Ariel Books, London, 1980.

Heater, D. B., *Political Ideas in the Modern World*, Harrap, London, 1960.

Hyman, H. H., *Political Socialisation*, Free Press, New York, 1959.

Lowe, P. and Goyder, J., *Environmental Groups in Politics*, George Allen & Unwin, London, 1983.

Parekh, B., *Contemporary Political Thinkers*, Martin Robertson, Oxford, 1982.

Plamenatz, J., *Ideology*, Macmillan, London, 1970.

Seliger, M., *Ideology and Politics*, George Allen & Unwin, London, 1976.

# 16
# Communication and participation

A comparatively high level of participation can be achieved provided that the type of participation called for is purely formal and symbolic as in elections to the Soviets in the USSR, or is limited to narrow choice as in liberal democratic elections. The term **'participation'** came into widespread use in the 1960s to express what the EEC calls 'the democratic imperative' defined as the principle that those who will be substantially affected by decisions made by social and political institutions must be involved in the making of those decisions. It is argued that the size and complexity of modern mass societies, the centralization of political power, the growth of bureaucracy, and the concentration of economic power mean that the traditional guarantees of democracy need to be strengthened and extended. This is necessary to check the advance of decisions affecting people's lives being made by small groups, often remote and not easily identified or called to account. They act in the name of the state, of a local authority, or of some large, impersonal business corporation.

The greater the degree of participation, the higher the level of legitimacy is likely to be. The fact that there are practical difficulties to be overcome, such as the excessive delays likely to occur when large numbers have their say, or the difficulty of getting free, unmanipulated, coherent decisions from large public meetings, are not insoluble. They are often perpetuated by the controlling groups for the very purpose of inhibiting wider political participation. The main point of argument is whether greater political participation is conducive to an enhancement of the legitimacy of the regime. Here participation is seen as introducing complications into the decision-making process, the frustrations of which reduce the efficiency and legitimacy of decisions and of those who make them. 'Excessive' participation creates conditions for the manifestation of discontent and dissension which would not have arisen had not the structure been created enabling them to be formulated and expressed.

Since 1945, there has been an apparent increase in people's readiness to participate in other ways, frequently disruptive and condemned as 'illegitimate' by many politicians. There is a whole spectrum of such unconventional activity from the orderly demonstration to riot and organized violence such as bombing and arson. There is controversy over whether unconventional behaviour achieves its ends. Denials of the effectiveness of direct action are loudest from those most inconvenienced by it. Today, there is a general predisposition to employ unorthodox methods of political action either as complements or alternatives to more traditional forms of group and party activity.

In the USSR, a high degree of participation is achieved by the comparatively high proportion of the population elected to the various levels of soviets in a representative capacity, while some 15 or 16 million of the population are Communist Party members and still others give up time and energy for various forms of political and social services. The Communist Party of the Soviet Union is seen as the party of the people and the people are represented in the organs of government through the soviets. The amount of really effective communication afforded is extremely limited. This is because of the overbureaucratized nature of the system causing delays and acquiring vested interests of its own, and because any real discussion and participation which does take place has to do so in private as it is considered imperative to preserve a show of outward unity. To Western understanding the lack of a public arena for political discussion is a serious disability in any regime which aims at really influential and widespread participation.

In spite of these criticisms there have been efforts to involve a high proportion of the population in some participation. albeit subordinate, in the administration. These efforts are based on control of the bureaucracy by the people. The local soviets have been revived as the main supervisory bodies for administrative effectiveness: for they are representative, nationwide in extent and embody a high degree of legitimacy.

In the United States, the basic measure of participation tends to be turnout in elections and this has been steadily declining since 1960. An important aspect of this decreasing turnout is the decline in the numbers of people identifying with a political party and a reluctance in the ability of parties to perform one of their traditional functions – that of mobilizing their supporters to vote. Yet there is an increasing willingness on the part of citizens to take direct action by demonstrations, sit-ins and marches. Single issue groups have increased in importance for, although having small membership lists, they are able to have increasing influence over politicians as turnout in general elections falls.

In Great Britain in the general elections since 1970 an average of 25 per cent of those entitled to vote did not do so. Non-voting is accounted for as much by factors like illness, or removal from the voting constituency, as it is by apathy or a conscious decision to withhold a vote as a protest. A study comparing rates of participation in Britain with those in Austria, West Germany, Netherlands and the United States found that Britain had the lowest proportion of people saying they were 'highly interested' in politics and the highest proportion of those saying they had 'no interest' in politics. This rather conflicts with the notion of liberal democracy as maximizing the opportunity for citizen participation in government. It has been frequently argued by proponents of liberal democracy that many people did not participate simply because they were content to leave politics to others and content also with their lot. An increased tendency for political action to take more direct forms in recent years has raised serious questions about this, as does the fact that many people who are non-active receive relatively few benefits from the political process by any definition of 'interest'. The general assumption made is that people act rationally and do not participate in politics because they calculate that the costs of doing so in terms of time, money and energy will outweigh the benefits they receive as a result of their activity.

In some countries a single party has a monopoly of legal political activity. Under such **one-party systems**, almost anyone who wishes to participate effectively in politics must join this party and try to rise in its ranks. Often a one-party system is combined with a dictatorship; competing parties are suppressed by force, the founding of new parties is punishable as a crime. If a one-party government is also willing and able to control all other organizations affecting public life, from labour groups to sports clubs – if it controls the mass media, education and even much of the leisure time of the population and if it makes no exception from its claim to power – then it is often called totalitarian, as in the Soviet Union.

In milder cases a one-party system may give the ruling party its formal political monopoly, but tolerate a number of other long established interest groups with political potentialities such as landowners, industrialists, the military and some major church organizations. It may then respect privacy for its citizens. These less extreme one-party systems are called authoritarian, e.g. Franco's Spain and Peron's Argentina.

A third group of one-party systems is involved in rapid change: such systems are often found in developing countries and existed in Turkey in the 1920s, in Mexico in the 1930s and in India in the 1970s, and even French Gaullists have perhaps attained this status. One-party systems tend to be most successful when the national supply of activists, top level political talent and of leaders and managers is small relative to the size and urgency of the tasks that a country faces.

When the number of political activists and potential leaders and the number and variety of active interest groups are much larger, not all participants can be accommodated within a single party. Under these conditions, a two-party system may offer twice as many opportunities for political participation. Each major party may represent a full team of potential leaders for the nation in its struggle against domestic or foreign difficulties.

In a two-party system, one party may specialize in initiating change and the other in slowing or consolidating it. Or one party may press for a more active foreign policy and the other may emphasize affairs at home. Most interest groups may find that neither party fits their needs perfectly. Compromise results, but its costs are the frustrations of interest groups, its rewards are what the party can get done for it.

A multiparty system such as is found in Western Europe is a mixture of parties of action and parties of expression. Its largest parties can get enough done to keep operating, but not enough to unite as many as half the voters and interests groups of the country. Its small parties voice sufficient protests and demands, interspersed with occasional bits of accomplishment, to hold the support of their specialized interests whether these are regional, occupational, religious or ideological. To govern the country, several parties, usually both large and small, must form a coalition. Such a coalition then agrees on a programme of legislation and on a distribution of government offices to be filled.

Coalition agreements on these matters often are made in writing, even though they are not always publicized. When the programme of the coalition has been carried out, or when agreement among members ceases for some reason, the coalition is dissolved and another is formed in its place. France, Germany, Switzerland and Italy have been governed by changing coalitions for almost a century.

In substance, formal coalition governments among several parties resemble the informal coalitions of interest groups within one- and two-party systems. They differ from the latter two in the relative ease with which coalition governments can be dissolved and reformed. Multiparty systems may be more flexible and less stable than one- or two-party systems, and they may offer a wider range of opportunities for political participation. This openness to participation, however, may depend primarily on the organization and quality of each party. The differences in openness and effectiveness among political parties often are as great as or greater than those among party systems as a whole.

## Transnational participation

Many transactions of the international system do not involve governments alone and much that happens across international boundaries is removed from sovereignty and intergovernmental negotiations. Despite the omnipresence of governments and official regulations, many international transactions occur on a people to people basis, or between one government and the corporations of another state. This is known as transnational participation and is a recent form of observation in international relations.

**Transnational interaction** is defined as 'the movement of tangible or intangible items across state boundaries when at least one actor is not an agent of a government or an intergovernmental organisation'. It may involve contact between two or more non-governmental actors, or between one official actor and one or more private actors. The non-governmental participants may be corporations, social organizations, interest groups, political parties, elite structures or formally instituted organizations designed to facilitate private relations.

While these forms of international contact have always taken place, their impact has traditionally been minimized because of state domination of the global system. Now it is acknowledged that such contacts contribute to the quality of coexistence either directly (by improving perceptions and tolerance) or indirectly (by affecting intergovernmental relations).

These interactions have six kinds of prospective impact. First, transnational contact is assumed to promote changes in attitudes among the actors; second, there is the promotion of international pluralism. Third, there are the creation of new avenues of dependence and interdependence and, fourth, the stabilization of relations among peoples with increasing intersocietal dependence, which may enlarge the peaceful contacts of governments and create for them new avenues of influence. Fifth, institutionalized transnational participation may create new influential autonomous or quasi-autonomous actors in the international system. Finally there is the gradual institutionalization of intersocietal transactions which may become the private counterpart of functional international organizations.

There are many types of transnational participation: the most informal are sociocultural, especially individual travel; then there is political transnational activity such as instigated by national communist parties and national liberation fronts. The most important transnational activities are in the economic realm. The transnational actor with the greatest power to affect national economies and the flow of international transactions is the transnational (or multinational) corporation. Its centre of operations is in one country, but it has subsidiaries in several others that have major effects upon international economies and upon host economies. In the mid-1980s there are over 4000 such corporations, many of them American.

At present, the sociocultural centre provides the greatest contribution of transnational participation to world stability. Governments, however, cautiously safeguard their prerogatives and prevent escape of political functions to external agencies. But the intersocietal linkages created by the movement of persons, information, goods and capital across national boundaries challenge the purely state-centred model of international stability. They may ultimately alter the supremacy of the state as an actor in the international system, though to date such transformation is minimal. Participation in political issues implies the need for a considerable development of interpretation of political issues.

## Interpretations

Interpretation is at the heart of politics – meanings can be signed to expressions of any formal language in politics; and areas in which this is most obvious include public opinion, pressure groups and propaganda.

In democracies opinion in the public realm can act diametrically against the wishes of the government in power. Government can be liberal at a time when majority opinion is illiberal, revolutionary at a time when the majority are reactionary and even reactionary when the majority opinion is mildly liberal. Consultation of public opinion can precede conciliation, for example, in many industrial disputes.

**Public opinion**, although closely associated with opinion polls and pronouncements through the media, is a distinct aspect of the political process. Public opinion cannot exist with totalitarian propaganda; and its utility has even been minimized in ostensibly democratic states.

**Pressure groups** are groups of people which seek to exert pressure on legislators, and public opinion, in order to promote their own ideas or welfare. Examples of these groups include the Confederation of British Industry, which tries to impress on the United Kingdom government the interests of the managerial class and the Trade Union Congress which looks after workers' interests. Pressure groups are at the centre of political activity, for politics can be defined as the activity by which differing interests within a given unit of rule are conciliated by giving them a share in power in proportion to their importance to the welfare and survival of the whole community. Conversely politics can be hindered by them. Any group which is open to regular consultation and which has enduring institutions and a body of legislation to protect its aims has ceased to be a pressure group, and has become instead part of the establishment, which comprises both power and authority.

Not all interest groups are, however, pressure groups: the difference is one both of intention and of power. Any interest group is united by common interest and has sufficient identity to act on its own behalf and to have some influence either on public opinion or on government. An interest group may have sufficient political access to become a pressure group, alternatively its influence in the political world may be only indirect, e.g. through the mobilization of popular support.

Since its first use in the seventeenth century, the term '**propaganda**' has come to denote any attempt to win acceptance for a cause, system or state, either by praise of the thing itself, or by vilification of its known and unknown alternatives.

The emergence of the 'propaganda machine' in the twentieth century has been related to the rise of communist and fascist ideologies. The central themes in all propaganda are the feelings of loyalty to friends and hostility to enemies which they inspire. The 'enemy' concept has alerted people to the ever present dangers by which they are surrounded. The development of television has widened the possibilities for the uses of propaganda.

**Parties and television**

The big change in the role of parties, especially in the Western world, came not from well-intentioned and non-partisan reform, but from the un-anticipated political impact of television. Mankind never anticipates all the consequences of technological innovation. Because candidates now could appeal to voters by means of television, rank and file party workers ceased to be very important. Television suddenly became important in politics in the 1950s, but it was also very expensive for politicians. In America, in particular, immense amounts of money had to be raised, not to pay the campaign expenses and to line the pockets of party loyalists, but to buy time on commercial television. Increasingly in America, Britain and France, the effective use of television time has meant the hiring of professional media people who know how to package the product. A candidate's personal appearance, his or her statesmanlike demeanour, apparent grasp of the facts, and ability to appear decisive and in command have become more important than before, and reduced even further the role assigned to substance and content in the shaping of voter perceptions. As winning elections has turned increasingly on personality and image, the candidates have leaned less on experienced partisans than on public relations consultants, press advisers and personal pollsters. Television has enabled the candidate to reach over the heads of party workers and to touch the interests of millions of voters in a brief flash of time. Thus the candidate has found himself or herself talking to massed video citizens with varied interests, not to relatively small groups of voters with clearly defined interests. The television message has the potential for reaching everyone.

Few have ever accused campaigning politicians of failing to promise the moon and the stars and everything in between. By extending the reach of candidates to all the people at one time, television has increased the risks of making specific policy commitments to specific groups of voters. Thus it is important for the candidate to elaborate endlessly on the themes that most television viewers can agree upon: punishing criminals, restoring law and order and morality; balancing the budget; reducing inflation; providing more jobs, and keeping the country strong. But television has reduced the frequency with which candidates openly confront the real issues, if only for the fear of alienating one group of voters while appealing to the other. On political and international political matters, television has made clear what may be a fundamental irony of human nature: that people are entertained more by bad news than by good news.

In the reporting of political events, television raises the interest value for viewers by focusing on personalities and on the real or apparent conflicts between them. Thus television reinforces the superiority of appearances over matters of substance in the eyes of the viewer. The candidate is raised above the level of the party, and television personalizes politics and so makes the party irrelevant.

## Public opinion

**Public opinion** as measured in a democracy is a complex issue. Within the public there are some people who care intensely about any given issue and others who care hardly at all. It is not even true that all people would want their judgements to be weighted equally. Often we feel that some things are not our business and should therefore be decided by those who are affected. On many issues wide segments of the public want only a positive outcome to any particular issue and have no definite view about how to achieve it. The public, for example, wants peace but few members of the public believe that their judgement on diplomatic moves to keep peace is better than that of the government. Thus, the relationship between the public's view at any moment about what the government does is far from a mirror image.

The measurement of public opinion is, in its simplest sense, finding out what people think. So defined, it is as old as society; and it developed, without being named, along with the other characteristics – language, the division of labour and habits of cooperative work – that marked the latter stages of the 'descent of man'.

It is helpful to differentiate between what might be called positive public opinion on the one hand, and mere acquiescence, on the other. It can be argued that all rulers of all time have needed the acquiescence of the masses, but not necessarily the support of positive public opinion. When the number of persons whose opinions count is very small, as in primitive societies and in tiny self-governing communities whether public or private, the opinions of all can be measured.

Size is a limiting factor to the direct measurement of opinion; and in cases where vast numbers of people are involved, the opinions of some people are measured, and from these measured opinions, deductions are made about the opinions of all. This is sampling and whether it is good or bad depends on whether accurate deductions can be made from the measurement of the representative group. Thus there can be both good and bad representation.

The measurement of public opinion is as important in a society as is the extent to which the support of the masses is necessary or is thought to be necessary for the legitimizing or operation of government. Briefly, the importance of public opinion depends on the degree of democracy in the society. In so far as there are theories that say that the people have a right to influence their governments, public opinion is important.

As a practical matter, political leaders are selective in their assessments of public opinion. They try to measure the opinions of those people who have the greatest influence on their own future. Whether opinion sampling is good or bad, it always involves asking, listening and reading. The endless measuring of opinion is a process in which we all share in various degrees, for opinion measuring is inevitable in every social situation.

In democracies, political actors are compelled to be attentive to the size, composition and behaviour of crowds. The possibilities of manipulating crowds are much reduced in democratic environments, mainly because in democracies other messages and stimuli compete with those given to crowds by the government. Nonetheless, the democratic politician needs large, enthusiastic crowds for three reasons: first he or she needs the support and votes of individuals in the crowd; second, he or she hopes for a bandwagon effect; and third, he or she needs the crowd for feedback in order to sense how he or she is doing.

**Straw polls** are unofficial canvasses of electorates to determine the divisions of popular sentiments on public issues or on candidates for public offices. One of the problems of such a poll is that it is almost impossible to ensure that the persons giving their opinions are representative of all the persons whose opinions are presumably being measured. There is no certainty that the microcosm (the sample) is like the macrocosm (the universe).

## Survey research

Modern public opinion has origins in the journalistic straw votes; in the field of market research; in the development of psychological testing; and in the application of the mathematical laws of probability and sampling to human behaviour. The objective of public opinion surveys is to obtain responses to uniform questions from a select number of persons (the sample) who, according to criteria thought to be relevant, are representative of the whole group of people (the universe) about whom one wants information. Public opinion surveys only require a positive or negative reply to any particular question but do not elicit from those questioned the means by which it can be believed. The opinion survey is a tool, with clear limits of usefulness. Public opinion surveys are expensive and care has to be taken with the size of the sample. Representativeness in a sample is ensured only by some combination of two alternatives: stratification and randomness. Questions asked in public opinion studies are of three kinds: dichotomous, multiple choice and open end. The questions can elicit direct facts, direct information, indirect or inferential material, or, lastly, elicit attitudes and material for background and richness in analysis. The ideal interviewer has to be understanding, intelligent, kind, insightful, patient, modest, well presented and soft spoken.

The question of truthfulness in public opinion polls is important. It appears to be true that persons will not always tell exactly what they think when asked. Whether truth will be obtained in any instance seems to depend on what the question is about, who asks the question and what the respondent thinks will be done with the answer. Validity in polling has to do with whether the respondents' real opinion is discovered. To the political scientist, reliability is probably more important than validity. Reliability is judged by the reproducibility of a measurement result.

Rousseau is sometimes considered to have been the first modern political thinker to make an extended analysis of public opinion. He exhibits not only a concern for the relations between governmental policy and the opinions of individuals but even in some places, a modern understanding of public opinion as it relates to majority rule and representation in a democracy. Thus he appreciates that opinions have their origin not in man's physical nature, or in supernatural causes, but in social relationships. He was aware that all governments rest fundamentally on opinion rather than on law or coercion and that in social change no government may be very far ahead of popular opinion.

Public opinion is the complex of beliefs expressed by a significant number of persons on an issue of public importance, i.e. a contemporary situation with a likelihood of disagreement. There must be a recognizable group of persons concerned with the issue; the 'public' of public opinion. Another factor in public opinion is the distribution of opinion on an issue. Then there is the expression of the various views that cluster around an issue. Lastly there is the size of the public that is interested in the issue. Public opinion requires there to be a significant number of persons – significance can be measured in part by effectiveness, or potential effectiveness, which are functions of intensity and organization as well as of sheer numbers alone.

## Democracy and the opinion–policy process

Public toleration is necessary for the continuation of any existing government and in this sense, despotic and arbitrary governments maintain their power only because non-governmental elements are unwilling or unable to change them.

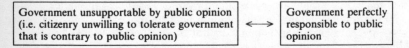

| Government unsupportable by public opinion (i.e. citizenry unwilling to tolerate government that is contrary to public opinion) | ⟷ | Government perfectly responsible to public opinion |

> Range in which public opinion
> tolerates government (left end
> of range) and is reflected by
> government (right end of range)

**Relationship between opinion and governmental policy**

Bertrand Russell (like Hegel) views human nature as self-interested, aggressive and above all, fearful. Yet self-interest is not always aggressive and passions can be channeled constructively by social institutions. Fear produces the three concomitants of conflict: the fear of nature, the fear of others, and modern social institutions, above all governments, aggravating fears and institutionalized aggression. Yet paradoxically he believed the United States, once the sole possessor of the atomic bomb, should have forced the rest of the world to disarm under the threat of nuclear punishment. Yet social controls are at best stopgaps; our fear of one another, turned inward as guilt and intrapersonal strife projected outward in war and conflict remains.

Einstein, a convinced pacifist, believed governments institutionalized aggressiveness and were bent on a collision and cataclysmic course.

Freud added psychological observations to Einstein's pacifism. Conflicts of interest are inevitably settled by violence, the superior individual being the winner, until the weak learn that unified they can outmatch the strength of the individual. Sovereign power, however, still rests on potential and/or actual violence. Court decisions and common law tend to reflect the interest of the strong who are ever on the alert to better their situation; while the weak or exploited press steadily and sometimes turbulently for justice. At the same time communities develop strongly supportive emotional and social bonds.

In the evolution of culture, it became popular to think in the mid-twentieth century of the progressive control of instinct by intelligence and the internalization of aggression. War is the grossest affront to cultural achievement and the psychological attitudes which this achievement has bred; the pacifist's commitment is thus grounded more profoundly than ever on an intellectual and emotional repudiation of war.

Writers in the latter half of the twentieth century challenged such views as too individualistic, negative or simplistic. For the most part, modern warfare has only a remote and indirect connection with an individual's hostility.

The opinion-policy process is the way in which what people think is related to what government does. Traditional democracy assumes that each member of the electorate is motivated by principle and does not make political decisions either on habitual or whimsical grounds. Another assumption is that the voter in making political decisions is aware of the relevant facts. Lastly, it is assumed that the voter makes his or her decision rationally – on reason alone, excluding emotion, prejudice and fancy.

The opinions that any individual holds are products of his or her unique experience as a person within an environment he or she shares with others. Opinions must be in some general and overall sense, comfortable to the individual. Except in extreme cases, opinions cannot be judged solely on their congruence with facts; the facts that give rise to public issues, and therefore public opinion, are not obvious, objective and palpable.

Although both common sense and theories of personality point in the direction of a meeting of minds between beliefs and behaviour, there are many occasions when behaviour will not be consistent with attitudes or opinions. The study of public opinion has to be paralleled by and compared in every possible way with the study of political behaviour. An individual's opinions are limited and conditioned by physical and chemical reactions within himself or herself and by the unique experiences of his or her own development.

In tightly culture bound societies the possible opinions that may be held on any issue are few. In modern societies the increasing intracultural diversity and the change of many cultural patterns from requirements to influences may be represented by the narrowing of choice by contrast to primitive patterns. Modern cultural patterns require fewer opinions, but they permit many more. Differences in political culture will demonstrably influence the kinds of attitudes and opinions held by the citizens of various nation-states.

Economic factors seem to have only a small influence on anti or pro democratic opinions and behaviour. Extremist and intolerant governments in modern society are more likely to be based on the lower classes than on the middle and upper classes. Economic factors are related to political activity and inactivity. The effects of economic factors on opinion holding are mediated and modified by organizations. Commitments to party membership, to group ideology, to role expectations of leaders and followers, and to other aspects of group behaviour will often significantly distort the more directly economic influences on opinion holding.

Although the mass media generally do not regard themselves as political phenomena – and although audiences do not want them to be or become such – political leaders think the mass media are highly political and politically very important. People who believe that they ought to have opinions tend to look to the mass media for help. There are differences in the self images of the media, and in the expectations of media performance held by citizens of various levels of political interest and activity.

Underneath public opinion lies private opinion. The expression of points of views on issues by significant numbers of persons (public opinion) is only possible if many individuals have preferences (however formed) that they are able and willing to make public (when they volunteer or are asked to do so).

People do not always say what they think and do not always act as they believe. Difficult as it is to discover attitudes and opinions, it is even more difficult to know when behaviour reflects attitudes and opinions. Opinions matter for policy. The reason is simple – opinions are usually reflected in votes and in a democracy votes make policy. Public policies evolve from governmental responses to human needs and desires. All public policies were once merely private ideas. Private ideas, when shaped by large numbers of individuals become proposals. Proposals when they are adopted by governmental authorities become public policies.

Beyond the general constraints of bureaucracy, the influence of opinion in policy making will vary with the specific organizational context within which the decision makers operate. The time demands of the decision situation will have important consequences for the opinion–policy process; and lastly the impact of opinions will vary with the personality characteristics of the decision makers. Political parties enter the opinion policy process in two ways: first, in their efforts to determine who the office holders will be in the official government, and, second, in their efforts to mediate and compromise the conflicts among interest groups. Ultimately, in any process of democratic government, individuals are free to form, hold and revise their opinions where their opinions may be openly expressed and where social institutions encourage opinion holding individuals to participate in public enterprise.

## Questions

### Participation

1  Account for the varying levels of participation.
2  How has participation been helped and hindered by the comprehensiveness of modern government?
3  Compare and contrast participation in the Soviet Union and United States.
4  Arguably, are coalition governments the best forms of government for the advancement of participation?
5  What is the value of transnational participation?

### Interpretations

1  Are pressure groups an advantage or a hindrance to the development of Western democracies?
2  Is propaganda necessary?

### Parties and television

1  Assess the impact of television on party politics.

### Public opinion

1  Is it possible effectively to measure public opinion?
2  Examine the Rousseau approach to the analysis of public opinion.
3  Discuss the constraints inherent in forming and judging public opinion.
4  Compare and contrast public and private opinion.
5  How do political parties enter the opinion policy process?

## Further reading

Arnold, G., *The Unions*, Hamish Hamilton, London, 1981.
Ayer, A. J., *Philosophy in the 20th Century*, Weidenfeld & Nicholson, London, 1982.
Ball, A. R., *Modern Politics and Government*, Macmillan, London, 1983.
Blondel, J., *Political Parties – a genuine case for discontent?* Wildwood House, London, 1978.
Bracher, K. D., *The Age of Ideologies. A History of Political Thought in the 20th Century*, Weidenfeld & Nicholson, London, 1984.
Carter, G. and Herz, J., *Government and Politics in the 20th Century*, Thames & Hudson, London, 1970.
Crespigny, A. de and Minogue, K. (eds), *Contemporary Political Philosophers*, 1976.
Dahl, R. A., *Modern Political Analysis*, Prentice-Hall, New Jersey, 1963.
Day, A. J. and Degenhardt, H. W. (eds), *Political Parties of the World*, Longman, London, 1980.
Deutsch, K. W., *Politics and Government, How People decide their Fate*, Houghton Miflin, New York, 1974.
Halebsky, S., *Mass Society and Political Conflict*, Cambridge University Press, 1976.
Heater, D., *Contemporary Political Ideas*, Longman, London, 1974.
Jones, W. S., *The Logic of International Relations*, Little Brown & Co., Boston, 1985.
Ponton, G. and Gill, P., *Introduction to Politics*, Blackwell, Oxford, 1984.
Robins, L., (ed.), *The American Way: Government and Politics in the USA*, Longman, London, 1985.
Stewart, M., *Modern Forms of Government*, George Allen & Unwin, London, 1965.

# 17
# Comparative and representative government – theory

## Constitutions and liberties

'**Constitutions** are codes of rules which govern the allocation of functions, powers and duties among the various governmental agencies and their officers and define the relationship between them and the public' (Finer). Morally, legitimacy flows to governments constituted in a manner that has previously been agreed, tacitly or explicitly by the electorate.

Britain does not have a written constitution, and since formal legitimacy in Britain is not spelt out, it is sometimes a matter of debate. Source elements of the constitution include constitutional documents, major statutes, constitutional conventions, case law and the works of major political writers. Some people objected to Britain's entry to the European Economic Community on the grounds that British governments do not possess the legitimate authority to cede certain state powers to an international organization. Generally people are able to separate notions of legitimacy and popularity. In the United States both politicians and the public have a highly developed sense of the importance of formal powers defined in the constitution and interpreted by the Supreme Court.

All constitutions are intended to be inherently conservative and they preserve a set of 'rules of the game' that enable the game to continue in the face of short-term pressures for change. If the method of passing constitutional laws is identical with the method of passing ordinary laws then the constitution can be considered flexible. Owing to the unwritten nature of the British constitution there has been a gradual transfer of powers of government from the monarch to the elected representatives of the people. Thus relationships in government should be left fluid so that they can be adapted easily to changing circumstances rather than written into constitutional law. With a flexible constitution no laws are regarded as fundamental laws. Conversely rigidity means that the principles enshrined in the constitution assume the character of fundamental law. Difficult amendment procedures mean that hasty alterations are impossible.

The flexibility in constitutions was admired by Montesquieu. What the French political theorist admired most in England was its high morale, which he connected with the constitutional safeguards that preserved it from corruption from the despot's caprice and from demagogic irresponsibility. From his observations of England he imported a new word 'constitutionalism' into the French language. Montesquieu's *Spirit of the*

*Laws* reasserted the need for legality and constitutionalism and in turn influenced the American revolutionaries.

Procedures are interrelated with conventions, and all political systems develop the latter to help their organization. Countries with flexible constitutions develop an enormous range of conventions which have come to fulfil certain needs. In Britain, the office of Prime Minister and cabinet government have emerged through need and have remained by convention. Such as the monarch calling the leader of the majority party to be Prime Minister after a general election and the non-partisan nature of the monarchy. If a government is defeated part way through its period of office, the Queen would appoint a caretaker Prime Minister until a general election could be called. Also if a Prime Minister dies or loses the confidence of his or her party some other party member would be nominated to fill the role without the necessity of a general election or the Queen's interference. In discussing conventions one has to take account of the separation of powers.

## Separation of powers

The theory of **separation of powers** was implicit in Aristotle. He advocated a form of mixed government, or polity, in which all citizens 'rule and are ruled by turn'. Aristotle also believed political obligation was founded in distributive justice – the principle uniting citizen to citizen and all to the state in which equals are treated equally. The theory was given greater expression by James Harrington, the seventeenth-century English political philosopher, who, arguing for a written constitution, spoke of the separation of powers. John Locke suggested that liberties could be more easily protected and the social compact upheld more effectively by a separation of powers – introducing a notion that was to have radical influence through the systematic theory of it given by Montesquieu. The Frenchman believed that the English constitution epitomized the separation of powers. The English model could create an effective balance of powers within the state, avoiding the despotic tendencies inherent both in absolute monarchy and in government by the common people.

Following Montesquieu the three powers normally considered to be separable in the exercise of government are

- *The legislature* which formulates policy and enacts it as law
- *The executive* which carries policy into action
- *The judiciary* which applies the law according to rules of procedural justice and resolves disputes.

Montesquieu argued that the sign of the despot was to subsume these powers under one and to hold that one power to himself. Despots and independent judiciaries do not go hand in hand. Montesquieu thus believed in the totality of separation of powers. The executive power should not be exercised by members of the legislature but by a monarch, subject to impeachment for actions performed *ultra vires*.

The differentiation of powers is not clear in the Western world; for example, in Britain executive power lies with the cabinet which is formed from members of the ruling majority party in Parliament, i.e. of the legislature, and which effectively controls the operation of Parliament. Guarantees of liberty contained in the British constitution cannot be attributed simply to a separation of powers. The American constitution does not separate the powers completely, nor indeed could it do so without destroying the necessary unity of government.

Government in the Western world at least would be impossible if the three powers ceased to function in unison. As Roger Scruton, the political lexicographer, states, 'laws enacted by the legislature must be applied by the executive, and upheld by the judiciary and if a judge acts ultra vires, it must be possible for the legislature to hold him to account and for the executive to remove him from office'.

If all three branches were united under a single head, the opportunity for an act of government to go through rapidly would be very much greater than if three individuals or sets of individuals had to concur before that act went through: and so the separation of powers imparts a brake to the activity of government. When all three powers act in concert the matters go forward: let one of them refrain and nothing can go forward at all. This means delay.

The Marxist–Leninist argument on the balance of power is that whoever holds the power alone is important. It is maintained that the people ought to hold the power and that the more unfettered that power, the easier it is for them to act in the purported interests of the state.

## Federal and unitary forms

A federal system of government exists in the United States in which a central government, both legislature and executive, exists side by side with the state or provincial government, again with both executive and legislative powers. Federal systems exist where the people are not ready to surrender all powers to a central government; and is adapted to states embracing wide areas, where there are sectional diversities of race, language, nationality, religion and geography. Switzerland has three nationalities, three languages and two religions. Australia's federalism has been built on historical development despite the unifying influences of common nationality and common language.

In the United States there is the division of the functions of government between the centre, represented by the governments of no less than fifty separate states. The functions which in Britain are exercised by the sovereign Parliament are in the United States divided in two: one half is handed to the governments of the individual states, the other remains in the hands of the federal or national government. Related to this factor is localism; the effective pyramid of power runs from below upwards, from the county to the state, and from the state to Washington itself.

The constitution is supreme in the federal system; and the central government supreme in cases of conflict. As exemplified in the West German system, certain powers are conferred on the central government and the remaining residual powers are left to regional governments. In West Germany, the powers of the Bund (federation) are enumerated, the rest of the powers remaining with the Lander (eleven regional units) according to the constitution. The legislature is bicameral – one house consisting of the representatives elected on a population basis, and the other representing on an equal basis the various regional units in the state.

The unitary system occurs in a society which is homogeneous in character with no sharp linguistic, racial or religious differences between sections of the population. Power and authority is in the hands of central government which controls the various areas into which the state is divided for administrative purposes, as in France. Powers and boundaries can be altered only by the legislature.

A **confederal system** is a loose federation in which certain powers are surrendered to a common government for the mutual advantage of the separate states, such as matters affecting trade and defence. Central government exists by virtue of agreement of the constituent states and can only make laws for them if they agree to accept them.

## Administration

Parties are organized to decide what things should be done. Executives are put into office to decide how they should be done. But it is the people on the spot, the administrators, who must do them.

No policy can be put into effect without administration. But the administrative machinery can continue to function by routine even when that routine has no apparent logic or sense. Only in the long term do decisions about consistency and policy become inevitable. Even the business of thinking about policy needs to be administered. The administrative personnel that serves this task are called staff. Officers or officials on the staff of an organization – private or public, civilian or military – collect and process current information and past decisions that are relevant for the decisions to be made. On the basis of all this information, the staff then advises the line executive or executive officer who makes the final decision.

Administration can make or break a policy. Bureaucrats can go through the motions of carrying out a policy or law while actually sabotaging it. If a policy is to work or if a leader or party is to have real power, it must have the support of a body of administrative personnel that is loyal and competent enough to give effect to its orders. While policies, leaders and parties change, bureaucrats remain. The question is asked many times – if a new policy is to be implemented, can the old bureaucracy be expected to administer it?

An answer to this question can perhaps be provided by the concept of a civil service, which nowadays occurs in most countries of the world. This notion goes back to the time of European monarchies when government officials were supposed to be primarily loyal to the king and not to any policy, party or special interest group. Civil servants were expected to be equally loyal and competent in serving any minister or policy that the king commanded. Later this loyalty of civil servants became oriented not to the king but to the crown – that is, to the state – for even kings come and go or make mistakes. Civil servants then were expected to be loyal to the interests of the state and its constitution, if need be against the errors of kings and cabinets. Under this tradition in Britain a Labour government or a Conservative government will expect to be served equally well by the non-partisan professionals of the civil service. Recruitment and promotion is usually carried out by means of some merit system in accordance with supposedly objective standards of training and performance. In practice, however, such standards favour members of particular social classes or particular ethnic groups. Certainly no fully objective standards for the hiring and promoting of government personnel have been discovered as yet.

In the United States, government offices were a matter not for specialists and experts, but for ordinary people. In the last century, any right thinking man was good enough to fill an office after his party had won the election, for 'to the victor belong the spoils'. This spoils system permitted the victorious party to fill administrative posts with its own adherents, who were expected to carry out its policy, and to be grateful to the party for getting them their jobs. Such officeholders were not politically neutral but intensely partisan. Few other countries went as far, but a part of the practice lingers on in the decision making politics of many American cities.

The class theory of administration was elaborated by Marx, Engels, and particularly Lenin. As they saw it, professional bureaucrats would serve different masters or policies equally well as long as the latter remained within the same ruling class and social system. As soon as a new government or policy went radically beyond the old class limits, the old bureaucracy could not be expected to serve it loyally. According to Lenin, socialist or Communist governments on coming to power would need to dismiss the old officials and replace them by new ones recruited from the working class and its allies. Even this new bureaucracy would have to be watched closely and purged often to prevent it from becoming a new middle class. Ultimately the communists would have to reorganize the whole machinery of government. The practical experience of the Soviet Union and other communist countries shows that communist bureaucracies have a way of becoming large and persistent. Dissident communists have complained bitterly of the rise of a 'new class of communist manager and bureaucrats'. The administrative machinery of communist countries has not yet become simplified enough.

The average citizen is likely to think of public administration primarily in terms of governmental regulation of individual and group conduct, overlooking the vast and varied forms of protection, assistance and services that governments in democratic countries provide. Public administration falls into four categories: the protection of society as a whole; promotional activities or assistance to particular economic and social groups; proprietary activities where a government owns and operates enterprises serving the public, and the regulation of particular businesses or activities.

Federal systems as in the United States, Canada, India, Australia and West Germany, require that certain administrative functions be discharged exclusively or mainly by the national government and others by the state. Human activities are so intermeshed that there is a vast amount of synchronization, dovetailing and cooperation among all levels and agencies of government.

All governments rely on a civil service of some sort, but finding a clear operational definition that distinguishes the public administrators from the politicians is not easy. There is no equivalent to the concept of civil service (the idea that senior officers of the state are servants of the public) in Western Europe. The phrase 'civil service' is only meaningful in a democratic society where it is possible to draw a clear distinction between politicians who are elected to office and who must face reelection from time to time, and civil servants who are appointed to offices which they will hold subject to good behaviour in the same way as any other employed person. A corollary of this is that the civil service itself has no right to make laws, policy and regulations, only to issue them. They exist only to advise and carry out the instructions of their political masters and are usually supposed to be non-partisan. In practice, these ideals are seldom achieved. Civil services everywhere have a great deal of political power, if only because governments are often totally dependent on their advice and a combination of time, pressure and the technical nature of legislation makes it difficult for politicians to question or check on the advice given by the civil service. Furthermore, in most countries there is little or no pretence that the upper levels of the public administration are non-partisan.

Even the word 'administration' has increasingly come to have more than one meaning. It can refer simply to the political part of the executive branch and is frequently used as such in the United States; whereas in Britain it describes the civil service or bureaucracy alone. An 'administration' also relates to the process of implementing decisions and organizing the government of a country; for example, one can talk of the administration of quasi-governmental agencies, nationalized industries and local authorities.

In recent years politicians have become concerned with the problem of governmental overload and the inefficiencies which result from an executive with too many responsibilities. One solution which seemed possible in the United Kingdom was devolution, the transfer of legal and political powers to some subordinate institution, while retaining in theory complete political control over the exercise, for example giving certain powers to the Welsh and Scottish assemblies. Across the Atlantic, deregulation has involved strict reviews of government rules and orders, and efforts to reduce or even remove government intervention and control.

A large question is whether the administration can be effectively controlled by the politicians. Accountability in democracies has two meanings. It involves the idea that those who exercise power whether as governments, as elected representatives or as appointed officials, are in a sense stewards, who have to show that they have exercised their powers and duties properly. Accountability can also refer to arrangements made for securing conformity between the values of a delegating body and the person or persons to whom powers and responsibilities are delegated. In Scandinavia and Britain, for example, the Commissioner for Administration, or Ombudsman, is thought to have improved the accountability of the administration by the scrutiny of administrative methods and inquiries into complaints against government departments.

Any delegation of power usually carries with it a requirement to report on how that power is exercised, and any institution seen as having power may be required to justify its operations to a superior authority. Thus in many Eastern bloc and Third World countries today, one can speak of the press, universities and trade union movements being accountable to governments. Some parts of states in liberal democracies have escaped the control of the governors, other parts are controlled by them, but the governors themselves are largely uncontrolled. There needs to be a more critical concept of authority, resting on stronger forms of consent and accountability. The growth of the administrative state, in the context of democratic politics is less an imposition of authority on the people than a practical response to their interests and demands. As these have become more complex, so have the organization, management and functioning of government, not notably the bureaucracy.

## Bureaucracy

Rule by administrative offices is a feature of all aspects of political life. In a bureaucracy, power is vested in those who are, from the legal point of view, administrative intermediaries between sovereign and subject. They (normally the civil servants, although they can also be military and religious bureaucracies) can delay or advance the causes of both sovereign and subject to an extent that gives them *de facto* control over major political transformations. Weber in *Wirtschaft und Gesellschaft* published in 1921, argued that the conflict between capitalism and socialism must be extinguished by the triumph of bureaucracy, which would prove indispensable for the rational attainment of the goals of any organization in industrial society. The result would be the creation of an increasingly centralized, increasingly impersonal, and increasingly 'routinized' kind of authority.

Since administrators can master their tasks only slowly, they must perforce remain in office longer than most politicians remain in power: their activities therefore impose a continuity on successive governments.

The term 'bureaucrat' or 'bureaucracy' has come to have distinct perjorative connotations.

**Bureaucracies** are described as full of small-minded time servers, indifferent to the public and incapable of initiative. Yet this was largely ignored by the original theorists of bureaucracy, and indeed refers only to a corrupt manifestation of a useful general principle for organization of efficient goal-oriented human interaction.

Those who feel benevolent towards senior bureaucrats would suggest that they are 'administrators' carrying on a vital and important task in government. There is a certain incompatibility and tension between the seeming inevitability of large scale administration as a part of the political system of the more 'developed' nations and the supposed evils of impersonal bureaucracy on this scale.

A corpus of theory about administration and about bureaucracy has evolved over the last few decades, which attempts to explain the behaviour of a set of 'actors'; individuals with distinct 'roles' whose performances can be isolated to some degree from others in the political system. In the English speaking countries these people are known as **civil servants**, but the generic term of **bureaucrat** commands universal acceptance.

The term is often extended to cover the work of those who take the decisions and cope with the paperwork in any large scale organization, whether it be a commercial enterprise, a trade union, an armed service or, of course, a governmental organization. Yet behaviour patterns are similar in certain respects in the administration of all big organizations. In the last century, J. S. Mill was critical of the education and selection of potential civil servants, while Walter Bagehot struck a gloomy note about their behaviour, commenting that 'it is an inevitable defect that bureaucrats will care more for routine than for results'. By the mid-twentieth century the massive size of the bureaucracies that underpin the governments of most modern nations, amounting often to something like 3 per cent of the labour force even at a conservative estimate, has led to the many attempts to distinguish between the conventional and the observed patterns of behaviour inside this branch of government.

For Weber, the essence of bureaucracy was its 'rational' character; it was governed by a set of rules that were easily discernible. After Weber's concern for the 'rational' character and professionalization of bureaucracy, he was intent to show how it related to human society at certain stages of its development in different parts of the world. The decisive reason for the advance of bureaucratic organization has always been its purely technical superiority over any other form of organization.

Societies that demand this level of technical superiority, mainly those that are more advanced economically, inevitably tend to support a bureaucratic structure sooner or later. Its durability is illustrated by the contrast between the bureaucratic content of the 'rational–legal' ideal type (of authority) and the more unstable world of the 'charismatic' leader. The only comparable form of legitimate authority to the 'rational–legal' model is that in which 'patriarchal' power flourishes, for bureaucracy is the counter image of patriarchal authority. Both provide a certain amount of routine and satisfy the need of a society for a degree of continuity in the dispensation of authority, but only bureaucracy with its aura of professionalization and specialization, its reliance on precedence and the written record, can cope with the constant rush of rule-making that can be observed in, say, Western European countries since Weber's day.

The increase of bureaucracy among the major nations of the world, especially over the last half century or so, implies the inevitable increase of the power of the bureaucracy within the individual polity.

Weber's medium for the control of possible bureaucratic excesses was parliamentarianism. The French appear to have preferred legal curbs; the Americans use the Congressional Committee as one of their main checks on the administration right up to members of the presidential cabinet. In Britain both varieties have been attempted. Recently interest has centred on the parliamentary specialist select committee, which seems to be a weapon of legislative control conceived within the Weberian mould.

Some post-Weberian thinkers, such as Karl Mannheim, believe that bureaucrats fail to see political problems as anything more than administrative ones, for they are taught to confine their appreciation of a given situation to the application of the rules or laws that govern the society to which they belong. Mannheim, like Weber, realized that bureaucracy had its positive side and that the good inherent in this type of organization could outweigh the potential evil. For example, it allowed the development of 'impersonal and classless justice' which was not present in earlier societies more dependent on personal rule exercised from the apex of a hierarchy. It should be possible to develop the inherent benefits of bureaucratic organization in government – efficiency and objectivity in particular – while restraining the inherent dangers, chief of which was its potential for dehumanizing situations that called for justice tempered with mercy, administration tempered with sympathy for the cause of those who are being administered. Carl Friedrich considered that six elements contained in a bureaucratic structure could be isolated. Three of these are organizational in aspect – centralization of control and supervision, which implies a distinct hierarchy present in the structure; differentiation of functions or, more simply, specialization; and qualification for the office. Objectivity is an ideal to which the administrative structure aspires. The expert or professional can be objective and suppress his or her personal views or feelings in a given situation much more easily than the layperson or administrator, who lacks the necessary training or conditioning. Precision and consistency make up another element: the former is self evident since it is essential to the communication of decisions to those who are closely affected by them, usually the general public. Consistency is important because legal or quasi-legal precedent is a key to the fair-play aspect that underpins the acceptance of much of what the bureaucracy imposes on this latter group. The most contentious of the behavioural traits is that of discretion, which in this context is a way of pointing out that bureaucracy works best when its main activities are cloaked in a degree of secrecy. The degree of secrecy is open to question, for while it is reasonable to use it to protect the legitimate rights of clients and even to see that unnecessary embarrassment is not caused to colleagues in the administration process, it is surely necessary on occasion to let a certain amount of publicity into the administrative processes if only to provide a check on the political effects of decisions made in the bureaucracy.

When one discusses bureaucracy as part of the political system there is a structure function problem in that the term is used interchangeably to describe either a group of actors, or a set of attitudes and roles among groups that might not necessarily be seen as 'bureaucrats' pure and simple. **Bureaucratic power** is very important to the modern state. Indeed among the structural components of political systems in modern society, the bureaucracy is the most pervasive and therefore one of the most powerful.

In newly independent nations, bureaucracies can exert change and play a major part in modernization because of their unique position as a reservoir of trained personnel who can seek appropriate social and economic objectives for the nation and who can also exert the necessary pressure to carry them through. The emerging bureaucracies are also the major instruments of social change and political socialization in their respective countries.

The attitude of an administrative system to change depends on a number of variables. These will consist of the social and political context in which

it finds itself, the behavioural characteristics that have developed as a result
of its history and the specific attitudes of its political directors. Where a set
of administrators have taken their values from a metropolitan culture, it is
quite likely that a limit will be placed instinctively on the amount of change
that is found to be acceptable. It is noticeable how military 'counter-
bureaucracies' assume much of the mobilization initiative.

Although one no longer believes that administrative structures are essentially neutral, it is equally unlikely that they will be uncontrollable. Except
in unusual or temporary phases of political development, there tends to be
some counter-balance to the power of the bureaucracy, even if only in
terms of a quasi-bureaucracy like the army or a monolithic political party.
The degree of expectations engendered inside and outside the bureaucracy
in terms of what an administrative organization in government can or
should effect in the direction of political outputs will inevitably be conditioned by cultural factors. There is little tendency to underrate the power
of bureaucracy. If anything the danger lies in the reverse, in the temptation
to see the bureaucracy as an inhibiting force in the development of responsible political institutions.

## Comparative government

There are many criteria by which governments can be compared and
categorized. Additional criteria can be created by which differences within
any main type of government can be identified, for instance, the differences
between the operation of the liberal democratic procedures in, say Britain
and Bulgaria, or Britain and Chile; or comparing the operation of totalitarianism between the USSR and China. Then similarities and contrasts
can be established across the main types.

Military regimes can be analysed on the basis of being direct, e.g.
Kampuchea, or quasi-civilized, e.g. Pakistan; the degrees of reliance on
coercion as opposed to other bases of power, e.g. Indonesia, and autonomy
for any groups within the state, e.g. Buddhists in Burma or Kurds in
Turkey. Sub-classified groups are

1  High sub-group dependency, e.g. Central African Republic and Burkina
   Faso (Upper Volta)
2  Moderate sub-group dependency, e.g. Peru and Syria, where priests,
   unions and students play significant roles
3  Low sub-group dependency e.g. Indonesia which functions along with
   various civilian action-groups; this category includes dual military
   regimes. e.g. South Korea, where the government or head of state draws
   support from two sources: the military and institutionalized civilian
   forces
4  Dynastic regimes, e.g. Kuwait and Saudi Arabia

Degrees of democracy can be classified as

1  Façade democracies, e.g. Morocco, where power and political influence
   combine with a highly politically pluralistic regime and actively competing political parties
2  Quasi-democracies, such as Guinea and Senegal

3   Totalitarian regimes. These include the Soviet Union and East European countries. Groups are institutional and include the party, civil bureaucracy, military, trade unions, the secret police.

Regimes can be distinguished by the degree of competitiveness. Groups can also be distinguished by the dependence-autonomy of associations other than the institutional ones, e.g. nationalities in Yugoslavia have emerged as partially autonomous entities which effectively check the central power; in Poland the Church enjoys a partial autonomy and acts as a critic of the regime and a rival focus of loyalties; and in Czechoslovakia the writers' circles have established a measure of autonomy.

Liberal democratic regimes vary from those functioning stably since 1945, including Finland and Belgium, to those functioning with periods of instability, e.g. Colombia and Turkey, to states such as Malta and Singapore, and lastly to those with a tendency to instability and one-party rule, e.g. Surinam and Nicaragua.

It has to be remembered that there are enormous differences between the way a liberal democratic regime operates in say the United Kingdom or Somalia. In liberal democracies, as in other forms of government, formal procedures and formal authority are important; while in totalitarian and military regimes, formal and juridicial norms are everywhere interpreted elastically and sometimes totally ignored. Note of the political process has to be taken in comparative analysis. This process is a contest through which the various social groupings seek, as far as possible, to universalize their own interests or values by getting them sanctioned by the authority of the state by giving them the status of law. The most significant procedures involve those in which individuals use or form groups to further or give political expression to or secure their objectives.

Relationships involve the systems of civil liberties representation and political expression plus inner governmental relationships.

Sub-groups in society can also be compared by reference to their access to the policy makers, specific interest and inner groups and the network of governmental agencies.

Social structure, wealth and communications and similar societal variables of course affect the way in which a country is governed. Social structure generates the substantive issues of politics. Harsh material conditions, low per capita income, glaring disparities in the distribution of wealth or status may set low limits to mutual forbearance.

## Questions

### Constitution and liberties

1   What are the main advantages of a pluralist democracy?
2   Outline the Dahl theory on pluralism.

### Administrative and civil service

1   Why are civil services necessary?

2  Compare and contrast administration in the West and communist countries.
3  Should civil servants be apolitical?
4  Under federal systems, is the civil service weakened?
5  Is governmental overload detrimental to the civil service?

**Bureaucracy**

1  Why does the term bureaucratic or bureaucracy have perjorative connotations?
2  Account for the spread of bureaucracy in the world.
3  Discuss the Weberian approach to bureaucratic issues.
4  Is Friedrich's 'compartmentalism of the bureaucracy' an accurate description?

**Comparative government**

1  Account for the variations in the types of constitutions.
2  Examine the interrelationship between conventions and procedures.
3  Critically appraise the Montesquieu model for the separation of powers.
4  Assess comparatively federal and unitary systems of government.
5  Produce your own criteria for comparing and categorizing governments in different parts of the world.

**Further reading**

Albrow, M., *Bureaucracy*, Macmillan, London, 1970.
Andrews, W. G., *European Political Institutions*, Van Nostrand, New York, 1962.
Brogan, D. W. and Verney, D. V., *Political Patterns in Today's World*, Harcourt Brace, New York, 1968.
Daalder, H. and Mair P. (eds), *Western European Party Systems: Continuity and Change*, European Consortium for Political Research, 1983.
Delury, G. E. (ed), *World Encyclopedia of Political Systems* (2 vols), Longman, London, 1983.
Finer, S. E., *Comparative Government*, Penguin, London, 1982.
Hitchner, D. G. and Levine, C., *Comparative Government and Politics*, Harper & Row, New York, 1981.
Ionescu, G., *The Politics of the European Communist States*, Weidenfeld & Nicholson, London, 1969.
Kellner, P. and Crowther-Hunt, Lord., *The Civil Servants: An Inquiry into Britain's Ruling Class*, Macdonald, London, 1980.
Roberts, G. K., *What is Comparative Politics?*, Macmillan, London, 1972.
Smith, G., *Politics in Western Europe*, Heinemann, London, 1983.

# 18
# Comparative and representative governments – the West

The political system of the United States has been marked by a large land area, a short history, a young and mobile people, a succession of moving frontiers and vast resources in wealth and opportunity. It has also been marked by competing individuals and interest groups; uneven and uncertain images of legitimacy and habits of compliance; great influence and power conceded to money; conflicting ideas and values often held by the same people; tolerance of a wide variety of surface idiosyncrasies and fashions; serious readiness to learn and change quickly and boldly in particular sectors; and widespread insistence on visible overall continuity of the nation's basic morality and culture. Political moods in the United States swing back and forth between optimism and pessimism; trust in education and distrust of the educated; and confident faith in the improvement of human beings through knowledge and kindness. Despite its diversities and inner conflicts the political system has preserved its unity; despite tragedies and errors it has often been a force for good in the world.

In terms of economic capability the United States is the largest political system in the world. The country has on a per capita basis one of the highest average living standards in the world. In population and in area the United States is the world's fourth largest political system. Only three countries – the Soviet Union, Canada and China – are bigger in area, and only three countries – China, India and the Soviet Union – are larger in population.

In less than two centuries the American political system has succeeded in organizing a country on the scale of a continent. The United States is the child of the eighteenth-century Enlightenment, the only secular ideology that has created a huge country and kept it intact. Its political system was shaped by the ideas of applied social scientists who were familiar with the most advanced theory of their time: Franklin, Jefferson, Hamilton, James Wilson and Madison – all were men who had studied carefully what was then called 'the science of government'. The American colonists were moulded into a new people by their common experience in the New World, the growing communication among the colonies, the distance from Europe and finally the growing revolutionary movement. Americans became recognizable as a people as they became more and more associated with certain distinctive traits – great geographic mobility, high degree of literacy and a high degree of political participation, in rural areas as well as in towns; and there was the habit of self government and the widespread ability to form and maintain self-governing groups for a variety of political, economic and social purposes.

The government of the United States is a **presidential form of government** based on the principles of separation of powers and checks and balances; the structure of the state is federal; the rule of law at least in principle supersedes the narrow self-interest of individuals and groups; the political process is marked by the competition of political parties and interest groups; and public opinion is an important if not always determining factor in the making of public policy. The growth of the regulatory power and administrative apparatus of government reflects the society's transformation from the life styles of small towns and farms to the life styles of big cities, factories and offices. Voting and policy making are based on the principles of universal suffrage and representative government; and elections are organized by the single member district, simple-plurality electoral system. The political party system is essentially two party, and the national legislature, the Congress, is bicameral and the houses are equal in their authority to pass legislation. Culture cleavage in the United States, most apparent in terms of religion and race, has had little impact on United States' politics, especially at national level. A culturally homogeneous elite has presided over United States' politics throughout the country's history, including the periods of political reform (democratization) and economic change (industrialization).

The Founding Fathers, who assembled in Philadelphia in 1787, brought to their task a notable heritage of political wisdom. From Britain and France (during the Enlightenment) came the inheritance of the notion of man's unlimited rational capabilities and the ideas of the rule of law. From the organization of governing institutions in the individual colonies, and after 1776 in the newly independent American states, the Fathers took as their model of good government a system that concentrated political power in representatives elected to a bicameral legislature, delegated administrative responsibility to a chief executive, restricted the suffrage to citizens who owned property, protected citizens' rights and liberties; all of which rested on the principles of popular sovereignty.

The men of liberty – those who wrote the Declaration of Independence – gave way to the men of order – those who wrote the Constitution. The Founding Fathers were confronted with a fundamental problem of political science: combining both strength and weakness in the same system of governing institutions and giving the newly constituted government the power to preserve but not the power to change its constitutional articles.

*Article 1*　The Congress; methods of selecting members of the House of representatives and Senate and powers of Congress.

*Article 2*　The President; method of selection; powers and responsibilities.

*Article 3*　The Supreme Court; types of cases falling under its jurisdiction.

*Article 4*　Rights and obligations of the states; admission of new states.

*Article 5*　Methods of amending the Constitution.

*Article 6*　The government's obligation to pay its debts; supremacy of constitution and federal law; state and national legislators bound by oath; the holding of public office not subject to religious belief.

*Article 7*   Ratification of the constitution.

Change in politics is possible but not easy, and this is shown in the proposed amendments to the constitution of which there have only been twenty-six in 200 years. This is owing to the fact that to be adopted, a proposed amendment to the constitution must be approved by two-thirds of the members of the Senate and House of Representatives and by a majority of representatives in the legislatures of three-fourths of the states. The first amendment of 1798 clarified the Supreme Court's original jurisdiction in cases involving states and foreign countries, and the last in 1971 lowered the voting age from 21 to 18 years.

The first ten amendments adopted in 1791 are enshrined in the Bill of Rights:

1  Freedom of religion, speech, the press.
2  Right of people to bear and keep arms.
3  Conditions for quartering soldiers in private homes in times of peace and war.
4  Freedom from unreasonable searches and seizures.
5  Rights of those accused of crime.
6  Rights of citizens brought to trial.
7  Right of trial by jury.
8  Protection against excessive bail and cruel and unusual punishments.
9  Rights of citizens remain valid whether or not protected by the constitution.
10  Powers not delegated to the federal government, or prohibited to the states, are reserved to the states or people.

According to the constitution, a bill becomes a law when the bill is passed by both the Senate and House of Representatives and signed into law by the President who thus formally registers his approval. The constitution establishes a form of representative government characterized by federalism (the powers of government divided between national and state governments) separation of powers of the legislative, executive and judicial branches of government; co-equal bicameralism to pass both houses of Congress; and judicial review with the courts having the authority to pass on the constitutionality of legislative and executive acts. Checks and balances are provided to prevent invasions of authority into each branch of government.

The presidency has become the centre of gravity in the political system. Legislative initiative on almost all public bills and the first steps in the definition of most major public policy positions comes not from Congress but from the executive branch of government.

The Supreme Court interprets the meanings of the constitution, and controls the economic regulatory powers of the federal government; where the power of Congress stops and the power of the President begins and the nature of the judicial process itself.

On party lines, Republican voters tend to be middle class (and upper class) white, better educated, Protestant, and middle aged or older. Democratic voters tend to be working class, less well educated, younger and drawn disproportionately from minority groups (blacks, Catholics, Jews and Hispanics).

The American political system is being held together by the high mobility of the population; the experience and expectation of joint rewards from the high national income; living standards and educational and social opportunities shared by most of the population; the social and cultural cohesiveness of the American people, by the interlocking of social roles, the similarity of expectations and experiences, and a community of habits, values, character and culture.

American government is also characterized by an informal separation of powers, which some political scientists call **pluralism**: a plurality of competing interest groups and a diversity of rival interests – regional, social, economic, religious and psychological. **Populism** can produce a consistent political will for limited populations, regions, periods of time and small sets of issues. This opinion was based on the fact that the will of a popular majority should prevail in all matters, including science, art and morals, and that neither experts nor minorities ought to have any valid claims against it. Here the popular initiative to move matters toward legislation and the referendum to decide on a new law by popular vote can be highly effective.

In its domestic politics the American system has more effective channels for the intake of information than does the political system of any other large industrial country. American political culture places high value on listening to people and on paying attention to the views at the grassroots. There are many channels bringing to the various levels and agencies of government a wide variety of information about domestic conditions, popular feelings, specific needs and demands of large interest groups and the problems of numerous small groups and individuals. Administrative officers and agencies receive a similar stream of information. The court system is also a channel through which complaints about alleged violations of legal and constitutional rights of individuals and groups can be raised and often brought to a decision. Then there are the lobbying organizations and lobbyists representing large corporate enterprise, industry, agriculture and various labour unions and public interest groups. In all these channels messages can be and often are initiated by parties at interest, that is, by individuals and groups outside the government. They can also be initiated by some part of the government that is in search of information. Other channels include the press and television, the universities and the churches and religious organizations.

As more Americans have become politically active, the political system has accepted a wider range of responsibilities. The American social and political habits that emphasize equality and mobility, respect for all kinds of work, including manual labour, and interest in discovery and practical solutions could be of real help to many societies whose politics have remained bound by more rigid barriers of class and status, tradition or ideology.

## France

France has a longer continuous development of being a liberal democracy than any other European country of its population, resources and world involvement, excepting Britain. Perhaps the best known image of the French between 1789 and 1960 has been one of individualism, unrest, ceaseless change and infinite variety. Its history is an almost classic example of political institutions that failed to adapt to new conditions of social life. Political change in France thus has been marked more by revolution than evolution.

Other images of France are that of the orderly French which sees them as precise, logical and bureaucratic; the segmentation of French life where changes in practices and habits rarely spill over quickly from one sector of activities to another; French elegance, taste, imagination and creativity; and French courage, loyalty and pride. French writers have stressed the distinction between *le pays legal*, the legal France, divided by disputes about politics and laws, and *le pays réal*, the real country, held together by a profound unity of tradition and culture.

The French were the first people on the Continent – and, after England, the second in Europe – to achieve a modern absolute monarchy for a large territorial state. A relatively modern centralized state was established before the industrial revolution and before any political middle-class revolution like those in Britain and the United States. The effects of the French revolution and the Napoleonic age further strengthened the power of the state and its machinery, partly modernizing it by increasing its claims to legitimacy and popular support. The result was a strong bureaucratic state that remained somewhat authoritarian in its dealings with people and somewhat remote from them.

The revolution had been the big catalyst for change. The Bourbon dynasty ruled by divine right and resisted any reduction in its absolute authority. The nobility lived in grandeur and maintained feudal prerogatives among the peasantry without providing the services traditional to the responsibilities of *noblesse oblige*. A new urban class of citizens was also developing. The wealth of the bourgeoisie (or people of the town), derived from money not from land (as in the case of the nobility) or from manual labour (as in the case of peasants). Yet the social status and political influence of the bourgeoisie did not coincide with its growing economic prominence. Mobilized by the financial crises of a bankrupt monarchy more interested in war than domestic reform, these several forces converged on the old regime in 1789, peasants burned the estates of the nobility while the lawyers, journalists, businessmen and intellectuals agitated for a new social and political order based on the rights of man – liberty, equality and fraternity. From 1789 to 1792 the constitutional monarchy struggled to maintain royal authority against the Constituent Assembly and the bourgeoise representatives. The execution of the King in 1793 helped to ensure civil war between royalists and revolutionaries. In many respects these two lines of reinforcing cleavages (clericals and monarchists against anti-clericals and republicans) laid the basis for much of the country's troubled history. France has produced many revolutions and many conservative reactions. Its revolutions flare up in Paris and a few other big cities and industrial areas. Its conservatism is supported by wealthy minorities in those centres, but draws its main strength from the small towns and countryside.

At many times the stakes in French politics have been unusually high.

In the post-revolutionary period these have included middle-class and peasant property rights against working claims for a more equitable distribution of income and welfare; a monarchic versus a republican form of government; a powerful church versus the separation of church and the state; civilian versus military rule; absolutism or dictatorship versus constitutional government; priority for domestic improvements versus military power politics in Europe or colonial expansion – all these were repeatedly at hazard in the political struggles often together with the character and future of the country.

Another stake in the politics from 1870 to 1945 was the fate of two major regions, Alsace and Lorraine, which had been annexed by Germany from 1871 to 1918 and 1940 to 1945, after having been French since the late seventeenth century, or earlier. An even larger stake during both World Wars and since 1945 has been the political and economic independence of the entire country, first *vis-a-vis* German attempts at conquest and occupation, and from the late 1940s into the 1980s against the spreading hegemony of the two superpowers of the period, the Soviet Union and the United States.

Political participation for a large part of the French people is more intermittent than it is in some other highly developed countries such as Britain or West Germany. Though local prefects concentrate a good deal of power in their hands, they are appointed from Paris, and they depend somewhat less on the political decisions of local voters and somewhat more on the plans, orders and regulations of the central government.

The current French Republic – the Fifth – was designed to avoid the weaknesses of its predecessors. Major executive powers were given to the President not to the Premier. The President has the right to dissolve the Assembly at will; the only limit is that it can be done only once a year. The President nominates the Premier and thus can control this minister and the cabinet. The President can call a referendum, issue decrees having the force of law, or declare a state of emergency. The constitution describes the President as the 'arbiter' charged with making the ultimate decision among conflicting interests and policies. During de Gaulle's period in office (1958–69) he also took on the role of 'guide' to the nation. The structure of the Fifth Republic is similar to the Third and Fourth, but the relative powers of its various organs have changed. There still is a two-chamber legislature, a Premier and cabinet, a President and a system of courts. Real power has shifted. The role of the Premier and the cabinet is weaker *vis-a-vis* the President, but stronger *vis-a-vis* the National Assembly. The Premier and cabinet members are appointed by the President, whom no legislative vote can overthrow. The legislature technically may force the cabinet's resignation but its powers are much less than they were under the Third and Fourth Republics. All cabinet decrees require the presidential signature.

The legislature consists of two chambers, the more important one being the National Assembly, members of which are elected directly by the people for five-year terms. The Assembly legislates on all matters of law, but these are enumerated restrictively by the constitution, which leaves all other matters to the rule-making power – the power to issue binding regulations – of the executive branch. Even the enumerated law-making powers may be delegated to the executive branch by an organic law – that is a law which affects the constitution and is passed by a majority of the members of both houses. The Assembly's order of business is determined by the administration.

The Senate's 283 members are elected indirectly by municipal and departmental councillors and representatives of the cities. The Senate has few powers – though a bill can become law only if passed in identical form by both houses. The real decision in the case of disagreement lies in the hands of the Premier, who is primarily an instrument of the President. It is elected for nine years and one-third stand for re-election every three years. The Senate has continued to represent the entrenched power structures of local government, which has remained a stronghold of the traditional political parties.

Other divisions of government have still less political power. The Constitutional Council supervises elections and referenda and decides disputes about them. It passes also on the constitutionality of any bill or treaty before promulgation, but only at the request of the President, Premier, President of the National Assembly or President of the Senate. Once a bill has become law, the council can judge its constitutionality only in restricted cases and on the request of the government.

French administration is organized like the British under ministries – the most important being Interior, Finance and Foreign Affairs. The key official in charge of the administration of each of the ninety departments is the Prefect; and the Corps of Prefects forms one of the five great bodies – les grands corps – of the French state. The mayor – *le maire* – of any of the 36,000 French communes is elected but then must represent not only that municipality but also the state. The tutelage of central government over all municipal authorities ensures a high degree of uniformity of administration throughout France. The Council of State advises the head of the state, and/or the government on matters of public policy and legislation and resolves conflicts within the administration. There is a proud and competent top-level bureaucracy, open in theory but largely closed in fact. The civil service and the armed forces form a heavy counterweight to the changing contest among the political parties of the right, left and centre that has moved France this way and that during nearly two centuries.

But although these general political tendencies seem perennial in France, issues and problems do change, as in other Western countries. Nevertheless in French society the middle class is strongest, but in French politics the centre seems weak. The politically active French are on the right and the left. In the middle are the politically passive – often about one-fifth of the electorate. As a result French politics is often deadlocked. As in other countries, only more so, French politics tend to oscillate between immobilism and emergency.

French elections come in two stages – on election day voters cast their first ballot for the candidate whom each prefers. If no candidate wins an absolute majority, a run off election follows: voters vast a second ballot for the compromise candidate whom they find most acceptable among contestants.

What of the new France? The country still has larger shares of its population working in agriculture, living in small towns and remaining self employed than does Germany or Britain. It still has a social structure that makes unity difficult and a political culture that encourages distrust of government and withdrawal from politics.

## United Kingdom

Two factors have influenced British politics and the behaviour of British people. These two major influences are their class structure and their history. Class distinctions in Britain are more marked and pervasive than in almost any other highly industrialized nation. Those who seek progress within and through the class system tend to support the Conservative Party, while those who believe the traditional class system to be unjust support the Labour Party. British voters cannot be persuaded to ignore class. The Liberal Party, and to a lesser extent the recently formed Social and Liberal Democrats, which have tried to do just that, have been limited to about 10 per cent of the national vote or less.

Traditionally there have been four main strata in British society: the aristocratic and imperial group – the establishment, forming 1 per cent of the population; the upper middle class including military officers, the professional people, employers and managers, forming 6 per cent of the population; the lower middle classes totally 34 per cent of the population, including tradespeople and non-manual workers; and lastly, forming 59 per cent of the population are the manual workers. From this society the British have produced a four-layer culture, at the top a libertarian culture of the avant garde; the Victorian respectability of the upper middle class; a tight lower middle class respectability and at the bottom an irrepressible working class. Thus, there is no single English character.

For more than a century this class structure changed slowly; but since the late 1950s the rate of change has been accelerated, and during the current decade radical alterations are taking place, particularly in attitudes to work and the spread of wealth. Current British politics has ebbed and flowed, but other changes in terms of a search for social identity have also occurred.

The British state is in some ways a unique combination of a response to given conditions and a political inventiveness. The state derived its flexibility from its geography, rich in its variety of coastlines, plains and mountains. Geography permitted options of basic policy: the British could choose whether they wanted the state to be strong or weak, centralized or decentralized.

The first modern state was built by the Norman conquerors in the eleventh century. For example, they established a sophisticated administration of royal taxes and spending called the exchequer. This was the first modern office of the treasury in Europe outside of Italy. Contracts everywhere in England could be enforced in the king's courts. Centralization and solidarity were the unique gifts of Norman administration and they became two of the key aspects of British government. The English refused to assimilate to its conquerors – rather the conquerors were assimilated to the people. The interplay of Normans and Saxons created in England a set of political institutions which continued to grow and function long after the differences between Normans and Saxons had faded. Institutions included from an early time the centralized monarchy, the exchequer and common law. There was in Norman times the tradition of inquiry – the systematic asking of questions, listening to evidence, and searching for facts. William the Conqueror, foreshadowing the best modern practice in government and social science, began his reign with a statistical survey. The results were recorded in his *Domesday Book* (1086), which counted every piece of real estate and every potential taxpayer as well as the population as a whole. It was an inventory of the national resources of England, a report that could have gone to a national resources planning board, had one existed at the time. The notion of enquiry lies at the heart of the British political and administrative tradition. *Magna Carta* (1215) marked the rise of the secular tradition that every individual's life and death matters – it secured the liberties of the English Church, the rights of the baronial classes, and restricted abuses of royal power. Parliament too developed from a tradition of enquiry. Arising out of the king's great council around 1240, it was based on the principle that 'what touches all should be approved by all'. This is still a reasonable principle of government. Hearings, consultations and eventually a grant to people of a widening share of decision making are characteristic of the British tradition of government and have had a profound effect on British society, e.g. the nineteenth-century Royal Commissions of Enquiry, and the creation of the welfare state immediately after the Second World War.

The English revolution took half the seventeenth century to run its full course. It was a real revolution for it did not merely replace some rulers by some others, but it also changed the habits and political culture of the people, the structure of many political and social institutions, and the structure of the relationships among them. It made England the first great modern nation. Its first phase – the war of Parliament against the King – and the days of Cromwell are called the **Great Rebellion** and its second period – the almost bloodless expulsion of the last Stuart king in 1688 is called the **Glorious Revolution**. The two waves of revolution left their invisible but real monuments in the world of ideas. The political theories of Thomas Hobbes and of John Locke are responses of the times, but they have influenced political thought and action, directly and indirectly, at many times and places ever since. In 150 years the reforms of absolute monarchs and two waves of revolution had merged England into Britain and made it the most modern country of the world. In the course of these events, kings lost power to the Crown, and the Crown lost most of it to Parliament.

Under the British system there are no legal limits on the power of Parliament. The country has neither a separation of powers nor a written constitution – both of which occur in the United States. Indeed, Britain has no such thing as judicial review of the acts of Parliament.

The two chambers of Parliament are the House of Lords and the House of Commons. The Lords represented and was composed of the peers of England; by contrast the Commons' members were elected. Power shifted to the Commons from the Lords increasingly in the eighteenth and nineteenth centuries. As the monarch became increasingly obliged to choose ministers only with the advice of the Commons and then to follow the advice of these Parliament-controlled ministers in his or her own political actions, the Commons gradually acquired the powers of the Crown. Additional power came from the fact that governments always need more money, and from early days the Commons alone could introduce money bills. In the nineteenth century it gained exclusive control over appropriation and this was formally recognized by law in 1911. Other types of legislation had to be passed by majorities in both houses, so the Lords had, in effect, a right of veto. This right gradually eroded. Ordinary people became less inclined to obey the Lords, but remained willing to support the Commons.

The primary result of these shifts in power has been the transformation of the cabinet from a council of advisers to the king or queen, chosen by and responsible to the monarch, into an instrument of the House of Commons. The cabinet is now the chief executive power headed by the Prime Minister, and is a committee of Parliament. In theory it is Parliament's creature. Parliament can make or unmake it. If Parliament votes no confidence in the cabinet, the cabinet must resign.

In practice the Prime Minister and the cabinet depend on the support of their party. To function well, the British system requires political parties and party discipline. Parties began to emerge among the still narrow political elites in the late seventeenth century. The **Whigs** (who took their name from Scottish lowland opponents of the monarch) favoured increasing the power of Parliament and reducing that of the monarch. They drew their support from urban and mercantile interests and a minority of the great landed families. The **Tories** (named after bands of outlaws favouring Catholicism and the traditional monarchy) formed the court party. They stressed the claims of the hereditary nobility and the divine right of kings. In the course of the nineteenth century the Tories became the modern Conservative Party and the Whigs the Liberals.

Candidates for the Commons depended on party support for election and re-election – and followed the orders of their party while in Parliament. Each party organized its members in the House into a disciplined group called the parliamentary party, in contrast to the national party outside Parliament. The parliamentary party elects party whips to instruct members how to vote. Free votes left to the discretion of each member are rare. The majority party designates the Prime Minister who is then formally entrusted by the monarch with the task of forming a government.

Specifically the Prime Minister chooses the members of the Cabinet and assigns them the tasks. He or she may change assignments or drop them from the Cabinet and replace them by others. In all this the Prime Minister needs the support of Parliament and above all his or her own parliamentary party. A Prime Minister is ordinarily the leader of his or her party both within and outside Parliament. But a parliamentary party may revolt against a Prime Minister or a national party may induce the members of the parliamentary party to do so. Members of the House of Commons do not like to risk their seats and hence do not overthrow governments lightly.

Within each party, especially over the past two or three years, pendulum swings can be detected. At present there are two kinds of Conservatives. One kind is highly traditional, nationalistic, nostalgic for empire, hostile to non-whites and indeed to most foreigners. The other wing of the Conservative Party favours modernization, reform, economic integration with Europe, cooperation with non-white countries of the Commonwealth and a continuation of the more moderate policies of the welfare state. The Labour Party has its own internal divisions. Its left wing is concerned with the ideology of socialism and advocates further nationalization of industry. It stresses class interests and the working class character of the party. It favours planning and distrusts the play of forces in the market. It opposes defence spending and the remnants of empire. The right wing of the Labour Party is strong among many of the better paid groups of labour and public employees as well as among a majority of intellectuals. Right wing leaders argue for pragmatism, reliance on market forces and consumer interests, greater cooperation with the United States and Western Europe, greater caution toward nationalization of industries and further expansion of the public sector. Common interest is stressed among classes and restraint urged in the further wage demands of trade unions. Both parties have to manage to work with both wings of the party and make heavy use of party discipline. The Labour Party can ill afford to quarrel too seriously with the Trades Union Congress, any more than the Conservative leadership can afford to quarrel too seriously with the financial interests in the City and industrial centres throughout the country.

The basic domestic arrangements about the distribution of economic wealth, political power, social status, educational opportunity and the future directions of British society and culture have become the main stakes of British politics. What national role has Britain to play? It has a choice between the dangers of underachievement and overcommitment. How much economic growth? Britain has grown less than most other major industrial countries. Many workers have chosen to strike at the expense of seeing a growth of the national economy, and the press has identified with the business community's point of view. Britain's wealth creators have been reluctant to invest in many branches of industry, fearing that these might be nationalized without adequate compensation or made un-profitable by too low wages and low productivity. British industries thus have less modern equipment, and the ingenuity of scientists and engineers fails to be applied and bear fruit in production. These failures tend to restrict exports and foreign exchange earnings and promote inflation, and keep real wages low in comparison with those in other countries. Other questions that are raised are: More equality or less? One work force or two? What about the problems of underpaid service jobs and immigrant labour? Traditional or change oriented culture patterns? These stakes are all interdependent and depend heavily on available means and capabilities.

If the end of the dominance of the two-party system is in sight then what of the alternative alliance parties? Problems have to be resolved be-tween Liberals and Social Democrats over issues of programmes, leader-ship and distribution of seats. This has already happened in the 1987 general election, the 1989 European Parliament elections and in some local elections. Once in power, will the Social and Liberal Democrats prove more capable than their predecessors of solving economic problems that have troubled most other countries in the industrialized world and that appear to be beyond the range of capabilities of modern governments whatever the governments' institutional characteristics? Thus over the next decade the advantage might shift to an ideologically purified and radical Labour Party whose far reaching alternatives to Thatcherism and 'muddling through' could prove attractive to a plurality of British voters.


## Hong Kong

Hong Kong is a colony of Great Britain whose principal administrator, the Governor, is appointed by the Queen and is responsible to the government in London, although in practice he or she and his or her subordinate officials enjoy a good measure of autonomy.

The legal basis for the existence of the colony is found in three treaties which Britain imposed on China following the latter's defeat in war. The first, the Treaty of Nanking (Nanjing) which followed the First Anglo-Chinese War, or 'Opium War', was signed in 1842 and ceded the island of Hong Kong to Britain. In 1860, the Kowloon Peninsula and Stonecutter's Island were annexed by the British under the First Convention of Peking (Beijing) which followed China's defeat in the Second Anglo-Chinese War in that same year. In 1898, after China's defeat in the Sino-Japanese War, the British pressed the Chinese to agree to the Second Convention of Beijing allowed them to occupy 365.5 square miles of territory North of the Kowloon Peninsula and on islands adjacent to the colony which were designated the 'New Territories'. The New Territories, some 90 per cent of the total land area, are held under a 99-year lease which expires in 1997. China has never recognized the legitimacy of the unequal treaties which created Hong Kong, and the collapse remains a symbol of the great humiliation China has suffered at the hands of foreign imperialists. Since 1949, the Chinese could have recaptured it with little difficulty but tolerated its existence for economic and political reasons. Indeed they spent years hoping for Britain to reach agreement on the colony's future which eventually was achieved in 1984.

In September 1984 representatives of the United Kingdom and Chinese governments initialled the draft text of an agreement on the future of Hong Kong – the outcome of two years of negotiations undertaken with the common aim of maintaining the stability and prosperity of Hong Kong. The agreements were formally signed in Peking in December 1984 and in London in June 1985. It is a formal international agreement, legally binding in all its parts.

The United Kingdom has agreed to restore Hong Kong to the People's Republic of China with effect from 1 July 1997. The Chinese agreed to establish a Hong Kong Special Administrative Region vested with executive, legislative and independent judicial power. The current social and economic systems are to remain unchanged and so is the lifestyle. The new Region is to retain the status of a freeport and an international financial centre with independent finances. Under the name Hong Kong, China, the Region may on its own maintain and develop economic and cultural relations and conclude relevant agreements with states, regions and relevant international organizations.

Hong Kong's government structure, with a colonial governor at its apex working in consultation with the non-elective official and unofficial members of the Executive and Legislative Councils, is typical for a British colony. The chief executive and head of government is the Governor, who is responsible for the administration of the colony and the conduct of its officials. He or she has the power to make laws 'for the peace, order and good government of the colony', in consultation with the Legislative Council. The governor establishes both the Executive and Legislative Councils.

The Executive Council meets weekly, advises the Governor on administrative matters, and the Governor is expected to consult on all but emergency issues. The Council consisted in 1980 of fifteen members, six official (the chief secretary, the financial secretary, the commander of British forces, the attorney general, the secretary for home affairs, the director of medical and health services) and nine unofficial members. Official, or *ex officio* members are appointed to the Council by virtue of being high officials. Unofficial members are prominent in private society and represent the interests of significant sectors of the population. The Governor has the final decision in all matters discussed by the Council.

The legislature of Hong Kong, the Legislative Council, is a consultative rather than a law making body. It is the Governor who makes laws, and submits bills to the Council only in order to obtain its 'advice and consent'.

Another feature of the Legislative Council is that its members are not popularly elected. They come from among the most prominent and influential members of Hong Kong's financial, industrial and professional elites.

The chief justice, judges of the High Court and justices of appeal are appointed by the Governor. The Urban Council is a local government body with 50 per cent popularly elected members.

Elective institutions are very limited, no significant political parties have been organized in the colony and there has been very little popular support or pressure for the initiation of democratic reforms. The nature of colonial government puts stress on executive authority and hierarchical administration. Another reason for the lack of parties is that the Chinese, who comprise 98 per cent of the population of Hong Kong, have no tradition of parliamentary institutions, preferring to work within and through their own voluntary associations rather than make demands directly on government. Another important factor in the people's apparent political apathy has been their lack of a citizen consciousness. The lack of a sense of allegiance to the political unit in which they live no doubt contributes to a lack of interest in political participation. The People's Republic of China has also held tremendous leverage over the colony and Peking does not wish to see the development of a democratic or independence movement which could lead Hong Kong in the direction of becoming a 'third China' (Taiwan being the 'second' China).

Business interests are of special importance in Hong Kong, which is considered one of the bastions of free-market capitalism.

In the post-agreement period, Hong Kong's future depends exclusively on the attitude of China. China is concerned to preserve Hong Kong's stability, and there is a feeling that Hong Kong will play a significant role in China's modernization.

The colony's stability will depend a great deal on continued success as a manufacturing and financial centre. A world economic crisis, a rise in protectionist sentiments, or the failure to remain competitive with such places as Taiwan, South Korea or Singapore could lead to unemployment, declining standards of living and great unrest.

## Australia

Liberal democracy is a British export and some states have maintained this form of government for well over a century. Australia has a mature political culture and its political consensus and degree of organization are high.

A nation of 15 million people it is both a federal and a parliamentary democracy. In 1901, six self-governing British colonies – New South Wales, Victoria, Queensland, South Australia, Western Australia and Tasmania – federated to form the Commonwealth of Australia. The six colonies remained as component parts of the federal system. There are also two territories – the Northern Territory and the Australian Capital Territory – directly administered for most of their history by the Commonwealth (national) government.

The Act of the British Parliament which authorized federation also provided Australia with a written constitution. This specified the allocation of powers between the Commonwealth and the states. The Commonwealth powers are mainly the obvious 'national' ones – currency, defence, foreign affairs, immigration, international trade, postal service, etc. Few of these powers are exclusive and most are concurrent with continuing state powers. The states retain all powers not exclusively transferred to the Commonwealth, leaving them with immediate authority over most personal and property matters.

There has been a gradual expansion of the significance of the Commonwealth government, partly achieved by constitutional amendment. Amendments are difficult to approve requiring the passage of a referendum by a majority of voters nationwide and a majority of voters in at least four of the six states. The High Court, which exercises judicial review over constitutional matters, also has assisted the increasing prominence of the Commonwealth government. The Commonwealth has been permitted to use the primacy of its concurrent legislation to monopolize the collection of income taxes and in turn made the states dependent on the 'reimbursement' of these funds through a revenue-sharing arrangement. In addition the constitution enables the Commonwealth to 'grant financial assistance' to any state on such terms and conditions as Parliament approved. The federal balance is thus largely a political rather than a strictly constitutional matter.

The federal system coexists with parliamentary institutions originally developed under the British unitary system. The national legislature (Parliament) consists of two chambers: a House of Representatives in which the majority party (following Westminster conventions) forms the government, and a Senate in which there is an equal allocation of seats to each state.

The Australian head of state is technically the British monarch whose role is carried out by the Governor-general, appointed by the monarch on the advice of the Australian government. It is the firm convention of the parliamentary system that this head of state acts only on the advice of his or her ministers and, in particular, of the Prime Minister.

The Prime Minister is by convention the leader of the majority party or coalition in the House of Representatives. Other ministers are drawn from either house of Parliament, mostly from the House of Representatives.

The Cabinet, chaired by the Prime Minister, is the central organ of government. All major decisions about policy and legislation are dealt with at this level. Because the government, by definition, controls the House of Representatives (and usually the Senate as well), the Cabinet is able to operate as the effective locus of decision making within the constraint of broad party expectations. Technically under the constitution, executive power is wielded by the Executive Council, consisting of the Governor-general and his or her ministers. In practice, the Executive Council meets only to satisfy this technical requirement, providing a forum in which the Governor-general follows ministerial advice in assenting to legislation, making proclamations and appointments and so on.

Ministers are nearly always given particular responsibility for a department or departments within the Commonwealth bureaucracy. The House of Representatives is the forum from which the government emerges. Under the constitution it must be double the size of the Senate and each of the six states must have at least five members. The Senate acts as the house of review on legislation originating in the House of Representatives, but the constitution states that the two houses shall have equal powers except in a few specific instances; the Senate, for example, cannot originate money bills.

Constitutionally, Parliament is the lynchpin of the democratic system, a great debating forum in which legislation is discussed and amended and policies debated and criticized. In practice, the locus of power is with the executive – owing to the retrenchment of Parliament of disciplined political parties, making no clear separation between the executive and its origins in the legislature; the growth of governmental activity, and the internal procedures of the Parliament itself.

The chief constitutional crisis which faced Australia occurred in 1975 when the opposition, which controlled the Senate, decided to force what it perceived as an unpopular government to resign and contest a new election. It refused to pass the budget in the Senate. The government, refused to resign. The situation was resolved dramatically and controversially by the unprecedented intervention of the head of state. The Governor-general dismissed the Prime Minister Gough Whitlam and his government. He installed the leader of the opposition as Prime Minister of a caretaker government, even though the leader of the opposition had only minority support in the House of Representatives.

The High Court exercises judicial review over matters relating to the constitution as well as being a final court of appeal from other jurisdictions. In many respects the High Court was directly modelled on the United States Supreme Court. In terms of providing essential services and of maintaining direct contacts with citizens, the states are the most visible level of government in Australia. The present state governments are the historical successors to the colonial governments whose federation created the nation. Services which in many Western countries would be provided by national or local authorities are in Australia firmly entrenched at state level.

State governments operate under their own constitutions, most of which date from the 1850s and which must now adapt to the existence of the Australian constitution. Each state operates under a parliamentary system, and in five of the states, the parliament is bicameral with the composition of the government being determined in the lower house. The Premier (the state equivalent of the Prime Minister) and his Cabinet are the visible focus of government, though again a governor acts as the formal representative of the monarch.

Australians directly elect representatives to a number of legislative bodies – two houses at the Commonwealth level, two at the state level and the local council. Registration and voting are compulsory; there is a long history of universal adult suffrage and the use of the secret ballot; and to avoid gerrymandering, electoral boundaries are drawn up by independent commissioners.

The emergence of the Labour Party in the 1890s served to solidify conservative interests. By 1901 the Australian Labour Party was opposed by two relatively coherent groups, the Free Traders and Protectionists, which fused in 1910 to form the Liberal Party. Thereafter the major party on the right underwent several changes in structure and name, absorbing various breakaways from the Australian Labour Party until in 1945 the modern Liberal Party was established. The Australian Labour Party and the Liberal Party remain the two most important parties today. The Liberal Party operates in coalition with the National Country Party, which remains a significant force. Nowhere is a party defined or made subject to any constitutional provisions. Neither are the Australian parties subject to any particular legal forms or requirements.

## New Zealand

New Zealand, a parliamentary democracy, has had a unitary government since the abolition of the federated provinces in 1876. Its constitutional framework is not a written document but a collection of acts of Parliament, British precedents and accepted conventions. The country was a British colony from 1841 to 1907 when it was granted dominion status and achieved complete autonomy in 1947.

Executive power resides in a Cabinet headed by the Prime Minister, who is leader of the majority party in Parliament. Only elected members of Parliament may hold portfolios in the twenty-member Cabinet. The head of state is the reigning sovereign of Britain represented by a Governor-general appointed for a five-year term, and he or she appoints judges, and cabinet ministers, including the Prime Minister.

Legislative power is vested in a ninety-two member unicameral Parliament, the House of Representatives, elected triennially. An appointed upper house, the Legislative Council, was abolished in 1950. Constitutionally, Parliament is a bipartite body, Cabinet and House share in the legislative process.

The judicial branch is independent of both government and Parliament. New Zealand was the first non-Scandinavian country to establish the office of ombudsman in 1962. The ombudsman investigates individual complaints against administrative decisions and is not concerned with official policy. Responsible to Parliament, the ombudsman does not serve as a constitutional check on government.

New Zealand is organized territorially into different classes of local authority depending on the concentration of population.

The structure of the electoral system is not part of the constitution. It is prescribed by statute alone and may be amended by Parliament. Each of the ninety-two electoral districts or electorates is represented by one member in the House of Representatives.

Since the late nineteenth century, the major political issues in New Zealand have been its long tradition of government intervention in the economy and the desirable extent of social legislation, in which the country has always played a pioneering role. The approach to these questions, by both the leftist parties and their right wing opposition, has generally been pragmatic rather than ideological.

New Zealand has maintained its two-party system through several realignments, the most recent in the 1930s, when Labour and National parties developed out of issues related to the world depression. The country's political tradition is British, and, as in Britain, the parties originated within Parliament. Parties are not banned because of extremist beliefs. Political organizations combine the elements of the mass-based and the cadre-based type of party. Parties draw up their own constitutions. Traditional Party loyalties have been declining since the 1950s.

New Zealand is currently facing a dilemma of its own ambiguous position in world affairs and declining position in the world economy. Its dilemma is whether to relax its traditional dependence on Britain; or renounce the United States alliance, and assume leadership of the Pacific Third World. There are also calls for parliamentary reform and proportional representation, and cracks are even appearing in the traditional high respect for authority found in New Zealanders. Maori self awareness is growing.

## Singapore

Singapore is a parliamentary republic in which one party, the People's Action Party (PAP) has been dominant since it first came to power in 1959. The territory consists of Singapore Island and about fifty offshore islets located at the southern tip of the Malay Peninsula. Out of a population of 2½ million, Chinese make up 76.2 per cent; 15 per cent are Malay, 7 per cent Indian or Sri Lankan and the rest Westerners.

The present republic had its origins in the British colony established by Sir Thomas Stamford Raffles in 1819. In 1957, Britain granted independence to the Federation of Malaya, and Singapore attained home rule two years later. Malayan leaders were reluctant to attempt a union with Singapore because of its large Chinese population and active left wing movements, but in 1963 the Federation was formed, which only lasted two years. Differences between the state government of Singapore and the central government in Kuala Lumpur and the governing parties led to the departure of Singapore from Malaysia in 1965. The Prime Minister, Lee Kuan Yew had hoped to keep the federation viable, but with its collapse he set about to assure the survival of the new Republic of Singapore. His policy was to create a 'multiethnic, multilingual secular state'.

Singapore's constitution is embodied in the following documents: the Constitution of the State of Singapore when it was part of Malaysia, certain articles of the Constitution of Malaysia considered applicable to the republic and the 1965 Singapore Independence Act and Constitution. With separation, the Governor of the State of Singapore was renamed the President of the Republic and the state legislature became the national Parliament. Singapore is unusual in that it shares with another state, Malaysia, certain provisions of its constitution; but this is not meant to compromise its independence.

The head of state is the President, elected for four years. He or she is in theory the chief executive and has the authority to appoint the Prime Minister and deny him or her request to dissolve Parliament. Below the President is the Presidential Council for Minority Rights, established in 1967, which reviews all legislation to determine whether it discriminates against the rights of any ethnic or religious group in the republic. The constitution requires that all parliamentary bills, with the exception of those involving the budget, national defence or public security, be examined by the Council, which also serves as an advisory body to the government on ethnic affairs. The Cabinet, headed by the Prime Minister, is the focus of real political power. The Prime Minister is designated by Parliament and answers to it for government policy.

Singapore has a single-chamber Parliament of seventy-five popularly elected members, and the legislature is presided over by a speaker. Parliament has a five year term. Singapore's judicial system is based on the British model and the Judicial Committee of the Privy Council in London is the ultimate court of appeal which can reverse decisions of the Singapore Supreme Court.

Given its small size, Singapore does not have formal structures of local government. The national government has established a number of institutions which serve to keep it in touch with the grass roots; the most important being the Citizen's Consultative Committees found in each electoral district, run on a theoretically non-partisan basis and directly the Prime Minister's responsibility.

## Questions

### USA

1   How has the political system preserved its unity?
2   What are the advantages and disadvantages of a presidential form of government?
3   What problems faced the Founding Fathers?

4   A Bill of Rights has both strength and weaknesses. Do you agree?
5   Assess the characteristics of American government.
6   Analyse the effective channels for the intake of information in the
    American system.

## France

1   Account for the swinging pendulum between left and right in French
    politics.
2   What have been the main repercussions of the revolution on French
    political life?
3   Discuss the reasons for the intermittent nature of political participation
    in France.
4   What are the unique features of the Fifth Republic?
5   Examine the nature of French administration.
6   Is there such an issue as the new France?

## United Kingdom

1   Why is class a dominating factor in Britain?
2   Account for the uniqueness of the English parliamentary institutions.
3   Describe the power of Cabinet government in Britain.
4   What are the pros and cons of the double feedback process in Great
    Britain?
5   Assess the reason for the demise of the two-party system.

## Hong Kong

1   Analyse the uniqueness of Hong Kong's politics over the past ninety
    years.
2   Assess the value and importance of the Hong Kong–China agreement.
3   Write an essay on Hong Kong's Executive Council and legislature.

## Australia

1   Describe the federal nature of Australian politics.
2   What were the issues behind the 1975 constitutional crisis?

## New Zealand

1   Analyse the extent of legislative and executive power in the politics of
New Zealand.

## Further reading

Palmer, Geoffrey, *Unbridled Power? An interpretation of New Zealand's
    constitution and government*, Oxford University Press, 1979.
Sinclair, Keith, *A History of New Zealand*, Penguin, London, 1959.

# 19
# Comparative and representative governments – the East

## The Soviet Union

The Soviet Union is proof that in government, as in magic, appearances can be deceiving. The Soviet constitution is highly democratic. There is universal suffrage and elections are held periodically. There are discernible differences in the structures and functioning of legislative, executive and judicial institutions. Citizens' liberties and rights are constitutionally specified and judicially protected.

But, there is only one party and it is doubtful that it deserves to be called a political party. Elections then are not competitive. There is no institutionalized opposition to the existing elite or its policies. Citizen access to top decision makers is limited if it exists at all. Much of the country's history has been characterized by one-man rule, terror and repression.

Russia is the dominant language group that, under the Muscovite regime, gradually extended its territorial and political control in the Middle Ages. The ethnic Russians constitute only a bare majority (52 per cent) of the Soviet Union's 275 million people. In fact seventy languages are spoken by ninety-two different ethnic Groups including Russians, Ukrainians, Uzbeks, Byelorussians, Kazakhs, Tatars, Azertis, Armenians, Georgians, Lithuanians, Yakuts and Gaguzis. Religions cover the spread from the Orthodox Christian faith to Muslim, Roman Catholic, Protestant, Jewish and Buddhist. Despite official atheism, religion does act as a form of social identity.

The Bolshevika who adopted the communist label after the 1917 revolution established a federal state based on the major nationality divisions of Russian society. The federalism of the Soviet Union is indicated by its official name – the Union of Soviet Socialist Republics (USSR). Less assimilationist than the czars, the communists nevertheless laid the basis for a quantitative reduction in nationalist identities. Internal migration, economic growth, natural demographic trends and the cultural changes effected by modern communications and transportation have all contributed to a progressive reduction of the number of nationality groups.

There are a number of links between the czars and the communists. Both are characterized by authoritarian regimes that have ruled their subjects through bureaucratic control. In a culturally heterogeneous society, the unity of the state first symbolized by the czars is now symbolized by the Communist Party. A bureaucracy that once ruled in the name of the czars now rules in the name of the party. Both czarist and communist states subordinated religion, or suppressed it, in the interests of the all-powerful state. Czars and communists have tolerated legislative institutions and elections only in so far as they reinforced the policy positions of an entrenched ruling elite. Both insisted on the conformity of intellectuals and artists to the interests and symbols of the regime, and both sought to stamp out dissent. To secure these ends both czars and communists used the repressive powers of the secret police, censorship of arts and media, exile to Siberia, forced labour camps, the execution of political enemies and the confinement of intellectual dissidents to asylums for the insane.

Each group built a centralized state that attempted to eliminate or hold within narrow boundaries any manifestations of cultural autonomy (whether from Ukrainians, Jews, Lithuanians or other cultural or nationality groups). They attempted to legitimate their autocratic authority in terms other than citizen consent, democratic elections and popular participation in policy making. The czars appealed to divine right; the communists appealed to the party's infallible interpretation of historical inevitability – thus political legitimacy is seen in terms of supernatural myth.

The revolutions in the United States and the Soviet Union were very different. The Americans began with a vision of plenty, they had a long tradition of local self-government of spontaneous organizations in small, self-governing groups, they envisaged the possibility of harmony or at least of a workable compatibility of interests within the country, they trusted the spontaneity of individuals and setting people free, and they had a tradition of moderation. In contrast the Russian tradition began with scarcity, in a poor country with many people and little capital. For many centuries, self-government was very limited at the village level and almost non-existent at any other. Violent conflict, like scarcity, had long been a basic assumption of Russian politics and the Russian revolution merely reinforced it. The Russian leaders who emerged from the revolution believed in discipline, direction and organization, and very much distrusted spontaneity. Whereas the American tradition stressed moderation, the Russian tradition stressed desperate ruthlessness.

The Russian citizen has typically been thought of by his or her rulers as more of a producer in the collective mass than a consumer with private interests. Thus there has been no political intellectual or ideological tradition separating individual rights from the prerogatives of the state. There was no middle class to foster the ideas of individual enterprise and humanism. Much of traditional Russian society was oriented toward collectivist styles of economic production and social organization.

It is interesting to compare Plato's view of politics in Greece in the fourth century BC and the Russian rulers today. Their first assumption is that there is an absolute truth; their second assumption is that the absolute truth can be known and their conclusion is that the absolute truth once known, must structure all beliefs, all behaviour and all social relationships. The political consequences are that those who know the absolute truth must rule, and their power and authority must be complete and unassailable. Marx, Lenin, Trotsky, Stalin, Khrushchev, Brezhnev and

Gorbachev, and all those associated with them, are convinced of the view that capitalism = exploitation = oppression = deprivation = alienation = misery (both physical and psychological). The alternative for these leaders has been the organization of economic production and distribution, and all other social relationships, in terms of the interest of all instead of the advantage of the few.

The Soviet state does not function like the governing institutions of a democracy. In the Soviet Union, the Communist Party makes policy. The state, as distinct from the Party, is primarily an instrument of administration. Thus the Party establishes the policies that are formally expressed through legislation passed by the state, or through administrative decrees implemented by the state bureaucracy.

A Soviet citizen may be represented by, and may elect deputies to, as many as six different levels of government. Each of these levels is defined by the population size and geographic extent of its jurisdictional authority. These levels are the soviet of the Union with over 750 deputies; soviets of the union republics with fifteen; soviets of autonomous republics, territories, regions and some major cities (*oblast*); soviets of national areas and autonomous regions (*okrug*), district soviets (*rayon*) with 223,000 deputies, and local soviets with over 2 million deputies.

In elections there is only one legal party which enjoys a constitutional monopoly on propaganda, prestige, power and access to the decision-making centres of government. Everyone nominated for government office is selected by the Party, is usually a member of the Party and serves only at the pleasure of the Party.

No government can function efficiently or long survive without the willing cooperation of a large majority of its citizens. This is true with regard to the Soviet Union, where government is accorded considerable legitimacy. One half of Soviet candidates standing at any particular election are nominated by the Party and its organizations for the first time. The sizeable turnover in the large number of candidates offers the state an opportunity to single out individuals for honour and distinction and provides many Soviet citizens with the chance of at least formal participation in the governing of the state. The 'legislative process' of the Soviet Union is one of ratification instead of policy making. The deputies elected to the Supreme Soviet and those at every level of government have been nominated by the Party because they represent some part of the Soviet ideal.

The Supreme Soviet is the highest organ of state power in the USSR and is directed and controlled by the Presidium. The Soviet meets twice a year and between sessions, the Presidium exercises many of the functions assigned to its parent body. The Presidium is granted an impressive array of executive, legislative and judicial powers – the chairman is formally identified as President. Soviet Presidents have sat in the highest councils of power within the Party and emphasize the subordination of the state's hierarchy to the Party's hierarchy.

The Council of Ministers is elected by and is responsible to the Supreme Soviet. When the Supreme Soviet is not in session, the Council of Ministers is responsible to the Presidium. In fact the lines of actual responsibility are reversed. The centre of legislative and administrative activity in the USSR is the Council of Ministers and the chairman and his informal 'inner cabinet' draft almost all the legislation submitted to the Supreme Soviet and supervise the day-to-day operation of the many ministries that administer the Soviet state. The Council of Ministers is in effect the chief executive authority of the Soviet Union.

In any revolutionary effort, the organization that captures power must undergo profound transformation as it attempts to consolidate power and to administer the state. The Communist Party reorganized Russia's military establishment around the Red Army; created a secret police apparatus, successively referred to as the Cheka, OGPU, NKVD, MVD, and KGB; the trade unions were subordinated to the Party in order to strengthen the Party's control over the workers; and establishing a network of auxiliary organizations designed to extend the Party's influence beyond the ranks of its immediate membership, each appealing to a different age group, e.g. from among youth and students, the Komsomol and Young Pioneers. Party members at the base indirectly elect Party elites to the top. One of the principles of political science is that the more indirect the electoral process the more elitist the result: the greater the opportunities for top executive and policy making personnel to manipulate nominations and elections in order to entrench their own positions. Each level of the party's organization is subordinated to its immediately superior level which controls the selection of personnel in the lower body and may intervene in any and all matters of decision making. The key instrument of central control is the vertical hierarchy of the party secretariats.

The history of the Communist Party confirms that whoever controls the implementation of policy controls the making of policy. The primary function of the Party is to chart the course of Soviet economic, political and social development. The party establishes general policy and oversees through overlapping personnel and close consultation with state and public authorities the implementation of general policy guidelines. The state apparatus is responsible for the more detailed elaboration and administration of Party policies, thereby freeing the party for a broader and supervisory role in socioeconomic development. The Party retains the right to intervene at every level of administration, and it is the keeper of conscience and vision that impels Soviet society to modernization and socialism and ultimately communism. This means that the individual Party member is expected to busy himself or herself with tasks that bring Soviet society closer to the goals established by the Party. Thus the Party member works long hours without direct compensation. It constitutes a mobilization elite responsible for leading the whole society ever upward and onward toward the regime's social and economic goals. The Party can be seen as an institutionalized elite that brings together the political activities and leading citizens of Soviet society.

One dimension of the Soviet society has not changed and probably never will: the planned economy.

The very definition of socialism in the Soviet Union includes the state's ownership of all the means of production which necessarily implies the state's supervision of economic activity. Private ownership of factories and land means exploitation, but ownership is placed in the hands of the state and if the state is representative of all the people, exploitation is abolished.

In 1921, Lenin introduced the New Economic Policy, but it was considered inadequate by the mid-1920s for rapid economic development. The basic assumption was that all details of production and distribution could be rationally planned by the state, and in the context of accelerated growth. The State Planning Committee (*Gosplan*) was ordered to draw up a five year plan to raise dramatically production of coal, iron and steel. With succeeding five year plans these production targets spread to other sectors of the economy.

**Collectivization** first occurred in the agricultural sector, as food had to be supplied to the growing cities and industrial centres. Agricultural production had to be made more efficient and mechanized, and mechanization in turn required the consolidation of small peasant holdings into large tracts of land. The resulting surplus of agricultural population would provide more workers for industry. The peasants were collectivized on farms (*kolkhozi*) and the richer ones who often refused (*kulaks*) were liquidated. The interests of both rural and urban consumers could continue to be subordinated to the demands of heavy industrial development. The problem which has bedevilled the Soviet economy is that once the heavy industrial base had been laid, planning mechanisms had to be adjusted to conform to an ever more sophisticated economy. It has always been difficult to programme all the details of a modernizing economy, and insistence on rigid centralization has tended to heighten inefficiency, waste and corruption. To increase economic efficiency centralized controls have to be relaxed (not necessarily eliminated), more autonomy delegated to managers, a system of distribution that adjusts supply to demand introduced in the strategic sectors of the economy, especially those related to consumer goods.

The distortions worked by rigid central planning are obvious in those categories of production and distribution which affect the living styles and consumption patterns of Soviet citizens. In a controlled economy it is difficult to measure the total cost of production, and even harder to measure the value of output. Any economic reform threatens bureaucratic power and once the planning system is in place, it develops an inertia of its own highly resistant to change.

What of the performance of the Soviet Union? On the positive side the regime has done things that had been thought impossible; for within forty years it transformed an underdeveloped country into a highly developed one. On the negative side the persistence of dictatorial government-decreed uniformity in many fields of opinion, culture and expression are manifest for all to see. The Soviet system has paid for its achievements with vast human costs.

There are many types of political problems. In the international arena of communist parties and regimes the Russians face a continuing problem of pluralism or polycentrism. The Russians no longer occupy the only communist country. Second, there is the question of the property of nations. Communists agree that in regard to means of production, individuals may not retain private property against the claims of the nation-state; but they are not clear whether a nation-state may legitimately retain the capital and land within its borders as its collective quasi-private property against the claims of poorer nations or of any international community. Third, there is the question of the Soviet military–industrial complex. The system is not monolithic and within the limitations set by political systems, groups vie for influence and power, and their share of the nation's resources. Fourth, there is the limited responsiveness to criticism: the population can write letters to the press; they can indulge in Bolshevist self-criticism – people at small Party unit meetings and larger meetings are supposed to speak up and criticize the practices of their own unit, their own group, the management of their factory, or the way the collective farm is being managed. Fifth, there are the particular units of the Party in which candidates are picked. Poetry and literature provide an indirect channel and there is greater autonomy and variety in present-day Soviet culture. As consumers become more affluent they insist on a wider range of choice, and this will mean a growing need for innovation.

There are signs of leaders in the country who wish to improve their own society and government and who wish to improve their ability to accept other nations – both communist and non-communist – as neighbours deserving genuine cooperation and equality.

## China

The power and vision of Mao Ze Dong (Tse Tung) made Chinese communism utterly unique – unique in world history and unique in the history of communism.

China presents the greatest challenge to an analysis of politics and government. It has a huge population of nearly one billion – more than all Europe and almost a quarter of all humankind. One of China's provinces, Szechwan, is roughly the size of Britain, France and West Germany. China is more than a nation among nations: it is at one time a continent, a state, and an idea.

The political idea of China is older than the idea of a unified Europe; but the Chinese successfully maintained their centralized government through many periods of disorder for more than two millenia. Though the structure of the government, its relationship to the population and to some extent its informing ideology have changed from dynasty to dynasty the concept of China as an indivisible political–cultural unit remains more alive than the often expressed idea of a reunified Europe. Analysts do face an 'inscrutability gap' in dealing with the region.

There are differences between traditional and modern political systems. Modern or developed systems have elections, parliaments, codified laws, political parties, rationalized public administrations and integrated national governments. Their citizens are politically conscious. By contrast, traditional systems lack elements of modern politics. Monarchs are absolute; governors are patrimonial; officials are privately corrupt; the populace is sharply stratified between literate city dwellers and illiterate peasants; and citizens are mere subjects.

In some political matters the Chinese were more advanced and progressive than the Europeans. In connection with a civil service type structure, China since the eighth century has possessed a system of official entrance examinations by which entrants to the career of mandarin (bureaucratic administrators of the empire) were recruited. There was an extensive network of bureaucracy and openness of competition for public office. The implicit faith in the value of education, the distrust of hereditary privilege, the belief that officials should be aware of the moral and environmental impact of their decisions were endemic in Chinese life. These were part of the broad tradition of Confucian statecraft named after Confucius (551–479 BC) who taught that he was merely rediscovering and extending the way of emperors.

At the core of the Chinese political tradition was the consciousness of the inseparability of political and social, economic or moral matters. At the heart of Confucius's concept of proper behaviour was the notion of social relationships, pictured as forming a coherent single unit. In accordance with the notion of the unity of all human relationships, the Chinese tradition assumed the unity of public and private realms. Officialdom was also an enduring characteristic of the Chinese tradition. Officialdom was divided into an extensive territorial hierarchy that reached down to the county level as well as into specialized ministries in the imperial capital. Another Chinese tradition was humanism which assumed that human beings naturally care more for those with whom they are in socially determined contact – a tradition which differs sharply from Western individualism.

The political history of modern China can be described as a response to the West, whose nations came to China unannounced and largely unwelcome, for trading purposes. The revolution of 1911 which overthrew the Manchu dynasty, declared China a republic and marked the end of a century of domestic turmoil over the way to respond to the Western challenge.

After the Bolshevik revolution in Russia and with the impetus imparted by the founding of the Comintern, the **Chinese Communist Party** (CCP) was organized in 1921. The small circle of intellectuals directing the CCP gave the party a Leninist orientation; its ideological appeal and organizational efforts were directed at members of China's proletariat, a relatively small social class in a society where 80 per cent of the population was made up of peasants, and the CCP was considered to be the necessary revolutionary vanguard both for capturing power and for constructing socialism.

In the mid-1920s the Party was allied with the Kuomintang, or Chinese nationalists, who had initiated China's republican revolution in 1911. The growing political and military strength of the Nationalists, whose leader after 1925 was Chiang Kai Shek, led to a dissolution of the alliance with the Party. The Party's position in China's urban areas and among the Chinese workers appeared to be hopeless and it was in this context that Mao Ze Dong captured the leadership of the communists and gave the Party an exclusively agrarian orientation.

Mao's strategy was to build a peasant-based army and to secure 'liberated' areas in the Chinese hinterland where the communists could enhance their appeal to the peasantry through agrarian reform. He demanded and got independence of his troops from the interference of Moscow and the urban-based Chinese Communist Central Committee; and resisted the demands of his superiors to waste his forces in futile attacks on the cities, outlining instead a strategy of building base areas in the remote mountains and in the broad countryside. After he gained full power over the Party during his army's heroic Long March (1934–5), which took them through thousands of miles of the interior, he moderated in his village work Moscow's hard line 'class struggle' doctrines, which had lost the Party considerable support. The Party carried out programmes of land redistribution, limited the exploitation of the peasantry by landlords and moneylenders, instituted progressive tax and welfare programmes, built factories and strengthened communist political and military organization. The civil war with the nationalist armies continued, but it was the territorial extension of Japan's military occupation of China after 1935 that laid the principle cornerstone for the eventual victory of Chinese communism. The communists proved more effective than the nationalists in fighting the Japanese, and Japan's defeat at the end of the Second World War opened the way for the advancing Red Army which finally forced the nationalists to flee mainland China for the island of Taiwan in 1949. The vast majority of the Chinese welcomed the chance to build their nation in peace. The Communist Party's skill in enlisting and utilizing popular aspirations in the game of politics was probably the most important cause of the revolution of 1949.

China's revolution of 1949 was similar to the Russian events of 1917 only to the extent that China also was a poor non-Western country ravaged by war and famine. The differences were striking: China's political traditions were rich and highly developed, its Communist Party far more mature and experienced in ruling, its social fabric far more torn by a century of disorder than even that of wartime Russia. In the 1950s the Chinese communist government exerted every effort to engineer a society and government that closely resembled the Soviet Union's. However, the Chinese were not to be fully satisfied with a mere carbon copy of Soviet government and politics – the Stalinist variety. For Marx, 'socialism' is possible only after the social and cultural transformations worked by mature capitalism and subsequently the dictatorship of the proletariat. For the Chinese communists, on the other hand, 'communism' had to be more broadly defined and its ultimate test was in the communalization of the production process and the elimination of private incentive in worker participation.

In the Great Leap Forward of 1958, the Party attempted to win the race with the Soviets to pure communism by communizing agriculture, which entailed the elimination of all forms of private property and the organization of all workers into production brigades, presumably inspired by the collective good of the whole society. More incentive for the individual producer meant greater reward differentials and by the mid-1960s Mao was faced with a weakening of his control over the Party and the development of a social structure that, in its growing status inequalities, was beginning to parallel that of the Soviet Union. The Party had worked hard on the development of political participation – the party line which bound the ordinary citizen more closely to the new political structure in the post-1949 period. There was an awareness of government and policy, and a much wider sharing in the output of government. The government explicitly demanded that in return for the real interests gained from the revolution, the citizenry be willing to participate actively in the new society.

Thus, the Great Proletarian Cultural Revolution 1966–71 was a major effort to reestablish Mao's political authority and the dominance of his most fervent supporters by eliminating the influence of the Party. The Party itself was to be rebuilt along the lines dictated by the youthful militant Red Guards, and especially by the Chinese Red Army. Second, the revolution inculcated in the collective consciousness of Chinese citizens the necessity of total social equality along with the socialist spirit of all for one and one for all.

Even before Mao's death in 1976 and the purging of the Gang of Four that sought to carry on Mao's radical policies, and especially by the early 1980s, it was clear that the great social experiment symbolized by Mao had failed. It proved to be impossible to modernize China's economy without accepting the traditional patterns of authority and status inequalities that mark the relationship between elite and mass. Raising the level of China's economic productivity meant providing more incentive to industrial and agricultural workers. Increased incentive meant greater reward differentials; and greater reward meant greater inequality.

The post-Maoist leadership also repudiated the Maoist cardinal principle of national self-sufficiency. Economic rationality, including the emphasis on planning as far ahead as the twenty-first century came to be stressed instead of revolutionary fervour. High standards of training and performance seemed to be preferred over political purity and proper worker-peasant-class origin. China began to open its doors to students and experts and to establish extensive commercial ties with the capitalist world. Heightened economic incentive entailed some measure of social and political liberalization.

The areas of accomplishment for China since 1949 have been in maintaining peace and the curbing of inflation, urbanization and overpopulation. The national economy has been revived to meet the requirements of an ever growing population and the desires of a nation-building elite. Recurring political strains still exist: generational in the fact that the leadership is septuagarian; regional since few of the current top leadership come from China's most industrialized regions. There is also tension between civilian and military rule – a dichotomy which is an element of the classical tradition that stressed rule by the word over the weapon.

## Questions

### The Soviet Union

1  Account for the success of the Bolsheviks in the 1917 revolution.
2  How different were the revolutions in the United States and Soviet Union?
3  What influence has the revolution played on Soviet politics?
4  Describe the 'legislative process' of the Soviet Union.
5  How does the Communist Party supervise the Soviet state apparatus?

6  Discuss the importance of political control over the economy.
7  What are the political problems facing the Soviet Union today?

**China**

1  Assess the differences between traditional and modern political systems with relation to China.
2  How relevant is Confucian thinking to today's world?
3  Describe Mao's politicization of the peasantry.
4  What did the Cultural Revolution achieve?
5  How far has China disavowed Mao's views in the last decade?

**Further reading**

Churchward, L. G., *Contemporary Soviet Government*, Routledge & Kegan Paul, London, 1975.

Finer, S. E., *Comparative Government*, Penguin, London, 1982

Griffith, E. S., *The American System of Government*, Methuen, London, 1954.

Lees, J. D., *The Political System of the U.S.A.*, Faber and Faber, London, 1969.

McCauley, M. (ed.), *The Soviet Union after Brezhnev*, Heinemann, London, 1983.

Macridis, R. (ed.), *Modern Political Systems in Europe*, Prentice-Hall, New York, 1978.

Neumann, R. G., *European and Comparative Government*, McGraw Hill, New Jersey, 1960.

Rose, R., *Politics in England*, Faber and Faber, London, 1980.

Wass, D., *Government and the Governed*, BBC Reith Lectures, 1983, Routledge & Kegan Paul, London, 1984.

# 20
# The Third World

This is a term generally applied to the developing countries, particularly those not associated formally with the American or communist alliance systems. It includes many former colonies of European empires. The term emphasizes the economic difficulties of these states, and their non-committed attitude towards the Eastern and Western power blocs. It consists therefore of those countries not in the first or second world. The first world consists of the leading Western industrialized countries of Europe, North America and the old British colonies which are of the same level of economic development. It is, in fact, the world of the industrial revolution. The second world covers the rest of the industrialized nations, mainly the Soviet Union and its European satellites. The Third World has very little homogeneity, exhibits vast social and economic differences and has little in the way of common political or economic interests. The phrase is largely the creation of the media. In fact it originally was a collective term of French origin (*le Tiers monde*) taken up by American writers. Many states of Latin America, Africa and Asia share a colonial past and a strong resentment against imperialism. They are poor and, thanks to the population explosion, are growing poorer by comparison with the industrialized nations. In foreign policy, following the Indian example, many have favoured neutralism (the policy or the advocacy of neutrality, at times when international relations show symptoms of bipolarity, as a means by which states can dissociate themselves from involvement in the ideological conflicts which produce these symptoms). Many commentators query whether India indeed is a Third World country – despite its poverty and its status as an ex-colony, it is a nuclear power in terms of energy and possibly weapons, and manages to run a political system not always very different from a Western parliamentary democracy. In recent years people have questioned the role of the oil-producing states of the Middle East as Third World members. Some of these states have enormous international political influence, while in other respects being obvious Third World members. Indeed many writers, who now include such countries as India and those represented in the Middle East in a Third World categorization, add the Fourth World in which are counted all the other underdeveloped countries which have no such resources and little if any prospect of development. Other writers subdivide the last World into fourth and fifth, the **Fourth World** comprising countries with potential for eventual economic development, e.g. Bolivia, Zaire, Zambia and Thailand; and the **Fifth World** consisting of those countries that have little hope for economic development because of a dearth of infrastructure, resources and skill. Niger, Chad, Somalia and Bangladesh represent the poorest of all classes of economic conditions.

The Third World accounts for about one-third of the membership of the United Nations. 100 countries are embraced in the Third World: with 48 per cent of the world's area; 45 per cent of the population; 14 per cent of the national income; 8 per cent of industrial output; and 22 per cent of the foreign trade.

The chief characteristics are: domination by colonial powers (and, a Marxist would add, imperialist and capitalist powers); in international relations the steering of a neutral or middle course, (although some of these countries more or less clearly align themselves with Western or the socialist power blocs); underdeveloped economies, with most populations being engaged in primitive agriculture and, in some cases, in mining; low national income per head (about US$700 compared with US$5000 in the West and US$1500 in the socialist bloc); early stages of social development with feudal, semi-feudal, or tribal relations prevailing in rural areas. Marxist or communist commentators add the class dimension and political orientation factors: the bourgeoisie constitutes 2–5 per cent; the urban proletariat 5–7 per cent; and the remainder representing socially unconscious rural masses of whom the vast majority turn to socialism in one form or another and Marxist ideology.

In assessing the role of the Third World economically and politically, recourse is made in many cases to the three worlds theory to make a comparative analysis of the economic (and to some extent political) conditions of the three worlds and attempt to understand the Third World, perhaps as an ideal type (in order to denote social arrangements peopled by ideally rational beings).

Poverty stricken states in the Third World have sided with other Third World states in an effort to restructure the international economic order; just as poverty stricken Third World states have invaded other poverty stricken Third World states. Such situations show that ideological criteria influence states to adopt certain ways of looking at the world and of defining their national interests, but ways that may, in fact, be overcome by other criteria for defining national interest. Different nation-states have different views of the various intergovernmental organizations and consequently pursue different policies toward them. The general American attitude toward the United Nations, for example, was supportive during the early years of existence of the United Nations. In recent years, however, as more and more Third World nations entered the United Nations, and as more and more votes in the United Nations opposed preferred American outcomes, American support for the United Nations cooled noticeably.

Many Third World states were willing to accept economic and military aid and technical assistance from whoever offered it, but chose to remain politically non-aligned – thus helping to break down bipolar politics which dominated the first two decades of the post Second World War era. This situation developed so quickly that by the beginning of the 1970s it was clear that, although the Third World was internally divided, it had become the major actor on the international scene. Since then the Western world believes that problems in the Third World were created by Third World incompetence or Soviet meddling. This view is perhaps not surprising in view of the autocracy and totalitarianism which have surveyed, confronted and been endemic in the Third World in recent times. The West, while realizing that development was a difficult process, often concludes that Third World states by their choices of policy have made future development even more difficult than it is at present. The Second World, that is the Soviet Union and Eastern bloc nations, asserts that progressive anti-imperialist forces predominate. Soviet spokesmen maintain they have a dynamic methodology with which to explain the vagaries of political, social and economic developments throughout the Third World.

The Soviet Union has been a vocal supporter of the Third World's call for a new international economic order because of a Soviet perception that the United States' overseas economic interests would be injured if such an order were instituted. Only after the Soviet Union turned to the pursuit of military diplomacy has its influence in the Third World expanded significantly. Moscow turned to military diplomacy during the 1970s because of the failure of its economic and ideological diplomacy. Thus it failed to take advantage of the Third World resentment of past and present colonial bonds which fitted almost perfectly with Lenin's interpretation of capitalist imperialism. The Soviet perhaps have taken comfort from the decline of Western controls in the Third World. The emergence of a Third World from colonial hegemony has forced the Soviet Union to recognize countries that are neither socialist nor capitalist. The country has accommodated its ideology to this reality by accepting the existence of national paths of development.

The main strengths of the Third World are in its natural, especially mineral, resources. Other than states, multinational corporations are the most prominent organizations that derive power from natural resources. Corporations are dependent on states to grant access, but because of the human expertise and financial income they provide, particularly to Third World states, corporations may exercise a disproportionate amount of influence within those states. Many of these states, for example certain Middle East states rely on corporations to provide expertise and capital for resource exploitation. Corporations were able to achieve such a position because despite the gradual emergence of newly independent Third World states most of the new states remained economically subservient to their former colonial rulers. Not surprisingly economic capabilities continued to be viewed as less significant contributors to power potential than military capabilities.

In Third World states, governments are opposed to free trade, arguing that infant industries need shelter from the trade of efficient industries in already industrialized states. From the Third World's perspective this is both a political and an economic argument. It is political in the sense that Third World states seek to escape the vestiges of colonialist and neo-colonialist dependence on the industrialized West, and it is economic in the sense that Third World states are seeking to allow their own industries time to become efficient producers. From the Western industrialized states' perspective, Third World states and Western states participate in a single international trading system on the same basis, with equal access provided to all economic institutions on the basis of wealth and capability. From the Third World's perspective developing states enter international trade in a clearly subservient position and therefore are not part of a Western system, but rather unwilling partners in a separate subsystem, that of North–South economic relations. Conversely, Marxists believe that through its international trade and exchange system, the West exploits the Third World economically even though political independence has been achieved by the Third World. Further foreign investment adds to local unemployment by introducing capital-intensive productive means. Foreign aid in this context to Marxists is simply exploitative because 'strings' are often attached to it, thereby perpetuating Third World dependence on the West.

Even some of those people opposed to Marxism observe that although foreign investment and trade do help Third World states improve their economic status, only a small sector of a Third World country's economy is in fact aided – the export sector. Therefore in Third World states investment and trade creates a dual economy, one aspect of which is relatively developed, that is, the export sector, and the other of which is underdeveloped.

Third World states have also been susceptible to changes in the price of world oil. Over the last decade to avoid a downturn in Third World trade, developing states have pushed for the creation of a new international economic order that would facilitate the transfer of wealth to Third World states for developmental purposes and create preferential trade arrangements for products of Third World states. These latter states have consistently argued for a restructuring of economic relations between developed and developing states.

Third World states believe they have remained economically dependent and politically subservient to developed states, at least in part, because of the inequalities built into the system. These inequalities include low valuation for the currencies of the Third World, poor and worsening terms of trade for the primary products produced by Third World states, and too much international emphasis on who has wealth as opposed to who needs wealth.

To the Third World economic strength is both desired and feared. Some perceptions of Third World states are rooted in historical memory. Few could deny that developed states exploited their colonies during the colonial era. Only rarely did colonial powers seek to improve the living conditions and economic standards in their colonial territories. These memories do cloud current realities and current Third World perceptions of those realities. Third World states also charge that the First World has been particularly parsimonious in its willingness to extend aid and assistance, at least in relation to the First World's available wealth. Thus to them, the current international economic system is biased in favour of developed states. Third World trade and financial problems are accentuated by reliance, in many states, on one or two primary products for their foreign exchange income. Economic might thus breeds political power as seen through Third World eyes. Change is requisite, Third World states conclude, and must be brought about. This change is desired in the economic structure of the current state system and not a change in the state system itself. Indeed one of the great paradoxies of Third World development is the clash between growing international economic interdependence and the desire for full national sovereignty.

In the face of this state of affairs, Third World unity is also eroding. During the last decade the most rapidly growing gap between domestic incomes in states was not between First World and Third World, nor between Second World and Third World or First World and Second World. It has been between Third World states and other Third World states. Most of the economically strong Third World states are OPEC countries, but others such as South Korea and Singapore derive their economic strength from new industrial bases.

The industrialized states of the East and West, as well as China, account for 75 per cent of the world's military expenditure, but Third World states have actively increased their military budgets as well. The flow of arms to Third World states has been accelerated by the widespread desire of those states to improve their military forces. Many Third World states see security challenges on or near their borders. Internal security provides another motivation for arming, and in addition developing states seek strengthened military forces because the military has historically been the measure of a nation. To many developing states, having one's own military forces is viable and tangible proof of independence, even if one's economy is controlled or influenced by others. Several Third World states nonetheless resent their continuing dependence on external sources for military equipment and arms and have, therefore, begun to develop their own domestic arms industries despite higher costs of limited production. Some, such as Brazil, have become weapons exporters. The heightened lethality of Third World arsenals may also lead to increased unwillingness on the parts of the world's great powers, including the two superpowers, to intervene in the developing world when their interests are challenged.

Third World views of international law are as critical as its views on international economics. Almost all chastize Western-dominated international law as granting economic preference and advantage to those very states that created most of the tenets of international law, the states of Western Europe and North America. The Third World is extremely supportive of the concept of sovereignty, but argues that because of the strictures of prevailing international law, Third World sovereignty is abridged by economic dependence on and penetration by the developed Western world. Under prevailing international law, the Third World believes such neocolonialism is not prevented, but rather encouraged. Third World states perceive that the institutions of the international community are established by and for the Western world to protect its own interest. Third World jurists themselves have advocated changes in international law such as the 'clean slate doctrine' which argues essentially that once a new state or government comes into being, all obligations of previous states or governments are ended. The jurists have also supported the doctrine of nationalization without compensation – which has been rejected by the West.

Demography does not favour continuing economic development in the Third World. Of the 6.3 billion people in the world in 2000, 5 billion will live in the Third World. Most of the areas' population by 2000 will be in or near their offspring-producing years; thus barring an unexpected and precipitous drop in birth rates, rapid population growth will continue with all its attendant political and economic implications. Governments find themselves hardpressed to maintain satisfactory living standards in urban areas; and the rural areas of the Third World are less well off in many cases than the urban centres. In several of these countries, efforts to control population growth are viewed as neocolonial plots designed to maintain Third World subservience to the First World. Third World governments have found it hard to repay loans from other countries in the Western or Eastern blocs and from international organizations such as the World Bank and International Monetary Fund.

Throughout man's many societies tensions exist between value systems that emphasize the responsibility of the individual to himself or herself and those that emphasize the responsibility of the individual to society. In simplistic terms this tension may be described as the conflict between individualism and collectivism. In the traditionalist societies of many Third World states life revolves around a collective body. In some cases that body is the tribe or village; in other cases it is the extended family. In all cases, however, the desires of individuals, as well as their rights and needs, are subordinate to the interests of the collective. Often rigid formal or informal rules and customs have been developed to assure primacy of the collective. In societies such as these, Western conceptions of individualism often have little relevance. This has major implications for Western relations with Third World states.

Traditional societies, nevertheless, are breaking down, succumbing to pressures of urbanization and development. Together urbanizaton and development disrupt traditional collective societies by challenging or rejecting old rules and customs and by weakening or destroying links within the collective. Within many states, masses of the population are adrift, their old traditional collective attitudes disrupted and replaced by little or nothing.

Although Third World states may individually be deciding whether to cast their lots with the individualist West or the collectivist East, or to follow their own line of thought to resolve the individual/collective dilemma, they are at the same time seeking to establish their own internal identities, called into question by the disruption of their traditional collective societies.

## The North–South conflict and Third World

The North–South conflict derives its name from the simple fact that, almost without exception, the wealthy nations of the world are in the Northern hemisphere, and the poorer nations lie to their South. Generally speaking the North, in terms of development, consists of the United States, Canada, Western Europe, Eastern Europe, Israel, the Soviet Union, Japan, South Africa, Australia and New Zealand. The remaining states of the world are in the underdeveloped South and have two attributes, that they have had a colonial past dominated by European powers, and they are poor.

The danger with the present economic order in the world is that the

North and South may find themselves even more deeply entwined in the rhetoric of confrontation and hostility. The South closely guards its newly won independence, fearing that economic ties to the North through either state agencies or private firms may increase economic dependency and political subservience. Despite its poverty the South is not without tools. Many of the resources that the industrial North requires are available primarily in the South. Realizing this, the South could turn to a strategy of resource deprivation and price increases in raw materials. The continued disparity in wealth could have a psychological impact on the collective psyche of the North, particularly in situations where starvation occurs.

The simple bipolarity of the post-Second World War era in East–West relations has been replaced by a more complex multipolar structure. The North and South never were unified in structure or objectives and other countries take a nonaligned view and try to be free of economic and political influences. Nevertheless, the political, economic, military and social confrontation between East and West and the struggle between North and South to achieve an equitable distribution of the world's wealth remain the centrepieces of contemporary international affairs. In one way or another, rightly or wrongly, most Third World states perceive that the current international system relegates them to a permanently inferior position, and they therefore seek to change or modify that system.

If one is sceptical regarding the Third World, one has to remember that only half a century ago colonialism and imperialism were acceptable and respectable. Today colonialism and imperialism are almost universally decried and reviled. This in itself is a significant change in international affairs, despite the fact that colonialism and imperialism have not been eliminated. The clear challenges which confront the human race are all to be found in Third World politics – population growth, food production, nuclear and conventional arms procurement and build up, inequitable wealth distribution, trade and exchange imbalances, mineral and energy scarcity, development and development aid, and value conflicts are just a few.

### India

In terms of population India is one of the largest countries in the world; but is also one of the poorest. Next to China it is the largest of the developing countries, and is home to one of the oldest continuous cultural traditions of humankind covering about 3500 years from the Bronze Age to the nuclear age. Politically it has been both independent and almost unified only twice: once in about 250 BC under King Ashoka who ruled two-thirds of the subcontinent, and again since 1947 after the secession of Pakistan. From the nineteenth century onward, British rule brought an end to local wars and there were important improvements in transportation, public health and education. The Indian Mutiny changed the political system of India. The British Government replaced the British East India Company as the political and administrative power. Educational reforms were started, universities founded, and a civil service organized. The lower ranks of the government administration became filled with native clerks. Hindus were the most successful in the results of examinations.

As India changed more Indians began to think of national unity and independence. In 1885 the Indian National Congress was founded, uniting Muslims and Hindus in their demands for more Indian self-government. Muslims came to demand a larger share of public jobs and other opportunities and to fear their minority status in a Hindu-dominated self-governing India. In 1906, the All India Muslim League was founded.

Gandhi's and Nehru's Congress Party tried to keep Hindus and Muslims together. Indian self-government was to be secular, and religion and the state were to be kept separate. At all times, some Muslim leaders held prominent offices in the Congress, side by side with Hindus, but other Muslims feared that majority rule would give power and privilege to Hindus. When India became independent in 1947 the regions with Muslim majorities apart from Kashmir seceded and formed the new state of Pakistan. In 1971, Pakistan broke up into two states – Bangladesh to the east of India and today's Pakistan to the west – each with more than 80 million inhabitants still including some Hindu minorities. Today, more Muslims are living as a minority in India than in either of these Muslim states. Partition in 1947 had a high cost in blood, and communalism still remains a political problem.

The life and death of millions of people affect and are affected by politics in India. Public health and life expectancy, famines and epidemics or their avoidance depend on public policy. Many issues press for political decisions: economic development; its orientation toward industry or agriculture; the interests of Indian and foreign corporations, of Indian big business, small businesses, labour unions and the unemployed, of landowners, big farmers, small peasants and the landless rural poor, of the highly educated, the merely literate and the illiterate majority. Many matters of family and personal life, of custom and culture press for political decisions – matters that in other countries are settled and stable. Politics in India has thus acquired greater intensity and personal relevance than is found in the politics of many other countries. The major developments of Indian political history are the creation of legislative councils in 1853; the introduction of local self-government in 1882; the enlarging of legislative councils in 1890 and increase in their powers reiterated by the Morley–Minto Act of 1909. In 1919 the Montague–Chelmsford report led to the Government of India Act of 1919 allowing for the election of council members. According to the principle of dyarchy (double rule) – important matters (defence, police and finance) were 'reserved' for the provincial government and the appointed British members of the executive council; the less important (health, education and agriculture) to be transferred to the Indian members. In 1932 the franchise was extended to members of the 'depressed classes' – the untouchables or harijans, whose leaders today still play a significant part in Indian politics. In 1935, the Government of India Act gave wider autonomy to the provincial legislatures but reserved emergency powers for the governors who remained British. A two-chamber central legislature in Delhi was created, consisting of a 'council of state' with thirty-four elected and twenty-six appointed members, and a 'legislative assembly' of forty appointed members and 105 members elected by the provincial assemblies. Defence, foreign affairs and certain financial powers remained under the Governor-general and hence in British hands.

Ultimately increased self-government and political opposition may have worked together. The slow extension of Indian self-government by the British rulers has given India four generations of political experience within a constitutional order. Motilal Nehru was an important political leader in the 1920s demanding dominion status for India; his son, Jawaharlal Nehru, was Prime Minister from 1947–64; Jawaharlal's daughter, Indira Gandhi, was Prime Minister from 1966 to 1977 and again from 1980 until her assassination in 1984, and Indira's son, Rajiv, has been Prime Minister since his mother's death. It was through their own growing efforts, organization, struggle and readiness to sacrifice that Indians developed the self-confidence and the moral and political capabilities for sustained self-government and independence within constitutional democracy.

Certain political realities prevail. Voting participation in national elections is high. Extremist parties of the right and left are small and civil rights remain popular. The Muslim and harijan minorities have remained strong; the linguistic diversity is eradicable, particularly between North and South. In foreign affairs, no major political group wishes to change India's policy of nonalignment with the great power blocs, West and East.

There are some interesting stable images in Indian political thought: first, the vastness and unity of India and the depth of the attachment of many people to it; second, the British idea of government by discussion, of playing by parliamentary rules of respect for individuals and civil rights; and third, the old Indian religious tradition of the holy man who lives in poverty but enjoys general respect and has great moral influence which is closely linked with Gandhi's ideas of civil disobedience, pacifism and non-violence. To this day success in Indian politics requires a moral basis.

There are many small frustrations in the process and machinery of government, often owing to poverty – but the country as a whole has grown and improved politically in the years since partition.

## Nigeria

Nigeria's cultural heritage emanates from several ancient kingdoms. Modern Nigeria, however, is the child of a short history. For several years prior to 1900 Lagos and the coast near it was administered by a private business corporation under British protection. Direct British colonial administration of this region commenced in 1900, and by 1914 the territories of present-day Nigeria were united under it.

The main peoples are the Yoruba in the south-west which includes Lagos, the Ibo in the south-east and the Hausa in the far north. The north is Muslim with elements of Arab cultural influence. Its main languages are Hausa and Fulani. Its society and politics are still characterized by aristocratic and feudal traditions supported by a traditional governing class and local rulers. This society contrasts with the more urban and decentralized political culture of the Yorubas and even more with the egalitarian, commercial and competitive traditions of the Ibos. A multitude of smaller groups, languages and religions supplements these three major groups and seems likely to persist.

## Growth towards independence

The Yorubas and the Ibos took relatively quickly to education, commerce, social mobility and eventually to labour unions, political parties and aspirations for independence from Britain. The north for a long time tended to remain proud, traditional, illiterate, socially conservative, and more or less content with British rule.

From 1914 to the 1950s, Nigeria's population grew and so did its cities and towns and the non-agricultural occupations within them. After 1945 there were increases in labour unions, newspapers and political agitation demanding more self-government and the eventual end of foreign rule. By the late 1950s, Britain was ready to concede legal independence to Nigeria and to replace colonial rule by the more indirect means of economic and political influence. But Britain wanted the country to stay together and expected the conservative north to exert a stabilizing influence throughout the country as well as to encourage the confidence of foreign investors. The federal independence constitution of Nigeria deliberately favoured the north. It assigned to the north a larger number of peoples so as to give it a majority of the population, legislature and armed forces of the new federation that was formally established in 1960.

Within a few years regional rivalries and political instability threatened the very existence of the federation. The effective head of government was a northener, Prime Minister Abubaker Tafawa Balewa. Southerners counted on the advantages of their own peoples in education and commercial and technical skills to shift the social economic and political leadership to them eventually. Particularly for the Ibos, these expectations soon seemed to come true. Their businesses prospered.

In 1966, a military coup instigated by a group of predominantly Ibo officers overthrew Balewa. A military government under Major General Ironsi was established, but in July anti-Ibo violence started in the north and culminated in another military coup under General Gowon.

Ibo opinion now turned to the idea of secession; the trend being reinforced by the recent discovery of oil deposits. Oil discoveries would be an economic reward for Ibo secession, but also promised a reward to the Nigerian government for preventing secession.

The result was civil war during the period 1967–70. The Ibos declared the independence of their region, calling it Biafra, and establishing a government headed by Odumegwu Ojukwu. The Nigerian government blockaded Biafra causing much starvation and eventually conquering the entire region. The unity of Nigeria was preserved; but at the expense of a vastly increased army and army involvement in politics which has persisted to the present day, apart from a short period of civilian rule by Shehu Shagari, the National Party leader.

Nigeria's government is federal and constitutional in form, but an authoritarian military regime in substance. The former regions, north, southeast and south-west have been replaced by twelve states in the hope of reducing the likelihood of conflict among large regions. After suppressing the attempt at secession, the Nigerian military government embarked on a policy of reconciliation, permitting the return from abroad of many political exiles and a few political leaders.

The oil fields have been developed and their output has grown. In the 1980s, Nigeria's politics remains independent from foreign rule, both in form and in substance. Domestic politics, rather than foreign influence, has the largest share in determining the distribution of incomes, investments and career opportunities among different regions, language groups and peoples. It also determines the size, intensity and nature of development efforts. Class politics and religious conflicts have so far been less prominent. Political participation is limited; much of the population being still uninvolved in politics. In addition the military government keeps a watchful eye on political organizations, intellectuals and students of all kinds. In the election which led to Shagari's victory in 1980, five parties were admitted to the electoral contest out of an original fifty-two. Shagari proved to be corrupt and lethargic in the field of economic development and he was overthrown by a military coup in 1984 which brought in Major General Bunari as Commander-in-Chief and Head of State.

Nigeria's political system is still weakly integrated. Civic loyalty and skills, communication channels between government and governed, administrative accountability and efficiency are still incompletely developed. Even so, Nigeria's performance since the Biafran war deserves respect. Since that time there has been relatively little bloodshed or repression, measured by the size of the country and the standards of many other developing nations. Economic gains have been matched by gains in education, e.g. the universities. Starting from a heritage of poverty and severe interregional cleavages in colonial days, Nigeria has done better than many observers expected. Only since 1983 has the economic growth faltered owing to global recession, which reduced demand for Nigeria's oil, and the debts to foreign creditors which were accumulated during the decade of development in the 1970s. It follows a non-aligned policy but is becoming a superpower of the African continent.

## Zimbabwe

Since 1980, Zimbabwe has been a multiracial parliamentary republic. Its government of national unity is dominated by the majority party, Robert Mugabe's Zimbabwe African National Union (ZANU), but it also contains representatives of other parties with both black and white support.

Zimbabwe is the former British colony of Southern Rhodesia which between 1923 and independence had been ruled by a virtually independent government of European settlers. While the British government granted independence to its other southern African colonies in the 1960s, it refused to do the same for Southern Rhodesia unless the government of Ian Smith's Rhodesian Front Party would allow provisions to be made for an end to white minority rule in the country. Smith's reaction was a unilateral declaration of independence (UDI) in November 1965. The Labour Government in Britain retaliated by declaring the Smith Government illegal and arranging economic sanctions against Rhodesia through the United Nations. The Rhodesian Front Government managed to survive for fifteen years, principally because of help from its white-dominated neighbours in South Africa, Angola and Mozambique.

A guerrilla war began several years after UDI. Black armies, aided by many of Rhodesia's neighbours, sought to overthrow the white government. The main guerrilla groups were linked to Joshua Nkomo's Zimbabwe African People's Union (ZAPU) and Robert Mugabe's Zimbabwe African Nationalist Union (ZANU). In spite of their differences the two movements joined forces in the Patriotic Front (PF) in 1977. More peaceful opposition to the Smith regime came from Methodist Bishop Abel Muzorewa's United African National Council (UANC). It was only in 1977 that Smith declared his acceptance of the principles of universal suffrage, and a rapid transition to black-majority rule and thus legal independence from Britain. The guerrilla forces still did not trust the Rhodesian Front Government and refused to cooperate. In May 1978, Muzorewa's UANC and Smith joined forces with the two other black movements, Rev Ndabaningi Sithole's faction of ZANU and Chief Chirau's Zimbabwe United People's Organisation (ZUPO) to form an interim Government to guide the people towards majority rule.

In 1979, a new constitution was approved by white voters and multiracial elections held, with Muzorewa's UANC achieving a clear victory in renamed Zimbabwe–Rhodesia. However, without the agreement and participation of the PF and its guerrilla forces, the new constitution stood little chance of domestic or international acceptance. Real hope of a lasting solution came with negotiations arranged in London in September 1979. The PF agreed to accept special representation for the white minority of Smith and Muzorewa in turn consented to free multiracial elections under British government supervision. In November 1979, the Parliament of Zimbabwe–Rhodesia voted to return the nation to its pre-1963 status as a British colony. This paved the way for a British controlled voluntary disarming of the guerrillas and for elections in 1980. The new Prime Minister, Robert Mugabe, led Zimbabwe to full independence in April 1980 with a coalition government consisting not only of ZANU–PF ministers but also four PF (formerly ZAPU) men (including Nkomo himself) and two white representatives. The intervening period has been dominated by quarrels between Nkomo and Mugabe, which has split the black parties. The white Rhodesian Front Party has also split over the issue of support for the government.

The head of state is a President, chosen by an electoral college consisting of the members of the Zimbabwe Parliament. The President appoints the members of the Cabinet on the advice of the Prime Minister. The tenure of the Prime Minister is limited by the term of the parliament, normally five years. The Cabinet consists of departmental ministers, a deputy Prime Minister and two ministers without portfolio. The legislature consists of two houses, the House of Assembly and the Senate – the former with 100 members and the latter forty members.

The highest judicial authority is the High Court divided into appellate and general divisions. The country is a unitary state with local government organized along pre-independence lines based on British structures.

The House of Assembly is directly elected; the President and Senate are chosen by elected legislators and traditional chiefs. There are twenty white roll constituencies where all whites, Asians and coloureds can vote, and the rest are common-roll constituencies open to all black Zimbabweans and black non-resident citizens who work in neighbouring countries. Voting in the white roll constituencies is preferential, the voter ranks the candidates according to his or her preference; in black constituencies each party presents a ranked list of candidates for each electoral province and voters choose a party list not an individual. A secret ballot is used, although there were allegations of corruption and intimidation by both black guerrilla groups and the mostly white government security services at the 1980 elections. The elections were supervised by British officials and police.

Mugabe has never made any secret of the fact that he would like Zimbabwe to become a one-party state, although only if the people consent to it.

### Malaysia

Malaysia is a parliamentary federation comprising, first, the eleven states of the Malay peninsula together with the federal territory of Kuala Lumpur the capital, which comprise West Malaysia, and, second, the states of Sabah and Sarawak on the island of Borneo, which comprise East Malaysia.

Large groups in the population of 15 million are Malay (47 per cent), Chinese (32 per cent), and Indian (9 per cent). It achieved independence from Britain in 1957 as the Malayan Federation then consisting of the states of the peninsula only. In 1963 Sabah, Sarawak and Singapore joined the federation, but Singapore seceded in 1965. The federal territory of Kuala Lumpur was created in 1974; and the present constitution has been effective from 1957, with only limited subsequent alterations. It provides for a parliamentary and cabinet system closely modelled on that of the United Kingdom.

The head of state serves for a term of five years and the office rotates according to precedence among the royal rulers of nine of the thirteen states of the federation, but accession to the office is confirmed by election among these nine rulers. The office thus constitutes a unique combination of monarchic rotational and elective principles. Although formally the head of government, the King is in practice a constitutional monarch with only very limited discretionary powers. The effective head of government is the Prime Minister working with and through the Cabinet. Members of the Cabinet are appointed by the King from either of the two Houses of Parliament on the advice of the Prime Minister. The Cabinet is required by the constitution to be collectively responsible to the Parliament.

The legislature consists of the King and the two Councils: the Senate and the House of Representatives. The Senate, which is the least powerful of the two houses, has sixty-eight members. Two members are elected by each state legislature, while the King, acting on advice from the Prime Minister, appoints an additional forty-two, including two to represent the federal territory. The House of Representatives has 154 members directly elected from single-member constituencies by simple majorities. A single majority in both houses is sufficient to carry legislation.

The Conference of Rulers, which meets three or four times a year, comprises the thirteen rulers of the states of the federation, including the nine hereditary royal rulers and the Governors of Penang, Malacca, Sabah and Sarawak. Since independence, the government coalition dominated by the United Malays National Organization has always held an absolute majority of the seats in the House of Representatives.

The Federal Court is the highest judicial authority in Malaysia, with the power to interpret the constitution and to adjudicate in disputes between states or between any state and the federal government. It is also the highest court of appeal in criminal cases for the federation.

The most distinctive feature of Malaysian political parties is that they are all ethnically based, but a second feature is a tendency towards consociation and coalition. The ethnic divisions are not only racial, but are also characterized by language, religion, culture, and to a considerable extent economic differentiation. Political parties are numerous, different in size and often limited to regions – but they are permanent associations sustained by membership dues and private donations.

The Secretariat of the Association of South-east Asian Nations was founded in 1967, with its Secretariat in Kuala Lumpur, to accelerate the economic growth, social progress and cultural development in the region and 'to promote regional peace and security'.

## Questions

### Third World

1 Why is there so much controversy about the term 'the Third World'?
2 What are the chief characteristics of Third World countries and why are they inherently politically unstable and economically weak?
3 Assess the main strengths of the Third World.
4 Account for the lack of unity in Third World countries.
5 Why is the Third World at the centre of the North–South conflict?

### India

1 What are the unique features of Indian politics?
2 Discuss the main issues at stake.
3 How far has respect for rules and tradition helped or hindered the development of political issues?

### Nigeria

1 Examine the role of tribal and ethnic issues in Nigeria's politics.
2 What are the chief characteristics of federalism in the Nigerian context?

## Zimbabwe

1 Account for the turmoil in Zimbabwean politics before and since independence.
2 Why has guerrilla warfare been an endemic feature of Zimbabwean politics?

## Malaysia and Singapore

1 What is the Malaysian Federation?
2 Describe the distinctive features of Malaysian political parties.
3 Examine the strengths and weaknesses of the Singaporean political system.

## Further reading

Legum, C., *Pan-Africanism: A Short Political Guide*, Pall Mall Press, London, 1962.
Sivard, R. L., *World Military and Social Expenditures*, World Priorities, Washington, USA, 1985.
*Third World Affairs 1985* Third World Foundation for Social and Economic Studies, London, 1985.

# Part 4  International Issues

# 21
# International relations

Every historical occurrence is of course unique. The situations in which statesmen construct alliances, decide to go to war, declare independence, or make peace are all different. Regardless of historical and geographical context, policy makers for different types of political units, whether tribes, city states, empires or modern nation states, have attempted to achieve objectives or defend their interests by fundamentally similar techniques – the most widely used being the use of force or the construction of alliances. Little has changed over the centuries in the types of threat and reward modern governments make in attempting to achieve their objectives, the techniques of diplomatic bargaining, and the concern governments have for their international prestige.

The main purpose of early authors such as Chinese philosophers, and Machiavelli, was not so much to provide general analyses of the relations between states as to offer advice on the most effective forms of statecraft. In the eighteenth and nineteenth centuries Europe's view was generally held by writers to be that the balance of power was a more or less fundamental law of politics at the international level. The subject of international relations took on a moralistic and legalistic orientation in the first two decades of this century, with emphasis on treaties and international organization. During and after the Second World War these views developed into the need to look at objectives such as security and expansion processes, trade and diplomacy, and propaganda and subversion. In the wake of a world war, the study of the phenomenon of nationalism, the influence of geography on a country's foreign policy, and particularly the effect of power (or lack of it) on a nation's fate became important. Since 1945, the study of international relations has seen important new developments. With the development of basic animosities between the United States and the Soviet Union, the Middle East states, and China and its neighbours, the creation of weapons of mass destruction and the rise of over fifty new states, policy makers have had to cope with extremely difficult, dangerous and in some cases unprecedented problems.

The current schools of study in international politics centre on four main theories. First, the traditional analysts study various states' foreign policies, certain international 'problems' and international institutions. Their purposes are to report and analyse current international problems and to speculate on sources and outcomes of various policy alternatives for specific states or for international organizations.

Second, there are the strategists, a group which has developed dramatically since 1945. Their main concern has been to understand the logic of deterrence in the nuclear age, to analyse the impact of new weapons systems on deterrence, and to develop strategies to maximize national security while minimizing the possibility of nuclear war.

Third, there are the grand theorists dominated by Hans Morgenthau. Unlike his predecessors who believed their task to be reporting on current events or pushing for their favourite peace panacea, Morgenthau argued that the diverse data of international politics could be made coherent within the terms of a model of power politics. His major contribution was to show that the field must seek to establish generalizations, not remain focused on unique events; that interstate relations in their essence display patterns of behaviour and recurrence, and that the core of the subject is to explore the sources of state behaviour (the search for power) and the resulting patterns of relations (the balance of power).

Middle-range theory is the interest of a fourth group of scholars. It seeks empirically to explain selected aspects of international politics and foreign policy. This group is problem oriented, searching for precise description and explanation of specific phenomena. Scholars are involved in research about the effects of public opinion on policy making, the origins and types of international conflicts, the conditions under which alliances are formed or disintegrate, and the relationship between the construction of alliances and the outbreak of incidence of war.

Lastly, there is **peace research** which combines the main characteristics of traditional analysis and empirical study: it is deeply concerned with the problems of peace and war. The objectives of the research are normative – devising ways to control processes leading to violence – and the techniques are scientific and systematic. Some of the work has made important contributions to understandings of such problems as the processes leading to war; escalation of violence; the relationship between individual personality characteristics and the phenomena of bigotry, prejudice, and national hostility; the economic consequence of disarmament and arms control programmes and the sources of public attitudes toward foreign countries and alien cultures.

## Interdisciplinary efforts

A unique feature of recent studies of international politics and foreign policy, aside from theoretical activity and attempts to create new research techniques, has been the extent to which they have become interdisciplinary, blending the data, concepts and insights of all the social sciences. In the past, historians, political scientists, geographers, and legal scholars monopolized the field of international relations; today, anthropologists, economists, sociologists and psychologists enrich our understanding of international relations by bringing their special skills to problems of common interest or opening previously neglected areas of inquiry. Sociologists and social psychologists help us to understand the nature and origins of public attitudes and opinions that affect foreign policy issues: they have also provided a vast literature dealing with individual behaviour in bargaining situations. Economists, aside from their interest in international trade and economic development, provide help in understanding political processes in underdeveloped countries. Anthropologists assist the development of the field by studying war and violence as cultural phenomena, characteristics of mediation and conciliation in primitive societies, and types of problems arising from cross-cultural contacts and economic progress in underdeveloped societies.

Some theorizing activity in the field is undertaken not for the purpose of constructing a predictive theory of international relations, but for creating ordering devices or approaches that help the investigator and student make some sense of the great diversity of facts and events in international relations. Two examples of popular models of international politics illustrate the issue of concepts and variables. First, the communist view of international politics is one in which classes not states are the main political actors. International and class relationships are typified by constant 'struggle'. Since the theory argues the state is the instrument of a society's ruling class, in a capitalist society foreign policy will merely express the monopolists' interests in gaining access to markets, fields of investments and raw materials. By its very nature a state that represents the interests of the monopolists is an imperialist state, though how imperialist it is depends upon the stage of capitalist development and class relations within society. Here is a simple theory of international politics that attempts to explain how foreign policy behaviour (dependent variable) varies with changes in domestic class relations and the stages of economic development (independent variables). Yet the theory does not account for such obvious phenomena as the great quantity of collaborative and cooperative relationships between states with highly developed and essentially private enterprise economies. The theory leads the analyst to the ludicrous view of seeing European economic integration as some form of collusion between monopolists to repress the working classes of the EEC countries.

Second, the power politics approach, popular in the mid-twentieth century, assumes that no matter what the long-range objectives of states, their immediate objective is power over other states. International politics is conceived as a struggle for power among all states, either for expansion or defence and protection. Because of its undue emphasis on power and struggle, the power concept conceals other important aspects of international politics. If some relations can be described as abrasive, this is certainly not true of Anglo-American relations. As interesting as the elements of power may be they do not determine how effective a state will be in its external relations. A state can be well endowed with all of the 'elements' of power, and still not achieve its objectives against even the weakest and smallest states.

## Levels of analysis

Each level of analysis makes one look at different things in international politics. For example, the classical theory of balance of power is an attempt to explain the behaviour of many states over a lengthy period of time. It proposes that states will form coalitions and countercoalitions to fend off hegemonic drives, and that a 'balancer' will intervene on behalf of the weaker side in order to redress the balance or restore the old equilibrium. The behaviour of individual political units is thus explained in terms of the state of the whole system (balanced or imbalanced) and the presence or absence of one aggressive state and a balancer. This type of analysis makes no reference to personalities, domestic pressures, or ideologies within states. Foreign policy behaviour is conceived as a reaction to the external environment, the state of balance or imbalance among all the units in the system.

If one looks at international politics from the perspective of individual states, rather than from the state of the system in which they exist, quite different questions arise. One can attempt to explain the behaviour of states by reference not just to the external environment (the system) but primarily to the domestic conditions that affect policy making. Wars, alliances, imperialism, diplomatic manoeuvres, isolation and the many goals of diplomatic action can be viewed as the results of domestic political pressures, national ideologies, public opinion or economic and social needs. Governments do not react just to the external environment or to some mythical balance or imbalance. Their actions also express the needs and values of their own populations and political leaders.

International politics can ultimately be studied by concentrating on the actions and behaviour of individual statesmen. This is the usual approach of diplomatic historians based on the sound point that when one says that 'states' behave, one really means that policy makers are defining purposes, choosing among courses of action and utilizing national capabilities to achieve objectives in the name of the state. This level of analysis focuses upon the ideologies, motivations, ideals, perceptions, values or idiosyncracies of those who are empowered to make decisions for the state.

The key concepts in the study of international relations are the systems or environments in which state action recurs; foreign policy outputs, ranging from orientations to actions; the factors that explain these outputs and the patterns of interaction between states as revealed in conflict and cooperation. International politics consists of a study of types of foreign policy and in such phenomena as diplomatic bargaining, deterrence and conflict; and not with the activities of any one state or group of states.

At what point if any does foreign policy become international politics? Distinction between the terms is vague, but it is roughly the difference between the **objectives** and **actions** (decisions and policies) of a state or states, and the interactions between two or more states. One who analyses the actions of a state toward external environment and the conditions – usually domestic – under which those actions are formulated is concerned essentially with foreign policy; the person who conceives of those actions as only one aspect of a pattern of actions by one state and reactions and responses by others is looking at international politics, or the process of interaction between two or more states.

As distinct from international politics and foreign policy, the term international relations may refer to all forms of interaction between the members of separate societies, whether government sponsored or not. The study of international relations includes the analysis of foreign policies or political processes between nations, but also all other facets of relations between distinct societies. Thus it would include as well studies of international trade unions, the International Red Cross, tourism, international trade, transportation, communication and the development of international values and ethics.

The student of international politics is not concerned with these types of relationships or phenomena, except where they impinge upon official government objectives, or where they are employed by governments as instruments of inducement to achieve military or political objectives. The student of international relations is interested in all aspects of international trade. In the field of international politics, one is concerned with international trade only to the extent that governments may employ economic threats, rewards or punishments for political purposes, as when they promise to lower tariffs *via à vis* another country in return for the right to establish a military base in that country.

## Biases

These are common in the field of international politics. First, many popular analyses of foreign policy and international politics reflect a preoccupation with essentially national problems. There is a tendency to regard the most important problems and conflicts in the world as those in which one's own country is involved. In the United States there is a tendency to view all international political problems in terms of Soviet–American rivalry. Hence, international politics becomes synonymous with the Cold War, and solutions become identified with the effective nuclear deterrents, the cohesion of NATO and effective foreign aid programmes. Threats all seem to emanate from the communist nations and all Western actions appear only as responses to those threats. A second prominent bias derives from the common interest in the unusual, the dramatic and the violent. Newspapers regularly distort reality in favour of violence and sensationalism. News media focus attention on great international crises while they systematically neglect to mention peaceful relations between states. A majority of transactions between states are peaceful, unexciting, stable, predictable and conducted with strict regard to treaty obligations. These transactions do not make news. An unceasing emphasis on violence and conflict naturally leads to perspectives that take 'power politics' and cold warfare as the norms of interstate behaviour, whereas they are really the exception.

Contemporary international relations are becoming increasingly complex and contradictory. Although traditional interpretations of international relations emphasizing the East–West conflict, the primacy of the nation state, and problems brought about by economic underdevelopment all remain valid, they by themselves are no longer able to explain events in the international arena. Capitalist states are no longer necessarily allied with capitalist states against what they perceive as communist expansionism. and communist states are no longer necessarily allied with other communist states against what they perceive as capitalist imperialism. Nation states have been joined by a huge variety of multinational corporations, international organizations, non-governmental organizations and even individuals as prominent actors in the international community. Economic backwardness continues to plague broad areas of the world, but within this panorama of underdevelopment some states are beginning to make economic strides forward, whereas others are sinking into even more abject squalor and poverty. The world is stranded between old conceptions of political conduct and a wholly new conception between the inadequacy of the nation state and the emerging imperative of a global community.

## Foreign policy objectives

People grouped into nation states and other types of political units have needs and purposes, many of which they can only achieve or meet by influencing the behaviour of other states. A large portion of foreign policy making is concerned with day to day problem solving as issues arise at home and abroad. Diplomats and foreign office officials are normally concerned with immediate mundane matters of narrow scope. However, most governments also have some objectives that they are attempting to achieve through the ordering of various actions that reflect needs and purposes. The objectives may be very specific, e.g. promoting a peace proposal for the Arab–Israeli conflict, or general, e.g. creating a common market in a given region.

There are five main objectives of **foreign policy**. First, the concept of internal national unity as opposed to national security includes the administration, control and governing of the territory and outlying dependencies (if any) of a state, including looking after its citizens both at home and abroad. Jurisdiction over land and people has to be maintained in any situation where national interests touch upon international problems. Moreover, the frames of policy have to seek psychological unity in strong public support of action taken in pursuance of negotiations with other countries. The principle of geographic unity presents three types of problems to the policy makers – maintenance of title to all areas claimed by the state; cession of certain areas, and the acquisition of new territories and possessions.

Second, there is the promotion of economic interests. The economic interdependence of nations has been dramatically shown by the world energy and food crises of the mid-1970s, and the recession and unemployment in the last decade. Even the greatest and most powerful nations on earth cannot enjoy economic prosperity and maintain a high standard of living while remaining isolated from the channels of world commerce. The prosperity of a state is contingent upon many complex and closely related factors. These may be divided into two categories: the state assets, including natural resources and population structure, and the manner in which the assets are exploited, which is a reflection of the state's cultural status.

Third, there is the provision of national security. The assumption that a nation's foreign policy must be developed to protect it from attack implies the possibility of danger. Because of the slow development of international law and international agencies to enforce it, each government is dependent upon its own resources in case of attack. Thus the framers of policy must provide a defence against any contingency that may arise. Governments wishing to retain territorial boundaries intact are said to follow *status quo* policies while those with designs on new territory develop revisionist policies, which can be executed by peaceful negotiations or by force.

Security involves at least three phases of preparedness – political, economic and military. Political awareness can be achieved by creating a treaty network that will serve the dual purpose of forming strong alliances and commitments with capable allies and consequently of isolating any potential enemy; utilizing international tensions to implement policy framing and prosecuting a positive, popularly supported and vigorous foreign policy; avoiding by negotiation the precipitation of an overtly hostile act that might cause war; and using international machinery for collective security. Economic preparedness involves either the possession of essential minerals, foodstuffs and other raw materials, or access to them; industrial capacity; the administrative, industrial and scientific know-how necessary to create the weapons and other equipment and facilities needed by the military services; and the financial capacity or natural wealth to underwrite all the foregoing activities without incurring internal economic collapse. Military requirements for the maintenance of national security include: a long-range strategic plan of attack and defence supplemented by constant study of possible tactical situations that might develop in encountering potential enemies; the organization and training of a fighting service that can efficiently utilize the modern engines of land, sea and air power; plans for coordinating civilian personnel and facilities to meet a war situation; and the provision of effective transportation and supply. Psychological preparedness is often a forgotten element – the morale of the population is a vital element in the maintenance of national security.

Protecting national prestige is the fourth fundamental principle. Just as individuals are concerned with their personal reputation in the community in which they live, so a state is obliged to consider its influence in relation to other states in international affairs. A state conducts its international affairs so that its pride and self-respect, or reputation, are maintained intact.

Developing power is the last guiding principle. Power is leverage; it is the ability to initiate and control events and to obtain results. Kings, dictators, and presidents are symbols of power, winning an argument or winning a war is the end result of the application of power. Power exists in social situations involving human relationships. Politics is a struggle for power because in any society, one group is in possession of the government and another seeks its control. Political power is the capacity in any human relationship to control behaviour and influence thought for the attainment of political goals. In this sense power is probably the most universal of all principles governing foreign policy goals.

Sometimes the term 'national interest' has been used (or abused) as a device for analysing nations' objectives. A normative or civic concept of national interest may refer to some ideal set of purposes which a nation should seek to realize in the conduct of its foreign relations. A descriptive meaning is the sense that the national interest may be regarded as those purposes which the nation appears actively to pursue. It might also be said that the national interest is what foreign policy makers say it is.

All too often policy is the product of random, haphazard or even irrational forces and events. Equally often it is the result of dead-locked judgements or an uneasy compromise formula. Often what appears on the surface as the nation's settled course of action may in fact be the result of indecision, unwillingness or inability to act. It may be no policy at all but simply a drift with events. Sometimes foreign policies are the products of statesmen's passive compliance with strong domestic political pressure – and thus products of contending political forces within the nation itself. Finally, policy may be owing to statesmen's abdication of choice and rational judgement in the face of ruthless and strong external pressures.

Governments often pursue incompatible private and collective interests and value objectives simultaneously. It is the task of policy makers to select among conflicting objectives, and determine which are feasible within a specific set of circumstances. Disarmament has been conceived by many governments as both an end in itself and a means to achieve increased national security from foreign military threats. Yet the implementation of any disarmament scheme would incur serious short-term risks to any nation's security.

Political units in the twentieth century have sought to achieve a range of comprehensive objectives. In some areas, state interests are still indistinguishable from dynastic interests. To them the primary objectives of foreign policy were to protect their ruling position and secure quantities of personal wealth and prestige. At the other extreme there are governments that commit national resources to the expansion of messianic philosophies, regardless of what the effects will be on the personal lives, prestige and fortunes of those who formulate these objectives. Between these extremes exist the vast majority of modern states, which seek to achieve collective objectives of national security, welfare of citizens, access to trade routes, markets and vital resources, and sometimes the territory of their neighbours.

What types of criteria do policy makers operate? There are three main ones: the value placed on the objective, or the extent to which policy makers commit themselves and their countries' resources to achieving a particular objective; the time limit set for its achievement; and the kinds of demands the objective imposes on other states in the system.

From these one can construct categories of **objective**. First there are 'core' values and interests, to which governments and nations commit their very existence and which must be preserved or extended at all times. People are willing to make ultimate sacrifices as such interests are related to the self-preservation of a political unit. These are short-range objectives because other goals obviously cannot be achieved unless the political units pursuing them maintain their own existence. Practically all policy makers in the twentieth century have assumed that the most essential objective of any foreign policy is to ensure defence of the home territory and perpetuate a particular political, social and economic system based on that territory. Some governments place equal value on controlling or defending neighbouring territories because these areas contain assets such as manpower and raw materials that can increase a state's capabilities or because they believe that the major threat to their own territorial integrity might materialize through adjacent lands. States with well-established frontiers corresponding to ethnic divisions, which protect their territories and social orders through ordinary defence policies, are not likely to disturb even their immediate neighbours. Those that seek more favourable strategic frontiers or ethnic unity normally do so at the expense of the 'core' values and interests of their neighbours, and thus create dangerous conflicts.

Second, there are middle-range goals which normally impose demands on several other states (commitments to their achievement are serious and some time limits are usually attached to them). Governments can attempt to meet public and private demands and needs through international action. Social welfare and economic development cannot be achieved through self-help, as most states have only limited resources, administrative services and technical skills. Instead of encouraging general expansion of trade or access to foreign markets, they might, under pressure from domestic groups or economic interests, undertake certain foreign policy initiatives that have little connection with the interests of society in general. Another objective is to increase a state's prestige in the system. In the past, as today, this was done primarily through diplomacy, ceremony and displays of military capabilities, but increasingly in our era prestige is measured by levels of industrial development and scientific and technical skills. There are also many different forms of self-extension or imperialism. Some states make demands for neighbouring territory even if that territory does not satisfy any important security or ethnic requirements. Others do not occupy foreign territory, but seek advantages including access to raw materials, markets and trade routes, which they cannot achieve through ordinary trade or diplomacy.

Lastly, there are long-range goals which seldom have definite time limits. In practice, statesmen rarely place the highest value on long-range goals and do not, consequently, commit many national capabilities or policies to their achievement – unless the goals are central to a political philosophy or ideology, in which case they may be considered 'core' or middle-range interests. States that work actively toward achieving universal long-range goals usually make radical demands on all other units in the system and thus create great instability. In pressing for middle-range goals states make special demands against particular states; in pursuing long-range goals, states normally make universal demands, for their purpose is no less than to reconstruct an entire international system according to a universally applicable plan or vision. The objectives do not necessarily determine the actions that will be used to achieve them. A frequent mistake is to assume that the only American objective abroad is to promote its liberal and free enterprise values or that every Russian diplomatic manoeuvre is part of a carefully formulated plan to communize the world. If a state wishes to secure more strategically advantageous frontiers at the expense of its neighbours it can do so using almost any technique from persuasion to aggression. To persuade it can offer a piece of its own territory as compensation, promise a friendship treaty, foreign aid or 100 other types of reward. To coerce it can build alliances or subvert the neighbouring regimes and establish puppet governments which would then cede the desired territory.

A government that sees itself as a bastion of the revolution will probably have at least some vague objective or plan to create a new revolutionary world or regional order. A government that sees itself as a regional collaborator will probably have an objective relating to the construction of a common market. Regional protector roles can be related to objectives of creating stable alliances, which test the wide ranging skills of decision makers.

## Questions

### International relations

1 What is meant by 'statecraft' in the medieval and modern contexts?
2 Discuss the four main theories of international politics.
3 Critically appraise the popular models of international politics.
4 At what point if any does foreign policy become international politics?
5 Account for international politics being beset by issues of bias.
6 Give reasons for contemporary international relations becoming increasingly complex and contradictory.

### Foreign policy objectives

1 Assess the main objectives in foreign policy formulation. Are there any perceived dichotomies?
2 Foreign policy relations between countries are often misunderstood. Do you agree?
3 Are governments' private and collective interests effectively incomplete?
4 Are the criteria adopted by policy makers considered to be too complex?
5 Are long-range foreign policy objectives self-defeating?

### Further reading

Banks, A. S. (ed.), *Political Handbook of the World*, McGraw Hill, New Jersey, 1979.
Chan, S., *International Relations in Perspective*, Macmillan, New York and London, 1984.
Day, A. J. (ed.), *China and The Soviet Union 1949–1984*, Longman, London, 1984.
Grenville, J. A. S., *The Major International Treaties 1914–1973*, Methuen, London, 1974.
Howard, M., *Ethics and Power in International Politics*, Council on Christian Approaches to Defence and Disarmament, London, 1978.
*International Yearbook and Statesman's Who's Who*, IPC Business Press Information Services Ltd, International Publishing Corporation, London, yearly.
Papp, D. S., *Contemporary International Relations, Frameworks for Understanding*, Macmillan, New York and London, 1984.
Schiavone, G., *International Organisation, A Dictionary and Directory*, Macmillan Press, London, 1983.

Stephenson, M. and Weal, J., *Nuclear Dictionary*, Longman, London, 1985.
Taylor, P. J., *Political Geography: World Economy Nation-State and Locality*, Longman, London, 1985.

# 22
# Decision making issues

## Decision making

A decision is a choice of goals or means of reaching some goal from among those seen to be available as alternatives at the time, for the purpose of reacting to the requirements of a specific complex issue, or some situation thought likely to occur in the future.

Analysis of decision making is a vital factor in political science and it involves the analysis of political systems, processes and behaviour in terms of political decisions which are made, including the structures involved in decision making, the factors influencing the outcomes of the process and the political costs of decisions, as well as the selection of actors for decision making roles.

**Decision making analysis** is distinguished both by its concern with decisions that are not in themselves policies, e.g. with voting decisions, or which are only part of a wider-ranging policy process, and by its concentration of attention on the political factors involved in decision making. Among the approaches to decision making analysis that have been employed are game theory, with its emphasis on the quantification of the results of decision strategies in certain types of competitive situation; and approaches derived from economics, including the analogies between economic and political decision making.

The **decision making approach** offers a way of studying international crises. This approach stresses the importance of the decision makers' perceptions and the manner in which their perceptions can affect the selection of policies. A crisis is a special kind of situation for decision makers. It is distinguished from normal situations by the officials' perception of a high degree of foreign threat, a feeling of urgency about the situation and a sense of surprise over its occurrence. In combination the pressures created by high threat, short response time and surprise can produce unsound policies. In a crisis situation, officials may be apt to make less rational or more belligerent decisions. As the Cuban Missiles Crisis made clear, the translation of the actual stimulus, (the Soviet introduction of missiles into Cuba), into a perceived stimulus, (the interpretation of the meaning of this Soviet action by American officials), may not always be accurate. In other words, the decision makers' perception of a situation may not correspond to the actual objective situation. Misconception can occur. In other cases the intended response of decision makers may not match their perceptions of a situation. Officials may miscalculate and make an in-appropriate policy choice. Yet again, the wishes or intentions of decision makers may not be faithfully or competently executed. For example, although President Kennedy ordered the United States' Navy to alter the coverage of its blockade of Cuba during the height of the missile crisis, this order was not immediately implemented.

Decision uncertainty is also a tricky situation but in the context of great power rivalry, escalations can be prevented. It is more difficult for policy makers to assess the probability of victory or defeat when there are many uncommitted states. On the other hand when states join alliances they make a public commitment to defend their allies. Therefore the formation of alliances helps to clarify the intentions of governments. When the number of states joining alliances increases, policy makers can be more confident in their assessment of the likely strength of the contesting groups and the probable outcome of the contest. This prediction in their decision uncertainty – especially when they feel that their side enjoys a decisive edge – can dispose officials to risk confrontations. The fear of war prompts policy makers to search for alliance partners. Yet those who support the balance of power theory believe alliances – to the extent that they help to preserve an equal distribution of power – tend to inhibit wars.

Paradoxically alliance commitments may also increase decision uncertainty. When a great power promises to defend a smaller ally it expands the number of situations in which it will go to war. Yet it lacks complete control over or knowledge of the conditions that can ensnare it in a war (e.g. when its ally is attacked by another state). Uncertainty is thus enhanced by the loss of capacity to make autonomous decisions.

## Environment and the nature of decision making

For a national government there are two kinds of feedback of current information. There is an external feedback about foreign policy and an internal feedback about what goes on inside the country. The latter is usually more important. Domestic politics tends to outweigh foreign policy in most countries most of the time, particularly in the modern age of mass politics. It is a commonplace of political experience that politicians ignorant of foreign policy who make gross mistakes in foreign affairs can get re-elected if they correctly gauge the realities of domestic politics. Today government policies are domestically determined more often than inter-nationally determined although most political decisions are a mixture of the two.

When all information comes in from the different streams of current intake, a decision must be made by the government. The more diverse intake streams of information a system has, the freer it is in making decisions. One of the most difficult and most important features of politics is how one makes decisions – especially decisions on policy.

Decisions are often broken into sequences. First, a decision is made about the general preferences, purposes or goals in regard to some class of problems. This is called a policy decision. Later, decisions deal with the means and methods of carrying out the policy. The difference between policy and its execution resembles that between strategy and tactics. Strategy consists in setting a long-run series of goals or targets; tactics consists in choosing and applying the short-run means to attain them. Generally, strategy looks farther ahead into the future and involves setting a larger class of goals, whereas tactics denotes choosing a more limited class of intermediate steps within the larger class. This orderly progress from policy to tactical decision occurs when there has been an accurate assessment of the consequences of each step. In practice, the decision-making sequence may easily degenerate into muddle, drift and worse as in the United States' involvement in the Vietnam War: the failure of early strategic and tactical decisions to produce the desired effects resulted in progressively widening the scope of the initial policy decisions to provide limited support to the government of South Vietnam. Policy also often implies the setting of a relatively distant goal or purpose that may have to be approached by a zig-zag course of short-run moves around several intervening obstacles.

In modern politics, policy is very controversial. Until the Second World War people talked of 'legislation' rather than 'policy'. When the eighteenth-century English philosopher and political theorist, John Locke, divided power among several authorities, he was primarily concerned about the power of legislative decision not the power of policy making. He wanted each legislative decision to be made very carefully at the appropriate time. He did not concern himself with setting policy as a general guide for the future conduct of the government. Nowadays people demand just that for they have become increasingly preoccupied with policy. Those in public life are very keen about being involved in policy making. This has become the really important task of government; legislation is looked down upon as a technical matter. The concern of important people is to decide policy. They then leave it to lawyers to work out the technicalities of the legislation involved.

At this point the interests of the 'important people' coincide with those of the 'people in the street'. They too know little about technicalities of legislation and are impatient with them. But they know what they like and often know what they want. They can make clear which goal or outcome they prefer. They can express their support for a policy, or opposition to it, and they can vote for a candidate or party that appears to stand for the policies they like.

Policy decisions involve particular objectives, and the more important the objectives are, the more important the decisions are. The definition of objectives, or goals, is a critical stage in policy making. **Policy** in short means goal setting or goal definition. It is a decision about what one's goals should be. One reason that discussions about foreign policy are usually unenlightening and futile is the lack of definition of a concept of foreign policy. It is not a clearly defined proposition. Often people have several goals that they find hard to reconcile, but cannot put into a clear and agreed upon rank order of importance. As a rule it is difficult to say what is the goal of the foreign policy of any modern democratic nation. All sorts of people in a democracy have different kinds of need and orientation and, hence, different preferences for national goals; each will try to make his or her definition prevail, and many have enough power to compel at least some consideration. Thus, by the very nature of the democratic process, long-range foreign policy will only rarely be real policy since usually it will lack an agreed upon, clearly defined goal. More modest short-range goals sometimes command easier agreement, because different groups may interpret them as steps toward different long-range policies and support them for different reasons. Something similar is true for domestic policy. Only if widespread agreement can be reached on well-defined specific goals – such as maintaining low unemployment or trying to end race discrimination – and only if such goals are realistic, will domestic policies have a chance to succeed. The same policy can often be supported by several groups for different reasons.

In domestic as in foreign policy, people may seek to attain several goals without being able to agree on which one to put first. Some political decisions are invisible. Often they are non-decisions, that is decisions not to discuss a problem or not to put a project on the agenda of a meeting. Techniques of deferring political intervention or making it selective are common. Such situations tend to benefit those groups which have the power and organizational skills to use them, and they mitigate against those groups which have not.

Almost every political decision or non-decision makes someone richer or poorer, more or less free to follow his or her desires, more powerful or less so. Political power also includes the power to be noticed, for politics also decides which problems are to be neglected or ignored, which ideas can be expressed with a chance of getting serious attention, which questions are not to be discussed, and which groups of people are to be forgotten or persistently overlooked. Occasionally when politics changes at some later time, these formerly unobtrusive groups and unmentionable questions then move into the focus of attention, and public opinion suddenly becomes aware of a new spectrum of light thrown on an issue.

## Systems analysis, policy analysis and leadership

Systems analysis represents one of the attempts to develop more detailed techniques for analysing public policies. Techniques such as mathematical models and human gaming have been used to find optimal or preferable solutions among a series of alternatives based on relative costs and benefits. Such efforts represent a reaction against policy recommendations or decisions made on the basis of untested hypotheses, unstated assumptions and uncertainties about the implications of alternative choices.

Operational research is the application of scientific methods and tools to problems involving the operation of a system. A problem is studied, a model made of a system, and experiments carried out, so that recommendations can be made to policy makers.

Model building in its widest sense means choosing from the jumble and chaos of life those aspects which are considered significant, and relating them to form a coherent picture or system. Models are sometimes drawn from 'cybernetics' (the study of systems of control and communications) and used in the study of political-decision making to emphasize the importance of feedback from the environment and of adjustment to avoid obstacles.

A system is a grouping of separate but interdependent parts which form a complex whole to achieve some objective. It can exist as a subsystem of a larger system. Each individual is an actor in a set of interlocking and overlapping systems, extending from the more exclusive, such as the family, through to the political system and eventually to the all inclusive nation state system.

All systems, an individual animal, plant, social group, have properties in common. Components of a system are related, in the sense that when the properties of one component change, the remaining components and the system as a whole are affected. A system maintains its character throughout a limited period of time.

The main premise behind a general systems theory is that different systems have much in common, and that regularities in one system will have a fair chance of being repeated in another. A country's domestic political system can be conceived as similar to an electronic computer which processes and transforms inputs into outputs while adjusting mechanisms allow for a feedback from the outputs to the input mechanisms. Just as organic systems adapt to their environment, states aim to do the same for the purpose of survival. Unless a system is closed (totally self-contained) it depends on links with the external environment to which it must adapt and from which it gains aid (feedback) to help it to survive. A political system survives if the government is able to obtain taxes from the people to pay the expenses of administration and is able to recruit staff to operate the system. By socialization it will try to gain public support. Various systems operate akin to a simplified stimulus–response situation. When the environment responds, an adjustment can be made on an expectation of how the environment behaves. If domestic or foreign policies meet with unfavourable reaction governments tend to make the necessary changes in policy.

General systems theory can be applied to the activities of people, especially in politics. A **social system** is characterized by a system of roles supported by norms and values concerning the appropriate behaviour and relationships between persons occupying the roles; and by shared values, symbols and beliefs which provide the basis for people who sometimes act together to pursue common goals. People can be involved in a number of systems, the boundaries between them distinguished by people's different roles or modes of behaviour. A political party is one example.

A **domestic system** can be defined as sets of interactions taken from the total behaviour of members of society through which values are authoritatively allocated for the society by government. The concept of system applies to foreign policy analysis as well as to domestic politics; taking into account certain domestic variables such as military and economic strength, political structure, interest groups and competing elites, and external aims of a military, political, economic and cultural nature.

There are limitations to the use of models, which are only as accurate as the elements introduced into them. The choice of assumptions is largely a matter of judgement and there is much in the behaviour of people, governments and states which cannot be predicted. The systems approach as applied to policy making cannot allow for various irrational and uncertain forces such as charisma and ideology or the propensity of actors to adopt high risk or low risk strategies.

Many of the wants or needs articulated by society are lost to the political system, for example reports and the work of pressure groups which are not implemented by the government. Some aspects recur, e.g. documentary evidence on which future ideas are built which may eventually be channelled into some concrete output of the political system. Considerable wastage can result in the political system. Human endeavour such as psychological, spiritual and ideational forces in speech, written form and activity often never results in anything positive.

## Policy making and policy analysis

Public policy making consists, as do other types, of a pattern of action extending over a period of time and involving many decisions. A distinction needs to be made between policy content, i.e. the substance of policy and policy process, which is the given set of methods and techniques by which a policy is made. The three main phases of policy making are initiation, formulation and implementation. Policy initiation involves the source of ideas for policy proposals drawn from the various inputs into the government machinery. Sources of ideas for new policy may come from the public, political parties, pressure groups, or as the result of feedback from the operating of existing policies. Input implies the total of the outputs from other domestic subsystems or from abroad, or the flow of effects from the environment into the inner political system of government.

Policy formulation involves the development of a policy in detail until it becomes accepted in some finalized written form. Implementation involves the carrying out of a policy once approved. A political system will collapse if subject to too much stress or lack of support and if excess demands are imposed upon it. To prevent this occurrence, policy analysts act in specialized consultant capacities to try and improve the quality of decision and policy making. Analysts are concerned with the causes, nature and consequences of political action at various levels of government and with all aspects of the policy making process.

## Leadership

**Leadership** is very important when considering decision making. Three types of leadership are, authoritarian (a person may like to plan and make decisions himself or herself, disliking delegation of authority and not accepting advice likely to contradict his or her own views); democratic (a person may like to share the problems involved in decision making and will tolerate discussion of opinions which differ from his or her own); and *laissez-faire* (an abdication of leadership inclined to be anarchical). The democratic style is likely to be the most successful general purpose pattern, for a balance is maintained between dictatorial management and participation. The autocratic style if abused can result in resentment, absenteeism and resignations. However, sometimes it may be necessary, and such leadership often gets the quickest results in the short term.

Qualities of leadership are valuable in political life. Special attributes include the abilities to make appropriate decisions expeditiously relating to the task undertaken and to command respect and support, showing consideration for the needs and feelings of others. Leadership requires certain ingredients such as intuition, vision, conviction, courage, integrity, vitality and endurance. It is crucial to have persons of sound stable personalities in vital positions.

Decision makers are interested in effective communication – in the methods, techniques, processes and barriers involved in the skilful conveying of ideas to others and in the factors which result in success or failure. The ability to convey messages effectively is an important factor in gaining and maintaining power. Successful communication depends not only on a common language but also on a common set of words as people vary in intelligence, experience and social position. With regard to political and institutional barriers, much will depend on the nature of the political system, whether it is closed or open, democratic or authoritarian, and on the characteristics of the bureaucracy. Personal idiosyncrasies or qualities of particular leaders are not as important as class or educational background, role requirements of a particular office, institutional constraints imposed by bureaucracy, or pressures and problems involved in decision making.

## Game theory

Human life is a sequence of continuous decisions made by the conscious individual. He or she is continuously confronted with the need for making choices, some of them narrow, others of very wide scope. In some cases he or she commands much information about consequences of a particular choice, in most he or she is quite uncertain. Some affect the immediate present, others involve commitment for a distant future. Some decisions are entirely his or her own and many are made with respect to nature. Many decisions are made by a group of individuals, and the group decision can be arrived at by a great variety of processes. Some decisions arise from a logical structure as in law.

Decisions must also be made when an individual plays a game. In playing the game, the individual follows rules which together with the decisions made usually determine the winner. In all cases the need for optimality (maximum rewards) will arise since clearly a decision is a choice among alternatives and the 'best' decision will be preferred over all others. Many different kinds of decisions occur in connection with games of various types, the number of different games being indeterminate since always new games can be invented. In order to establish the behaviour of individuals and to evaluate their choices, criteria have to be known or be established.

**Game theory** represents a rigorous mathematical approach towards providing concepts and methods for making reasonable decisions in a great variety of human situations.

Games, as far as both their origin and development are concerned as well as their scientific analysis, have a long and varied history. Their roots go back into the animal kingdom and to primitive society. Games are present in all civilizations in great varieties of form and in disguises such as in ceremonies, liturgies, diplomatic customs or war, the latter being especially visible during the time of maintenance of expensive private mercenary armies. In Roman imperial times public games were a great burden on the state. In modern ages the money transactions, say in the United Kingdom from football pools, exceed those of some of the largest corporations.

It was not until the sixteenth century that games became a subject of scientific inquiry. The fundamental notion of probability was developed by Geronimo Cardano; from which time Galileo, Blaise Pascal, Christiaan Huygens, the Bernoullis, Pierre Simon de Laplace and many others of equal distinction have extended our understanding of this basic concept. Probability theory is characterized by the simultaneous appearance of several independent but interacting human agents each pursuing his or her own goal. Probability theory first explained chances in particular games: Gottfried Leibnitz in 1710 first foresaw the possibility of simulation of real life situations by indicating that naval problems could be studied by moving appropriate units representing ships on manoeuvre boards.

Games can be classified into two broad but sharply different categories – games of chance and games of strategy, the latter of which contains chance games, as a simple special case. In the former, the outcome is totally independent of the action of the playing individual, whereas in the latter the outcome is controlled neither by chance alone, nor by the individual player alone, but by each player to some extent. It is the entirety of the actions of the players which determines the outcome and the equilibria. In the course of a play the interests of the players are sometimes opposed to each other, sometimes parallel. Thus with game theory suitable games can be identified with the important human actions which they model.

A purpose of social science, of law, of philosophy, has been for a long time to give meaning to the notion of rational behaviour to account for irrationality. Rationality is predicated on two things – the identification of a goal in the form of preferences formed (possibly stated numerically); and control over all the variables that determine the attainment of the goal. The control factor is of primary concern: if nature intervenes in his or her intended behaviour, the individual can control an indifferent nature by means of statistical adjustment. It is an entirely different matter if among the variables there are some that are controlled by other individuals having opposite aims. This lack of complete control is clearly the case in zero-sum (winnings compensate losses exactly) two-person games of strategy, but also in business, in military combat, in political struggles and the like.

The purpose of a theory of decision making or specifically of game theory is to advise a person how to behave by choosing optimally from the set of his or her available strategies, in situations subject to the theory. If he or she decides knowingly to deviate from the indicated course he or she has either substituted another goal, or dislikes the means (for moral and other reasons). It is then a matter of terminology whether he or she is still considered to be a rational actor. Clearly some technical available strategies may be inadmissable in legal, moral and other respects. In some cases these questions do not arise: chess is played equally whether the opponents are rich, poor, Catholics, Mohammedans, communists or capitalists. But business or political deals are affected by such circumstances. Advice can be given with or without constraints which involve morals or religion.

The description of a **game of strategy** involves a number of new concepts.

Obviously games are first classified by virtue of the number of players or participants. When the winnings of some are compensated exactly by the losses of others, the game is zero-sum. The sum can also be positive (when all gain), negative (when all lose), constant or variable. Games are 'essential' when there is an advantage in forming coalitions which can happen even in zero-sum games. Games are inessential when there is no such advantage, in which case each player proceeds independently for himself or herself.

Games are played according to rules which are immutable and must be known to the players. A tacit assumption is that the players agree to play. They do this without doubt when playing for pleasure. When games are used as models it may however happen that one's participation in the modelled situation is not voluntary. For example, a country may be forced into a military conflict: or, in order to survive and to earn a living, a person may have to engage in certain economic activities.

In games of chance the task is to determine and then to evaluate probabilities inherent in the game; in games of strategy we introduce probability in order to obtain the optimal choice of strategy. The problem now arises how a social equilibrium can be described when there are more than two decision makers. When a coalition wins the proceeds have to be divided among the partners and these then find themselves in the same kind of conflict situation which arises for the players of a zero-sum two-person game. The totality of all payments to all players is an 'imputation'. In order to determine an equilibrium it appears to be necessary to find a particular imputation that is better or more acceptable from among all possible ones than any other. Such an imputation then dominates all other imputations. That would be the case in inessential games. Only for those is there a unique social optimum, a division of the proceeds of the game played by society which cannot be improved upon and which therefore is imposed or imposes itself upon society as the best stable arrangement. But since cooperation is a basic feature of human organization, these games are of little interest.

Thus the hope of finding a uniquely best solution for human affairs is in vain: there is no stability for such arrangements. Political, social and economic schemes have been proposed under the tacit assumption that they are possible when people organize themselves freely. Only the isolated individual or a fully centralized (usually dictatorial) society can produce a scheme that it considers better than any other and that it hopes to be able to enforce. So there is in general no better all dominating scheme of distribution or imputation.

In political science there are many applications of game theory. Great strides for example have been made in assessing voting procedures, many of these steps resting on the theory of weighted majority games. In addition political power play, with favours granted, side payments made, bluff, promises kept and broken, is as ideal and fertile a field for the new concepts as one could wish, but the path is thorny, especially because of the preliminary difficult quantification of matters such as 'political advantage' and the like. Of particular significance is the illumination of the bargaining and negotiating process. Points have to be borne in mind; namely how the contracting parties should deal with disclosure of their own utility functions in the process of negotiating. Furthermore in the situation of two bargaining parties the one will get the upper hand which has the finer utility scale, a better discernment of advantages. Negotiation is always possible except when there is full antagonism, which exists only in a zero-sum two-person game. In all other cases negotiations are possible whether the game be zero-sum or not, to manage and resolve the conflict.

### Conflict studies – management and resolution

Interactions between states in the contemporary system are numerous and diverse, and can be classified according to issue areas; trade, international security, tourism, technical cooperation, colonialism, control of nuclear weapons, etc. The intensity of war as measured by frequency and duration of battles, number of combatants, casualties, costs and the like, has increased dramatically. The number of participants has also increased. Conflict that 'threatens the peace' is a problem important enough to warrant both scientific study and implementation of plans and proposals to keep it within 'acceptable limits'.

### Characteristics of violent conflict

Conflict leading to organized violence emerges from a particular combination of parties with incompatible positions over an issue, hostile attitudes, and certain types of diplomatic and military actions. The parties to an international conflict are normally, but not necessarily, the governments of nation states. Parties seek to achieve certain objectives, such as additional or more secure territory, security, access to markets, population increase, prestige, alliances, world revolution, the overthrow of an unfriendly government, changes in United Nations' procedures and many other things. In seeking to achieve or defend these objectives their demands, actions or both will run counter to the interests and objectives of other parties.

An issue field is the subject of contention between the parties, and includes the positions they are attempting to achieve, e.g. over actual territory. There may also be incompatabilities of position on such a political issue as tariff structures, legal rights in Berlin, the proliferation of nuclear weapons, the treatment of minorities in a state, or the powers and duties of the United Nations' Secretary General. Conflict may arise in these areas because one government wants the problem solved in a manner incompatible with the wishes of another party or parties.

A crisis is one stage of the conflict, its distinguishing features include a sudden eruption of unexpected events caused by previous conflict. The characteristics of crisis are unanticipated surprise actions by the opponent; perception of great threat; perception of limited time to make a decision or response and perception of disastrous consequences from inaction. None of these events or perceptions is likely to occur unless there has been a preceding conflict.

In the twentieth century, seven major types of state objective or source of conflict can be identified. Limited territorial conflicts occur where there are incompatible positions with reference to possession of a specific piece of territory, or to rights enjoyed by one state in or near the territory of another. Conflicts can, second, be concerned with the composition of a government. Third, conflicts can occur in which one state is attempting to secure territorial rights or privileges from another state in order to protect its security interests – this can be classed as strategic imperialism. Fourth, national honour conflicts occur in which governments undertake military threats or actions to vindicate some alleged wrongdoing. Fifth, unlimited imperialism is in evidence when one government seeks to destroy the independence of another state, usually for a combination of ideological, security and commercial purposes. Sixth, liberation conflicts or revolutionary wars can be fought by one state to 'liberate' the people of another state. Lastly, conflicts can arise from a government's objective of unifying a divided country.

Generally, incompatible positions in the fields of territorial jurisdiction, rights on teritory and control over ethnic minorities are a major source of international conflict. Ideological confrontations between the great powers concerning the composition of governments in small states are a hallmark of the Cold War.

## Attitudes

Certain attitudes and psychological predispositions typically surround any serious conflict or crisis. First, suspicion is directed toward the opponent, his intentions and the motives underlying his actions. In conflicts or crises sudden changes in relationships are likely, as well as high degrees of uncertainty and unpredictability. Suspicions colour speculation as to the other side's intentions and peace gestures, for example, will probably be rejected as a trick. Issue escalation is another attitude common to policy makers operating in a crisis or conflict. They tend to attach symbolic importance to interests that, from a commercial or strategic point of view, are not worth very much. A feeling of urgency surrounds the policy makers, at least during the crisis stage of an international conflict. Under the feeling of urgency and the uncertainties surrounding the enemy's motives and actions, policy makers perceive fewer alternative courses of action open to themselves than to the enemy. Policy makers perceive the crisis, if not all conflicts, as a turning point in the relationship between the parties and sometimes in the history of the world. In a crisis, perceptions of threat are more salient than perceptions of the opponent's relative capabilities.

The presence of these and other attitudes – hostility, lack of trust and nationalism – are directly linked to the propensity of people to overreact to provocations. Studies help to explain why armed force is frequently the action that is ultimately taken in crisis, though other action may precede the use of force. In the early stages of conflict or crisis, protests, rejections, denials, accusations, demands, warnings, threats, and symbolic actions are likely to occur, whereas formal negotiation is more likely in the settlement stage of the conflict or crisis.

Forms of action can include protest notes; denials and accusations; calling ambassadors home for consultations; withdrawal of the ambassador assigned to the enemy capital; threat of serious consequences if certain actions by the opponent do not cease; threat of limited or total economic boycott or embargo; extensive official denunciation of the opponent; application of limited or total economic boycott or embargo; formal break in diplomatic relations; formal blockades, exemplary limited use of force and reprisals; and war, of which there may be a great variety according to the nature of the objectives, level of force and geographic scope. A conflict or crisis may involve any of these actions and many may be taken simultaneously. Conflicts and crises do not necessarily escalate from one step to the next; it is possible that policy makers will decide to go from denunciation warnings straight to the use of military force.

A conflict can be settled by means of conquest – with virtually no diplomacy except perhaps in drafting the terms of surrender – or it may be resolved by means of some official compromise arrived at after extended negotiations and mediation. A compromise is only one of six possible outcomes or settlements – the others are avoidance or voluntary withdrawal, violent conquest, forced submission or effective deterrence, award and passive settlement.

When the incompatibility of goals, values, interests or positions is perceived by both sides, one possible solution is for one or both parties to withdraw from a physical or bargaining position, or to cease the actions that originally caused hostile responses. It is probably the most common behaviour among governments that normally maintain friendly relations.

Conquest requires overwhelming the opponent by means of the use of force. Even the termination of violent conquest can involve some agreement and bargaining between the antagonists. One side must be able to realize that peace, even under the terms of unconditional surrender, is more desirable than the continuation of conflict. One side may achieve this goal by forcing the others to realize that the possibilities of achieving even reduced objectives or successfully defending itself have disappeared.

In submission or deterrence, one side withdraws from a previously held value, position, or interest because the opponent makes effective threats to push it out by the use of force. There can be some compromise in which both sides agree to a partial withdrawal of their initial objectives, positions, demands or actions. The withdrawal need not be of the same magnitude to both parties. The main problem in arranging a compromise settlement is to get both sides to realize that the price of continued conflict is higher than the costs and consequences of reducing demands or withdrawing from diplomatic or military positions.

A complicated outcome based on a previous compromise is the award, wherein the opponents agree to a settlement achieved through non-bargaining procedures. An **award** is any decision effected by an independent third party (e.g. a court) or criterion (e.g. majority rule) which sets out the substantive terms of settlement. Most conflicts are not of course resolved by means of awards, because procedurally they involve a surrender of bargaining and require a willingness to resolve the issues on the basis of some impartial criterion, such as law, under which there can be only a winner and a loser.

Often international conflicts have no formal outcome (deterrence, avoidance, compromise, conquest or award) but persist for a long period until the parties implicitly accept a new *status quo* as partially legitimate.

**Institutions and procedures for resolving international conflicts**

Conquest, forced submission and deterrence are outcomes usually achieved by manipulation of the instruments of violence. Three basic procedures for arranging compromises and awards are: bilateral or multilateral negotiations among the parties directly involved; mediation, wherein a third party with no direct interest in the issue areas under contention intervenes in the bargaining processes; and adjudication wherein an independent third party determines a settlement by means of some type of award.

Direct negotiations among opponents are as old as conflicts between organized societies. Techniques of diplomatic bargaining have remained essentially the same over time. Bilateral discussions between special emissaries or professional diplomats have been the historical rule, but as many conflicts involve more than two parties, multilateral conferences have been used extensively as well.

The essence of the bargaining process involves the establishment of commitments to essential positions, determination of areas where concessions can be made, commissioning of credible threats and promises, and maintaining patience. The necessary condition for the success of any negotiation is a common interest on the part of the opponents to avoid violence.

**Compromises** or successful negotiations are more likely to result if (a) the issues or objectives under contention are specific and carefully defined rather than vague or symbolic; (b) the parties avoid use of threats; (c) in their general relationships, the states in conflict have many other common interests; (d) the issues are defined in such a way that pay-offs can be arranged for both sides, or that the rewards for both parties will increase by means of cooperation; (e) in disarmament negotiations, at least, the parties are equal militarily and similar negotiations have led to previous compromise outcomes.

One of the potential consequences of international conflict is the spill-over of violence between two or more parties into the territory or issue fields of third parties. It is recognized that in any social conflict between two nation states, the attitudes and patterns of behaviour commonly exhibited during the crisis stage are precisely those most likely to lead to violence and destruction. Thus the most important functions of the third party – a party outside the 'emotional field' of the conflict – are to restore communications between the disputants, impose cooling-off periods, investigate conditions in the area of conflict, and provide, if necessary, a variety of services to the parties in conflict. From a bargaining point of view, third party intervention into a conflict or crisis may provide a feasible avenue of retreat for governments that wish to withdraw gracefully, without appearing to back down before threats from the main opponents. A compromise yielded to the third party may be easier to arrange than withdrawing in the face of the enemy. Distrust and suspicion are among the hallmarks of policy makers' attitudes during a conflict and a neutral third party can help to dispel them. The extent to which third parties 'penetrate' a conflict depends upon many variables, none of which alone could explain success or failure. Since pacific settlement procedures in contemporary international organizations are based on the principle of voluntarism – both parties to a conflict must accept the role and functions of the third party – it is the protagonists themselves, through their responsiveness and willingness to be influenced, who ultimately determine the third party's success. Power does not seem to be particularly relevant in mediation efforts.

The final procedure for resolving international conflicts is adjudication and arbitration, whereby the parties, by prior agreement, submit the issues under contention to an independent legal tribunal. The court is supposed to decide the case on the basis of international law, and jurisdiction usually extends only to legal issues. A legal issue can be defined loosely as the interpretation of a treaty; any question of international law; the existence of any fact that, if established, would constitute a breach of an international obligation, and the nature or extent of the reparation to be made for the breach of an international obligation. International tribunals can take a case only if both parties agree to its jurisdiction.

In crises where violence has broken out and where the parties have previously agreed to a ceasefire or truce, the United Nations has been active in separating combatants through interpositionary forces or truce observation teams. This is usually the action taken following the Security Council or General Assembly organizing an investigatory body followed by the appointment of some agent to attempt diplomatic intervention. Of all the activities and tasks that the United Nations undertakes to cope with crises, conflicts and disputes, mediation is the most difficult in the sense that only about two out of five attempts succeed. Nevertheless many difficult crises and conflicts have been brought to a conclusion essentially in accordance with United Nations' objectives because of the mediatory activities of various commissions or individuals.

Information gathering and service functions of the United Nations have been on the whole more successful than mediation. Fact finding and reporting, which come at the early stages of conflict, have been hampered only in cases where governments have refused to permit investigating groups to conduct their operations in the territories where the sources of conflict existed. Various service and supervisory functions normally come at the latter stages of a crisis or conflict, when the parties have already agreed to a ceasefire or to accept more substantive terms of settlement.

The high number of ceasefire violations and armistice line incidents shows that many agreements are built on flimsy foundations. Others are at best truces rather than real settlements.

All the reporting, bargaining or supervisory activities of the United Nations have been aimed primarily at relieving or managing crises, not at resolving underlying conflicts. Except for easing the transition from colonialism, this organization has been effective primarily as an agent for controlling crises.

**Conflict resolution** has had mixed success. Conflicts involving two small states, non-cold-war issues and a combination of bilateral negotiation and Secretary General mediation have most likely resulted in a successful outcome. Conflicts involving the major powers, cold war issues and mediation outside or within the United Nations' structure have the least likelihood of reaching a successful outcome. 'Open' states are more likely than 'closed' states to utilize the major institutionalized structures for resolving conflicts, though 'closed' states use the United Nations slightly more often than 'open' states. In cases submitted to the courts, the initiator is usually the stronger of the two states involved in the conflict or dispute.

Most conflicts arise over incompatible positions in various issue areas. If the incompatible values and positions of both parties are perceived as fundamental, the parties' behaviour, buttressed by hostile, distrustful and suspicious attitudes, may well be violent. Unless stalemate, obsolescence, or effective third party intervention occur, the outcome is likely to be physical conquest or forced withdrawal. The critical point in the conflict is when the actions of one state lead the government of another to consider the possibility of using force. Mild threats, pressures and reprisals can often be controlled, but if tensions are high enough and the actions perceived as extremely threatening, a crisis situation, where a decision to use organized force may be required, results. In a crisis, symbolic communication often increases while overt bargaining and negotiation decrease; and the behaviour of policy makers may well be vitally affected by the pressures of time, perceptions of threat and the need to act quickly. Violence often results. It is in this situation that the fact-finding, mediation, interposition and supervisory tasks developed in international organizations become important. One of the most discouraging facts about international organizations has been their inability or unwillingness to cope with conflicts before they reach the crisis stage.

In dealing with terrorism and similar anti-state activities, international organizations in general have been weak.

## Questions

### Decision making

1  Examine the distinguishing issues in decision-making analysis.
2  Discuss the role of misconception and overreaction in conflict escalation.
3  What were Locke's views of decision making?
4  Why is the definition of objectives a critical stage in policy making?

### Systems analysis, policy analysis and leadership

1  What are the advantages and disadvantages of systems analysis?
2  How can a general systems theory be applied to the political activity of people?
3  Examine the distinctions between policy content and policy process.
4  Why are qualities of leadership valuable in political life?

### Game theory

1  Define game theory.
2  How can game theory be applied to political issues?

## Conflict studies – management and resolution

1 Examine the chief characteristics of violent conflict.
2 Account for the variety of state objectives or sources of conflict in the twentieth century.
3 What are the rational and irrational characteristics of crisis behaviour?
4 Assess the value of the bargaining process in the resolution of conflict.
5 Outline the process of procedures for resolving international conflicts.
6 Critically appraise the value of the conflict resolution process.

## Further reading

*Europa Year Book*, Europa Publishers London, 1982.
Freedman, L., *Atlas of Global Strategy*, Macmillan, London, 1985.
Holsti, K. J., *International Politics, a Framework for Analysis*, Prentice-Hall, London, 1974.
Martin, L., *The Two-Edged Sword*, Weidenfeld & Nicholson, London, 1982.
Ward, H., *World Powers in the 20th Century*, BBC, London, 1985.

# 23
# Antistate activities

## Terrorism

**Terrorism** is the systematic application of violence by governments and organizations in pursuit of specified goals. Accordingly, terrorist activities are directed against individuals or groups, or their representatives, real or potential, who oppose or interfere with the execution of desired policies by governments or organizations. These organized activities include personal injury, death and destruction of property.

Terrorism is utilized by governments, political parties and other groups, including those organized specifically for this purpose, who seek a fundamental change of political power. The disputed areas may differ widely and include the domination of one nation over another, the oppression of one economic class by another, supporters of one system of government against those favouring another system.

Anti-government organizations use terrorism to generate in the entire society, including the government itself, an awareness of impending large-scale upheaval; thus, its effect is to express widespread discontent, possibly neutralize pro-government elements, challenge the established authority and show its vulnerability and instability. Where the government is stable and has popular support, terrorism is relatively ineffective.

Widespread publicity aids terrorists by instilling fear in many more people than those directly affected and by demonstrating the capability of the terrorists. Sometimes the discriminatory acts of terrorism can be counterproductive; for example, when a previously indifferent population becomes aroused and active in support of the government against the terrorists. The common failing of terroristic organizations has been the lack of popular response for their causes.

Throughout history terrorism has been conducted for a variety of purposes. In Czarist Russia terrorism was advocated for revolutionary purposes by anarchists and proponents of the 'propaganda of the deed'. Terrorism is a tenet of Marxism–Leninism–Stalinism and an instrument of communist control. Mao Ze Dong in China claimed revolution to be an act of violence whereby one class overthrows another. In South Vietnam, the Viet Cong, supported by communist North Vietnam, employed tactics of guerrilla warfare and brutal terrorism throughout the country against all segments of society in order to generate fear and the myth of invincibility, and to obtain ultimate control.

Terrorism has been utilized to gain self-determination and also to deny it. The Anglo-Irish War of 1919–21 is an illustration. Brutalities were perpetuated by both the Sinn Fein (Ourselves Alone) society, Irish nationalists who demanded independence, and the British who opposed it. The latter used their military police and the hated auxiliaries (Black and Tans) to suppress the Irish. The reign of terror (1793–4) was the period in the French revolution during which opponents of the revolutionary regime were tried and thousands executed under the authority of the Law of Suspects. Ultimately the reign of terror devoured its own and ended when Robespierre was guillotined in 1794. From the inception of the Nazi movement, Hitler was a strong advocate of terrorism, concomitant with inflammatory propaganda as the most powerful instruments to achieve his objectives. Concentration camps and mass murders, especially of Jews and gypsies, attest to his diabolical calculations. Terrorism as an instrument directed against the enemy, including brutality against prisoners of war, and the effect it would have on German troops, was employed in military operations.

Since the Second World War, terrorism has transcended national boundaries in its exercise, ramifications, effects and prosecution. Terrorism feeds on itself and is self-breeding. There are many interrelated aspects of terrorism as we know it today – the act or threat of violence, the emotional reaction to such a threat and social effects resultant from acts and reaction. Mankind has to try and improve its understanding of the terrorism problem against the background of contemporary international relations and ideological conflicts. Terrorism manifests a multipolarity of international conflicts. Liberal democracies are prone to infiltration and attack by international and transnational terrorists; and terrorism has posed a clear and present danger to the lives of innocent people, social peace and order. Terrorists are increasingly availing themselves of modern warfare capabilities, highly sophisticated weapons, communications and transport capabilities and opportunities and advances in science and technology. Group acts enhance the political terrorists' sense of political purpose and direction. Psychologically, terrorists resist what they see as societal oppression and controls. Political terrorism aims to disorientate and psychologically isolate individuals in the populace. In so doing, terrorists lead a life of uncertainty and strain. The Palestinian Arabs' cause, for example, is fomented by the psychological trauma of humiliation and victimization. Arabs have resorted through mass media to psychological warfare and propaganda.

To many people it is axiomatic that the force used by a democratic state against the terrorist is legitimate, while the violence of the terrorist is not legitimate. It has become not an ideology but an insurrectional strategy that can be used by persons of very different political convictions. It has ceased to be a technique, for its philosophy has transcended the traditional dividing lines between political doctrine, and has become all purpose and value free. Terror, inflicted from above, is the manufacture and spread of fear by dictators, governments and management, and an attempt of the powerful to exert control through intimidation. Terrorism imposed from below is the manufacture and spread of fear by rebels, revolutionaries and protestors. More than any other form of aggression terrorism stems from and depends in its motivation, its perpetration, and its short and long term effects on the general social context of the political situation, the choice and value of victims, time and place of deed, the anticipated public reaction and many other such factors.

Terrorists aim to frighten, and by frightening to dominate and to control. They want to impress. They play to and for an audience, and solicit audience participation. They are convinced that in desperation, society needs them because they have the simple answers society searches for with its complex questions.

The mass media, willingly or unwittingly, are the spokesmen of the terrorists, the transmitters of the terroristic message, and the instrument through which terroristic deeds with all their excitement and insignificance instantaneously become known to a world audience.

Although separatist and nationalist objectives are important motivators for such people as the Palestinians, Irish republicans and Basques, almost all terrorist groups active today either find or rationalize their *raison d'être* in Marxist ideology or anarchist schools of thought. As a result of commonalities in sociological background and political outlook, a shared ideology and training experience, and floating membership of individual terrorists between and among groups, links between individual terrorists and terrorist groups have increased significantly.

Terrorism has been used when all else fails and frustration peaks. Terroristic violence as such is an act of the will. It is this characteristic that always has separated terrorists from the orthodox Marxists who insist on orderly progression toward eventual proletarian revolution.

In the short term at least terrorism works, for it is efficient and cost effective. If this was not the case the resources and urgency devoted to this problem could be more productively employed elsewhere. Other evidence of the realization that terrorism works can be found in increased hostage taking by individuals with various personal grievances or mental problems. This indicates that a portion of the population which is not politically motivated or inveterately criminal has turned to pseudo-terrorism as a way out of frustrations brought on by various causes. Terrorism has become a pseudo-ideology for some groups with nihilist aims, while other political groups consider resorting to terror for 'attention getting' qualities. The effects of relatively small amounts of violence will tend to be quite disproportionate in terms of the number of people terrorized.

Even the whole issue of nuclear terror provokes thought about the ambiguities of the future world we are entering. Defining the future threat of nuclear terrorism exposes inadequacies in the theory and reality of human behaviour, psychology and contemporary international relations. The trend to nihilism is hard to stop in an age of high nuclear technology. So terrorism is a weapon that has peculiarities of its own. It is a weapon that can and does get out of hand among those who use it, especially in urban settings. By initiating and participating in terrorism, leaders are releasing human potential for destructiveness over which they do not have full control. The terrorists themselves can never predict the level and intensity of violence to which they will be subjected, either as possible killers or as victims.

So terrorism can be either indiscriminate, as a nuclear attack would make clear, or highly selective in terms of a specific killing task. **International terrorism** can be classed as any attack with international repercussions and outside diplomatic norms; narrow identifiable acts or different definitions proposed by national governments.

Terror is as old as civilization itself. The use of sporadic and relentless non-government political and ideological violence is principally but not exclusively seen as part of a parochial or transnational revolutionary strategy which is characteristic of the age of terrorism. Thus, to protect itself against coercion and to protect its people's lives and possessions, a society needs awareness of what the terrorists are trying to achieve and a high degree of public cooperation with police and soldiers in whichever part of the world this may occur. Terrorism is a battle of wills between society on the one hand and those who oppose it on the other.

**Political terrorism** is a distinctive disorder of the modern world. It is criminal with concentration on murder, assassination, extortion, arson, maiming; it is politically motivated with violence against innocent people to erode political stability, seek publicity and attention, redress grievances, liberate colleagues in foreign jails and get money to buy arms; and ultimately it transcends national boundaries. To combat terror one has to forestall by learning in advance the plans of the terrorists; provide physical security of target installations and people; and the apprehension and punishment of terrorists. Terrorism is a crime and intolerable in a civilized community, and is considered by many to be the first step on the road to conventional war and ultimately to nuclear war.

## War and militarism

General images of war have always been extremely varied. The history of ideas about war and militarism is mainly one of combinations of prevailing ideas in political, social and moral philosophy. Modern war is an armed conflict among states. Yet war predates states and remains an expression of so pervasive and traumatic a feature of mankind's evolution that ideas about the origins of war-like tendencies are discussed in classical and neo-classical military literature.

Ideas about war are peculiarly though not uniquely affected by historical events and social problems. The need to train large numbers of men to engage in potentially self-destructive acts grew greater after the French revolution had shown the military value of more popular armies and after the industrial and agricultural revolutions had increased the material resources and manpower which could be devoted to warfare. In the twentieth century compulsory education for a peaceful life in an industrial society increased the citizen's preparation for and his or her personal resentment of military training.

Carl von Clausewitz developed some of the foremost views about the nature of war, more explicit assumptions about its origins in human nature, society or the state system, and a set of ideas for its management. This gave military scientists positive goals during a century of peace, 1815–1914, in which the major European military events were involvement in the Crimean War by Britain and Russia, and Prussia's victories over both

Austria and France, which heralded the birth of the German nation in 1871.

Three images of the relations of man are the state, war, and war's origins in human nature. As soon as man enters into society he loses the sense of his weakness, equality ceases, and then commences the state of war.

Militarism became a nineteenth-century liberal perjorative label for systems which overvalue the military virtues, glorify war, or give inordinate power or rewards to soldiers. These evils became clearer as more uniform states replaced the feudal orders and as national and democratic armies replaced bands of mercenary military artisans. These measures were touched upon in writings by Sun Tsu, Frederick the Great and Machiavelli. Clausewitz's work *On War*, published in the 1830s, reflected on the primitive violence of war free from any conventional restrictions. He saw war as a great affair of states being not merely a political act but a political instrument. This view of war was shaken in the twentieth century. Failures in the First World War came from unscientific evaluation of weapons. The Allied victories in the Second World War confirmed a new faith in scientific mechanization. Absolute nuclear and biochemical weapons and assured delivery systems revived doubts about war as a political instrument.

In the realms of classical warfare, observers of primitive warriors stressed not only their courage but also their treachery and indiscipline. Graeco–Roman political and social institutions were partly based on kinship groups but civilized men saw few analogies between themselves and barbarians, perhaps because they had so largely overcome the restrictions which tribalism placed on military and political efficiency, and perhaps because the technological gap between civilized and barbarian peoples even in metallurgy remained relatively small. War began with plunder. Both Hellenes and barbarians were commanded by powerful chiefs who took this means of increasing their wealth and providing for their poorer followers. The Romans managed the most efficient city-smashing, land-grabbing, slave-catching machinery of antiquity.

Aristotle related constitutions to military systems. Cavalry's replacement by infantry had been democratized. The then modern ideas of militarism came after the technology which ended the dangers of barbarian incursions had threatened to make wars self-destructive. Disciplined and efficient soldiers were necessary for a state's survival in fighting barbarians with very similar hand weapons. The Romans benefited from the abundance and convenient accessability of their military supplies but they also glorified war. Soldiers often fought each other for political power.

Images of pacifism mirror a society's image of violence. Early Christians rejected a society founded on coercion rather than on love. An established Church regarded those who felt that it should not defend itself as naive and sinful. As long as the military and technological balance between civilized and barbarian remained relatively even, both needed the necessity for an enemy to be envied, feared, hated, enslaved and plundered.

Although militarism is a nineteenth-century term, its meaning received little attention from writers on war. De Tocqueville, however, believed that the inevitable growth of democracy would lead to despotism and militarism. He believed no protracted war could fail to endanger the freedom of a democratic country, if only because it must increase the powers of civil government. Hegel on the other hand believed modern war fostered unselfishness and did not lead individuals to hate individuals.

By 1914, Clausewitzian ideas on the scientific management of war dominated military thought and Napoleonic military ideas were uniformly widespread. The transformation of war had been owing to the importance of national industrial potential: and the institutionalization of and innovation in research laboratories, universities and general staffs.

The most common definitions of militarism are Prussian in origin. It was seen as permeating all society and becoming dominant over all industry and arts. Military authority rested on belief. The rhetoric of twentieth-century fascism was flamboyant in imposing new orders on masses which had been deliberately led to hope for more revolutionary results from their sacrifices. The totalitarian powers' evaluations of air power – the most important new weapon of the interwar era – were no more scientific than the evaluation of seapower. The idea that militarism chiefly affects great powers which have accomplished something by war is supported by those who see contemporary American militarism as an outgrowth of her crusades against war, fascism and communism. Contemporary research on militarism takes in developing societies in which militarism is mainly internal, as well as developed ones, and tries to fix the degrees of political and social power held by soldiers. Some advanced democracies now need only an internal or international constabulary for peacekeeping purposes. The soldiers of some totalitarian popular democracies may well be quite realistic conservatives, but they are still subject to political interference in their professional affairs. In a liberal society political involvement hampers professional soldiers who seldom get the expertise to compete with its political, profit making and technological professionals.

The descent into covert or overt military rule begins with threats of mass resignation or non-cooperation. Then come vetoes of particular policies or politicians, manipulating or delaying elections in the interest of public order, or the preventive detention or the murder of opposition politicians. Contemporary views on militarism deal with the scientific management of war in an atmosphere of popular fears of absolute weapons and revolutionary passions. While great powers are deterred from direct attacks on each other, this may produce non-events which seem like victories, and old ideas of influence spark wars in which irresponsible small powers may manage their sponsors.

Many writers believe that in an age of civilization, war was a stable social institution, and for mankind as a whole, a tolerable one. In the twentieth century the system of international relations based on unilateral national defence has broken down because of the change in the fundamental parameters of the system, and war has therefore become intolerable. Military science is so rooted in the particular actions of individuals and groups in so wide a variety of circumstances that the history of ideas about the causes of war and militarism remains one of new combinations of old political and philosophical insights and ideas.

## Civil disobedience

The concept of **civil disobedience** presupposes, first of all, some formal structure of law, enforced by established governmental authorities, from which an individual cannot dissociate himself or herself except by change of citizenship. Civil disobedience consists in publicly announced defiance of specific laws, policies or commands of that formal structure which an individual or group believes to be unjust and/or unconstitutional. The defiance may also take the form of disobedience of just laws if such disobedience appears to be an effective way to focus public attention on unjust laws. The defiance must be publicly announced, since the point of it is to bring the unjust and/or unconstitutional laws, policies or commands to the attention of the public for the purpose either of stirring its conscience or of frightening it into helping repeal the laws, change the policies, or mitigate the commands; or to get the attention of the courts so that their constitutionality can be judged. The defiance may take the form of doing what is prohibited or of failing to do what is required. The defiance, moreover, must be a premeditated act, understood to be illegal by the perpetrator, and understood to carry prescribed penalties. Willingness to accept such penalties is a crucial part of that sort of civil disobedience which hopes to stir the public conscience, while eagerness to escape punishment is perfectly compatible with that sort of civil disobedience which aims to pressure and frighten the public. The defiance, finally, may be either non-violent or violent and still count as civil disobedience.

The question arises why anyone should be civilly disobedient. The higher law doctrine asserts that God's law takes precedence over civil law whenever it can be shown that the two come into conflict. People are ordinarily duty bound to obey the civil and criminal law since the benefits of orderly government are large indeed; on the other hand they cannot, out of higher duty, obey civil and criminal law which command them to break the word of God. While the higher law doctrine was never wholly absent from thought and practice during most of the history of Western civilization, it was usually sporadic and individual in nature. For the most part, people were happy to accept the higher law concept without resorting to its painful corollary of civil disobedience. The most sustained development of the concept was by the anti-slavery abolitionists.

The notions of natural rights and human rights are by no means identical since the former usually involves an absolutistic and rationalistic outlook in moral philosophy and is usually based on a theological foundation such as 'God-given rights' while the latter does not usually entail such conceptions but leaves open the possibility at least of basic rights. The concept of human rights is the one usually used these days, not simply because ours is a more voluntaristic and humanistic era but because this concept includes many social and economic freedoms which seem important to our age, along with the more traditional concept of freedom as 'freedom from' various restraints. For example, the **Universal Declaration of Human Rights**, adopted by the United Nations in 1948, recognizes among others the rights to life, liberty, personal security and equal protection of the law; freedom from slavery and degrading punishment; freedom of thought, conscience, speech, religion and peaceful assembly; and the right to an education, choice of one's own employment, favourable working conditions and protection against unemployment.

The concepts of natural and human rights, with all their differences, still have a core of common meaning, namely, that there are certain rights which belong to a human being independent of his or her position in a civil society. Since society does not bestow these rights, it cannot justifiably take them away. Thus such rights are inalienable. The function of society, far from interfering with these rights, is to sustain and protect them and to adjudicate conflicts that arise in the common pursuit of these rights. If a civil government subverts these rights in a wholesale fashion, it is not fulfilling its proper role and hence the people are justified in overthrowing that spurious government (with the least violence possible) and erecting a legitimate one in its place. It follows as a corollary of this general principle that if a government which on the whole respects its proper role nevertheless infringes or denies some specific rights, either to a majority or minority of people, then they have the right civilly to disobey the offending laws, policies or commands (either non-violently or violently, depending upon further arguments). The democratic principle envisaged by most of the architects of the Bill of Rights of the United States constitution and of the Declaration of Human Rights of the United Nations is that the rule of the majority is the best way known of adjudicating the conflicts which inevitably arise in the common pursuit of their human rights by millions of people.

The concept of human rights provides the principal justification of civil disobedience in the humanistically oriented modern world. Yet prudent considerations are offered by believers in the concept to soften the commitment to civil disobedience. Thomas Hobbes represented the extreme position of accepting the concept of natural rights and yet, out of fear of anarchy, rejecting not only civil disobedience but even dissent. David Hume provided a utilitarian approach to the relative limits of obedience and disobedience to civil magistrates, and adopted a libertarian position. Later out of fear of anarchy again he recommended 'exact obedience' to the law of the land and the authority of its administrators.

In the view of Jeremy Bentham, each situation and political context had to be carefully studied in its own right and the likely consequences predicted. If the prediction is for fewer overall mischievous consequences by disobedience than by submission then it is the duty, not simply the right, of the conscientious citizen to resist the government. In Bentham's opinion, if a person is so concerned about civil stability that he cannot conceive any conditions that would justify disobedience, then he really has abandoned any tenable concept of human rights.

Writers on civil disobedience have pondered whether it should be non-violent in nature or if the use of violence is ever justified.

The defence of **non-violence** has taken two radically different forms; one prudent in nature and the other a matter of principle. The prudent view holds that if government forces are so strong and oppressive that they would retaliate tenfold against any violence, then they should be opposed only non-violently or by passive resistance. If the situation changes, if the strength of the oppressive regime declines, then it may be violently resisted.

The most important defenders of the non-violent as a matter of principle were Leo Tolstoy, Mohandas Gandhi and Martin Luther King. The principle usually invoked to justify non-violence was the religious and moral belief that love is necessarily good, and hence that violence by its very nature is evil; that only love of others brings happiness and the realization of a moral self, while anger and violence debase the character of the agent as well as wounding and killing others. Gandhi argued that the lawbreaker should openly and quietly disobey unjust laws and suffer the consequences of such disobedience with dignity. However, Gandhi also felt it was legitimate to dissent from unjust policies and commands of a government by disobeying laws which were not themselves unjust provided that breaking these just laws did not itself violate principles of conscience.

Many people in America offer a justification of non-violent dissent which does not view violence as necessarily wrong in all societies but as unnecessary in a free society. There is no need for disruption and destructive violence since there are constitutional and rational means of dissent in American society unparalleled in character and constitution anywhere in the world. Universal suffrage allows the majority of people to express their dissent by voting out of office those officials whose policies and commands are objectionable. Moreover, individuals and groups are guaranteed the right to bring pressure to bear on their government by writing, speaking, organizing, picketing and demonstrating, provided only that laws governing public safety are obeyed. They may also challenge laws which they consider unjust through the courts, claiming that the laws are unconstitutional as well as unjust. And when they sue the state or its officials, they are equals with the state in court, and have the protection of elaborate procedural rights. This is possible because the courts are totally independent of the executive and legislative branches of government.

There is a widespread feeling in the free world, however, that no progress has been made and that there has been, in fact, double-dealing in the civil rights area, which has led to the fall of the great tradition in civil disobedience. The common theme in the campaigns of the blacks, the young and the poor is that they want more participation in the decisions which are always being made for them by someone else. They want more participatory democracy whether it be in the United States or South Africa, because they feel that their representatives and public servants have produced sham progress and usually apply double standards.

Rejection and alienation are frightening symptoms in the body politic as well as in the individual. Grievances have to be taken seriously to avoid the risk of producting further uncivil disobedience and an increase in movements of protest.

## Protest movements

The relationship between ideas and protest in history has always been complex. Before modern times most protest ideologies were religious and few were specifically intended for social protest. This suggests the common distinction between the grievances that caused popular unrest and the ideologies that might be invoked by it. In modern times there has been the rise of explicit protest ideologies.

The more sophisticated forms of protest require organization. Protest ideas and intellectual leaders could help shape such organization, but the requirements of effective organization could force ideological compromises, even radical distortions as well. The evolution of protest movements, has more often been an accommodation of ideas to the demands of electorates and of organizations than an application of any undiluted ideology.

Until the late eighteenth century religion was almost always the link between formal ideas and popular social and political unrest. Christianity could serve as a vehicle for social protest for a variety of reasons. Like any effective protest ideology it could combine bitter denunciation of the present order, and belief that a better way, even a utopia, could be found for the future; and it could overlay these with deep emotion and a passionate confidence that could sustain leaders and inspire followers as well. The egalitarian message of gospel Christianity recurred in many types of protests from the peasant jacqueries of the late middle ages through the levellers and diggers of the English civil war, to the late nineteenth-century peasant uprisings in Southern Europe. The common people now and again claimed in violent uprisings that Christ had condemned the rich and preached the sharing of goods.

Christianity as a protest ideology differed in many ways from the protest ideologies of the last two centuries. The Christian churches including all the major Protestant sects were set against protest. The Christian message to the common people with its focus on heavenly rewards lulled discontent more often than inflamed it. This ambiguity with regard to protest has some parallels in modern ideologies; socialism, for example, quickly developed an institutional outlook that discouraged violent protest.

From the Enlightenment onwards the principal ideologies of protest were non-Christian and often explicitly anti-Christian. Liberalism, radicalism and socialism differed in crucial respects but as protest ideologies had important points in common. They were very political, seeing alterations in the organization and control of the state as a basis for achieving social justice; only a few Enlightenment-derived ideologies, such as syndicalism, dissented from this point of view. They were avowedly progressive and spent little time measuring the present by the past. Often, as in Marxist socialism, the existing order was admitted to be in many ways an improvement over the past. Their main point was that a very good society could be built in the future. The new ideologies also countenanced protest directly, even urged it in many circumstances. They were, at least in the early stages of existence, truly protest ideologies and did not have to be reinterpreted or taken out of the mainstream to be used as such.

The new ideologies depended heavily on formal intellectuals not only for their articulation but also for their adaptation to actual protest efforts. This was part of the broader transition from Christian to secular culture and helps explain the extraordinary proliferation of protest ideas. Intellectuals moved to spread political awareness and build massive organizations out of protest movements. Their concern about their status and their relationship with society frequently became in itself a motive for protest. The sheer expansion of protest ideas and ideologists clearly related to a rising of actual unrest was as important as the new stress on secular progress. In the nineteenth century the first new functional connection between ideas and protest was at the level of leadership. From the ranks of intellectuals or their immediate adherents, the self-proclaimed advocates of protest emerged for the first time. At the extreme the professional revolutionary came from this environment, armed in some cases with devotion to disorder and little else. But the revolutionaries' organizational notions, particularly their stress upon a strict hierarchy descending from central control to small local unit and something of their spirit influenced more elaborate protest ideologies and more successful leaders.

There were also signs that ideas were getting increasingly involved in popular protest, a natural result of the radical intellectuals' efforts to be relevant and of the unrest caused by population growth and industrialization. Every modern revolution involved one or more ideologies. There was in fact something of the ideological build-up before each revolution. This consisted of an increased outpouring of dissenting ideas and a growing diversity in the ideas themselves resulting from a new or newly-important left wing. The proliferation of political tracts which were increasingly specific in content and the birth of socialist theory helped prepare the French revolution of 1789. Histories of this revolution, stressing its liberal or radical or socialist legacy, combined with rising agitation in the press and pamphlets to set the stage for the revolutions of 1830 and 1848. Dissemination of ideas before a revolution also helped create organizations capable of taking charge of the revolutionary effort once it began.

Ideologies played an increasing role in protests that fell short of revolution. There had always been, and continues to be, lower class agitation without any connection with formal doctrine. Bread riots and banditry, for example, were directed at specific targets and needed no larger goals; or at most they expressed a traditional belief in natural justice and a hatred of the rich. In the nineteenth century, traditional rioting declined, partly because elements of the lower classes gained a new contentment, but also because better organized outlets developed. For the working men, strikes became the chief form of protest. Socialist and syndicalist leaders had growing contacts with ordinary workers and persuaded many of them of the importance of ideas.

Nevertheless, from about 1900 strikes for ideological goals became more common, even before the leading labour organizations became ideologically inspired. Not only did rioting come under the influence of ideas for socialists, but nationalists were also able to instigate riots by the later nineteenth century. Protest voting added a new dimension to lower class agitation and was open to ideological direction.

The growing connections between protest ideas and protest movements developed partly because of the growing experience of the lower classes and their exposure to new conditions in the cities and in industry. Rising literacy and new freedoms of the press and of association obviously aided the process.

Beneath the broad patterns of modern protest movements the role as well as the specific content of the leading ideologies varied greatly. The multiplicity of protest ideas was itself an important new development. Until the late nineteenth century there was no necessary connection between the birth of an ideology and a real protest movement. Utopian socialists, for example, spent more time appealing to industrialists than to workers, but even those who went to the factories found few supporters.

Liberalism and radicalism were the first significant ideologies of protest, partly because both could appeal to rising middle-class elements, capable of sensing and airing grievances, and yet not close to the door to lower-class participation. Liberals wanted specific reforms in law and economy; furthermore their demands for parliaments and extensions of the suffrage implied an overturning of the ruling class that could be genuinely revolutionary. On the other hand, liberalism as a protest ideology had a number of crucial weaknesses. Liberals disliked disorder and violence, preferring evolutionary reform, partly because of their ideas and partly because most of them were prosperous property owners. Hence liberals started very few violent protests; more often they were in the position of countenancing a protest already under way and were trying to pick up the pieces to their own benefit and that of public order. Hence, liberal revolutions almost always failed for liberals lacked the toughness of spirit and authoritarian stamp to carry them through.

Muscle was given to the liberal protest ideals by radicalism – a vague designation for a number of movements which preached more vigorous methods such as massive demonstrations. In preaching democracy with a hint of social reform, radicals sought far more sweeping changes than did liberals. Political nationalism also spurred agitation, particularly in areas under foreign rule. Nationalism did not significantly touch the lower classes before the later nineteenth century, but it could unite the upper classes, including aristocrats, and move them to direct violence as liberalism never could. For liberals and many radicals direct protest had proved ineffective but sufficient gains had been won to permit work through the existing order. There were three clusters of protest ideologies from the later nineteenth century onward: socialism – communism, radical nationalism – fascism, and anarchism – syndicalism: a trio more diverse than that of the earlier period. All tried to reach the masses and a social message was carried which, with the partial exception of fascism, outweighed political demands. Violence was preached at some point, and all paid attention to the methods and organization of protest. These developments reflected the shift from the middle to the working classes as the most numerous and persistent constituents of a protest movement; and the pre-eminence of social issues. All recognized the difficulties of revolution against an industrial state; hence the concern for tactics which ranged from assassination through small scale gang violence to general strikes and protest voting. In fact none of the new protest ideologies produced a true revolution in an industrial country.

Socialism most resembled the liberal–radical ideologies of previous decades. It was progressive, rational and political; and as a result, like liberalism, it rather rapidly turned away from protest to evolutionary reform. This process dissatisfied the guardians of the revolutionary socialist ideas and led to many divisions, including the development and spread of communism. Yet even communism underwent a similar process within twenty years, if not in accepting piecemeal reforms alone, at least in renouncing revolution in favour of political action.

Certain factors turned socialism and ultimately communism from per-

284 Politics Made Simple

sistent protest. The constituency of the moment, primarily the working classes, was interested in sweeping rebellion but only when economic misery prevailed. Generally, it expected limited but rapid gains from the socialists. The socialists' commitment to politics also dulled the edge of protest. Finally, learning both from Marx and from the necessities of resisting an initial hostile society, socialists and, later, communists stressed strong organizations. Initially designed as a basis for protest, the organizations rapidly asserted their own imperatives requiring administrators rather than idealists' routine, and accommodation rather than revolutionary zeal; their very existence gave leaders and members a stake in the existing order. Only where repression inhibited the development of extensive organization did socialism remain a revolutionary force in Europe.

Anarchism and syndicalism, hostile to any kind of extensive organization from the state down, avoided the perils of bureaucracy but at the price of effective action. Theirs were the most radical protest doctrines developed in the modern era, for they rejected the whole doctrine of industrial society, and often urged individual and collective violence virtually for its own sake. They appealed to artisans and peasants in areas where industrialization was just beginning to take hold. The glorification of violence was particularly manifested in fascism which must be ranked as one of the most effective of all protest ideologies, for it attracted many groups that prided themselves on their respectability and had hitherto shunned any form of protest. It did this with a deliberately vague set of ideas that combined a radical attack on modern society from ethics to economics, a high level of emotion and unprecedented attention to tactics and organization.

The growing diversity of protest ideas and the groups to which they appealed increased radicalism and the explicit focus on the act of protest itself. The most successful of modern protest ideologies helped reduce direct and particularly non violent protest; this was one of their most basic if unexpected contributions to the character of industrial as opposed to pre-industrial society. Their advocates helped wean the common people from the traditional largely spontaneous forms of agitation, replacing them with strikes and political action that depended upon formal leadership. As the leadership became bureaucratic and turned from ideological impulse, the followers could only follow; apart from sporadic wildcat action they too had learned that strength lay in organization. At the same time of course, strikes and political action won important gains. Finally, socialism, and particularly communism, created something of a separate world in which the most discontented could find comfort even when the rest of society still seemed hostile.

From the early nineteenth century a multitude of theories and theorists started with an opposition to rationalism and went on to oppose the whole tenor of industrial life. They logically opposed liberalism and socialism as well. Resistance to machines and commercialism and the corruption of parliamentary politics had potential popular appeal.

Aside from this, the anti-industrial philosophies failed to produce a real protest movement. They came too late for Western Europe, where adaptation to industrial society had considerably advanced. The advocates of such philosophies failed to organize, for they sensed that this would necessitate some compromise. They often alienated the common people, which a successful protest ideology, dependent on numbers and violence that only the common people can produce, cannot afford to do.

In the 1890s and again in the 1960s, it won masses of students and this led to rioting. Yet at least until the 1960s this current of rejection of modernity separated its advocates from the rest of society, including potential rebels on other grounds. This is yet another reason why the association of ideas and protest, so vigorous in the nineteenth century, has declined in the twentieth century.

There is a very fragile link between formal ideas and protest. The difficulty in judging the relationship lies in the separate strands of causality involved. The development of protest ideas, although not independent of economic factors, rests primarily on the interpretation of previous movements of ideas by intellectuals, and on their concern with their own special status in society. **Popular protest** depends on its goals as well as in its timing on economic conditions above all. In its most elaborate expressions it rebels against the organization and even the guiding motives of the economy, rather than against material hardship, but it remains dependent on economic trends. This means that the most active protests have done without formal ideas. Many protest ideologies have never developed into protest movements, and many protest movements do not intend what the formal ideas involved seem to intend. Often a successful protest ideology leads to quite diverse protest movements in different regions among different social groups, even among different personality types.

Ideologies, then, can never fully define or describe a protest movement. The association became particularly complex during the last two centuries when ideas were modernized more rapidly than popular attitudes and intellectuals were moved, whether consciously or not, by growing uncertainty about their social role. Antistate activities and the increasing complexity of decision making issues are going to dominate politics in future.

## Questions

### Terrorism

1  Provide an acceptable definition of terrorism.
2  Why is terrorism conducted for a number of purposes?
3  'The use of force by a democratic state against the terrorist is legitimate, while the violence of the terrorist is not legitimate'. Discuss.

### War and militarism

1  Why are ideas about war a central theme in the behaviour of states?
2  Account for the interest displayed by the founders of political theory in classical warfare.
3  Write an essay on militarism.

## Civil disobedience

1  Why are people civilly disobedient?
2  Analyse the concepts of natural and human rights.
3  Compare and contrast the Hobbesian and Benthamite approach to rights.
4  Does the concept of non-violence have any relevance in the world today?
5  Is the success or otherwise of civil disobedience dependent on political fortunes?

## Protest movements

1  Are protest movements necessary?
2  Critically appraise the role of ideologies in protest.
3  What role did liberalism and radicalism play in protest movements?
4  Why have protest ideologies failed to produce a true revolution in any industrialized country?
5  Examine factors which turned socialism and communism from persistent protest.
6  Account for anti-industrial philosophies failing to produce real protest movements.
7  Discuss the fragile link between formal ideas and protest.

## Further reading

Barbrook, A., *Patterns of Political Behaviour*, Martin Robertson, Oxford, 1975.
Chandler, R., *Public Opinion*, R. R. Bowker & Co., New York and London, 1972.
Cranston, M., *What are Human Rights?* Bodley Head, London 1973.
Day, A. J. (ed.), *Border and Territorial Disputes*, Longman, London, 1982.
Degenhardt, H. W., *Treaties and Alliances of the World*, Longman, London, 1981.
Hennessay, B. C., *Public Opinion*, Wadsworth Publishing Co., USA, 1968.
King, P., *Modern World Affairs*, Heinemann, London, 1984.
Mason, P., *Base Relations*, Oxford University Press, Oxford, 1971.
Tivey, L. (ed.), *The Nation-State*, Martin Robertson, Oxford, 1981.
Thornton, A. P., *Imperialism in the 20th Century*, Macmillan, London, 1978.

# 24
# Politics – the future

Generally, when writers and politicians have tried to forecast the future in idyllic terms their vision has appeared as a positive utopia. Such writers, for example, predicted the post-war world in 1945 as one of peace, abundance and steady progress within the confines of dependable law. Yet the politics of the present, and perhaps of the years ahead, seems characterized by a feeling of great fear – a vague dread of impending changes. The changes the world has lived through in the last half century have been gigantic and the changes to come will no doubt be even more momentous.

In years to come, the first need of a political system will be to preserve a sense of identity and continuity for its people. Members of groups, committees and nations need a sense of belonging in order to face the dangers, the opportunities, and the tasks of reorientation which they will encounter. Many old landmarks, old governments, old institutions, and old beliefs will disappear. Since it was these landmarks toward which people oriented themselves in the past, the future will impose a continuous task of reorientation. Each and every one of us has to preserve a sense of identity as a group, as a people and as a country. For all time the world will be inhabited by different peoples; each with its own culture, institutions and social system. The Russians will remain Russians, the Americans, Americans, the Germans, Germans and to the English there will always be an England. Some day there will come a decisive and ever increasing orientation toward the values of humankind. A sense of country, of position and of individual and collective selfhood will have to be maintained in the midst of great changes.

For the first time in history humankind has the possibility to commit suicide as a species. An all-out war involving the detonating of large numbers of nuclear weapons, can end all or most of civilized life, and quite possibly all life on this planet. The growth of life has also reached unprecedented heights of effectiveness and power. Human reproduction has become a vast problem, and more slowly an increasing responsibility of both individuals and government. The sheer numbers of people, and the amounts of energy generated and resultant effects of pollution have produced effects which are qualitatively as well as quantitatively new. Humankind has grown too big and too powerful for its own old habits.

The difference between poverty and riches has persisted. Among a few countries the difference has narrowed. In others it has widened. But though the gap between poor and rich is an old story, now for the first time many millions of people in poor nations are gaining access to enough science, technology and power to do something about it. Taking into account the significantly higher economic base of the richer countries, it is probable that differing growth rates alone will not reduce significantly the gap between poor and rich peoples for many decades to come. For the first time in history mass migration has stopped on a global scale. People are penned in by the frontiers of their own states and by the unwillingness of other states to receive large numbers of immigrants. Rich, relatively empty countries such as the United States, Canada, the Soviet Union and Australia face poor crowded ones, such as India, Bangladesh, China, Egypt and Indonesia. Other countries are both poor and empty. They have abundant land but lack capital and human power; Brazil, Argentina and much of Latin America, the islands of Borneo and New Guinea, the Union of South Africa, and much of the rest of Africa all fit this description. Finally, a few countries are both rich and crowded. Lacking land, they have more than enough capital to make up for the shortage of square miles. Great Britain, Germany, Belgium, the Netherlands and Japan all have proved that people can make a living in densely populated countries if they have enough machines and enough skills to use them.

In most parts of the world, the importance of cities has decisively increased. During the 1970s the majority of humankind had become urban in residence and non-agricultural in occupation. In many highly developed countries, cities used to be surrounded by countryside. Now the countryside is becoming surrounded by cities. Nearly everyone can be reached by the mass media, and the majority of the urban and industrial part of the world can be reached by air transport within a few hours.

The industrial revolution of the eighteenth and nineteenth centuries has been followed by an **information revolution**. This revolution has had two aspects. First, it has increased the number of people working in information – processing industries of all kinds, from clerks and librarians to telegraph and telephone operators, and to operators of computing machines and other sophisticated technological equipment. Second, there has been the increasing intellectualization of society. All industrial growth requires even more raw materials and other ingredients. People must discover new ways for making the goods they need. In addition to inventions, there will be need for innovations, for changes of habits among millions of people to make them actually act in line with the new techniques. A strain on humankind will be the speed of information changes. Rapid change creates a gap between generations – the rapidity of change bewildering old and young. Distrust of experience, fear of highly developed technology, and impatience with the sustained thought needed to understand complex processes and systems all add up to the risk of massive intellectual failure. If we distrust anything that seems too complicated, we may be unable to deal with the realities we cannot afford.

Our age of physical and intellectual dangers is also an age of growing intellectual resources. For the first time in centuries, humankind has a plurality of social systems existing at approximately the same level of technology. Differences between the social systems of private enterprise and communism are more profound in some respects than differences between countries and the medieval world. Each of these different social systems has many variants. There are four kinds of communism in the world: Russian, Chinese, Yugoslavian and Vietnamese. North Korea may be a fifth. There are a number of different kinds of capitalism in the world, most of them allied in varying proportions with the institutions of the welfare state, e.g. the systems of United States, Britain, France and Canada. Finally, there are the countries whose societies, although based predominantly on private enterprise, have large public sectors and governments that avowedly favour democratic socialism. For many different policies one can find experiences in a plurality of social systems and institutions.

One of the most important changes in the world has been the change in political participation and political culture. By 1980 more than one half of the world's population had engaged in a vote of some kind. Never before in history had there been voting participation on so grand a scale. One has to remember that not every vote in every country means the same thing. In some countries an election is a choice among genuine alternatives, such as different candidates and different parties, while in other countries it is mainly an appeal by the government for some expression of popular support or loyalty.

There has been an increase of autonomous groups which take action in many aspects of social life having political significance. Industrial workers the world over now join trades unions; farmers in many countries are organized in farm organizations; interest groups for business people and management have arisen in a number of places. In general, the political activity of autonomous small groups as well as of large organizations is much greater than ever before. Many of these groups and movements are orientated not only to pursuit of the routine interests of their members but also to the bringing about of some more far-reaching kind of change in their society.

Agents of change, both public and private, are at work in the world today on a wide scale. A century ago, people debated whether the world could be changed. Fifty years ago they debated whether change was desirable, today they mainly debate how change can best be accomplished.

With many people entering politics, outside intervention becomes even less effective. Every year sees foreign loans, foreign ambassadors or even foreign armies less able than formerly to exercise control over a distant country. No longer can the world be governed from a distance either by a conqueror or an ideology. The days when a government could do things for its people and expect them to remain duly passive and grateful are disappearing. More and more it has become necessary to do things with people rather than merely for them.

In a way which debunks Orwell, in country after country, the inclination to take people for granted has become increasingly impracticable. Rather it has become important to consider the responses of those affected by public policy and to include their reactions in the planning of policy. Abraham Lincoln's notion of 'government of the people, by the people, for the people', is even truer today than 120 years ago.

The most dangerous thing the world today can do is to continue politics as usual. Very few leaders of today are either young enough or flexible enough in their thinking to be able to accept the full significance of nuclear weapons and nuclear energy. As a result we are, in the 1980s, still governed by the only generation of statesmen that will ever have the power to control nuclear weapons, but who have not fully grasped the significance of the new changes. Most statesmen who come to power in the 1980s will be people who were only teenagers in 1945 and who have accepted the nuclear age fully.

The most dangerous thing next to a nuclear war would be to try to press all humankind into the mould of a single ideology. The governments of the communist-ruled countries do not fully understand either the economics, the politics or the sociology of communism even though they understand enough to stay in power. In private enterprise countries, inflation, unemployment and recession as well as the large economic and social trends are not fully understood by either management or unions, or governments or voters.

In terms of fighting, the international community will have to try to get together to stop it. Though limited war is increasingly unrewarding and impractical it may continue for a time. It seems safe to say that it will rarely bring its participants the rewards they expect. Civil wars may be harder to cope with. Too many backward institutions, too many ideological and religious conflicts, too much impatience and intolerance and too much poverty make it unlikely that all political and social change will be peaceful for the rest of the century. What seems more reasonable to hope for is the limiting of civil wars and revolutions to the populations directly involved.

Another emergency task is the abolition of hunger. Food supplies have grown a little faster than world population, but as shown in north-east Africa, this advance has not been evenly spread. To unite the nations of the world and help them in the struggle against hunger will not be a luxury but a necessity. Beyond the immediate need to reduce and end famine lies the more far-reaching goal of eliminating poverty.

On a smaller scale, many countries can reduce poverty by doing a better job in integrating their large cities. The politics of big cities have become more like international relations, as their populations have become recruited from many ethnic groups. The instruments for doing most of these things will still be the governments of our nation states. These include all levels of the machinery of government – local, federal and national. Beyond them greater use will have to be made of regional organizations such as the Common Market in Western Europe and the United Nations with all its specialized agencies, as well as the many non-governmental international organizations such as the International Red Cross.

These measures perhaps can be implemented through the principle of self-determination of peoples. In so far as the population of an area is a people – a cohesive group of persons capable of communicating and cooperating with each other with a high degree of solidarity – its members are likely to demand their rights to demonstrate their capacity and take their fate into their own hands.

The most important task for national states, national governments and entire peoples will be the effort to increase their cognitive capabilities. Both in relations of nations among one another, which require the avoidance of war, and of peoples toward their natural environment, which require a more effective control of science and technology, they need to know much more than they now know in order to act in a way that prevents destroying themselves. In the West this could also include an increase in integrative capabilities – that is in the capabilities to enable people of different races, languages, religions and geographic and other background conditions to work together effectively.

Two other problems are population growth and the need to cope with the opportunities and dangers of the great breakthroughs in science and technology that have been made in our lifetime or are now in the making. Breakthroughs have occurred in breaking the sound barrier, and in rapid modes of transport and in humanity's conquest of new habitations on the bottom of the sea or in laboratories in outer space. New energy sources have become available from nuclear fission, although with dangerous by-products. Safer and cleaner sources of energy are now available from nuclear fusion and from solar energy. Chemistry and biochemistry have given us new materials, such as synthetic fibres, antibiotic drugs and drugs altering the state of a person's mind, while molecular biology has created the possibility of manipulation, i.e. the production of controlled changes in the genetic code, microorganisms, and eventually in plants and animals. A further two breakthroughs have not increased human material powers, but have tended primarily to enhance humanity's powers of awareness and of thought. Ultimately humankind has started to use the entire electro-magnetic field – from micro to macro waves – as a source of our perceptions. The development of large computers has permitted us to deal with much larger amounts of information much faster and more effectively than before. The progressive miniaturization of such computers through transistors and microcircuits is making them steadily more mobile and available for many new uses.

Each of these breakthroughs, and all of them together, offer a great aid to our power of thinking and acting. But they are not and cannot be a substitute for human thought and human actions.

People cannot act well together if they cannot also make sense of lives as individuals. Thus the twenty-first century can be an age of personal self-determination much as the twentieth has been the age of self-determination of entire peoples. If the inner space of the human mind and spirit is explored, people may become more effectively mindful of the feelings and emotions of every individual. This will also involve some continuing changes in the position of women and the young in many coutries and cultures. It may also be necessary to develop more devices for defending individual freedom and controlling governments by means of checks and balances.

Freedom of the individual and freedom of opinion are essential parts of freedom in the search for knowledge and the search for knowledge is an indispensable element in humankind's search for security and livelihood. Systems of government that are respectful of the individual, protective of minorities and permissive of new discoveries and individuals changing their minds about them, will be a necessity for the future growth of humankind. Where constitutional government and individual freedom already exist it may be worthwhile to guard and develop these traditions and guarantees now, because all mankind will need them at sometime in the future. Public opinion is only dimly aware of the way in which their prospects and everyday life are determined by complex chains of events which may be initiated thousands of miles away. Effective insulation or isolation is becoming a near impossibility, while at the same time such political direction as exists may appear to be more and more inaccessible and unaccountable as it moves beyond the confines of the single nation state and its political process.

## Questions

1  Is politics too complex to have any future in the patterns that we have known?
2  Assess the impact of the Third World on world political issues.
3  Discuss the main changes between rural and industrial politics.
4  Why is it dangerous to continue politics as usual?
5  What in your view is politics about in the world today?

## Further reading

Finifter, A. W. (ed.), *Political Science: The State of the Discipline*, The American Political Science Association, Washington, USA, 1983.
Rathbone, C. and Stephenson, M., *Guide to Political Quotations*, Longman, London, 1985.
Stewart R., *A Dictionary of Political Quotations*, Europa Publications, London, 1984.

# Index

Coventry University Library